Corporate Social Responsibility and Governance

Corporate social responsibility (CSR) has developed into a crucial corporate and organizational issue around the world. It has been incorporated into various sectors and countries, and includes many types of activities and dimensions. It is a common notion that organizations are more inclined today to broaden and shift their performance focus from short-term goals towards long-term social, environmental, and value-based perspectives.

Under the framework of corporate governance, organizations and companies are motivated to promote fairness, transparency, ethics, and accountability in their transactions while concurrently maintaining enhanced standards of governance. This means that organizations and corporations must align their activities with community aspirations, which is an issue falling within the sphere of CSR. Increased attention has been placed on the organizations regarding their approach toward the needs of various stakeholders. However, a crucial issue that this book attempts to address is the association, intersection, and inter-relationship between governance and CSR within the EU region, which are not adequately established in the existing literature. The book will show that governance and CSR are highly connected. With the purpose of studying the association of CSR with legal, managerial, and empirical aspects of governance in corporations and not-for-profit organizations in various sectors of the economy, the book also intends to provide useful policy implications, as well as to offer constructive directions for future research.

This book will be of value to researchers, academics, practitioners, policymakers, and students in the fields of CSR and governance, organizational theory, marketing management, business ethics, and human resource management.

Panagiotis Dimitropoulos is Member of the Department of Sport Organization and Management at the University of Peloponnese, Greece.

Efthalia (Elia) Chatzigianni is Associate Professor in the Department of Sport Organization and Management at the University of Peloponnese, Greece.

Routledge Studies in Corporate Governance

For more information about this series, please visit www.routledge.com/
Routledge-Studies-in-Corporate-Governance/book-series/RSCG

Corporate Social Responsibility and Governance

Stakeholders, Management and Organizational Performance in the European Union

Edited by Panagiotis Dimitropoulos and Efthalia (Elia) Chatzigianni

Routledge
Taylor & Francis Group

NEW YORK AND LONDON

First published 2022
by Routledge
605 Third Avenue, New York, NY 10158

and by Routledge
4 Park Square, Milton Park, Abingdon, Oxon, OX14 4RN

Routledge is an imprint of the Taylor & Francis Group, an informa business

Library of Congress Cataloging-in-Publication Data
A catalog record for this book has been requested

ISBN: 978-0-367-71590-8 (hbk)
ISBN: 978-0-367-71593-9 (pbk)
ISBN: 978-1-003-15275-0 (ebk)

DOI: 10.4324/9781003152750

Typeset in Sabon
by Apex CoVantage, LLC

Contents

Contributors

Niki Alexandrou

Niki is Counsel at global legal practice, Norton Rose Fulbright LLP, advising on a broad range of international finance transactions. She is an accredited leadership coach by the US International Coaching Federation (ICF) and a member of the World Business & *Executive Coach* Summit (WBECS) group of executive coaching and leadership. She is also Regional Co-leader (Greece) for the international women empowerment organization "Lean In". In 2002, Niki was called to the Bar of England and Wales. She holds a postgraduate certificate on "Sustainable Leadership" from the University of Cambridge, a Master of Laws (LLM) from University College London, and a degree (LLB) from the University of Bristol.

Antonopoulou Panagiota

Panagiota Antonopoulou is Associate Professor of Communication, Media, and Sport/Political Environment at the Sport Management Department, University of Peloponnese (UoP), and Director of a Postgraduate Program on Modern Sport Communication, Journalism, and Photo Press. She is also a visiting lecturer (SEP) at the Greek Open University (EAP). She earned her doctoral degree from Panteion University (Grade: Excellent). She worked for more than two decades as a journalist and served as Director of three Greek, daily, newspapers. She is a member of the Journalists' Union of Athens Daily Newspapers (ESIEA, member of International Federation of Journalists) and an associate member of the International Press Union of Greece. She has been honored with significant awards for her journalist activity. She has also served the field of social insurance, as the President of the Consolidated Insurance Fund of Media Stuff (ETAP MME) for four years, and as a member of the Temporary Board of Directors of Greek Consolidated Fund for Social Insurance (EFKA).

Chatzigianni Efthalia (Elia)

Efthalia (Elia) Chatzigianni is Associate Professor of International Organizations and other forms of cooperation in the field of sport at the Sport Management Department, UoP, Greece. She holds a BA in Sociology from the Panteion University of Social & Political Sciences, Athens, Greece, an MA in International Politics from the Université Libre de Bruxelles, Belgium, and a PhD in International and European Studies from the Panteion University of Social & Political Sciences, Athens, Greece. She is the author of two books: *Sport Governance: Globalization International Organization and Politics* (2018, Athens: Sideris) and *Lobbying: Interest Promotion Mechanisms* (2007, Athens: Papazissis). Her current research interests lie in the areas of global sport, sport policy and politics, sport governance, sport lobbying, gender issues in sport, sport and the environment, and the Olympic Games. She has lectured in various undergraduate and graduate academic programs and published numerous articles and book chapters in English, Greek, French, and German. She was an international visiting scholar and instructor (2017–2018) at the Sport Management Department, Brock University, Canada, and a visiting professor (2013 and 2014) at CERES, Munk School of Global Affairs, and the Faculty of Kinesiology and Physical Education, University of Toronto, Canada. Among others, she has participated in many international conferences as well as in the organization of various sport events, including three Olympic Games (1996, 2002, 2004). She is a member of various NGOs.

Colibăşanu Oana – Antonia

Oana – Antonia Colibasanu is a senior lecturer in economic diplomacy and geopolitics at the National University for Political Studies and Public Administration in Bucharest, Romania. She is also the Chief Operating Officer of the US-based firm Geopolitical Futures. Prior to joining Geopolitical Futures, she worked for more than ten years with the global analysis firm Stratfor in various positions, including Partner for Europe and Vice-President for International Marketing. Among other academic credentials, she holds a doctorate in international business and economics from Bucharest University of Economic Studies, where her thesis focused on country risk analysis and investment decision-making processes within transnational companies. She also holds a master's degree in international project management.

Dimitropoulos Panagiotis

Panagiotis Dimitropoulos, Ph.D., is a teaching and research associate in accounting and finance in the Department of Sport Organization and Management, UoP. His research interests include financial and managerial accounting, sport finance, and financial management. He has published several papers on top-tier academic journals (*European Sport Management Quarterly, British Accounting Review, R&D Management, Journal of Economic Behavior and Organization, Corporate Governance: An International Review,* among others). He is the author of three books and has presented numerous studies on international conferences.

Douvis John

John Douvis received his Ph.D. in Sport Management from the University of Connecticut. His corporate experience includes several organizations like the NBA, the "Athens 2004" Organizing Committee for the Olympic Games, the Greek Ministry of Tourism Development, the Board of the UoP, the Hellenic Tennis Federation, and the AEK Basketball Club. For several years he was Greek national champion in the sport of tennis. Since 2002 he has been a member of the marketing board of the Hellenic Olympic Committee. Currently, Dr. Douvis is a professor in the Department of Sport Management of the UoP, teaching sport marketing. He is also the cofounder of an internationally acknowledged master's program in sport management.

Kastrinaki Zafeira

Zafeira Kastrinaki is Senior Lecturer of Strategy, Entrepreneurship, and International Management at Brunel University Business School, London. Prior to joining Brunel University in January 2018, she held academic positions at the Universities of Bath and Warwick and Imperial College, London, as well as professional consultancy positions in the private sector. Zafeira conducts research at the intersection of strategic (risk) management and corporate finance, and she has published in top-tier academic journals such as the *Business Ethics Quarterly, Oxford Bulletin of Economics and Statistics,* and *Economics Letters.* She has also been involved in consultancy work on various antitrust and merger control investigations.

Kourtesopoulou Anna

Anna Kourtesopoulou received her Ph.D. in Sport Management from the UoP and her MBA from the Open University of Cyprus. Her current areas of research interest include human resource management, business ethics, organizational culture, and leadership development.

Kyriakis Vaios

Vaios Kyriakis is a Ph.D. candidate in the Sport Management Department, UoP. He graduated from the Department of PE and Sport Science, National Kapodistrian University of Athens (UoA), and received his master's degree (sport management) in 2013 from UoP. Since 2001, he has been working as a PE teacher in public education. He is also a part-time grassroots Alpine Ski Coach. Currently, Kyriakis is PE and school sports coordinator, Attica's Eastern Prefecture, Greece. His research interests include CSR in sport organizations and educational settings.

Mallen Cheryl

Cheryl Mallen is Associate Professor of Sport Management, Faculty of Applied Health Sciences, Brock University, Canada. She researches sport facility and event management, along with environmental sustainability (ES) performance. She has generated an ES measurement tool for sport events, examined best practices, challenges, trends, and interpretations of ES by the International Olympic Committee, studied sport facility renewable energy, and developed a framework for debating the future of ES in sport. Her research manuscripts can be found in a variety of sport management journals.

Strigas Ethan

Ethan Strigas was born in Athens, Greece. He graduated from the Department of Physical Education and Sports Science of the National University of Athens and earned a Master in Sports Organization and Management (MS) from Western Illinois University (USA), a Master in Business Administration (MBA) from Indiana State University (USA), and a Ph.D. in Sports Organization and Management from Florida State University (USA). For many years he taught organization and management, marketing, and sports finance at public universities in the United States. He has received international recognition for his scientific research and work in sports volunteering. Since 2013 he has been working at the UoP as an associate professor in the field of organization and management of volunteers in sports. His interests and activities extend to issues of health and physical activity, people with disabilities, and diversity and women's leadership.

Triantafyllidis Stavros

Stavros Triantafyllidis is Director of the Sport Management Programs and Assistant Professor at the Department of Health and Human Performance at The Citadel. He teaches courses at both the undergraduate and graduate levels. Stavros completed his Ph.D. in Sport Management with an emphasis on environmental sustainability and sport events from the University of Florida. He also earned a Master of Science in Sport Administration and Education from the University of Miami and a Bachelor of Science in Environmental Science from the University of Aegean (Greece). Dr. Triantafyllidis' research focuses on sport and sustainable development. Currently, he is actively involved in research projects with his students. Specifically, Stavros investigates with his students how sport can be an effective platform for sustainable development interventions at the personal, social, and environmental levels. His research also explores how the sport world can become more sustainable in its operations, such as events and transportation.

Tsagdi Christina

Christina Tsagdi studied at the Democritus University of Thrace in the Department of Physical Education and Sports Science. In 1998 she completed her master's thesis, and in 2003 she was awarded a doctorate by the same department. She is a research associate at the volunteer laboratory for sports and social services of the UoP and a research associate for education issues of the Hellenic Taekwondo Federation. She has participated in seminars and conferences related to her professional capacity and has given many lectures on volunteering. She has worked as a project manager for the General Directorate of Education and Training of the Organizing Committee of the Athens 2004 Olympic Games, aiming at the implementation of the Olympic Education Programs and the co-writing of books related to the sports of the Olympic Games.

Illustrations

Figures

Tables

1 A Conceptual Orientation of Corporate Social Responsibility and Governance

Panagiotis Dimitropoulos and Efthalia (Elia) Chatzigianni

Introduction

The European industry is "the motor of growth and prosperity in Europe", as has been argued by the president of the European Commission in 2020. The activities of companies have significant implications on all aspects of life of the European citizens including – but not limited to – the environment, social policy, health, human rights, gender issues, distribution of wealth, etc. In other words, company actions influence human development and well-being by a great extent. Given this, as well as the significance of European industrial leadership to the rest of the world, European industrial policy and related decision-making processes have a major impact on corporate social responsibility (CSR) and governance all around the world. CSR has received increased attention from business managers and executives, international organizations and researchers over the last decades, especially due to their significant impact on the organizational operations.

Several research studies have documented that businesses and organizations have stakeholders who exert pressure on the activities of firms owing to the concern for human rights, labor standards, and environmental issues (Dimitropoulos & Koronios, 2021). Moreover, the European Commission has defined CSR as "the responsibility of enterprises for their impact on society and therefore should be company led".

Under this framework, CSR has been utilized as a tool for competitive advantage, allowing firms and organizations to differentiate themselves from their competitors. CSR includes corporate activities, and policies, incorporated within daily business activities, decision-making processes, and organization structures (Dimitropoulos & Koronios, 2021). Several scholars have distinguished between the internal and external dimensions of CSR, where in the internal level organizations establish their priorities according to the needs of the internal stakeholders such as skills, training, education, workplace safety, equal opportunities, and other issues.

DOI: 10.4324/9781003152750-1

The external dimension of CSR (which has received more attention in the literature) focuses on the organization's duties as citizens and targets the external stakeholders and the environment.

Moreover, governance as a term is widely discussed – among others – in relation to the organization's performance. In this framework, the most acceptable description of governance is that of a system by which organizations are directed and controlled. Beyond that, governance encompasses the sense of compliance (laws and regulations), transparency, and accountability (based on codes of conduct). Practically, governance sets the framework under which power is exerted and decisions are reached within the organizations. Recently, a more extended and broader governance concept has given emphasis to an organization's responsibilities toward its various stakeholders who provide vital resources for organization's survival and longevity. Under these theoretical lenses, managers are not only responsible toward the owners, but also toward suppliers, their employees, local communities within which they operate, customers, and other indirect stakeholders. Good governance includes areas such as strategic setting and leadership, transparency, and honesty. Those areas are tightly connected with public acceptance and legitimacy, employee trust and commitment. In summary, governance revolves around a number of attributes such as stakeholder accountability, mechanisms for managerial control, and organizational structures that ensure that organizational behavior is abiding to laws and regulations, is answerable to stakeholders, and incorporates both shareholder and stakeholder value leading to enhanced accountability and organizational performance. Corporate governance may also determine the degree and impact of the organization's lobbying intensity and activities (Mathur, Singh, Thompson, & Nejadmalayeri, 2013).

Despite the increased interest of CSR and governance on various business sectors, those concepts have been extensively examined separately as two different or distinct mechanisms of organizational behavior, despite that fact that those two issues are inherently associated. Good governance should recognize CSR, and effective CSR must accommodate governance structures. When considering the broader concept of governance, it is clear that efficient governance includes responsibility and due regard of all main stakeholders. CSR and governance overlap on that direction as both mechanisms consider stakeholder relations as a crucial factor for sustaining and adding value to the organization. Several CSR scholars are admitting that internal CSR includes the highest standards of internal governance. Moreover, both concepts are reaching out to organizations to recognize their fiduciary duties and responsibilities toward stakeholders, advancing governance and CSR strategies as core activities targeting to regain the trust of the society at large. Thus, both disciplines are considered as necessary prerequisites for sustainable growth and long-term benefits.

Another reason justifying the examination of the governance–CSR interconnection is the fact that governance can be considered as a pillar of CSR and vice versa; CSR can be considered as a dimension of governance. According to the resource-based view (RBV) of an organization, the value creation process involves utilization of humans, stakeholders, and environmental capital through an effective governance system. In other words, governance is the main foundation for integrated CSR activities. On the contrary, CSR is also considered as a dimension of governance that makes the scope of governance even wider and more inclusive. This opinion posits that good governance is responsible for ensuring that the organization operates in a socially responsible way, and so there must be a clear ethical base for complying with the accepted social norms. In other words, being responsible to the society and to the employees is a quality that should be embedded in governance structures and mechanisms.

Origins of CSR and Social Innovation

CSR was conceptually created during the decade of 1950 and was considered as a phenomenon of social activity which started to alter the way firms (mainly of the developed world) were considering their environment and interacted with it. According to Blowfield and Frynas (2005), CSR is a generic term which was viewed as a social commitment of the enterprises, a strategic process, or even as a cultural issue that evolved over the years and transformed itself into a paramount factor of business decisions. A basic definition of CSR was initially documented by Carroll (1979, 1991) connecting the legal, economic, ethical, and philanthropic behavior of modern organizations. Practically, firms need not only be conforming to laws and regulations but they have to move beyond the necessary activities obliged by law as well, so as to be seen as being socially responsible. Several researchers have provided many definitions on CSR most of which seem to converge into the economic, social, environmental, and ethical behavior of organizations and corporations (Maignan & Ferrell, 2004; Sarkar & Searcy, 2016; Dahlsrud, 2008; Turker, 2018).

This dynamic evolution of the CSR concept, moving from a more generic notion of "doing the right thing" during the mid-1950 to the enhancement of ethical behavior (1960s), in turn led to the stakeholder management processes during the 1990s (Turker, 2018). Today, CSR incorporates strategic decisions encompassing firms' institutional environment including all direct and indirect stakeholders of the organization. This ongoing process of CSR development has impacted both businesses and regulators (such as the European Union) on the definitions they have provided over the years by including all forms and shapes of corporate activities leading to the so-called environmental, social, and governance (ESG) nexus of corporate activities often termed as "corporate sustainability" (Brockett & Rezaee, 2012; Dimitropoulos & Koronios, 2021). Academic researchers have also tried to approach CSR from various methodological and epistemological lenses providing new conceptual frameworks, theories, and even empirical studies (Turker, 2018).

Despite the collective efforts on defining and structuring the concept of CSR, its application within the private business sector presents significant differences among developed and developing countries. Cramer, Jonker, and van der Heijden (2004) and Dimitropoulos and Koronios (2021) all point that CSR perceptions and activities (and even strategies) are presenting a different pace and effectiveness of implementation between more-developed EU member countries (old EU members) compared to their less-developed counterparts. The reasons for these differences are the distinct cultural, legal, and even structural features of those nations that yield support (or not) toward CSR interest and implementation within the corporate world (Jamali, 2007).

Furthermore, CSR has been considered as a form of social innovation (Turker, 2018). The implementation of CSR activities from organizations includes the development of ideas, new projects, decisions on resource allocation, and the creation of new products and services, so as to respond to new economic, environmental, or social challenges and problems. Those decisions pertain to various organizational stakeholders ranging from employees and customers to local communities and the natural environment. Consequently, CSR could be considered as both the determinant and the product of social innovation as it can create and steer innovations within the social sphere. This fact allows companies to make a positive contribution to society and communicate their behavior as a good corporate citizen to the public. Moreover, social innovation (via CSR) could be a fruitful mechanism for resolving stakeholders' conflict of interest and generally enhancing corporate reputation and relation with local communities. Since the solution of social and environmental issues requires the collaboration of various actors, CSR allows the understanding of the interconnected relations between governmental, nongovernmental organizations and corporations, thus reducing the barriers of communication and enhancing opportunities for collaboration (Wood, 1991).

CSR and Sustainability

Corporate sustainability has received increased attention internationally due to the enhanced international awareness of the public regarding the planet's global warming, water and air pollution, social integration, and sustainable production and consumption during the previous decades. This fact urged corporations to shift their attention and actions toward these issues, as they were strongly connected with social cohesion and approval of their corporate activities.

During the early years of 2000, the issue of sustainable development started to emerge within the discussion of CSR and its implications for firms and organizations. Initially, the two concepts were sharing the same meaning or they were being used interchangeably within the academic and practitioner fields. According to Bansal and Song (2016) and Turker (2018), sustainability research was motivated by CSR scholarship by introducing a more systemic perspective on its theory and practice; thus CSR and CS were theorized as a system of inputs and outputs. The inputs of this system are distinguished on the basis of individual or managerial characteristics (educational background, gender, leadership, values, and personal ethics among others), organizational characteristics (corporate governance, strategy and firm culture), and contextual (global and institutional environment) features. These inputs are processed within the organization taking into consideration their stakeholders, daily operations, and firms' responsibilities in order to produce outputs captured by CSR strategies and activities or operationalized via corporate sustainability goals (Turker, 2018).

Business sustainability, in other words, is a concept which distinguishes stakeholders between those that have a direct legal claim to the firm (shareholders and lenders) and thus bear the risks of corporate activities, and other stakeholders who may have a contractual relationship with the firm (creditors, customers, employees, etc.). CSR and CS should be incorporated within operational practices, strategies, and decisions on functional areas of the organization relating to production of products and services, marketing policies, human resources, and even financial management. Corporate sustainability activities (social and environmental type of initiatives) could affect the well-being of those stakeholders, and so a weak social or environmental sustainability performance may expose stakeholders to a threat or a deterioration of their well-being. This fact exerts a pressure on future corporate endeavors which are crucial for enhancing the efficiency of firms' prospects.

CSR and Governance

Modern organizations and corporations are governed by executives and board members who have been appointed by the shareholders with the aim to protect their interests and enhance the value of the firm. Corporate Governance (CG) determines the systems, principles, processes, and procedures by which organizations are governed. CG determines and describes the relationships among the principal and agents of the organization, which shape the strategies, directions, and activities of the organization (Jensen & Meckling, 1976). Putting it differently, CG addresses issues related to the boards' fiduciary duties; the responsibilities of executives, board members, and managers; and the procedures with which the board members and other board committees' members are elected and appointed to specific duties and positions (Turker, 2018). It is the responsibility of the organization to create and foster an environment characterized by ethical and accountable behaviors among all stakeholders involved so as to enhance the reputation of the organization.

Multiple international organizations (including the World Bank, the Organization for Economic Co-Operation and Development-OECD among others) have accepted that CG includes all the official processes and procedures that form the basis of an organization's control and management. It includes distribution of responsibilities, duties, and rights (of shareholders, creditors and other stakeholders) and sets the rules for decision-making within the organization (European Central Bank, 2004). Efficient CG helps organizations to enhance their abilities to access external capital sources by contributing to sustainable financial growth. According to OECD (2004), efficient corporate governance can create more efficient and transparent financial markets by protecting the rights of investors and shareholders with equal treatment of all shareholders (minority, institutional, foreign, and majority shareholders). It also allows the cooperation of the organization with stakeholders (by mutually benefiting agreements) so as to enhance employment levels, income, and wealth within the economy, achieving an overall financially sustainable environment. Moreover, CG can improve the transparency by allowing timely and accurate financial information to be made publicly available and finally allowing the effective monitoring of managerial decisions by the shareholders (and other interested parties) through board and executives accountability to the shareholders (Turker, 2018).

All these issues are further discussed in the framework of "good governance" that involves a number of aspects that occur in the process of governing an organization. Aspects of good governance are mainly linked to the values of the public, which strengthen the legitimacy of the organization, and the trust between all stakeholders involved including employees, employers, and shareholders. Good governance enhances the reputation of the organization and maintains the trust of investors and other stakeholders (Nadaf & Navi, 2016). To achieve good governance, organizations need to identify areas of improvement in corporate governance issues following guidelines developed and promoted by a number of international organizations such as the OECD and the EU. Corporate governance principles were first articulated in the "Cadbury Report" (Jones & Pollitt, 2004) and further elaborated in the OECD Principles of Corporate Governance (Camilleri, 2017). Both intended to help organizations to acknowledge and improve their corporate governance standards and, thus, their efficiency and reputation.

Practically, OECD (2004) created a framework of CG which encompasses all areas of organizational and corporate operations. Special focus has been put on the recognition and protection of shareholders (and investors) rights, enhancing the accountability and transparency of executives and board members on decisions they make on daily operations. Along the years, CG extended its scope from having a shareholder-centered focus to having a stakeholder-centered focus. This fact was motivated by the perception of the public that businesses and corporations must also meet the needs and expectations of stakeholders. CSR seems to be an effective answer to this task by incorporating the interests of various stakeholders into daily operations, thus leading to the integration of CG with CSR.

Hancock (2005), Ho (2005), Bhimani and Soonawalla (2005), Jamali, Safieddine, and Rabbath (2008) and Turker (2018) stress that there are three main theoretical models on the association between corporate governance (CG) and CSR. The first suggests that CG is a basic pillar of CSR; on the contrary, the second theoretical argument addresses CSR as a feature of CG or as a strategy that is incorporated within the mechanisms through which the organization is governed (including policies and processes). At the end, the third theoretical model considers both as different or distinct mechanisms that tend to coexist and complement each other and jointly contribute to corporate transparency, accountability, and sustainability.

The majority of the empirical studies lean toward the second theoretical model and consider CSR as a feature of CG since all decisions relating to CSR activities are discussed and received within the board, and even corporate boards are forming specific sustainability (or CSR) committees responsible for drafting, organizing, and executing the corporate CSR strategy (Dimitropoulos & Koronios, 2021). Recently, several studies have followed the third theoretical model and considered CSR and CG as complementary mechanisms. However, this complementarity is existent only within developed financial markets and countries and is less visible in developing countries (Rahim & Alam, 2014). The lack of the relative regulatory framework and the required institutional mechanisms within the developing countries raises barriers on the incorporation of CSR with CG mechanisms. This fact is not beneficial for stakeholders and is even more difficult for organizations to survive under difficult economic conditions and even unexpected financial crises.

Structure of the Book

The book is structured into three parts. The first part is dedicated on the theoretical and legal framework of CSR and governance. Chapter 2 aims to provide the theoretical background on CSR, the evolution of different theories and their contribution on mapping the CSR research landscape, and finally offers a brief perspective on contemporary models and development of CSR. Chapter 3 extends our understanding of theories and definitions of governance and explores the theoretical framework that applies to both corporate and nonprofit governance. In sum, this chapter provides an opportunity to learn about the notion of governance and begins with a presentation of various definitions of both governance and good governance, with the three key areas of governance, including board composition, relationships, and effectiveness explained. The fourth chapter is devoted to a discussion the European Union's (EU) regulations and policies on governance and CSR. The chapter provides a comprehensive analysis on the first rules on governance started back in 1992 and moves on into more contemporary policies relating to European firms and their relations with key stakeholders and other firms within and outside of the EU. Also, the chapter provides information on corporate social performance indicators of EU-domiciled firms, the evolution of this performance of the last fifteen years, and its disaggregation among country and business sectors.

The second part of the book provides both theoretical and empirical investigations of corporate governance and CSR within the EU. The fifth chapter investigates the role of board of directors as a core element of corporate governance in corporate philanthropic activities, a strand of CSR, followed by the sixth chapter which examines the impact of corporate sustainability performance (both social and environmental performance) on total executive compensation while considering the existence of a voluntary CSR-sustainability committee within the board of directors. The sixth chapter utilizes a large sample of listed and unlisted corporations from 24 EU countries over the period 2003–2018. The seventh chapter describes some contemporary principal challenges for directors in the context of UK law and discusses the statutory obligation of directors to promote their company's success and examines good practice examples of leadership and corporate governance available to support directors in their decision-making. The eighth chapter offers a discussion on the ethical dimension of CSR by stressing the perception of socially responsible corporation outlines and the need for fair treatment and protection of shareholders' rights, integrity, and ethical behavior of directors and executives. At the end, the ninth chapter provides an empirical analysis on the impact of CSR activities and performance on corporate financial performance taking into consideration the potential endogeneity problem between the examined factors and their bidirectional association, evidenced by previous studies on the field.

The third section of the book provides a thorough discussion on several managerial aspects of CSR and governance in the EU. Starting with Chapter 10, which investigates the existing correlation of two important research areas for business management, corporate governance and CSR, it also considers the evolution of gender and diversity studies into a key element that is increasingly connecting the two fields. Chapter 11 contributes to the broad debate on CSR and governance, media and communication under common European policy, using the geometric shape of the pyramid in order to describe the interdependent relation between them. Followed by Chapter 12, which offers a cross-sectional literature review converging elements and findings regarding the concept of CSR in governance at professional sport and sport organizations, it also focuses on issues concerning various critical marketing aspects, necessary for the viability and sustainability of sport organizations in a global but fragmented market. Following Chapter 12, Chapter 13 connects CSR with volunteering in organizations and the efficient use of human resources on CSR and sustainability activities. At the end, Chapter 14 discusses the elements of governance, sustainability, and CSR and further explores the current literature on the relationships between governance with sustainability and CSR.

References

Bansal, P., & Song, H. C. (2016). Similar but not the same: Differentiating corporate responsibility from sustainability. *Academy of Management Annals*, *11*(1), 105–149.

Bhimani, A., & Soonawalla, K. (2005). From conformance to performance: The corporate responsibilities continuum. *Journal of Accounting and Public Policy*, *24*(3), 165–174.

Blowfield, M., & Frynas, J. G. (2005). Setting new agendas: Critical perspectives on corporate social responsibility in the developing world. *International Affairs*, *81*(3), 499–513.

Brockett, A., & Rezaee, Z. (2012). *Corporate sustainability: Integrating performance and reporting*. Hoboken, NJ: Wiley.

Camilleri, M. A. (2017). *Corporate sustainability, social responsibility and environmental management*. Cham, Switzerland: Springer.

Carroll, A. B. (1979). A three-dimensional conceptual model of corporate social performance. *Academy of Management Review*, *4*, 497–505.

Carroll, A. B. (1991). The pyramid of corporate social responsibility: Toward the moral management of organizational stakeholders. *Business Horizons*, *34*(4), 39–48.

Cramer, J., Jonker, J., & van der Heijden, A. (2004). Making sense of corporate social responsibility. *Journal of Business Ethics*, *55*(2), 215–222.

Dahlsrud, A. (2008). How corporate social responsibility is defined: An analysis of 37 definitions. *Corporate Social Responsibility and Environmental Management*, *15*(1), 1–13.

Dimitropoulos, P., & Koronios, K. (2021). *Corporate environmental responsibility, accounting and corporate finance in the EU*. Cham, Switzerland: Springer Nature Switzerland.

European Central Bank. (2004). *Annual report: 2004. ECB: Frankfurt*. Retrieved April 22, 2021, from http://stats.oecd.org/glossary/detail.asp?ID=6778

Hancock, J. (Ed.). (2005). *Investing in corporate social responsibility: A guide to best practice, business planning and the UK's leading companies*. London: Kogan Page.

Ho, C. (2005). Corporate governance and corporate competitiveness: An international analysis. *Corporate Governance: An International Review*, *13*, 211–253.

Jamali, D. (2007). The case for strategic corporate social responsibility in developing countries. *Business and Society Review, 112*, 1–27.

Jamali, D., Safieddine, A. M., & Rabbath, M. (2008). Corporate governance and corporate social responsibility synergies and interrelationships. *Corporate Governance: An International Review, 16*(5), 590–602.

Jensen, M. C., & Meckling, W. H. (1976). Theory of the firm: Managerial behavior, agency costs and ownership structure. *Journal of Financial Economics, 3*, 305–360.

Jones, I., & Pollitt, M. (2004). Understanding how issues in corporate governance develop: CadburyReport to Higgs review. *Corporate Governance: An International review, 12*(2), 162–171.

Maignan, I., & Ferrell, O. C. (2004). Corporate social responsibility and marketing: An integrative framework. *Journal of the Academy of Marketing Science, 32*(1), 3–19.

Mathur, I., Singh, M., Thompson, F., & Nejadmalayeri, A. (2013). Corporate governance and lobbying strategies. *Journal of Business Research, 66*(4), 547–553. ISSN 0148–2963. https://doi.org/10.1016/j.jbusres.2012.01.003.

Nadaf, S., & Navi, B. (2016). Corporate governance: Issues, opportunities and challenges. *International Journal of Commerce and Management Research, 3*(7), 66072.

Organization for Economic Co-Operation and Development (OECD). (2004). *OECD principles of corporate governance.* Paris: OECD Publications.

Rahim, M. M., & Alam, S. (2014). Convergence of corporate social responsibility and corporate governance in weak economies: The case of Bangladesh. *Journal of Business Ethics, 121*(4), 607–620.

Sarkar, S., & Searcy, C. (2016). Zeitgeist or chameleon? A quantitative analysis of CSR definitions. *Journal of Cleaner Production, 135*, 1423–1435.

Turker, D. (2018). *Managing social responsibility.* Cham, Switzerland: Springer Nature Switzerland.

Wood, D. J. (1991). Corporate social performance revisited. *Academy of Management Review, 16*, 691–718.

Part I

Theoretical and Legal Framework of Corporate Social Responsibility and Governance

2 Corporate Social Responsibility

Stakeholder Theory, and Conceptual Framework

Panagiotis Dimitropoulos

Introduction

Corporate social responsibility (CSR) has been included in the agenda of international organizations, multinational and local corporations and organizations and also has been examined under the lens of several theories and perspectives. At its initial phases of development, CSR was examined as a facet of corporate or business behavior that impacts on local societies and the environment. This fact evolved over the years under the term "sustainable development", and corporate sustainability is the outcome of enhancing the awareness of corporations and individuals on environmental and social issues (Wang, 2013). The first broad definition of corporate sustainability (and sustainable development eventually) was provided by the World Commission on Environment and Development (WCED, 1987) as a form of development that does not compromise the ability of future generations to meet their needs, while simultaneously providing the necessary for the present needs of the society.

This perspective portrayed corporate activity within a more socially and environmentally sustainable focus, considering the economic impact of business behavior on the environment and how these three issues (society, environment, and economy) are inherently interconnected. This means that the human economic activity must be in accordance with nature and should not exhaust natural resources, while achieving economic growth. Also, current generations must pursue enhanced development and consumption yet at the same time must shape the necessary ground for allowing an equal opportunity to their descendants. Abrams (1951) was among the first who echoed his disquiets about the responsibilities of managers toward their customers, employees, and the society as a whole. In a similar direction, Bowen and Johnson (1953) argued that corporations constitute important centers of power, and so their activities have repercussions on lives and well-being of citizens.

Under this framework, CSR was initially considered as a form of corporate benevolence and for that was associated with theories of business ethics, stewardship, and philanthropic principles of business behavior

DOI: 10.4324/9781003152750-3

(Camilleri, 2017). Early theoretical arguments by Drucker (1984) point to the utilization of CSR as a mechanism to address social issues in order to yield positive economic results. This view contradicted the dominant paradigm of corporate action which focused mainly on shareholder wealth maximization as the only responsibility of corporations (Levitt, 1958; Friedman, 1962, 1970). Since the mid-1980s, the concept of CSR developed further by including all key stakeholders who affect and even determine the existence and viability of a corporation. Freeman (1984) argued that those key stakeholders (except shareholders) must be acting as a sincere apprehension for managers and corporations. In other words, CSR has started to be considered as a logical economic justification for doing the "right thing" or what is good as portrayed by McWilliams and Siegel (2001).

Moreover, Carroll (1979) argued that corporations had a commitment to the society and should engage themselves on ethical, legal, and benevolent activities. As society provides a legitimacy to corporate activities and their mere existence, corporations should give something back to the community. On a later work, Carroll (1991) depicted CSR in a form of a pyramid where the economic responsibility being placed at the top at the pyramid, while legal responsibility (conforming to laws and regulations), ethical responsibility (involving key stakeholders within decision-making processes), and philanthropic responsibility (involving charitable behavior toward the local communities) formed the base of that pyramid.

Eventually, CSR gained significant momentum in the managerial and economic literature as it was considered by several scholars as a tool for competitive advantage, differentiation, innovation, and opportunity for businesses (Porter & Kramer, 2006), and not only a way to do "just good" to the society and the environment. Today, CSR activities are expressed via multiple ways by benefiting other organizations, groups, local communities, and individuals on several issues including health, cultural, and social problems and even sport activities and education (Camilleri, 2017). Those activities create significant economic and social outcomes including enhanced reputation, social trust toward the firm, financial performance and viability (Wang & Choi, 2013; Ameer & Othman, 2012; Orlitzky, Schmidt, & Rynes, 2003). According to Camilleri (2017), corporations can benefit themselves via enhanced social and environmental performance as they can accrue significant financial and strategic results such as cost reductions and operational efficiencies.

In the literature, there are several definitions of CSR; yet, none seems to have gained significant momentum or dynamism on prevailing over the other. For example, Davis (1973) argues that CSR is the response of a firm to issues beyond the narrow economic, technical, and legal requirements in order to achieve certain social and environmental goals and all those under the notion of balancing the concerns of different stakeholders. In the same vein, the World Business Council for Sustainable

Development (WBCSD, 1999), the International Organization for Standardization (ISO, 2010), and the Business for Social Responsibility (BSR, 2003) – all refer to CSR as the corporate commitment toward contributing to societal and environmental sustainability by applying transparent and ethical behavior without neglecting their economic responsibility toward their investors and shareholders (Chang et al., 2017).

Despite the fact that numerous academics and researchers have dedicated themselves on CSR research, there is still no consensus on a general definition of CSR (Dahlsrud, 2008). As previously discussed, CSR has been related with many concepts including business ethics, accountability, corporate citizenship, sustainability, social and environmental performance, stakeholder theory and stakeholder commitment, value creation, and even strategic orientation of social behavior (Camilleri, 2017, p. 6). Several scholars have distinguished between the internal and external dimensions of CSR, where in the internal level organizations establish their priorities according to the needs of the internal stakeholders such as skills, training, education, workplace safety, equal opportunities, and other issues. The external dimension of CSR (which has received more attention in the literature) focuses on the organization's duties as citizens and targets the external stakeholders and the environment.

The scope of this chapter is to shed further light on the vast literature on CSR by performing a structured analysis on CSR theories from the perspectives of business ethics, corporate legitimacy and institutional theory, social contract theory, and corporate citizenship theory and by providing a thorough discussion on the theoretical frameworks that shaped CSR and its successor, "corporate sustainability". We believe that this chapter will provide to the reader a sound theoretical base for evaluating CSR under different lenses and connecting the association between governance and CSR more efficiently (as will be done in the following chapters of the book). The rest of the chapter is organized as follows: in the following section, we provide the theoretical background of CSR and its relation to business ethics. The third section is devoted to analyzing the various theoretical foundations (various theories) of CSR. The fourth section discusses new theoretical models and developments on the CSR literature, while the last section concludes the chapter.

Theorizing on CSR and Business Ethics

The decade of the 1980s was characterized by an immense attention on ethical business conduct, and the notion that businesses should be accountable not only to their owners gained more and more thrust from academic literature. Thereafter, relative concepts and theories were developed focusing on corporate social performance, stakeholder theory and management, and the interaction of public policy with businesses on corporate social responsiveness (Freeman, 1984; Frederick, 1986; Wood, 1991).

This trend was actually fueled by several academics arguing that modern corporations must consider their stakeholders' ethical concerns on their strategy and activities (Goodpaster, 1991). Thus, businesses were guided to form an acceptable corporate social behavior through the establishment of communication channels and debate with key stakeholder groups (Camilleri, 2017). Over the years, more and more firms were becoming aware of the significant effect that responsible corporate behavior may have on their performance and thus tended to report information relative to their social or environmental performance.

According to Parker (2014), CSR is a dynamic concept that contains several dimensions and infuses ideas and theories from several fields, and this is the reason that there is not a consensus on what CSR actually includes (Frederick, 1994). One of the first attempts to define CSR was made by Carroll (1991) who argued that CSR is crafted from four pillars of philanthropic, ethical, legal, and economic responsibility. Other scholars argue that environmental performance is another important dimension of CSR not fairly represented on the CSR theories (Dahlsrud, 2008), and even more recent arguments by Sarkar and Searcy (2016) have extended the theoretical framework of CSR by incorporating societal and sustainability objectives within the definition of CSR.

According to Johnstone (2018), CSR initially originated from forces outside from the firm. Social and environmental practices, systems, and policies on CSR matters were actually implemented after pressures from external stakeholders. So firms aimed to enhance their reputation, image, and social acceptance through enhanced social performance. These activities improved stakeholders' trust toward the firm, a fact that corroborated arguments within stakeholder and legitimacy theories (Hassan & Ibrahim, 2012; Moore, 2013; Pondeville, Swaen, & De Rongé, 2013). Nevertheless, literature recently introduced broader definitions of CSR that consider it as a system of interactions, where businesses expand their range of stakeholders, while considering financial, social, and environmental goals on their operations (Costa & Torrecchia, 2018). Thus, CSR includes operational and strategic features which are formed inside and outside of the organization. Hence based on Johnstone's (2018) opinion, the goal of CSR stems from internal and external causes that interact dynamically with each other. Consequently, the main theoretical framework of CSR is structured via the intersection of legitimacy theory, stakeholder theory, and institutional theory.

Legitimacy Theory

The legitimacy theory originates from the neoclassical schools of thought (during the 1970s) on the goals of any for-profit organization, which must not be focused solely on increasing revenues and profits but to adhere to social expectations, needs, and problems (Dowling & Pfeffer, 1975).

Legitimacy theory argues that corporate disclosures react to several factors of the external environment (such as economic, social, and political), and in turn such disclosures provide legitimacy on corporate activities (Preston & Post, 1975). This theory is pillared on the premise that corporations operate within a society under a "contract" that urges firms to behave responsibly and ethically (through socially desired activities) in return for an approval on their strategies and goals and ultimately for its own existence and survival (Pfeffer & Salancik, 1978; Woodward, Edwards, & Birkin, 1996; Gary, 2002; Wang, 2013). In other words, changes in social norms, values, and concerns motivate firms to change so as to gain organizational legitimacy. O'Donovan (1999, 2002) argues that environmental activities are able to restore legitimacy on firms that have violated certain laws, regulations, and even social perceptions on environmental protection.

According to O'Donovan (2002) and Johnstone (2018), the views on corporate activities and responsibilities have shifted from considering not only owners and investors, but also social and environmental issues. Also, Deegan (2014) mentions that legitimacy does not merely refer to the activities of organizations but actually is what the members of local communities and the society at large perceive as being legitimate that actually shapes the corporate behavior. Nevertheless, those premises are all leading management teams of every organization to decide on how to act under these circumstances (Pfeffer, 1981; Ashforth & Gibbs, 1990). Putting it differently, legitimacy theory posits that firms can be penalized if they do not operate in a way that expresses society's expectations, values, and even concerns. When a disparity exists between the firm's activities and societal values, it threatens company's legitimacy, and so if firms want to continue operating into a dynamically changing social and economic environment, they must behave within the boundaries that society considers as being acceptable (Dowling & Pfeffer, 1975; Wang, 2013).

All the above-mentioned scholars set the pillars for considering legitimacy as a significant corporate resource manifested through managerial activities arguing that firms inscribe into a social contract with their social environment. This contract is actually the motive for building ethical relations between firms and the society, as it signals to the firms' information about social expectations (Suchman, 1995). At the end, legitimacy theory provides an explanatory value responding to the question on why corporations implement CSR for achieving specific financial goals or even sustaining strategies which are formed from managerial decisions.

Institutional Theory

A second theoretical framework that has contributed to the notion of CSR is institutional theory, which sees institutions as rules (the regulatory environment), ideas, and comprehensions that are created within detached contexts, as proposed by Zucker (1987). Despite the fact that the concept of institutionalization was initially developed during the 1980s and 1990s by the works of Epstein (1987) and Frederick (1994), it was not positioned within the developing CSR literature and was under-represented relative to stakeholder and legitimacy theories (Johnstone, 2018). None the less, institutional theory gained significant momentum in the CSR literature since 2010s, after several researchers have considered the dynamism of CSR and its interconnections with governance and public policy (Brammer, Jackson, & Matten, 2012). Within the CSR literature, institutional theory asserts that firms are forced (or pressured) by regulators and other external legislative forces to consider any negative social or environmental externalities arising from their activities. Thus, social responsibility issues become rooted into firm's strategy as an institutionalized procedure (Contrafartto, 2014; Johnstone, 2018).

In total, institutional theory provides a direction so as to mount social responsibility reporting and communicate it to external stakeholders for achieving strategic or moralistic goals (Higgins & Larrinaga, 2014). Consequently, under the institutional theory's lenses, CSR is considered as the boundary of governance and self-regulation accepted by firms due to external forces (Campbell, 2006; Vogel, 2010; Gond, Kang, & Moon, 2011). Thus, legitimacy and institutional theories (along with the most prominent theory of all – stakeholder theory) form the backbone of knowledge referring to the determinants that affect corporate decisions to engage in CSR behavior.

Stakeholder Theory

The stakeholder theory is the third most important theoretical framework that shaped the evolution of CSR literature. It originated from strategic management theoretical arguments made by Freeman (1984), and its focus and responsiveness on multiple stakeholders groups actually changed the way that CSR was theorized and implemented. Stakeholder theory extended the legitimacy concerns of corporate managers into a more responsive behavior toward various stakeholder groups. CSR eventually started to refer to the level and capacity of such responsiveness. It was believed that if firms started to behave responsibly, they will avoid redundant pressures from stakeholders and even regulators. So stakeholder theory pushed executives to consider their moral duties toward societal concerns, similar to a normative theoretical perspective (Jones, 1980). This is the main reason that stakeholder theory is considered to be more robust, sound, and applicable, as it questions the role of contemporary business on the society (Frederick, 1994). According to Evan and Freeman (1993), stakeholder theory is based on two main principles, the corporate rights principle that states that the corporation is obliged to respect and not violate rights of other stakeholders and the corporate effect principle that states that firms are responsible for the outcome of their activities.

According to Johnstone (2018), stakeholder theory is grounded on the premise that managerial decisions (as managers are key actors within firms) must consider various legitimacy concerns from different societal groups. Nevertheless, both legitimacy and stakeholder theories share the view that organizations are part of an extended social system (Deegan, 2014), and in fact stakeholder theory extends legitimacy concerns according to social values and apprehensions. Based on that premise, CSR has started to incorporate several groups of stakeholders (not being fully represented on the past) such as employees (beyond management personnel) and internal governance procedures (Sundin & Brown, 2017; Chang et al., 2017).

Moreover, Henriques and Sadorsky (1999) emphasize four main stakeholder groups whose concerns need to be considered by modern corporations. Those are the regulatory stakeholders (government, associations, and other members of social networks such as NGOs), the community stakeholders (local community members, environmental groups, and other activities which can affect public opinion), the organizational stakeholders (customers, employees, creditors, investors, suppliers, and shareholders), and the media that influence societal perception on several social issues (Wang, 2013). So it is apparent that failure of corporations to incorporate the power and interests of stakeholder groups can jeopardize their value creation process. So managers and executives have to seriously consider opinions of stakeholder groups when crafting and managing the firms' social behavior (Jones, 1995; Nasi, 1995).

Nonetheless, stakeholder theory does not come without hindrances. Even earlier studies by Jones (1980) have openly admitted that firms were difficult to address all concerns by stakeholders because it is hard to reach a consensus as to what is perceived as being socially responsible behavior and also because stakeholder theory considered stakeholder interest as being equally important, a fact that may not be factually true (Camilleri, 2017). Additionally, there was not suitable representation of the various (or even diverse) stakeholder groups within the firms' decision-making process (relative to the representation of shareholders). This created difficulties in justifying and implementing CSR and even corporate governance structures that involved stakeholders within them (Etzioni, 1999). Moreover, several researchers posit that stakeholder engagement aimed at satisfying managerial goals, opportunism, and image-building instead of actual interest on social issues and problems (Phillips, 2003; Marcoux, 2000; Jensen, 2000).

Consequently, the evolution of the legitimacy, stakeholder, and institutional theories has shaped the modern framework of corporate social performance (CSP), which, according to Garriga and Mele (2004) and Wartick and Cochran (1985), is the outcome of firm's application of CSR policies and programs of social responsiveness to stakeholder concerns. Carroll (2000) argues about the inclusion of philanthropic and ethical activities within CSP that firms engage in, in order to improve the societal well-being. So CSP includes issues of environmental responsibility, activities of social policy, and even efficient stakeholder management. Thus under this framework, CSP is a useful mechanism for communicating firms' commitment and responsiveness to socially responsible values which are shared and aspired by stakeholders (Brammer, He, & Mellahi, 2015).

Additional Theoretical Frameworks on CSR

Beyond the aforementioned three dominant theoretical frameworks (legitimacy, institutional, and stakeholder theories) that shaped the contemporary CSR literature, all three main frameworks are originating from social contract theory. Social contract theory emerged during the Enlightenment period, and those theorists believed that the proper functioning of a society requires its members to reach into an agreement (social contract) on their responsibilities and rights of both state and citizens (Rawls, 1971; Gauthier, 1990; Locke, 2003). For the social contract to produce its expected outcomes, every member of the society must agree to its terms and avoid any violation of it. Social contract theory manifests within several contemporary theoretical frameworks of CSR research and behavior as it recognizes the level of human control and domination on the planet.

Practically, we have entered into a period of significant changes in the human communities. These global changes have urged regulators, academics, and citizens to reconsider their role and their relations with one another in a more systematic way. This fact actually expresses an obligation of science and society's members to exploit their power in order to discover new knowledge, provide an integrated understanding of the public sphere, and ultimately assist society to achieve a more sustainable development (Wang, 2013). According to Lubchenko (1998), through this social contract, societies can be more economically, socially, and environmentally sound and just.

Contemporary environmental issues emerged during the last two decades, alongside the immense interest from regulators, scientists, firms, and the general public on environmental issues, and the theory of circular economy were developed as a way to balance corporate behavior and environmental awareness. According to Zhang (2004) and Ren and Wu (2005), the economic system is grounded on material circulation and energy flows, a fact that requires individuals to coherently apply environmental protection laws, which will provide the framework for social and environmental responsible behavior of firms. This theory extended the issue of environmental protection to almost all significant sectors of the economy by considering both environmental protection and economic operations as integrated and associated facets of the society (Wang, 2013).

The main characteristic of the circular economy theory is that it requires firms to organize their economic activities within a process of resources usage – outcomes produced – renewable resources, where there is a constant flow of materials within a certain cycle. Therefore, practically this theory posits a more efficient and environment-friendly method for the exploitation of waste that simultaneously is less harmful to the environment and also provides enhanced economic and employment opportunities by allocating the economy's scarce resources more efficiently. The second feature is the importance of science and technology in assisting individuals and corporations to use less harmful production techniques and methods, to reduce raw material and energy consumption, and to even create the sufficient infrastructure for developing social and environmental innovation (Feng, 2007). The third characteristic is that the circular economy theory reliably believes in combined interests of social actors by promoting rational use of resources and the continuous recycling of materials, instead of the system of mass consumption and mass production. Put differently, via circular economy, coordination of economic, social, and environmental benefits is attainable. By this way, the value produced toward the society is maximized by reducing waste, energy consumption and environmental damage. Finally, the fourth feature is the fact that circular economic activity is not feasible from the corporations only. Governments, as well as citizens contribution is necessary. It requires the most significant stakeholders to be engaged with it in order to maximize social benefits.

Similar to the circular economy theory is the externality theory which at first was developed by economist Alfred Marshall and further was substantiated by Pigou (1920) and Coase (1988). It simply states that under the increasing complexity of the modern economies, every economic activity creates some unwanted side effects (either positive or negative) to stakeholders that inherently were not associated with those activities, a fact that has to be considered from regulators and corporations. From the beginning of the 1970, externality theory started to be incorporated within environmental and social economics. Baumol and Oates (1988) were among the first who considered externalities on environmental issues by arguing that the one who receives the externality has been affected by it without having any consideration of that, while simultaneously the applier of the externality affects other without compensating for it. This means that environmental externalities have significant explanatory power and sometimes markets may lead to failures without being able to solve this damage. Thus regulatory intervention is warranted under these circumstances.

A more recent theoretical framework on CSR is corporate citizenship which describes corporations as a social institution which shares prerogatives and responsibilities as any other citizen within a country. Even though corporate citizenship is rooted in political sciences, has gained significant momentum within the management and economic literature because it promotes the social and environmental behavior under a globalized context (Matten & Crane, 2005; Crane & Matten, 2007; Frederick, 2008; Camilleri, 2017). Put it differently, corporate citizenship consists an allegory of firm's participation within the society by strengthening the social and ethical conduct of business activities (Moon & Chapple, 2005).

The fact that corporations worldwide are engaging on several social activities voluntarily, without being forced by laws and regulators, has reinforced corporate citizenship theory as an acceptable theoretical framework which can help the general public to assess and even affect corporate social behavior. Within academia, several scholars were arguing about the necessity to look at the firm as being a citizen where its behavior is manifested through socially responsible organizational activities (Carroll, 1979; Davis, 1973; McGuire, 1963). Since then, several research have tried to examine how managers behave within the firm and if they are concerned with ethical and socially sensitive issues, how employees perceive ethical conduct and whether they can influence CSR (Hunt, Wood, & Chonko, 1989). Nevertheless, other researchers consider corporate citizenship as a completely different concept from CSR because corporate citizenship is dependent on firm's philanthropic stances and managerial discretion (Windsor, 2001).

Despite the different opinions and propositions as to what corporate citizenship actually means and refers to, there is an increasing agreement on the fact that this theory paved the way for the creation of new themes within the CSR literature such as responsible investments, corporate social policy, social partnerships and other discourses. Corporate citizenship theory created a framework for assigning to CSR a more strategic focus because it was understood that it could produce positive results for the firms and their societal stakeholders (Lantos, 2001). So CSR was not seem simply as a cost creating activity simply done for marketing or public approval purposes, but as a strategy that adds value to the firm leading to the abandonment of other non-value-adding projects. Initial empirical studies conducted on this issue by McWilliams and Siegel (2001) and Orlitzky et al. (2003) pointed that firm's engagement within social and environmental responsibility actions could benefit them in the long run. Eventually, firms realized that CSR could be oriented based on their goals and needs and direct their social investments to such sectors that were beneficial for them. Thus, strategic CSR provided the opportunity for firms to gain enhanced legitimacy and credibility, as well as to add value to their shareholders by connecting social actions with long-term strategic goals (Jamali, 2007; Camilleri, 2017).

New Theoretical Developments on CSR

Based on the abovementioned theoretical frameworks, CSR has expanded its scope and focus by incorporating additional features and discourses such as the shared value principle. Porter and Kramer (2006) argued that CSR can add value not only to the society at large but also to firms engaged on it. The shared value perspective created new opportunities for businesses by opening up new markets, improving competition and enhancing financial performance. Their premises are that when organizations are doing well, this creates more employment opportunities, higher revenues for the state and a growth potential for the national GDP in the long term. This position further developed the notion of corporate sustainability which according to Dyllick and Hockerts (2002) relied on environmental and social efficiency, effectiveness, sufficiency and ecological equity. In the same vein, Visser (2011) pointed that sustainability should focus on economic growth, stakeholder salience and environmental responsibility. So those merits have transformed the modern corporation into a sustainable organization which adds value not only to itself but also to local communities and the environment (Camilleri, 2017).

This theoretical evolution on corporate responsibility contributed to a more holistic apprehension of CSR beyond the classic contribution of legitimacy and institutional theories. According to Dillard, Rigsby, and Goodman (2004), institutional theory presents some important disadvantages in terms of processing elements of CSR because it is weak at explaining its development process. Thus they proposed a structuration process which is more dynamic in nature, for explaining CSP facets. This theory originates in Giddens (1984) and assumes that every organization acts as an agent with its extended institutional environment and social structures. So structuration theory in CSR provides a more holistic framework for explaining its value through the consideration of the institutional and organizational perspectives. According to Johnstone (2018), structuration theory moves beyond the use of stakeholder, legitimacy and institutional theories at explaining the strategic behavior of organizations, by recognizing that modern corporations make agency decisions beyond CSR decisions. Thus, structuration theory assists researchers in assessing how firms are affecting and are affected by their institutional environment. Also, structuration theory considers individual agents beyond executives (employees, unions etc.) to be fundamental for the adoption and implementation of CSR strategies (Sundin & Brown, 2017).

According to Chang et al. (2017), recent theoretical contributions to CSR have pointed toward a focus on how sustainability can be promoted within firms instead of what actually sustainability means. This fact is depicted on co-evolution theory (which originates from Darwin's evolution theory) on management and tries to explain how the behavior of interacting agents within firms is evolving (Hodgson, 2010; Abatecola, 2014). Johnson, Price, and Van Vugt (2013) and Porter (2006) argue that co-evolution theory asserts that corporations and their environment evolve in relation to one another. In the similar vein, Foxon (2011) presented a co-evolutionary theory in order to explain environmental awareness of firms and how they implemented emission reduction policies. He recognized that business strategies, corporate practices, regulations and technologies are the main evolving systems that research has to consider for examining firms' sustainable behavior. Also, Geels (2014) proposed a Triple Embeddedness Framework (TEF) for explaining the co-evolution of firms and their external environment. As he explains, the social and political environment along with the economic environment are two factors that exert pressure on firms to address social and environmental issues. This framework actually hypothesizes co-evolutionary relations between firms and their environments.

Furthermore, several interdisciplinary approaches have also made themselves present in the literature. For example the abovementioned TEF framework by Geels (2014) is the outcome of evolutionary economics, economic sociology and institutional theory. Also, Lozano, Carpenter, and Huisingh (2015) proposed the Sustainability Oriented Theory (SOT) which incorporates various theoretical frameworks regarding the organization of corporations. Rotmans, Kemp, and Van Asselt (2001) and Loorbach (2010) based their theoretical contributions to governance and complex systems' theories in order to explain corporate changes toward sustainability and CSR. Thus, Transition Management (TM) theory was evolved as an effort to govern CSR transitions of firms.

Finally, the constantly evolving nature of CSR and corporate sustainability led the way to the green economics policies and toward more extended systems of CSR analysis. According to Smith, Voß, and Grin (2010), corporate focus steadily changed from social management strategies to sustainability activities and to green economics (broader concepts of sustainability). The outcome of such broader perspectives on CSR was the formation of the Multi-level Perspective (MLP), which moved beyond the firm level of analysis (Chang et al., 2017). This broader perspective views changes as nonlinear, which happen through the interaction of local innovations, established practices and rules, and the external social and technological environment (Geels, 2005). Consequently, recent theoretical and empirical developments on corporate CSR tend to theorize using several frameworks in order to gain a far-reaching perspective on the issue. This book will try to provide a similar perspective to the reader within the following chapters.

Conclusion

CSR has received increased attention from academics, executives and international organizations over the last decades, especially due to their significant impact on the operation of the organizations. Several studies assert that every firm -regardless of the business sector- has some primary (employees and customers) and secondary (communities, local governments) stakeholders who both assert increased pressure to the firms, as arising out of a growing concern for human rights, labor standards and environmental concerns. CSR has been developed as an important strategic mechanism through which organizations are trying to differentiate themselves from their competitors.

The current chapter presented a thorough theoretical background on CSR theories and perspectives offered in the literature. We started our analysis from the concepts of legitimacy, institutional and stakeholder theories as the cornerstones of CSR. Then we focused on additional theoretical frameworks (circular economy theory, externality theory and corporate citizenship theory) along with interdisciplinary approaches and broader systems of CSR analysis and behavior. These interventions and the increased public awareness on the issue of social responsibility created a wave of socially and environmentally responsible investments. Today it is even more coherent that social responsibility does not mean a waste of scarce corporate resources but on the contrary it can create value for both shareholders and stakeholders, leading to a win-win situation for all related parties.

References

Abatecola, G. (2014). Research in organizational evolution. What comes next? *European Management Journal, 32*, 434–443.

Abrams, F. W. (1951). Management's responsibilities in a complex world. *Harvard Business Review, 29*, 29–34.

Ameer, R., & Othman, R. (2012). Sustainability practices and corporate financial performance: A study based on the top global corporations. *Journal of Business Ethics, 108*, 61–79.

Ashforth, B. E., & Gibbs, B. W. (1990). The double-edge of organizational legitimation. *Organization Science, 1*(2), 177–194.

Baumol, W. J., & Oates, W. E. (1988). *The theory of environmental policy* (2nd ed.). Cambridge: Cambridge University Press.

Bowen, H. R., & Johnson, F. E. (1953). *Social responsibility of the businessman*. New York: Harper.

Brammer, S., He, H., & Mellahi, K. (2015). Corporate social responsibility, employee organizational identification and creative effort: The moderating impact of corporate ability. *Group and Organization Management, 40*, 323–352.

Brammer, S., Jackson, G., & Matten, D. (2012). Corporate social responsibility and institutional theory: New perspectives on private governance. *Socio-Economic Review, 10*(1), 3–28.

Business for Social Responsibility (BSR). (2003). *Overview of corporate social responsibility*. Business for Social Responsibility Organization. Retrieved from http://www.bsr.org/BSRResources/IssueBriefDetail.cfm?DocumentID=48907

Camilleri, M. A. (2017). *Corporate sustainability, social responsibility and environmental management: An introduction to theory and practice with case studies*. Cham, Switzerland: Springer International Publishing AG.

Campbell, J. L. (2006). Institutional analysis and the paradox of corporate social responsibility. *American Behavioral Scientist, 49*(7), 925–938.

Carroll, A. B. (1979). A three-dimensional conceptual model of corporate social performance. *Academy of Management Review, 4*, 497–505.

Carroll, A. B. (1991). The pyramid of corporate social responsibility: Toward the moral management of organizational stakeholders. *Business Horizons, 34*(4), 39–48.

Carroll, A. B. (2000). Ethical challenges for business in the new millennium: Corporate social responsibility and models of management morality. *Business Ethics Quarterly, 10*, 33–42.

Chang, R.-D., Zuo, J., Zhao, Z.-Y., Zillante, G., Gan, X.-L., & Soebarto, V. (2017). Evolving theories of sustainability and firms: History, future directions and implications for renewable energy research. *Renewable and Sustainable Energy Reviews, 72*, 48–56.

Coase, R. H. (1988). *The firm, the market and the law*. Chicago: University of Chicago Press.

Contrafartto, M. (2014). The institutionalization of social and environmental reposting: An Italian narrative. *Accounting, Organizations and Society, 39*(6), 414–432.

Costa, M., & Torrecchia, P. (2018). The concept of value for CSR: A debate drawn from Italian classical accounting. *Corporate Social Responsibility and Environmental Management, 25*, 113–123.

Crane, A., & Matten, D. (2007). *Business ethics* (2nd ed.). Oxford: Oxford University Press.

Dahlsrud, A. (2008). How corporate social responsibility is defined: An analysis of 37 definitions. *Corporate Social Responsibility and Environmental Management, 15*(1), 1–13.

Davis, K. (1973). The case for and against business assumption of social responsibilities. *Academy of Management Journal, 16*, 312–322.

Deegan, C. (2014). An overview of legitimacy theory as applied within the social and environmental accounting literature. In J. Bebbington, J. Unerman, & B. O'Dwyer (Eds.), *Sustainability accounting and accountability* (pp. 248–272). Abingdon, UK: Routledge.

Dillard, J. F., Rigsby, J. T., & Goodman, C. (2004). The making and re-making of organization context: Duality and the institutionalization process. *Accounting, Auditing and Accountability Journal, 17*(4), 506–542.

Dowling, J., & Pfeffer, J. (1975). Organizational legitimacy: Social values and organizational behavior. *The Pacific Sociological Review, 18*(1), 122–136.

Drucker, P. (1984). The new meaning of corporate social responsibility. *California Management Review, 26*, 53–63.

Dyllick, T., & Hockerts, K. (2002). Beyond the business case for corporate sustainability. *Business Strategy and the Environment, 11*, 130–141.

Epstein, E. M. (1987). The corporate social policy process: Beyond business ethics, corporate social responsibility, and corporate social responsiveness. *California Management Review, 29*(3), 99–114.

Etzioni, A. (1999). *A communication note on stakeholder theory*. Heidelberg: Springer.

Evan, W., & Freeman, R. (1993). A stakeholder theory of modern corporation: Kantian capitalism. In T. Beauchamp & N. Bowie (Eds.), *Ethical theory and business* (pp. 166–171). Englewood Cliffs, NJ: Prentice-Hall.

Feng, Z. (2007). Normalization theory study on circular economy. *China Population, Resources and Environment, 17*(4), 10–11.

Foxon, T. J. (2011). A co-evolutionary framework for analyzing a transition to a sustainable low carbon economy. *Ecological Economics, 70,* 2258–2267.

Frederick, W. (1986). Toward CSR: Why ethical analysis is indispensable and unavoidable in corporate affairs. *California Management Review, 28,* 126–141.

Frederick, W. (1994). From CSR1 to CSR2: The maturing of business-and-society thought. *Business and Society, 33*(2), 150–164.

Frederick, W. (2008). Corporate social responsibility: Deep roots, flourishing growth, promising future. In A. Crane, A. McWilliams, D. Matten, J. Moon, & D. S. Siegel (Eds.), *The Oxford handbook of corporate social responsibility*. Oxford: Oxford University Press. doi:10.1093/oxfordhb/9780199211593.003.0023

Freeman, R. E. (1984). *Strategic management: A stakeholder approach*. Boston: Pitman.

Friedman, M. (1962). *Capitalism and freedom*. Chicago: University of Chicago Press.

Friedman, M. (1970). A Friedman doctrine: The social responsibility of business is to increase its profits. *The New York Times Magazine, 13*(1970), 32–33.

Garriga, E., & Mele, D. (2004). Corporate social responsibility theories: Mapping the territory. *Journal of Business Ethics, 53,* 51–71.

Gary, O. (2002). Environmental disclosures in the annual report: Extending the applicability and predictive power of legitimacy theory. *Accounting, Auditing and Accountability Journal, 15,* 344–371.

Gauthier, D. (1990). *Moral dealing: Contract, ethics, and reason*. Cornell: Cornell University Press.

Geels, F. W. (2005). The dynamics of transitions in socio-technical systems: A multi-level analysis of the transition pathway from horse-drawn carriages to automobiles (1860–1930). *Technology Analysis and Strategic Management, 17,* 445–476.

Geels, F. W. (2014). Reconceptualizing the co-evolution of firms in industries and their environments: Developing an inter-disciplinary triple embeddedness framework. *Research Policy, 43,* 261–277.

Giddens, A. (1984). *The constitution of society: Outline of the theory of structuration*. Berkeley and Los Angeles: University of California Press.

Gond, J. P., Kang, N., & Moon, J. (2011). The government of self-regulation: On the comparative dynamics of corporate social responsibility. *Economy and Society, 40*(4), 640–671.

Goodpaster, K. E. (1991). Business ethics and stakeholder analysis. *Business Ethics Quarterly, 1,* 53–73.

Hassan, A., & Ibrahim, E. (2012). Corporate environmental information disclosure: Factors influencing companies' success in attaining environmental awards. *Corporate Social Responsibility and Environmental Management, 19*(1), 32–46.

Henriques, I., & Sadorsky, P. (1999). The relationship between environmental commitment and managerial perceptions of stakeholder importance. *Academy of Management Journal, 42*(1), 87–99.

Higgins, C., & Larrinaga, C. (2014). Sustainability reporting: Insights from institutional theory. In J. Bebbington, J. Unerman, & B. O'Dwyer (Eds.), *Sustainability accounting and accountability* (pp. 273–285). Abingdon, UK: Routledge.

Hodgson, G. M. (2010). Darwinian co-evolution of organizations and the environment. *Ecological Economics, 69*, 700–706.

Hunt, S. D., Wood, V. R., & Chonko, L. B. (1989). Corporate ethical values and organizational commitment in marketing. *The Journal of Marketing, 53*, 79–90.

International Organization for Standardization (ISO). (2010). *Guidance on social responsibility*. Geneva, Switzerland: International Standard.

Jamali, D. (2007). The case for strategic corporate social responsibility in developing countries. *Business and Society Review, 112*, 1–27.

Jensen, M. C. (2000). Value maximization and the corporate objective function. In M. Beer & N. Nohria (Eds.), *Breaking the code of change*. Boston: HBS Press.

Johnson, D. D., Price, M. E., & Van Vugt, M. (2013). Darwin's invisible hand: Market competition, evolution and the firm. *Journal of Economic Behavior and Organization, 90*, S118–S140.

Johnstone, L. (2018). Environmental management decisions in CSR-based accounting research. *Corporate Social Responsibility and Environmental Management, 25*(6), 1212–1222.

Jones, T. M. (1980). Corporate social responsibility revisited, redefined. *California Management Review, 22*, 59–67.

Jones, T. M. (1995). Instrumental stakeholder theory: A synthesis of ethics and economics. *Academy of Management Review, 20*, 404–437.

Lantos, G. P. (2001). The boundaries of strategic corporate social responsibility. *Journal of Consumer Marketing, 18*, 595–630.

Levitt, T. (1958). The dangers of social responsibility. *Harvard Business Review, 36*, 41–50.

Locke, J. (2003). *Two treatises of government and a letter concerning toleration*. New Haven, CT: Yale University Press.

Loorbach, D. (2010). Transition management for sustainable development: A perspective complexity-based governance framework. *Governance, 18*, 161–183.

Lozano, R., Carpenter, A., & Huisingh, D. (2015). A review of theories of the firm and their contribution to corporate sustainability. *Journal of Cleaner Production, 106*, 430–442.

Lubchenko, J. (1998). Entering the century of the environment: A new social contract for science. *Science, 279*(23), 491–497.

Marcoux, A. M. (2000). Business ethics gone wrong. *Cato Policy Report, 22*, 10–12.

Matten, D., & Crane, A. (2005). Corporate citizenship: Toward an extended theoretical conceptualization. *Academy of Management Review, 30*, 166–180.

McGuire, J. (1963). *Business and society*. New York: McGraw-Hill.

McWilliams, A., & Siegel, D. (2001). Corporate social responsibility: A theory of the firm perspective. *Academy of Management Review*, 26(1), 117–127.

Moon, J., & Chapple, W. (2005). Corporate social responsibility (CSR) in Asia: A seven country study of CSR website reporting. *Business and Society*, 44, 415–441.

Moore, D. R. (2013). Sustainability, institutionalization and the duality of structure: Contradiction and unintended consequences in the political context of an Australian water business. *Management Accounting Research*, 24(4), 366–386.

Nasi, J. (1995). What is stakeholder thinking? A snapshot of a social theory of the firm. In J. Nasi (Ed.), *Understanding stakeholder thinking* (pp. 19–32). Helsinki: LSR Publications.

O'Donovan, G. (1999). Managing legitimacy through increased corporate environmental reporting: An exploratory study. *Interdisciplinary Environmental Review*, 1(1), 63–99.

O'Donovan, G. (2002). Environmental disclosures in the annual report: Extending the applicability and predictive power of legitimacy theory. *Accounting, Auditing and Accountability Journal*, 15(3), 344–371.

Orlitzky, M., Schmidt, F. L., & Rynes, S. L. (2003). Corporate social and financial performance: A meta-analysis. *Organization Studies*, 24, 403–442.

Parker, L. D. (2014). Corporate social accountability through action: Contemporary insights form British industrial pioneers. *Accounting, Organizations and Society*, 39(8), 632–659.

Pfeffer, J. (1981). *Power in organizations*. Boston, MA: Pitman.

Pfeffer, J., & Salancik, G. (1978). *The external control of organizations: A resource dependence perspective*. New York: Harper and Row.

Phillips, R. (2003). Stakeholder legitimacy. *Business Ethics Quarterly*, 13(1), 25–41.

Pigou, A. C. (1920). *The economics of welfare*. London: MacMillan and Co.

Pondeville, S., Swaen, V., & De Rongé, Y. (2013). Environmental management control systems: The role of contextual and strategic factors. *Management Accounting Research*, 24(4), 31–332.

Porter, M. E., & Kramer, M. R. (2006). Strategy and society: The link between competitive advantage and corporate social responsibility. *Harvard Business Review*, 84(12), 78–92.

Porter, T. B. (2006). Coevolution as a research framework for organizations and the natural environment. *Organization and Environment*, 19, 479–504.

Preston, L. E., & Post, J. E. (1975). *Private management and public policy: The principle of public responsibility*. Englewood Cliffs, NJ: Prentice Hall.

Rawls, J. (1971). *A theory of justice*. Boston: Harvard University Press.

Ren, Y., & Wu, Y. (2005). Discussion on connotation and relevant theoretic issues of the concept of Chinese circular economy. *China Population, Resources and Environment*, 15(4), 131.

Rotmans, J., Kemp, R., & Van Asselt, M. (2001). More evolution than revolution: Transition management in public policy. *Foresight*, 3, 15–31.

Sarkar, S., & Searcy, C. (2016). Zeitgeist or chameleon? A quantitative analysis of CSR definitions. *Journal of Cleaner Production*, 135, 1423–1435.

Smith, A., Voß, J.-P., & Grin, J. (2010). Innovation studies and sustainability transitions: The allure of the multi-level perspective and its challenges. *Research Policy*, 39, 435–448.

Suchman, M. C. (1995). Managing legitimacy: Strategic and institutional approaches. *Academy of Management Review, 20*(3), 571–610.

Sundin, H., & Brown, D. A. (2017). Greening the black box: Integrating the environment and management control systems. *Accounting, Auditing and Accountability Journal, 30*(3), 620–642.

Visser, W. (2011). *The age of responsibility: CSR 2.0 and the new DNA of business.* Chichester: Wiley.

Vogel, D. (2010). The private regulation of global corporate conduct: Achievements and limitations. *Business and Society, 49*(1), 68–87.

Wang, H. (2013). Theory foundation of corporate environmental responsibility. *Advanced Materials Research, 726–731,* 4203–4211.

Wang, H., & Choi, J. (2013). A new look at the corporate social-financial performance relationship: The moderating roles of temporal and inter-domain consistency in corporate social performance. *Journal of Management, 39,* 416–441.

Wartick, S., & Cochran, P. (1985). The evolution of the corporate social performance model. *Academy of Management Review, 10,* 758–769.

Windsor, D. (2001). The future of corporate social responsibility. *The International Journal of Organizational Analysis, 9,* 225–256.

Wood, D. J. (1991). Corporate social performance revisited. *Academy of Management Review, 16,* 69–718.

Woodward, D. G., Edwards, P., & Birkin, F. (1996). Organizational legitimacy and stakeholder information provision. *British Journal of Management, 7,* 329–347.

World Business Council for Sustainable Development (WBCSD). (1999). *Corporate social responsibility: Meeting changing expectations.* Geneva, Switzerland: WBCSRD report.

World Commission on Environment and Development (WCED). (1987). *Our common future.* Oxford: WCED.

Zhang, K. (2004). Discussion on circular economy theory. *China Population, Resources and Environment, 14*(6), 48.

Zucker, L. G. (1987). Institutional theories of organization. *Annual Review of Sociology, 13*(1), 443–464.

3 Definitions and Theoretical Frameworks of Governance

Efthalia (Elia) Chatzigianni and Cheryl Mallen

Defining Governance

Governance as a term is widely discussed. In the recent years, the concept of governance has been at the center of attention of scholars, policymakers, and practitioners who aim to succinctly define it for public policy and management discussions. Yet, despite the significance of governance to contemporary society and its organizations, there is no one generally accepted definition of the term. Interestingly, Schneider (2004, p. 25) notes that the success of the term "governance" is partially due to its vagueness as a concept. So, let's examine what has been proposed in the various attempts to define governance. It must be noted that the notion of corporate governance should not be confused with the notions of corporate responsibility and corporate management even though they are all related.

We begin with Weiss, who notes academics and scholars use the term "governance" as a means to suggest "a complex set of structures and processes, both public and private" (2000, p. 795). Next, Fasenfest (2010, p. 771) links government and governance. He defines government as "the office, authority or function of governing" and governance as an array of "decisions and processes made to reflect social expectations through the management or leadership of the government". In contrast, Richards and Smith (2002) makes a significant distinction between government and governance. They define government as administration, law-making and regulation, financial jurisdiction, and use of force and consider governance as a policymaking tool with nonregulatory characteristics and growing significance in the field of public policy and administration. Meanwhile, Hague and Harrop (2013) purported that government consists of institutions that hold the responsibility for collective decision-making on behalf of society; as a term, in its narrower meaning, it refers to the highest political level of this institutional construction. For them, governance is a process of collective decision-making where government may be absent.

DOI: 10.4324/9781003152750-4

It must be noted, however, that government is not governance, even though the former may be part of the latter, given that governance is a dynamic process and government can become part of the process at the initial or any subsequent stage of it. This leads us to Rosenau (1992, 1995), who purported that governance is not as restricted as government because it encompasses more policy actors and processes, including non-governmental institutions and mechanisms, formal and informal, that aim to promote their interests in policymaking and implementation processes through various channels. The policymaking and implementation of governance can encompass an organization's responsibilities toward its various stakeholders, who provide vital resources for organization survival and longevity. This implies that managers are responsible not only to the owners but also toward suppliers, their employees, the local communities within which they operate, customers, and other indirect stakeholders. The boundaries of governance are, thus, extensive, and this suggests the need for flexibility for including particular constituents and their needs within each organization.

The definition offered by Rhodes (1996, p. 652) encapsulates this flexibility as "a new process of governing; or a changed condition of ordered rule; or the new method by which society is governed". He further purports that the term is used in six different ways: "as minimal state, as corporate governance, as the new public management as good governance, as a socio-cybernetic system, as self-organizing networks" (Rhodes, 1996, p. 653). It is important to note that Rhodes also reflected on the works of Kjaer (2004) and Pierre (2000) and determined the existence of the different meanings of governance in the various scientific disciplines gives support to the conclusion by Carroll (1965, p. 269), who proposed: "when I use a word it means what I choose it to mean – neither more nor less".

The authors of this chapter discuss corporate governance; they promote governance as a system by which companies and organizations are directed and controlled. Beyond that, governance encompasses the sense of compliance (laws and regulations), transparency, and accountability (based on codes of conduct), and in a practical sense, governance sets the framework under which power is exerted or distributed and decisions are reached, along with accountability within the organizations (Halfani, McCarney, & Rodríguez, 1994, Graham, 2003, Asaduzamman & Virtanen, 2016). Now, what is good governance?

Defining Good Governance

Good governance involves a number of aspects that occur in the process of governing. For example, good governance can include leadership that supports transparency in the decision-making process, honesty, inclusion, and racial equality, along with the avoidance of conflicts of interest.

Aspects of good governance are tightly connected with values and actions that are acceptable to the public and that strengthen the legitimacy of the organization, employee trust, and commitment. Additionally, good governance revolves around multiple aspects, including mechanisms for managerial control and organizational structures that ensure organizational behavior is in tandem with laws and regulations. Further aspects include that good governance means being answerable to stakeholders and incorporating both shareholder and stakeholder value. Additionally, good governance develops the reputation of organizations and "inspires, strengthens and maintains investor's confidence by ensuring company's commitment to higher growth and profits" (Nadaf & Navi, 2016, p. 67). If governance is good, then that "helps to prevent corporate scandals, frauds, and potential civil and criminal liability of the organization" (Nadaf & Navi, 2016, p. 67).

Overall, this means that good governance is linked to what we term as "democratic accountability" or, in the words of Jem Bendell (2006, p. 5),

> the quality of being accountable to those with less power who are affected by one's actions or decisions, when they in turn exhibit the same accountability, where accountable means both justifying to and being regulated by those to whom one is accountable.

It must be noted that the complexity and vagueness of a definitive definition doesn't only apply to the notion of governance; it also applies to the notion of "good governance". In an effort to further guide leaders toward good governance, practices worldwide have been enhanced since the 1990s with the issuance of *Codes of Good Governance*. This involves setting standards for behavioral best practices by members of an organization. The United Nations was the first to issue such a Code in 1978, serviced by the United Nations Centre on Transnational Corporations (UNCTC) as a means to establish a mutually respected framework for cooperation among transnational corporations and host-country governments in terms of rights and responsibilities (Sauvant, 2015). Later, in December 1992, in the UK, following the collapse of two publicly listed companies (PLC) in the London Stock Exchange (LSE) and scandals related to two others,[1] the Committee on the Financial Aspects of Corporate Governance, established in May 1991 by the Financial Reporting Council, and the Stock Exchange, along with the Accountancy Profession, issued their report – known since then as the *Cadbury Report* – as a means to regain the trust of investors in the companies listed in the LSE (The Committee on the Financial Aspects of Corporate Governance, 1992). The report, which defined corporate governance as "the whole system of controls, both financial and otherwise, by which a company is directed and controlled" (1992, para 2.5.), identified three important principles of corporate governance; these are openness, integrity, and accountability. In this framework, by 2008, 196 codes of conduct have been issued for use in 64 countries around the world (Aguilera & Cuervo-Cazurra, 2009). Such Codes have been the framework guiding corporate governance. As of March 2021, the International Finance Corporation (IFC), which is a global development institution and member of the World Bank Group, states that corporate governance codes can be found in more than 140 countries around the world (IFC, 2021).

Corporate governance policies and practices define the performance of an organization. The main pillars of corporate governance are accountability, transparency, fairness, and disclosure (Bhasin, 2013). The performance of companies and organizations in relation to these pillars determines their overall evaluation in terms of *good governance.*

The definitions of governance and good governance are now folded into a discussion of corporate and nonprofit governance. The boards of directors are mainly responsible for the governance of companies and organizations. According to the Institute of Directors (IoD, n.d.), an organization founded in 1903 in the UK with the aim to set the standards for corporate governance, lobby the government(s), and promote free enterprise, the role of the board is crucial in the company's prosperity and well-being not only in the field of directing the company's affairs but also in the areas of safeguarding the interests of shareholders and related stakeholders. The board, along with the top management, is responsible for the creation of an ethical and accountable corporate environment (Paine, 1994). Additionally, according to Bradshaw, Murray, and Wolpin (1992), the key management aspects of good governance encompass the following dimensions: structure (composition), process (in this case the focus is on practices impacted by board relationships), and board performance (effectiveness). In this framework, after a quick definition of corporate governance and nonprofit governance, the chapter will discuss the three dimensions that frame the role of the board: (i) board composition (such as organizational structures, mechanisms for managerial control, and stakeholder accountability), (ii) board relationships (including between the board members, managers and staff), and (iii) board effectiveness.

Governance of Corporate and Nonprofit Organizations

In general, there are three sectors: the corporate, government, and the third sector, or nonprofit organizations. According to the Organization for Economic Cooperation and Development (OECD), the corporate sector comprises the nonfinancial and financial sectors: the nonfinancial sector consists of public and private companies that produce and provide nonfinancial goods and services to the markets, whereas the financial sector covers forms of corporations (resident and quasi-corporations) principally engaged in financial intermediation and related activities (OECD,

2004, 2015). Meanwhile, nonprofit organizations, also positioned as "the third sector" (Hodges & Howieson, 2017, p. 69), following the corporate and the government sectors, encompass an array of local to international service-based organizations, such as charities, volunteer sport organizations, cooperatives, social organizations (Hodges & Howieson, 2017), along with many trade associations, and federations (Young, Bania, & Bailey, 1996). Governing such organizations, however, has been noted to be difficult due to their complexities (Minciullo & Pedrini, 2020). The difficulties stem from the variety of stakeholders and their interests, especially when the service or nonprofit organizations have for-profit donors "as the business-oriented interests may conflict with the altruistic interests" (Minciullo & Pedrini, 2020, p. 531). Despite the issue of complexity, much service is provided globally by these organizations, which have adapted to their specific conditions.

With the variety of definitions articulated in the previous chapter, it stands to reason that corporate governance can mean different things to the management of the various corporations/organizations, whether corporate or nonprofit. Profit and not-for-profit organizations are obviously entities with different responsibilities. Yet there are corporate governance principles applicable for both entities related to most areas of governance such as organizational performance, accountability, and transparency. In this text, corporate governance is positioned to involve decision-making concerning areas that apply to corporate governance in general such as compliance (with laws and regulations), transparency and accountability (based on codes of conduct), and excellence in resource allocation for efficient and effective action.

The boards of directors play a significant role in the overall management and control of corporations and organizations. While the precise impact of their performance is difficult to measure, given the differences across boards, firms, countries, even periods, the role of the boards is directly correlated with governance practice and is of outmost importance in the understanding of corporate behavior and agenda-setting and formulation (Adams, Hermalin, & Weisbach, 2010). Thus, we begin to further articulate governance in practice, presenting the main features of the boards of directors: composition, relationships, and effectiveness.

Governance – Board Composition

A corporate board of directors is generally the oversight body that ensures the company's performance meets the owners' or stakeholders' expectations and helps manage/resolve disputes in the process (Minciullo & Pedrini, 2020). The board composition may vary. Some include a single-tiered board of directors with a key supervisory role. Others utilize a two-tiered system, with a board of directors and an executive board that is in charge of the day-to-day management (Nadaf & Navi, 2016).

Multiple factors impact the board composition, such as social culture, government policy, economic environment, and the capital market system in the particular country (Nadaf & Navi, 2016). Additionally, rules and regulations for particular regions impact the composition. For instance, in the United Kingdom and the United States, the Anglo-Saxon model of corporate governance requires that listed firms must possess unitary boards, independent external directors, and board committees (Pande, 2011). Overall, a board is structured for efficient and effective control and accountability of the actions and directions in the process of seeking to achieve the established goals and objectives (Nour, Sharabati, & Hammad, 2019) with management oversight (Minciullo & Pedrini, 2020) and the harnessing of a compendium of relationships

Meanwhile, nonprofit board composition differs from corporations discussed earlier as there is an absence of owners, such as financial shareholders (Van Puyvelde & Raeymaechkers, 2020). This means that the structure for governance needs to be adapted for each organization and its particular context. As such, Browning (2012) noted that "the boards of for-profit and nonprofit organizations have different governance models, characteristics, and decision-making styles" (p. 82). The nonprofit sector can establish a hierarchical organizational governance structure (Van Puyvelde & Raeymaechkers, 2020) that follows a typical corporate style of governance (Svensson, Mahoney, & Hambrick, 2019). It has, however, generally transitioned to using a philanthropic model of governance (Vermeiren, Raeymaeckers, & Beagles, 2019). A philanthropic model represents a movement away from vertical governance power structures to using a network of committees and working groups that are concerned with a narrow topic of focus (Cornforth, 2011) and generating entrepreneurial endeavors (Browning, 2012). This type of network structure places internal members of the organization, such as management members and accountants, as working directly with external members or stakeholders, such as volunteers and financial contributors (Cornforth, 2011). Multiple hybrid structures stem from these networks (Billis, 2010) as the various network members enhance stakeholder inclusion, along with the dissemination of decision-making power in an effort to build trust, and contribute to the organizational functional service requirements. Overall, nonprofit organizational composition options may be advantageous as being "more flexible and better suited to try new things" (Svensson et al., 2019, p. 393). Both corporate and nonprofit governance is influenced by the board relationships. This is now our next topic of discussion.

Governance – Board Relationships

It has been noted that "what distinguishes exemplary boards is that they are robust, effective social systems" (Sonnenfeld, 2002). In other words, the success of a board depends on the relationships of the members of the board between them and the roles they all perform in order to fulfill the board's mission in terms of advising the CEO, monitoring the company's performance, and functioning as intermediaries between the company and the society. In this framework, board relationships can encompass a variety of internal and external groups. Internally, the relationships can include, for example, those between board members, with managers, and with staff/employees. Examples of external group relationships can include suppliers, governmental and nongovernmental institutions, banking institutions, and the general public. Research literature indicates that relationships are a key element in corporate good governance as they aid to protect both the investors and the corporate outcomes. For instance, it has been purported that protecting the investor advances the value of a firm (Campbell, Campbell, Sirmon, Bierman, & Tuggle, 2012) and aids to achieve better returns (Boulton, Smart, & Zutter, 2010), and countries that effectively protect their investors find that the efforts result in more effective corporate environments (Cline & Williamson, 2016). As such, excellence in establishing, managing, and maintaining corporate relationships is key for board effectiveness.

In contrast, relationships within the third-sector or nonprofit organizations are critical for generating good governance (Bauer, Guenster, & Otten, 2003), including organizational effectiveness (Browning, 2012). A key reason is that relationships impact the diversity of ideas generated for providing services (Willems, 2015). The exchange of ideas is a critical component within networks as it aids in forming "the basis of collective team actions and decision making" (Willems, 2015, p. 571). This exchange of ideas occurs between management and, generally, a body of volunteers. The relationships are paramount as the nonprofit must continuously be cognizant of the need for volunteers. Nurturing board relationships, thus, is a critical task that needs to encourage the sharing of ideas that aid in diversifying options and decision-making. These critical relationships need an effective recruitment process, training, individual and team-based motivation (without offering a regular pay check), management, retention, and recognition of the volunteers. Additionally, there is a need to build consensus and advance common beliefs and attitudes to ensure they are not incongruent (Kearns, Livingston, Scherer, & McShane, 2015). The relationships in nonprofits are complex as they include

> connecting and weaving relationships within the agency and across boundaries in the community, engaging in continuous learning, experimenting, risk taking, collaborating, integrating change, being creative with limited resources, fostering an adaptive organizational

culture, and inspiring, facilitating, and supporting agency and community members to do the same.

(Hopkings, Meyer, Shera, & Peters, 2014, p. 421)

If the volunteer working environment is not right – or is toxic – then volunteers can walk away from the organization, leaving them in a desperate shortage of human resources to complete their tasks. Successful governance within a corporation or nonprofit organization is influenced by board effectiveness. This topic will now be outlined.

Governance – Board Effectiveness

Effectiveness is noted as being able to be negotiated based on the repeated corporate interactions with internal and external groups and the working environment (Balser & McClusky, 2005). Researchers have also noted that there are several key aspects that impact board effectiveness. One aspect is that regulatory frameworks that are strict can positively impact the mechanisms of governance (Col & Sen, 2019). Another involves the adoption of good codes of governance (Aguilera & Cuervo-Cazurra, 2004). Further, European firms that fared better during recent financial crisis had advanced legal frameworks (Van Essen, Heugens, Otten, & Van Oosterhout, 2012). Overall, academic research indicates that organizational effectiveness stems from the board of directors acquiring the necessary information to make specific choices and decision outcomes (Minciullo & Pedrini, 2020) that impact overall corporate governance and board effectiveness. Such academic research also indicates that we can learn about governance with the application of theory.

In addition, the effectiveness of governance encompasses many dimensions that may be applicable to corporations as well as not-for-profit organizations, such as the implemented strategies, the policy process, and the accountability of organizations (Zollo, Laudano, Boccardi, & Ciappei, 2019), along with the extent to them being impacted by the size of the board and its composition and types of network members and their relationships (Willems, 2015). Further, effectiveness can be based on the combination of board priorities, multiple directives, and decision authority that can be influenced by multiple actors (Van Puyvelde, Caers, Du Bois, & Jegers, 2012). Board effectiveness can, in turn, influence organizational "planning, oversight, and accountability functions" (Browning, 2012, p. 83). This means that a number of aspects should be assessed to determine overall effectiveness – making the issue complex, especially for nonprofit governance (Willems, 2015). Adding to the complexity of the latter is that, over time, a nonprofit's board of director priorities, directives, and decisions can shift for a number of reasons, such as the maturing of the board members in their role, changing members of the board (Browning, 2012), or funding opportunities. The point in time of an assessment of board effectiveness is, thus, critical.

Researchers have articulated some additional key challenges, particularly for nonprofit organizations, in their pursuit of finding effectiveness. The range of challenges for nonprofits is expanded because stakeholders are diverse and include not only the board of directors, managers, staff, and suppliers but also volunteers, taxpayers, and interested community members (Minciullo & Pedrini, 2020). With the number of stakeholders, it can be difficult to meet the expectations of all parties (Van Puyvelde et al., 2012). Other key challenges stem from filling the emerging leadership with a critical eye on adapting to the future. This is because the leadership "is still in a state of flux as its workforce and services respond to drivers for change" (Hodges & Howieson, 2017, p. 76) and the "rapidity of . . . change" (Hopkings et al., 2014, p. 421). Examples of the drivers of change include the leadership needs to adapt to new requirements (Bligh, 2016), such as an increasing demand for accountability, including for "stakeholders-with-governance-rights" (Taylor, 2015, p. 161), as well as the "social, economic, and political change" (Hodges & Howieson, 2017, p. 76) that occurs throughout Europe. Adding to the complexity of the situation, these changes do not impact all third-sector organizations, such as those within European nations, in the same manner (Pape, Brandsen, Pahl, et al., 2020). Additional challenges include the need to manage "insufficient financial, human, and technical resources . . . in the face of government and foundation cutbacks" (Hopkings et al., 2014, p. 419); the need for the managerial team to update their competencies for the evolving nonprofit organizational environment (Hopkings et al., 2014) that includes an increasing "demand for services" (Hodges & Howieson, 2017, p. 69); and attempting to evaluate organizational performance without the appropriate measurement tools (Minciullo & Pedrini, 2020).

Overall, there has been a push for changes in organizational leadership structure, relationships, and roles to meet the many contemporary challenges in the governance spectrum of corporations and organizations. This is a manageable challenge to tackle for the majority of corporations, but the situation has left many nonprofit organizations in a survival mode (Hodges & Howieson, 2017), each struggling to stay viable due to the "enormity of the challenge" (Hodges & Howieson, 2017, p. 76). Further, additional researchers indicate that what nonprofits face may be beyond what any individual organization can manage (Comforth, Hayes, & Vangen, 2015; Svensson et al., 2019). Achieving effectiveness is, thus, a challenge. A strategy for success may lead to industries working together and may advance hybrid structural composition for governance.

To meet the challenges, researchers have offered recommendations concerning nonprofit organizations moving forward into the future.

The first to be outlined is that "much greater attention needs to be paid to building leadership capacity and that will require a shift in investment" (Hodges & Howieson, 2017, p. 76). Next is a recommendation that promotes leadership being "able to usher in technical and innovative organizational change at a pace that organizational stakeholders can manage" (Hopkings et al., 2014, p. 420). Also, Von Schneubein, Perez, and Gehringer (2018) "suggested three new clusters for future comparative research: investment and growth, participation and social impact, and social cohesion and civil society" (p. 437). This is because there is a lack of an abundance of research on nonprofits. To overcome a lack of research, theories can be used in examinations of governance. There are multiple theories that can be applied. We present six theories as a means to understand corporate and nonprofit governance.

Governance: Learning from Theories

There are numerous theories, and their characteristics can be used to frame examinations of governance at corporations and nonprofit organizations. Additionally, each theory has the potential to advance our understandings concerning the key challenges within governance. For instance, one such challenge involves the ability to attract and retain such human capital, as these resources are critical to the corporation (Nadaf & Navi, 2016). Another is the issue of maintaining the relationships between all parties (Nadaf & Navi, 2016). The relationships can require short-lived to long-term relationship-building and can be intertwined with the corporation's ability to ensure accountability, including the amount of disclosure and to whom, along with managing risk over time and maintaining a positive reputation. Additionally, an upcoming challenge is predicted to involve emerging technologies that can be used in the process of working toward efficient disruptive and advantageous. Hilb (2020) and Bolander (2019) predict a transition from decisions being made by the board of directors to being managed through artificial intelligence. Developing understandings concerning the way forward for efficient and effective governance with any issue, including emerging technologies, can be helpful in the process of working toward efficient and effective governance.

Theoretical examples will now be outlined for use with evaluations of corporate and nonprofit governance, including agency theory, stewardship theory, resource-dependency theory, stakeholder theory, and transaction cost theory. Additionally, cognition theory is outlined as it applies to nonprofit organizations. This chapter provides a brief overview of the main theories of corporate governance and highlights the main arguments. Each theory can be used as a framework for an evaluation in the pursuit of understandings concerning governance efficiency and effectiveness.

Agency Theory and Corporate Governance

To begin, agency theory is a long-standing theory that was first introduced by Adam Smith in 1776 and thoroughly discussed in the 1932 writings of Berle and Means, which see the agency as originating from the distinction between ownership and control (Pande, 2011). Thus, it discusses issues arising from control versus ownership, or, in other words, challenges and problems resulting from the fact that the board of directors has the control and monitoring authority of a company, while the owners of the company are the shareholders. Agency theory, thus, encourages a focus on separating an organization's ownership and management in a way that successfully aligns the interests of both parties. The theory indicates that safeguards are necessary to ensure such an alignment as the objectives of the investors may not consistently support the objectives of those governing the corporation or organization, and vice versa. Such differences can involve, for instance, the strategies utilized and the awards pursued (Van Purvelde et al., 2012). In summary, the theory reflects that governance needs to include safeguards concerning the appropriate and profitable use of funds (Shleifer & Vishny, 1997), and one such strategy could involve adopting codes of conduct. The characteristics of this theory can be applied as a framework for evaluating, for instance, the effectiveness of the separation of ownership and management and ensuring their interests align. Among others, the theory has been used to discuss the effective monitoring of the CEOs by the board of directors (Bonazzi & Islam, 2007), the impact of government regulations on corporate boards of directors (Bryant & Davis, 2012), the role of the board as a monitor of organizational activity in nonprofit management (Miller, 2003), and the impact of corporate governance on corporate environmental performance (Rubino & Napoli, 2020).

Stewardship Theory and Governance

Stewardship theory has been positioned as an alternative to agency theory (Subramanian, 2018). This theory presumes that the shareholder and management interests are aligned (Van Puyvelde et al., 2012). First developed by Jensen and Meckling (1976), the theory involves both a sociological and psychological approach to governance (Davis, Schoorman, & Donaldson, 1997). The approach positions governance as being "trust-based" (Schillemans & Bjurstrøm, 2020, p. 650). This implies that shareholders trust those within the governance structure to act in their best interests and with their values. This theory encourages empowering those in governance roles to make trusted decisions (Donaldson & Davis, 1991). The decisions need to be supported by the structure of the board, along with the determination of the roles and duties assigned to those acting within the structure (Donaldson & Davis, 1991). The theory further encourages assessments be conducted on the elements within governing, including the "empowerment-oriented processes such as responsibility, autonomy, engagement, involvement, and shared culture and norms" (Van Puyvelde & Raeymaechkers, 2020, p. 935), along with the implemented activities (Schillemans & Bjurstrøm, 2020). All activities are seen as elements that can aid in the alignment of the parties. The characteristics of this theory can be applied as a framework for evaluating, for instance, the effect of government regulations on the board of directors (Bryant & Davis, 2012) and the necessity of board accountability (Keay, 2017).

Resource-Dependency Theory and Corporate Governance

The resource-dependency theory (RDT) provides an evaluation framework (Udayasankar, 2008) that can assess governance based on it being "an open system, dependent on contingencies in the external environment" (Hillman, Withers, & Collins, 2009, p. 1404). First developed by Pfeffer and Salancik (1978), this theory positions those governing as having an understanding of the context in which they operate or knowing "the ecology of the organization" (Pfeffer & Salancik, 1978, p. 1). Further, there is an ability to evaluate and adapt to the multivariant contextual factors, such as understanding the institutional influences, interactions, impacts, resources, and awards (Udayasankar, 2008), and the critical aspects surrounding the dependence on resources, access to resources, and the associated agreements (Drees, Pursey, & Heugens, 2013). Such agreements can focus on a variety of contextual areas, such as safeguarding the natural environment and mitigating environmental impacts (Hillman et al., 2009), the utilization of human resources (Udayasankar, 2008), or advancing corporate reputations (Udayasankar, 2008). The RDT as an evaluation can bring forth advanced understandings concerning the governance system in effect.

Stakeholder Theory and Corporate Governance

Stakeholder theory involves three key aspects. The first aspect is that the priorities for each stakeholder must be articulated (McGahan, 2020). This involves a descriptive approach whereby the interests of each party are outlined as "the corporation as a constellation of cooperative and competitive interests possessing intrinsic value" (Donaldson & Preston, 1995, p. 67). This is followed by an instrumental approach that "establishes a framework for examining connections, if any" (Donaldson & Preston, 1995, p. 67). Additionally, the normative approach is used that considers "stakeholders are persons or groups with legitimate interests in procedural and/or substantive aspects of corporate or organizational activity. Stakeholders are identified by their specific interests" (Donaldson & Preston, 1995). The second aspect is that managers are accountable to the multiple stakeholders and their needs/expectations (deVilliers & Dimes, 2020). This implies that the board of directors can play a mediator role within the process of acting "as trustees of the diverse stakeholders of a corporation" (Amis, Barney, Mahoney, & Wang, 2020, p. 500). Third, stakeholder theory promotes that managers should work to reduce any conflicts of interests between the various stakeholders (Velte & Gerwanski, 2020). This implies that there is a need to develop a framework that supports stakeholder conflict resolution (Amis et al., 2020). Overall, stakeholder theory offers a framework to evaluate the negotiating between parties on their interests (Krishna & Serrano, 1996). The theory also promotes the continuous creation of opportunities for negotiating between the many parties (Amis et al., 2020).

Transaction Cost Theory and Corporate Governance

Transaction cost theory (TCT) has been positioned as an alternative to agency theory. The focus is on governance from the framework of corporate or organizational assets and their deployment. (Martins, Serra, Leite, Ferreira, & Li, 2010). This theory indicates that there are six types of assets, including "site specificity, physical asset specificity, human asset specificity, dedicated assets, brand name capital, and temporal specificity" (Williamson, 1989, pp. 141–142). Founded by Ronald Coase (1937), and further developed by Williamson (1975, 1985, 1989), this theory has been in practice for over more than eight decades (Rindfleisch, 2019) and has promoted that the most effective governance structure for any corporation or organization relies upon the variety of characteristics that stem from their asset transactions. This means that understanding one's assets leads to the generation of the necessary forms of governance for the corporation or organization (Williamson, 1979, 1981, 1985, Martins et al., 2010). Understandings can stem from examinations based on the characteristics of transaction cost theory, such as on the way transactions are conducted (Rindfleisch, 2019), the consequences of the transactions on governance (Drees et al., 2013), the boundaries, logic, and significance of network for the transaction (Martins et al., 2010), and the cost of each transaction (Williamson & Ouchi, 1981). This discussion on theories and governance outlined several key aspects that impact board effectiveness in the corporate and nonprofit sector.

Cognition Theory and Nonprofit Governance

One additional theory is proposed for the specific ownership situation in nonprofit organizations. The cognition theory brings into play that it is not one owner who is guiding the organization but it is the combined actions and decisions of a collective network of members that leads the way – this is a typical strategy for governing nonprofit organizations. This theory can, thus, add to an evaluation framework due to its focus on the need to "form the basis of collective team actions and decision making" (Willems, 2015, p. 571). Being effective in this area is vital to enticing critical volunteers to join and remain in the organization (Zollo et al., 2019) and ensuring that their roles are effectively defined and linked to an appropriate balance of power that aids work to be completed in an efficient manner for success (Cornforth, 2011).

Overall, multiple theories can be applied to advance understandings of governance in corporate and nonprofit organizations. Each theory offers a specific focus and can expand the development of knowledge concerning aspects of governance. This implies that the multidirectional aspects of governance make full understandings complex and require examinations of multiple indicators. Despite the complexity, understanding governance and working to ensure its efficiency and effectiveness are important to every corporation and nonprofit organization.

Conclusions

This chapter provided definitions of governance, good governance, and corporate and not-for-profit governance, including discussing board composition, relationships, effectiveness, and challenges. Additionally, six theories were outlined for use to frame examinations of organizations and their governance that can lead to advanced understandings of specific aspects of a corporation or a nonprofit's efficiency and effectiveness in practice. There are many ongoing and future issues in governance, and there is a need to build leadership that can shift to manage each of these challenges. This leadership will need to understand the emerging technical and innovative advances as well as be able to usher employees and volunteers to a new era. Much work continues to be required in the area of governance.

Note

1 The first two companies were the wallpaper group Coloroll and Asil Nadir's Polly Peck consortium. Both of them had previously healthy published accounts. The two scandals were the collapse of the Bank of Credit and

Commerce International and consequent exposure of its criminal practices, and the posthumous discovery of Robert Maxwell's stealing of £440 million from his companies' pension funds (University of Cambridge, The Cadbury Report. Available at: http://cadbury.cjbs.archios.info/report).

References

Adams, R. B., Hermalin, B. E., & Weisbach, M. S. (2010). The role of boards of directors in corporate governance: A conceptual framework and survey. *Journal of Economic Literature, 48*(1), 58–107.

Aguilera, R. V., & Cuervo-Cazurra, A. (2004). Codes of good governance worldwide: What is the trigger? *Organization Studies, 2004, 25*(3), 415–443.

Aguilera, R. V., & Cuervo-Cazurra, A. (2009). Codes of good governance. *Corporate Governance: An International Review, 17*(3), 376–387.

Amis, J., Barney, J., Mahoney, J., & Wang, H. (2020). From the editors – Why we need a theory of stakeholder governance – And why this is a hard problem. *Academy of Management Review, 45*(3), 499–503.

Asaduzamman, M., & Virtanen, P. (2016). Governance theories and models. In A. Farazmand (Ed.), *Global encyclopedia of public administration, public policy and governance.* SpringerLink. doi:10.1007/978-3-319-31816-5_2612-1

Balser, D., & Mcclusky, J. (2005). Managing stakeholder relationships and nonprofit organization effectiveness. *Nonprofit Management & Leadership, 15*, 295–315.

Bauer, R., Guenster, N., & Otten, R. (2003). *Empirical evidence on corporate governance in Europe: The effect on stock returns firm value and performance.* Retrieved from https://link.springer.com/article/10.1057/palgrave. jam.2240131

Bendell, J. (2006). *Debating NGO accountability.* New York: United Nations.

Bhasin, M. L. (2013). Corporate accounting scandal at Satyam: A case study of India's Enron. *European Journal of Business and Social Sciences, 1*, 25–47.

Billis, D. (Ed.). (2010). *Hybrid organizations in the third sector: Challenges of practice, policy and theory.* Basingstoke, UK: Palgrave.

Bligh, M. (2016, May 12). How followers create and sustain leadership. *Research Seminar.* London Henley Business School, Greenlands Campus. Henley-on-Thames.

Bolander, T. (2019). What do we lose when machines take the decisions? *Journal of Management and Governance, 23*, 849, 867.

Bonazzi, L., & Islam, S. M. N. (2007). Agency theory and corporate governance. *Journal of Modelling in Management, 2*(1), 7–23. doi:10.1108/17465660733022.

Boulton, T., Smart, S., & Zutter, C. (2010). IPO underpricing and international corporate governance. *Journal of International Business Studies, 41*(2), 206–222.

Bradshaw, P., Murray, V., & Wolpin, J. (1992). Do nonprofit boards make a difference? An exploration of the relationships among board structure, process and effectiveness. *Nonprofit and Voluntary Sector Quarterly, 21*, 227–249. doi:10.1177/089976409202100304

Browning, J. (2012). Corporate governance: How non-profit boards influence organizational decisions. *Board Directors and Corporate Social Responsibility*, 82–100. doi:10.1057/9780230389304

Bryant, P., & Davis, C. (2012). Regulated change effects on boards of directors: A look at agency theory and resource dependancy theory. *Academy of Strategic Management Journal*, 11(2), 1–15.

Campbell, J., Campbell, T., Sirmon, D., Bierman, L., & Tuggle, C. (2012). Shareholder influence over director nomination via proxy access: Implications for agency conflict and stakeholder value. *Strategic Management Journal*, 33(12), 1431–1451.

Carroll, L. (1965). *Alice through the looking glass*. Harmondsworth: Penguin Books.

Cline, B., & Williamson, C. (2016). Trust and the regulation of corporate self-dealing. *Journal of Corporate Finance*, 41(3), 572–590.

Coase, R. (1937). The nature of the firm. *Economica*, 4, 386–405.

Col, B., & Sen, K. (2019). The role of corporate governance for acquisitions by the emerging market multinationals: Evidence from India. *Journal of Corporate Finance*, 59, 239–254.

Comforth, C., Hayes, J. P., & Vangen, S. (2015). Nonprofit-public collaborations: Understanding governance dynamics. *Nonprofit and Voluntary Sector Quarterly*, 44, 775–795.

The Committee on the Financial Aspects of Corporate Governance and Gee and Co Ltd. (1992). *The financial aspects of corporate governance*. Great Britain: Burgess Science Press. Retrieved from https://ecgi.global/sites/default/files//codes/documents/cadbury.pdf

Cornforth, C. (2011). Nonprofit governance research. *Nonprofit and Voluntary Sector Quarterly*, 41(6), 1116–1135. doi:10.1177/089976401142795

Davis, J., Schoorman, F., & Donaldson, L. (1997). Toward a stewardship theory of management. *Academy of Management Review*, 22(1), 20–47. doi:10.2307/259223

deVilliers, C., & Dimes, R. (2020). Determinants, mechanisms and consequences of corporate governance reporting: A research framework. *Journal of Management and Governance*, 25(1), 7–26. Retrieved from https://link.springer.com/article/10.1007/s10997-020-09530-0#citeas

Dey, P., Petridis, N., Petridis, K., Malesios, C., Nixon, J., & Ghosh, K. (2018). Environmental management and corporate social responsibility practices of small and medium-sized enterprises. *Journal of Cleaner Production*, 195, 687–702.

Donaldson, L., & Davis, J. (1991). Stewardship theory or agency theory: CEO governance and shareholder returns. *Australian Journal of Management*, 16(1), 49–64.

Donaldson, T., & Preston, L. E. (1995). The stakeholder theory of the corporation: Concepts, evidence, and implications. *Academy of Management Review*, 20(1), 65–91.

Drees, J., Pursey, P., & Heugens, A. (2013). Synthesizing and extending resource dependence theory: A meta-analysis. *Journal of Management*, 39(6), 1–33. http://doi.org/10.1177/0149206312471391

Fasenfest, D. (2010). Government, governing, and governance. *Critical Sociology*, 36(6), 771–774. doi:10.1177/0896920510378192

Graham, J., Amos, B., & Plumptre, T. (2003). *Governance principles on protected areas in the 21st century. A discussion paper.* Dublin: Institute on Governance, the Fifth World Bark Congress. Retrieved from www.files.ethz.ch/isn/122197/pa_governance2.pdf

Hague, R., & Harrop, M. (2013). *Comparative government and politics: An introduction* (9th ed.). Basingstoke: Palgrave Macmillan.

Halfani, M., McCarney, P. L., & Rodríguez, A. (1994). *Towards and understanding of governance: The emergency of an idea and its implication for urban research in developing countries.* Toronto: The Center for Urban and Community Studies, University of Toronto.

Hilb, M. (2020). Toward artificial governance? The role of artificial intelligence in shaping the future of corporate governance. *Journal of Management and Governance, 24*(4), 851–870.

Hillman, A., Withers, M., & Collins, B. (2009). Resource dependence theory: A review. *Journal of Management, 35*(6), 1404–1427. doi:10.1177/0149206309343469

Hodges, J., & Howieson, B. (2017). The challenges of leadership in the third sector. *European Management Journal, 35*(1), 69–77. doi:10.1016/j.emj.2016.12.006

Hopkings, K., Meyer, M., Shera, W., & Peters, S. C. (2014). Leadership challenges facing nonprofit service organization in a post-recession era. *Human Service Organizations: Management, Leadership & governance, 38*, 419–422. doi:10.1080/23303131.2014.977208

Institute of Directors. (n.d.). *IoD.* Retrieved from https://www.iod.com

International Finance Corporation. (2021). *Corporate governance codes and scorecards.* Retrieved March 5, 2021, from www.ifc.org/wps/wcm/connect/topics_ext_content/ifc_external_corporate_site/ifc+cg/topics/codes+and+scorecards

Jensen, M., & Meckling, W. (1976). Theory of the firm: Managerial behavior, agency costs and ownership structure. *Journal of Financial Economics, 3*(4), 305–360.

Kearns, K., Livingston, J., Scherer, S., & McShane, L. (2015). Leadership skills as construed by nonprofit chief executives. *Leadership & Organization Development Journal, 36*(6), 712–727.

Keay, A (2017). Stewardship theory: Is board accountability necessary? *International Journal of Law and Management, 59*(6), 1292–1314.

Kjaer, A. M. (2004). *Governance.* Cambridge: Polity Press.

Krishna, V., & Serrano, R. (1996). Multilateral bargaining. *Review of Economic Studies, 63*, 61–80.

Martins, R., Serra, F., Leite, A., Ferreira, M., & Li, D. (2010). *Transactions cost theory influence in strategy research: A review through a bibliometric study in leading journals.* Presented at EnANPAD 2010, held in Rio de Janeiro, September 25–29, 2010. Retrieved from www.anpad.org/br/admin/pdf/eso82.pdf

McGahan, A. (2020). Where does an organization's responsibility end? Identifying the boundaries on stakeholder claims. *Academy of Management Discoveries, 6*, 8–11.

Miller, J. L. (2003). The board as a monitor of organizational activity: The applicability of agency theory to nonprofit boards. *Nonprofit Management and Leadership, 12*, 429–450.

Minciullo, M., & Pedrini, M. (2020). Antecedents of board involvement and its consequences on organisational effectiveness in non-profit organisations: A study on European corporate foundations. *Journal of Management and Governance*, 24, 531–555.

Nadaf, S., & Navi, B. (2016). Corporate governance: Issues, opportunities and challenges. *International Journal of Commerce and Management Research*, 3(7), 66072. ISSN: 2455–1627.

Nour, A. I., Sharabati, A.-A., & Hammad, K. M. (2019). Corporate governance and corporate social responsibility disclosure. *International Journal of Sustainable Entrepreneurship and Corporate Social Responsibility*, 5(1), 20–41. doi:10.4018/IJSECSR.2020010102

Organization for Economic Cooperation and Development (OECD). (2004). *OECD principles of corporate governance*. Retrieved January 25, 2021, from www.oecd.org/corporate/ca/corporategovernanceprinciples/31557724.pdf

Organization for Economic Cooperation and Development (OECD). (2015). *G20/OECD principles of corporate governance*. Paris: OECD Publishing. doi. org10.1787/9789264236882-en.

Pande, S. (2011). *The theoretical framework of corporate governance*. International Conference on Gandhian Values: Sustainability and Corporate Governance. Bangalore, 8 October 2011. Retrieved from www.slideshare.net/spande1952/the-theoretical-framework-for-corporate-governance

Paine, L. S. 1994. Managing for organizational integrity. *Harvard Business Review*, 72(2), 106–117.

Pape, U., Brandsen, T., Pahl, J., et al. (2020). Changing policy environments in Europe and the resilience of the third sector. *VOLUNTAS: International Journal of Voluntary and Nonprofit Organizations*, 31, 238–249.

Pfeffer, J., & Salancik, G. R. (1978). *The external control of organizations: A resource dependence perspective*. New York: Harper & Row.

Pierre, J. (Ed.). (2000). *Debating governance: Authority, steering and democracy*. Oxford: Oxford University Press.

Renz, D. (2006, Winter). Reframing governance. *Nonprofit Quarterly*, 13(4), 6–11.

Rhodes, R. A. (1996). The new governance: Governing without government. *Political Studies*, 44, 652–667. doi:10.1111/j.1467-9248.1996.tb01747.x

Richards, D., & Smith, M. (2002). *Governance and public policy*. Oxford: Oxford University Press.

Rindfleisch, A. (2019). Transaction cost theory: Past, present and future. *Academy of Marketing Science Review*, 10(5), 1–13.

Rosenau, J. N. (1992). Governance, order, and change in world politics. In J. N. Rosenau & E. O. Czempiel (Eds.), *Governance without government: Order and change in world politics*. Cambridge: Cambridge University Press.

Rosenau, J. N. (1995). Governance in the twenty-first century. *Global Governance*, 1(1), 13–43. Retrieved from https://sta.uwi.edu/iir/normangirvanlibrary/sites/default/files/normangirvanlibrary/documents/Governance%20in%20the%20Twenty-first%20Century.pdf

Rubino, F., & Napoli, F. (2020). What impact does corporate governance have on corporate environmental performances? An empirical study of Italian listed firms. *Sustainability*, 12(14), 5742. https://doi.org/10.3390/su12145742

Sauvant, K. P. (2015). The negotiations of the United Nations code of conduct on transnational corporations. Experiences and lessons learned. *The Journal of World Investment and Trade*, 16, 11–87.

Schillemans, T., & Bjurstrøm, K. (2020). Trust and verification: Balancing agency and stewardship theory in the governance of agencies. *International Public Management Journal, 23*(5), 650–676.

Schneider, V. (2004). State theory, governance and the logic of regulation and administrative control. In A. Warntjen & A. Wonka (Eds.), *Governance in Europe*. Baden-Baden: Nomos.

Shleifer, A., & Vishny, R. W. (1997). A survey of corporate governance. *The Journal of Finance, 72*(2).

Sonnenfeld, J. A. (2002). What makes great boards great. *Harvard Business Review*. Retrieved March 14, 2021, from https://hbr.org/2002/09/what-makes-great-boards-great

Subramanian, S. (2018). Stewardship theory of corporate governance and value system: The case of a family-owned business group in India. *Indian Journal of Corporate Governance, 11*(1), 88–102.

Svensson, P. G., Mahoney, T. Q., & Hambrick, M. E. (2019). What does innovation mean to nonprofit practitioners? International insights from development and peace-building nonprofits. *Nonprofit and Voluntary Sector Quarterly, 49*(2), 380–398.

Taylor, K. (2015). Learning from the co-operative institutional model: How to enhance organizational robustness of third sector organizations with more pluralistic forms of governance. *Administrative Sciences, 5*(3), 148–164.

Udayasankar, K. (2008). The foundations of governance theory: A case for the resource-dependence perspective. *Corporate Ownership & Control, 5*(4), 164–172.

Van Essen, M., Heugens, P. P. M. A. R., Otten, J., & Van Oosterhout, J. (Hans.). (2012). An institution-based view of executive compensation: A multilevel meta-analytic test. *Journal of International Business Studies, 43*(4), 396–423.

Van Puyvelde, S., Caers, R., Du Bois, C., & Jegers, M. (2012). The governance of nonprofit organisations. *Nonprofit and Voluntary Sector Quarterly, 41*(3), 431–451.

Van Puyvelde, S., & Raeymaechkers, P. (2020, October). The governance of public-nonprofit service networks: Four propositions. *Nonprofit and Voluntary Sector Quarterly, 49*(5), 931–950.

Velte, P., & Gerwanski, J. (2020). Current integrated reporting knowledge and future research opportunities – the impact of governance on integrated reporting – A literature review. In C. De Villiers, P. K. Hsiao, & W. Maroun (Eds.), *The Routledge handbook of integrated reporting*. London: Routledge.

Vermeiren, C., Raeymaeckers, P., & Beagles, J. (2019). In search for inclusiveness: Vertical complexity in public-nonprofit networks. *Public Management Review, 23*(1), 1–21.

Von Schneubein, G., Perez, M., & Gehringer, T., (2018). Nonprofit comparative research: Recent agenda's and future trends. *VOLUNTAS: International Journal of Voluntary and Nonprofit Organizations, 29*, 437–453.

Weiss, T. G. (2000). Governance, good governance and global governance: Conceptual and actual challenges. *Third World Quarterly, 21*(5), 795–814. doi:10.1080/713701075

Willems, J. (2015). Building shared mental models or organizational effectiveness in leadership teams through team member exchange quality. *Nonprofit and Voluntary Sector Quarterly, 45*(3), 568–592.0899764015601244

Williamson, O. (1975). *Markets and hierarchies, analysis and antitrust implications: A study in the economics of internal organization.* New York: Free Press.

Williamson, O. (1979). Transaction cost economics: The governance of contractual obligations. *Journal of Law and Economics, 22*(2), 233–261.

Williamson, O. (1981). The economics of organization: The transaction cost approach. *American Journal of Sociology, 87*(3), 548–577.

Williamson, O. (1985). *The economic institutions of capitalism: Firms, markets, relational contracting.* New York: Free Press.

Williamson, O. (1989). Transaction cost economics. In R. Schmanlensee & R. Willig (Eds.), *Handbook of industrial organization* (Vol. 1, pp. 136–182). Amsterdam: Elsevier Science.

Williamson, O., & Ouchi, W. (1981). The markets and hierarchies program of research: Origins, implications, prospects. In A. Van de Ven & W. F. Joyce (Eds.), *Perspectives on organizational design and behavior* (pp. 347–406). New York: John Wiley & Sons.

Young, D., Bania, N., & Bailey, D. (1996). Structure and accountability, a study of national nonprofit associations. *Nonprofit Management and Leadership, 6,* 347–365.

Zollo, L., Laudano, M., Boccardi, A., & Ciappei, C. (2019). From governance to organizational effectiveness: The role of organizational identity and volunteers' commitment. *Journal of Management and Governance, 28,* 111–137.

Websites

www.ifc.org
www.iod.com
www.oecd.org

4 Governance and Corporate Social Responsibility Regulations and Policies in the EU

Efthalia (Elia) Chatzigianni and Panagiotis Dimitropoulos

Governance

Since the 1990s, corporate governance issues have been receiving increasing attention as a result of globalization, transformation of firms' ownership, growing demand for legitimization, and efficiency of corporate practices. As a process corporate governance requires the participation, coordination, and monitoring of a variety of actors who participate in the governance of a company or organization with the aim to improve organizational performance and pursue the interests of a variety of stakeholders or shareholders while, at the same time, maximizing their value.

The European Union (EU) definition of corporate governance follows the one adopted by the 1992 *Report of the Committee on the Financial Aspects of Corporate Governance* (European Commission, 2011). This report, also known as the *Cadbury Report*, defined corporate governance as "the system by which companies are directed and controlled" and as the number of relationships among the company's management, its board, its shareholders, and its stakeholders. Corporate governance has been at the center of discussions of EU public policy since the beginning of the new millennium.

Given the similarities in their corporate governance structures, the United Kingdom, the United States, and Canada have adopted a unitary model of corporate governance. Companies in the European countries, though, operate within different corporate regimes and with different approaches to governance. Throughout the European territory, the corporate landscape is not uniform; companies have different structures, legislative and regulatory requirements, ownership status, and board practices. Consequently, this plurality and diversification of European companies do not allow the establishment of a unified model of corporate governance, one similar to the Anglo-Saxon model of corporate governance. Accordingly, the EU has adopted since 2000 an approach to corporate governance that links effective governance to accountability and shareholder responsibility in a framework of "principles-based

DOI: 10.4324/9781003152750-5

comply-or-explain regime for member state – based corporate governance codes" (CFA, 2016, p. 7).

Given this, the EU corporate governance framework for companies that are listed within the EU involves a synthesis of legislation and "soft law" tools, which include recommendations, directives, and corporate governance codes. The European policy corporate governance framework is set by the European Commission White and Green Papers as tools of policy initiation and implementation. The White Papers (WPs) are Commission documents proposing EU action in a specific area, and they are often followed by Green Papers; the Green Papers are consultative documents that stimulate dialogue at the European level on several topics of interest to the EU members. In most cases, the Green Papers provoke legislative developments, as they result in actions plans that finally turn into European law, directives, or recommendations.

EU Key Policy Developments

In July 2001, the European Commission adopted the White Paper (WP) on European Governance (European Commission, 2001). The WP was available on the Internet and distributed as brochures; it was open to public consultation and had initiated several debates, conferences, and discussions regarding the future of European governance. Some of the key messages from the public consultation were related to the adoption of principles such as accountability, legitimacy, openness, and participation in European governance (European Commission, 2003a). These principles linked to good governance mechanisms in organizations – which first aimed at the operation of European institutions – and further initiated and promoted the adoption of a new regulatory logic and culture in European business.

The Commission 2001 WP resulted in the publication of the 2003 European Commission first green paper on corporate governance. As a consequence of the global financial crisis (2007–2008), several questions were raised with regard to corporate governance. The Commission tried to address them with the publication of the *Green Paper on the Corporate Governance of Financial Institutions* in June 2010, followed by the *Green Paper on Corporate Governance* of all European corporations in April 2011. Both Green Papers dealt with similar issues of corporate governance, mostly related to shareholders, board of directors, gatekeepers such as auditors and regulators, as well as codes of conduct (ECGI, 2011).

Specifically, with the publication of the *Green Paper on the Corporate Governance of Financial Institutions* in 2010, the Commission has addressed the need for the establishment of a new European System of Financial Supervision presented in the *de Larosière Report* (2009). The report focused on the deficiencies of the European financial system that were reflected in the crisis generated by the bankruptcy of the Lehman Brothers: lack of efficient company management control mechanisms, inadequate corporate governance, insufficient risk management practices and supervision, and absence of an effective regulatory framework. Overall, studies and reports of that period stressed on the fact that the principle of self-regulation for institutions with major systemic significance endangered the stability of the system and that new capital allocations and a macro-prudential approach was required to address the systemic risks (Borio, 2005, Brunnermeier, Crockett, Goodhart, Persaud, & Shin, 2009, Tumpel-Gugerell, 2009).

In 2010, the Commission published the Green Paper on Audit Policy as a means to enhance the impact of the audits on increased financial stability in the framework of financial market regulatory reform (European Commission, 2010a). The Green Paper focused on the role and scope of auditors, including appointment, remuneration, and mandatory rotation. The aim of the Commission was to assume leadership in the field of audit policy and, in cooperation with the Financial Stability Board and G20, to ensure that audit, along with corporate governance and supervision, contributes to the financial well-being of European companies and the reestablishment of trust and confidence in the European market.

Furthermore, in 2011 the European Commission published the Green Paper on *Corporate Governance in Financial Institutions and Remuneration Policies*, initially triggered by the financial crisis that originated from the bankruptcy of the Lehman Brothers. The Green Paper aimed to improve corporate governance practices as a response to the financial crisis and lessons learned from it. The Commission paper followed the G20 decision at its meeting in Washington on 15 November 2008 to enhance good governance practices and financial stability within financial institutions, and it was accompanied by the Commission Staff Working Paper on *Corporate Governance in Financial Institutions: The Lessons to Be Learned from the Current Financial Crisis and Possible Steps Forward* (European Commission, 2010b). Following the Green Paper and online consultation, on 12 December 2012, the Commission presented an Action Plan on *European company law and corporate governance – a modern legal framework for more engaged shareholders and sustainable companies* (European Commission, 2012). The Action Plan included 16 initiatives on corporate governance and corporate law rules and regulations to be implemented through directives, to a certain extent through nonlegal measures, along three parameters: enhancement of transparency between investors and enterprises, motivation of long-term shareholder engagement, and amelioration for the framework of cross-border cooperation. Specifically, the Action Plan, included, among others, the following measures and initiatives to be undertaken by the Commission:

In the area of enhancement of transparency in EU companies:

- A proposal, or even an amendment to the Accounts Directive, with the purpose to enhance disclosure requirements concerning policies and procedures of the board in the field of diversity as well as risk management measures and strategies.
- The recommendation to ameliorate the quality of company reports on corporate governance, especially sections related to the explanation of "comply or explain" principle.
- Initiatives to enhance the visibility of shareholders (in relation to the Commission's legislative work program in the field of securities law) and on disclosure of voting, engagement policies, and voting records of international investors.

In the area of stakeholders' engagement in EU companies:

- Initiatives to include strengthening of transparency on directors' remuneration and related policies, the improvement of shareholders' control over related-party transactions, and the improvement of transparency and conflict of interest frameworks applicable to proxy investors.
- Cooperation with the European Securities and Markets Authority (ESMA) and relevant national authorities to develop and provide guidance on investor cooperation for corporate governance purposes and "acting-in-concert" under the Takeover Bids Directive and the Transparency Directive.
- Promotion of the development of transnational employee share ownership schemes in Europe.

In the area of EU cross-border cooperation and cross-border operations of EU companies:

- Enhance consultation and information campaigns in cooperation with relevant authorities and bodies.
- Assess the need for European initiatives in the field.
- The improvement of European law in general.

The Action Plan further aimed for the Commission to work in the area of codification of EU company law and directives.

In an effort to tackle challenges related to corporate governance short-comings in the EU, such as transparency and limited shareholder engagement, the Commission published on 9 April 2014 a proposal for the Revision of the Shareholders' Directive (2007/36/EC). The proposed provisions focused on issues related to the promotion of long-term sustainability of listed companies as well as the promotion of an accountable and transparent environment for shareholders, identification of shareholders, investor transparency, and facilitation of voting rights. The Directive was further revised in 2017 [Directive (EU) 2017/828)] with the aim to promote long-term engagement of company shareholders as a means to safeguard the long-term stability of the company and its consideration of social and environmental issues in decision-making processes. The Directive mainly focused on regulation and improvements in the areas of transparency in company activities and transactions, including directors' remuneration and improvement of information flow among stakeholders, especially between shareholders and the company. The Commission implemented related regulation as of 3 September 2018 (European Commission, 2018).

The aforementioned European initiatives in the area of corporate governance are indicative of the intention and willingness of the European institutions to contribute to the improvement of corporate practices within the EU. Changes in the European legislative landscape, though, are continuous and are not limited to the ones presented in this chapter. For example, in the area of sustainable governance, the European Commission launched between October 2020 and February 2021 a public consultation on sustainable corporate governance with the aim to encourage long-term sustainable and responsible corporate behavior as indicated in the European Green Deal, one of the six Commission priorities for the period 2019–2024 (European Commission, 2019a).

European Initiatives and Regulations in the Field of Corporate Governance

EU corporate governance in the framework of EU company law deals with issues related to the operation of companies listed in the stock exchange market, such as the protection of interests of shareholders and other parties, branches disclosure, mergers and divisions, minimum rules for single-member private limited-liability companies and shareholders' rights, the constitution and maintenance of public limited-liability companies' capital, and legal forms of undertakings such as the European Economic Interest Grouping (EEIG) and the European Cooperative Society (SCE) (European Commission, 2012, p. 3, note 17).

The European mobilization has resulted in a significant number of European initiatives and subsequent regulations in the field of corporate governance along the parameters discussed earlier. Some examples are the following:

- The 2004 Directive on Transparency Requirements for Listed Issuers, which aims at the harmonization of transparency requirements related to information about issuers whose securities are admitted to trading on a regulated market.
- The 2004 Directive on Takeover Bids, which focuses on minimum standards for takeover bids and protecting minority shareholders and employees.
- The 2004 Recommendation on Remuneration, which discusses long-term performance-based pay, public disclosure, remuneration committee, and shareholders' roles.
- The 2005 Recommendation on Boards about board independence and committees.
- The 2005 Amendments on 4th and 7th Company Law Directives, which provides updated guidance for annual corporate governance statements, disclosure on risk management, and material Related Party Transactions (RPTs).
- The 2005 10th Company Law Directive on Cross-Border Mergers, which aims to facilitate cross-border mergers of limited liability companies in the European Union.
- The "CRD-IV Package" on new prudential requirements for financial institutions, which includes the Directive (Directive 2013/36/EU) (EU, 2013a) and Regulation on Capital Requirements (Regulation (EU) No 575/2013) (EU, 2013b).
- The Directive (EU) 2017/828 (encouragement of long-term shareholder engagement), according to which shareholders have a vote on the remuneration policy and report, as well as related party transactions (EU, 2017).
- And, recently | (since July 2020–ongoing), the Commission initiative on sustainable corporate governance [Ref. Ares(2020)4034032–30/07/2020], which aims to enable European companies to focus on long-term sustainable goals with "the objective to 'ensure environmental and social interests are fully embedded into business strategies', in the context of competitive sustainability contributing to the COVID-19 recovery and to the long-term development of companies" (p. 1). Rather than managing sustainable-related matters, such as with a focus on short-term benefits, this initiative targets company value creation in the management of sustainable issues such as climate change, environment, human rights, and diversity. The consultation phase of the initiative ended on 8 February 2021.

European initiatives in the area of corporate governance had significant impact on the field of governance planning and strategy of corporate entities in Europe. Consequently, corporate governance within the EU requires a commitment to accountability and transparency and the implementation of procedures that abide to these principles. Corporate entities must provide to all stakeholders involved a clear framework of company operation and be willing to publicly clarify the role of the management and boards of directors.

Corporate Governance Principles and Codes

Corporate governance codes are the main indicators of governance practices of firms in various countries. A corporate governance code may be defined as "a non-binding set of principles, standards or best practices, issued by a collective body, and relating to the internal governance of corporations" (Weil et al., 2002, p. 1). Corporate governance codes, as elements of soft law (Kubíček, Štamfestová, & Strouhal, 2016), demonstrate best practices used in corporate governance taken into consideration among other issues such as board selection, membership and composition, board practices, relationships with shareholders, auditing, and information disclosure. Although there is a slight variation in the content of corporate governance codes across various countries, all of them aim at the improvement of companies' board performance as well as the increase of company accountability to shareholders and parallel maximization of shareholder or stakeholder value (Aguilera & Cuervo-Cazzura, 2004).

One of the most important research questions in the field of corporate governance is the debate concerning the convergence or divergence of corporate governance codes (Krenn, 2016). In the framework of European countries, corporate governance is increasingly perceived as a way to guarantee that the corporate sector exercises its economic power in accountable and legitimate terms. Regardless of the differences attributed to the significance of shareholder and stakeholder interests by the various theories and discussions, the majority of corporate governance codes in the EU countries acknowledge a co-dependency and intertwinement between corporate success and the satisfaction of all corporate stakeholders involved, including shareholders and employees (Weil et al., 2002). A study undertaken by Hermes et al. in 2006 discussed the impact of external and domestic forces and determinants on the contents of codes of governance in the EU countries; the research has shown that the majority of the codes of European countries at the time were not in full accordance with the guidelines and priorities set by the European Commission with COM-284 (European Commission, 2003b) and could not identify the forces determining the content and shape of codes. Another study by Kubíček et al. (2016) on the analysis of cross-country codes in the EU further suggested that although there was strong evidence of quality improvement of governance codes within EU countries in accordance

Table 4.1 A non-exhaustive list of corporate governance codes and principles that may be considered as milestones in the field of corporate governance

USA	Business Roundtable	1978	First code on good governance – On the Role and Composition of the Board of Directors of the Large Publicly Owned Corporation
Hong Kong	Hong Kong Stock Exchange	1989	Code of Best Practice, Listing Rules
Ireland	Irish Association of Investment Managers	1991	Statement of Best Practice on the Role and Responsibility of Directors of Publicly Listed Companies
UK	The Cadbury Report	1992	Financial Aspects of Corporate Governance in the UK
Global	International Corporate Governance Network	1995 (last updated 2013)	Global Governance Principles
Global	OECD	1999 (revised 2004)	Principles of Corporate Governance
USA	Sarbanes-Oxley Act	2002	Public Law/SEC Actions & SEC-related Provisions Creation of the Public Company Accounting Oversight Board
United Nations/ Global	The International Finance Corporation & the UN Global Compact	2009	Corporate Governance: The Foundation for Corporate Citizenship and Sustainable Business
Global (currently adopted by 116 institutions in 37 countries including Spain, France, Germany & the Netherlands)	Equator Principles	2010	Risk management framework for financial institutions

European Union	European Shareholders' Rights Directive (SRD) I & II	2007 2019–2020	Improvement of corporate governance in companies whose securities are traded on EU-regulated markets

Note: *Table 4.1 shows there is a gap between the first and the second code; after 1989 more codes steadily appear. The impact of the Cadbury Report was a significant landmark for the emergence of numerous codes in the EU and worldwide.*

with international standards and best practices, there was no certainty regarding the impact of the European Commission recommendations on this quality improvement.

CSR as a Manifestation of the Broader EU Social Responsibility Framework

In July 2001, the Commission of the European Communities presented the Green Paper entitled "Promoting a European Framework for Corporate Social Responsibility". The aims of this document were, first, to launch a debate about the concept of corporate social responsibility (CSR) and, second, to identify how to build a partnership for the development of a European framework for the promotion of CSR (Lenssen, Gasparski, Rok, Lacy, & Eberhard-Harribey, 2006).

The Green Paper defines CSR as "the concept by which companies voluntarily incorporate social and environmental concerns into their business and contacts with other stakeholders", as they become increasingly aware that responsible behavior leads to sustainable business success. CSR is also about managing change at the company level in a socially responsible manner. This happens when a company seeks to set the trade-offs between the requirements and the needs of the various stakeholders into a balance, which is acceptable to all parties. If companies succeed in managing change in a socially responsible way, there will be a positive impact at the macroeconomic level.

CSR is a concept whereby companies integrate social and environmental concerns in their business operations and in their collaboration with their stakeholders on a voluntary basis. The main function of an enterprise is to create value through producing goods and services that society demands, thereby generating profit for its owners and shareholders as well as welfare for society, particularly through an ongoing process of job creation. However, new social and market pressures are gradually leading to a change in the values and in the future of business activity. Currently, there is a growing perception among enterprises that sustainable business success and shareholder value cannot be achieved solely through maximizing short-term profits, but instead through market-oriented yet responsible behavior. Businesses know that they can contribute to sustainable development if the way they are managed promotes economic growth and increases competitiveness while ensuring environmental protection and promoting social responsibility as well as consumer interests (Van Marrewijk, 2003; Matten & Moon, 2005; Dahlsrud, 2008).

Corporate environmental responsibility (CER) in the context of a broader CSR is the least that could be offered today by a company to society, regardless of size. The ethics that should surround this mission should be taken for granted, as should the fact that the contribution of each company should reflect both the size of the organization and its carbon footprint (Mazurkiewicz, 2004).

Although the ethics of any contribution should not be dominated by financial terms or economic-technical analysis, in the context of large investments these could be considered legitimate on the basis of an initial assessment of alternatives and prioritization. Obviously, a Life Cycle Cost Analysis and environmental impact are required in such cases, as an investment could be seemingly economically viable and environmentally beneficial, but in the course of its life cycle it may ultimately have a negative sign. It is for this purpose that, for example, the selection of optimal solutions for saving resources and energy, utilization of renewable energy sources, recycling methods and proper waste management, and so on should not be taken on the basis of a simple cost-benefit study but a broader one that will take into account both economic and technical sustainability, as well as social and environmental benefits, on the basis of a life cycle analysis.

CSR is not just about big business. Any business, large or small, has an obligation to the environment and society. The application of simple methods of saving resources and energy in the basic operations of the company, the transition to alternative energy forms that are environmentally friendly, the implementation of a waste recycling strategy, the proper management of waste, the selection of suppliers and partners who have adopted corporate social policies and environmental responsibility, and the protection of employee rights are just some of the things that even a small business could implement for its own contribution to the environment and society in general (Cai, Cui, & Jo, 2016).

In short, CSR includes all those initiatives that a company takes to improve its impact on the environment and society. Such initiatives can be changes in the company's products or in the techniques used for their production, the adoption of policies to reduce energy consumption and waste production, the use of renewable energy resources, community engagement, responsible production processes, and so on (Wahba, 2008; Gunningham, 2009).

It is becoming clear that CSR is another step toward achieving the overall goal of sustainable development. An economy based on sound environmental and social actions has both ecological and economic benefits. CSR and sustainable development are concepts that continue to play an increasingly important role in the global economy, and it is therefore necessary to take action to implement them (He & Chen, 2009). The EU has developed multi-annual environmental and CSR action plans, which apparently determine, inter alia, the activities of companies, regardless of size, based in its Member State, as defining the framework for future actions in all areas of environmental and social policy. They are integrated into horizontal strategies and are even considered in international environmental and social negotiations. Therefore, their implementation is equally crucial. These include, among others, the EU Energy Efficiency Directive, the Integrated Pollution Prevention and Control Directive, the European Pollutant Release and Transfer register (E-PRTR), and the EUs Emissions Trading Scheme. All these directives made social responsibility a core element of business activity and coordinated EU member states efforts to improve nonfinancial reporting and transparency (Camilleri, 2017).

EU Initiatives and Directives on CSR Activities and Reporting

In the last decade EU has initiated a significant effort to create a framework for corporate reporting of social activities. EU officials recognize that companies' activities have a significant impact on citizens' lives, not only via the production of services and products, but also through decisions on human rights, working conditions, and environmental degradation. Therefore, this raises the expectations of EU citizens toward companies to recognize their societal and environmental impacts and act vigorously toward reducing the negative side effects of their activities. Hence, in 2011 the EU Commission issued the renewed strategy for CSR that aimed to promote CSR activities within different areas and social issues, including the environment, transparency reporting, human rights, and social inclusion (EC, 2019b). However, this framework (EU, 2011) does not provide a unified solution to the issue, nor is it compulsory for corporations.

Nevertheless, the tools of social responsibility reporting have been developed by several nongovernmental organizations and other stakeholders (Camilleri, 2017). Thus, in September 2014 the European Council provided some amendments on the type of nonfinancial information disclosures that corporations operating within the EU must publish. This information included details on community activities, environmental protection, emission reduction, anti-corruption matters, and other issues of social interest. This initiative affected directly only listed corporations and banks and insurance firms. Moreover, that EU initiative motivated firms to utilize key performance indicators for assessing their performance, focusing not solely on financial returns but also on social and environmental activities. Since 1995 the EU Eco-management and Audit Scheme (EMAS) set the ground for corporate reporting on environmental performance by introducing such core performance indicators. On the same direction, the EU accounts modernization directive, which was initiated in 2005, urged firms to report on both financial and nonfinancial indicators (social and environmental type of information) which contain significant information on business risks and prospects.

Thus, the EU commission gave more emphasis on the transparency and materiality of nonfinancial information while allowing a certain level of flexibility on those requirements. Taking a step further, in June 2013 the EU adopted the 2013/50/EU directive, which included several stakeholder concerns on corporate reporting, and so introduced the ESG (Environmental, Social and Governance) disclosures, which had a more mandatory character, especially for listed firms. Even though the aforementioned directives did not cover specific requirements on the type of performance indicators that should be included in the reports, several member countries' parliaments have taken initiative to provide guidance for their firms. Those guidelines were not characterized by general conformity, yet they steadily introduced ESG reporting as a core element on statutory financial reports.

France was the first EU country to introduce such rules on corporate financial reporting practices back in 2001. The French government proposed a framework for establishing social and environmental standards for benchmarking purposes among firms. The UK followed closely when the Company Act was modernized in 2006 and mandated large firms to provide information on strategies, risks, and performance indicators in their annual reports. Similarly, listed corporations had to disclose information regarding their employees and social and community activities. Later in 2008 the UK government enacted the Climate Change Act, which among other things regulated the disclosure of environmental footprint information and emission reduction activities by listed firms. This fact was obligatory for corporations and directed them to publish a *Footprint Report* on their energy consumption and carbon emissions. Sweden dictated in 2008 that state-owned companies need to publish sustainability reports following the internationally renowned Global Reporting Initiative (GRI) framework. Today, Sweden is the second European country to lead the rank on corporate GRI sustainability reports. The same year (2008) the Netherlands also mandated CSR reporting for large listed corporations (with assets more than 500 million euro), which allowed them to publish nonfinancial information on a "comply or explain" basis.

In 2010 Spain and Portugal incorporated social and environmental disclosure requirements for state-controlled organizations, which were forced to publish sustainability-related information. In the same vein, the Irish Credit Institutions Act of 2008 introduced the issuance of CSR reports by financial services firms, and steadily this was expanded within firms listed in the alternative market. This report was based on a "comply or explain" basis as in the Netherlands (Camilleri, 2017; Knopf et al., 2010). The Czech Republic took a step further and initiated a CSR award for firms that have published respective reports submitted to the government and evaluated by independent assessors (auditors). This award was proposed as a form of promotion and motivation for firms to engage and report their CSR activities and performance assessment.

Similar CSR ranking and independent assessments were set in Germany by the German Council for Sustainable Development. This ranking was created not only for promotion and CSR engagement motivation but also to help firms benchmark themselves against their competitors. This fact could help firms to enhance communication between stakeholder groups and so to stimulate fruitful competition between companies. In Italy, several nongovernmental organizations worked together to create a set of nonfinancial reports related to sustainability and CSR. As a result, firms have their CSR reports ranked and appraised for their creditworthiness if they present sustainability information under a true and fair view, thus assisting investors and stakeholders to assess future firms' prospects and risks. Additionally, the Belgium federal government initially introduced the ISO 26000 standard within government agencies, and then it was connected to GRI sustainability reporting guidelines for private corporations (Camilleri, 2017). Finally, the Greek government created a framework for CSR reporting in 2014, including a national strategy and specific goals. These goals were related to the workforce (human capital), local communities, transparency and business ethics, product responsibility, and environmental protection.

In conclusion, there is a vast wave of regulatory interventions on most EU member countries that has taken place during the previous decade. Some countries lead this effort while others lag behind, yet they have made initial steps into introducing specific guidelines and procedures for motivating firms to engage in CSR activities and reporting. The following section provides descriptive evidence on CSR performance of EU firms over a period of 15 years, in order to present to the reader a quantitative assessment on how European firms perform on several facets of CSR performance.

CSR Performance in EU Countries and Sectors

This section is aimed at providing a decomposition of main corporate social performance data of listed firms domiciled in the EU countries. The analysis is performed comparatively between countries and economic sectors, as well as during the research period 2003–2018. The main social performance indicators have been extracted from the Datastream database (ESG-Refinitiv data) on an annual basis. The respective scores include STRAT, which denotes each company's CSR strategy score, which reflects the firm's practices to communicate the integration of socially responsible activities into its daily operations and decision-making processes. WORK denotes the company's workforce score estimated via their efforts and effectiveness in job satisfaction, creating a healthy and safe working environment, promoting diversity and equal opportunities for its employees. HUMAN denotes the firm's human rights score and indicates its effectiveness in adhering to the fundamental human rights conventions. COMM is the company's community score measuring the firm's commitment to being a good citizen by protecting public health and promoting business ethical behavior. PROD is the firm's product responsibility score reflecting a firm's ability to create quality products and services by protecting customers' health, safety, and private data privacy protection. SHARE is the firm's shareholder score measuring the firm's effectiveness on treating their shareholder's equally by incorporating anti-takeover devices. Finally, we have estimated another variable, CSR, which is the firm's annual firm-specific average of the aforementioned six scores. All social responsibility scores range between zero (0) and 100; so the higher the score the more socially responsible and efficient is the firm.

Table 4.2 and Figure 4.1 present the total averages (for the whole sample period 2003–2018) of the CSR performance score by country. As we can see, Malta, Poland, and the Czech Republic are among the countries where firms have the lowest CSR scores. On the contrary, Spain, Slovenia, and Hungary have the highest CSR scores among the sample countries. Workforce score is the main CSR pillar that has the highest average practically among all sample countries, suggesting that European firms have paid enhanced focus on protecting employee rights and improving working conditions. Overall, the lower-ranked countries on the average CSR score (Malta, Poland, and the Czech Republic) suggest that corporations in these countries have not fully been investing on social responsibility activities and performance. The fact that these are countries which have joined the EU recently may be a valid reason for lagging behind the oldest EU member countries on those merits. Moreover, Slovenian firms have the highest score (almost 69.5), followed by Spanish and Hungarian firms (both of them present an average CSR score close to 69). The rest of the countries are placed between those top and bottom ranked countries. Overall, there seems to be significant discrepancies between EU member countries, where some are at a slower pace in incorporating relative regulations on social responsibility activities, so firms in those countries take time to follow the new standards.

Moreover, Table 4.3 and Figure 4.2 indicate the evolution of the average CSR score over the period 2003–2018 per country. Malta and Poland

Table 4.2 Average of social performance scores per country (2003–2018)

COUNTRIES	STRAT	WORK	HUMAN	COMM	PROD	SHARE	CSR
Austria	52.06	64.29	52.32	40.26	54.57	49.75	52.70
Belgium	55.10	55.63	58.76	44.96	47.22	51.52	52.33
Bulgaria	55.35	64.00	72.72	39.78	47.90	51.26	55.97
Cyprus	62.29	74.25	57.20	58.23	63.71	48.84	63.14
Czech Republic	43.52	48.63	45.06	55.00	51.64	49.63	48.77
Denmark	55.83	64.41	73.06	39.92	48.03	54.37	56.25
Finland	56.48	65.19	74.22	51.19	59.67	48.85	61.35
France	54.02	77.97	74.84	52.28	68.62	49.06	65.55
Germany	59.14	77.45	71.60	57.14	66.72	49.32	66.41
Greece	56.67	56.25	58.19	42.22	59.91	54.22	54.65
Hungary	52.37	73.52	66.48	74.88	70.13	67.14	67.47
Ireland	55.63	59.90	52.67	63.23	55.05	55.11	57.30
Italy	58.54	66.49	67.95	57.84	63.44	61.23	62.85
Luxembourg	60.67	67.53	66.10	63.82	66.93	65.74	65.01
Malta	46.35	30.45	38.67	19.15	25.81	26.31	32.08
Netherlands	59.17	64.90	76.69	73.70	62.46	64.85	67.38
Poland	54.22	42.28	44.80	30.02	46.33	45.17	43.53
Portugal	52.92	63.21	67.55	56.27	75.49	61.25	63.09
Romania	61.79	59.79	89.58	49.17	41.21	43.22	60.31
Slovakia	56.22	63.95	72.53	39.03	47.81	50.22	55.91
Slovenia	50.00	85.35	67.50	78.92	65.35	64.84	69.42
Spain	54.99	73.61	77.01	63.33	75.87	64.87	68.96
Sweden	55.17	65.16	73.93	60.94	57.09	56.74	62.46
UK	54.07	68.08	66.26	50.48	58.07	63.49	59.36

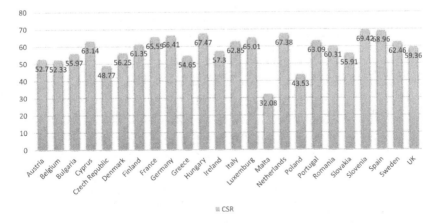

Figure 4.1 Average CSR performance per country over the period 2003–2018

Table 4.3 Average CSR score per country and sample year

Countries	2003	2004	2005	2006	2007	2008	2009	2010	2011	2012	2013	2014	2015	2016	2017	2018
Austria	53.09	53.25	53.00	52.92	53.13	52.86	53.00	52.87	53.39	51.96	52.91	52.58	52.13	52.33	51.78	52.17
Belgium	51.52	51.51	51.80	52.29	52.32	52.71	52.54	53.06	52.97	53.34	53.19	52.08	51.74	51.85	51.28	51.60
Bulgaria	55.24	55.36	54.39	55.93	56.54	55.70	55.22	56.56	56.80	56.43	57.02	57.28	56.10	57.80	53.78	54.40
Cyprus	63.66	60.29	61.88	64.43	63.84	62.70	63.40	64.81	65.77	64.40	63.82	63.00	63.18	64.84	61.24	60.48
Czech Republic	48.08	49.17	49.07	49.16	49.17	48.44	48.21	49.09	48.42	49.39	49.49	49.18	48.18	47.84	47.46	47.64
Denmark	53.92	57.47	57.29	55.98	56.86	54.12	54.20	54.90	56.01	56.01	56.64	57.20	56.20	57.67	56.51	57.50
Finland	61.90	62.32	62.45	61.59	60.97	60.75	60.78	60.42	60.64	60.78	60.58	60.72	61.76	61.99	62.16	62.26
France	63.84	65.40	65.56	65.18	65.83	66.00	66.03	65.75	65.12	65.75	65.95	65.91	65.47	65.61	64.83	65.07
Germany	63.33	65.88	67.69	67.44	67.73	67.78	67.67	68.94	66.68	65.16	64.85	64.97	65.55	64.51	65.07	66.15
Greece	53.87	54.90	54.78	55.04	55.36	55.38	55.33	53.67	53.98	53.91	54.45	54.31	54.52	54.70	54.98	54.54
Hungary	71.22	68.37	68.35	67.27	66.70	66.56	66.21	66.54	67.60	68.48	68.53	67.52	67.25	67.58	66.08	67.67
Ireland	56.08	56.75	58.02	57.81	56.85	56.73	56.60	56.93	57.29	57.21	56.89	57.49	57.77	57.77	57.51	58.08
Italy	59.47	63.37	63.02	62.46	61.99	62.04	62.14	62.74	62.65	61.57	62.65	63.02	63.01	64.18	64.26	64.31
Luxembourg	66.53	65.21	65.62	64.29	63.96	64.07	63.89	64.84	66.21	65.45	64.41	65.35	64.94	64.86	65.72	65.59
Malta	31.41	31.67	31.97	33.70	30.60	32.37	33.39	31.09	30.02	31.20	31.86	31.63	32.07	31.74	33.28	34.57
Netherlands	65.01	66.92	67.22	67.22	67.33	67.44	67.29	67.46	67.71	67.65	67.74	67.49	67.59	67.47	67.74	67.92
Poland	43.86	44.13	42.82	43.71	42.53	42.56	42.01	40.78	42.92	41.97	44.63	45.53	44.88	44.22	45.58	47.07
Portugal	63.08	63.80	64.17	63.74	63.93	62.93	62.51	61.57	62.90	62.87	62.08	62.53	62.96	62.86	63.18	63.77
Romania	52.11	58.60	68.39	53.70	47.49	69.71	67.07	60.39	56.38	58.16	55.85	68.13	62.78	60.39	61.05	67.95
Slovakia	56.90	57.85	56.47	53.99	49.65	51.09	50.94	50.97	54.44	55.27	56.56	56.43	59.54	61.08	63.41	65.42
Slovenia	68.14	69.42	69.42	69.43	69.43	68.15	67.55	63.15	66.84	67.49	68.44	69.34	69.02	68.78	69.55	68.86
Spain	68.71	69.72	69.65	70.01	69.92	69.41	68.83	68.29	67.95	68.02	67.76	68.56	69.38	69.20	68.83	68.82
Sweden	65.47	63.27	63.36	63.03	62.55	61.43	60.79	61.33	61.72	61.92	62.81	62.35	62.19	62.50	63.53	63.40
UK	55.27	58.84	58.84	59.38	60.15	59.01	59.28	59.12	60.05	59.56	59.49	58.60	59.11	59.46	60.25	60.28

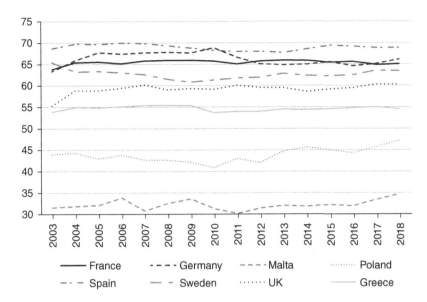

Figure 4.2 Time-series evolution of average CSR score of some EU countries

(which score among the lower-ranked countries in terms of CSR) indicate significant fluctuations in CSR over the sample period. Specifically, Polonaise firms reduced their overall social performance up until 2010, and then an upward trend is evidenced yet is characterized by rather small growth. Firms in Malta present a rather moderate positive upward trend (with fluctuations from one year to another), but for the whole period of investigation the average CSR score spans between 30 to 35.

French and Greek firms present the most stable evolution of CSR performance, which averages around 65 and 55 respectively for the whole period under investigation. The same picture is also evident for the highly ranked countries such as Spain, Germany, and Sweden, where in all of those countries we observe a stable fixed time-series of average CSR for the sample period, indicating that firms on those countries have incorporated robust social responsibility strategies.

Furthermore, Table 4.4 and Figure 4.3 present the evolution of the six social responsibility performance sub-scores from 2003 to 2018 for all countries. All scores present a stable evolution over the years (with a small reduction up until 2012 and a rather moderate increase afterward). Human rights score (HUMAN) and workforce score (WORK) present the highest averages among the main six indicators, followed by product responsibility score (PROD). It seems that EU firms invest more on improving conditions relating to their human capital and

Table 4.4 Average of social performance scores per year (2003–2018)

YEAR	STRAT	WORK	HUMAN	COMM	PROD	SHARE	CSR
2003	54.33	64.99	65.78	55.84	61.25	49.76	60.44
2004	55.68	65.87	67.49	55.85	61.58	50.15	61.30
2005	55.85	66.01	67.73	55.76	62.00	49.69	61.47
2006	55.86	65.78	67.28	55.66	61.78	50.46	61.27
2007	55.72	65.80	67.26	55.45	61.57	50.68	61.16
2008	55.86	65.49	66.98	55.24	61.05	50.98	60.92
2009	55.60	65.21	66.81	55.25	61.06	50.65	60.79
2010	55.52	64.87	66.75	55.44	60.99	50.34	60.71
2011	55.58	65.18	66.86	55.48	61.40	50.37	60.90
2012	55.63	64.82	66.87	55.37	61.18	50.22	60.77
2013	55.81	65.02	67.09	55.47	61.19	50.26	60.92
2014	56.09	65.21	67.02	55.52	61.19	50.54	61.00
2015	55.90	65.41	67.19	55.73	61.34	50.45	61.11
2016	55.99	65.57	67.34	55.78	61.73	50.72	61.28
2017	55.97	65.42	67.48	55.76	61.33	50.47	61.19
2018	56.11	65.82	67.61	56.11	61.74	50.47	61.48

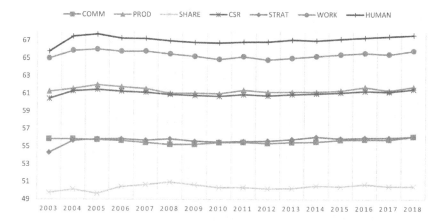

Figure 4.3 Time-series evolution of average social responsibility scores in the EU countries

protecting human rights because those scores have a direct impact on their daily operations, competitive advantages, and profitability potential. Shareholder score (SHARE) presents the smallest numbers yet with a stable trend over the sample years. This could be attributed to the fact that European firms are more stakeholder-oriented organizations relative to US firms, which focus mainly on protecting shareholders' rights and set priorities toward this interest group (Dyduch and Krasodomska, 2017).

Additionally, in order to examine the decomposition of the six social performance indicators in more detail, we estimated the average of the six scores after distinguishing firms following the Statistical Classification of Economic Activities of the European Community (NACE Rev. 2), so as to assign each firm into a specific sector. Eleven sectors were determined, as presented in Table 4.5, and we estimated the average CSR performance scores for the whole period 2003–2018. As we can see in Table 4.5, human protection score (HUMAN) and workforce score (WORK) are the highest CSR scores within all economic

Table 4.5 Average social performance scores per economic sectors (2003–2018)

SECTOR	STRAT	WORK	HUMAN	COMM	PROD	SHARE	CSR
Communication Services	55.19	64.68	66.08	55.41	60.59	51.03	60.39
Consumer Discretionary	56.95	67.36	68.64	57.33	62.50	50.00	62.56
Consumer Staples	55.33	64.72	66.67	55.15	61.31	51.48	60.63
Energy	56.54	64.76	67.03	54.95	61.00	50.32	60.86
Financials	55.98	64.65	67.59	55.49	61.58	49.77	61.06
Health Care	54.52	64.70	66.16	52.88	59.53	49.89	59.54
Industrials	56.18	65.39	67.69	56.25	61.80	50.76	61.46
Information Technology	55.07	66.31	68.28	55.52	62.81	49.85	61.60
Materials	54.47	64.68	65.46	54.48	60.81	51.05	59.98
Real Estate	55.55	65.63	67.42	57.39	61.68	49.74	61.53
Utilities	55.82	65.62	65.57	55.05	62.21	50.65	60.85

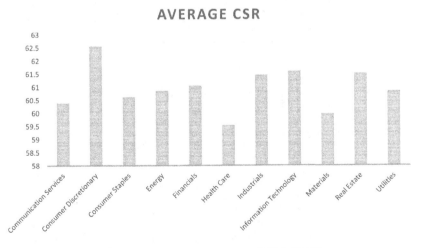

Figure 4.4 CSR performance averages per sector (2003–2018)

Table 4.6 Average CSR score per economic sector and sample year

SECTOR	2003	2004	2005	2006	2007	2008	2009	2010	2011	2012	2013	2014	2015	2016	2017	2018
Communic. Services	59.48	60.46	60.95	60.43	60.30	60.18	60.91	60.79	60.58	59.87	59.14	60.26	60.32	60.60	60.14	60.51
Consumer Discret.	62.12	62.81	62.78	62.51	62.50	62.27	61.98	62.23	63.10	62.62	62.28	62.68	62.24	62.50	63.45	63.02
Consumer Staples	57.46	59.84	59.33	60.18	60.46	60.20	60.41	59.48	61.39	60.37	62.24	60.97	61.74	61.61	61.17	61.34
Energy	59.62	61.76	61.74	60.77	60.11	60.40	60.17	61.07	59.18	59.87	60.30	61.09	61.42	62.05	62.13	61.15
Financials	61.06	60.93	61.56	61.10	60.66	61.08	60.56	61.36	61.23	61.03	61.16	61.24	60.95	61.00	61.39	61.07
Health Care	59.62	60.54	61.46	60.47	59.20	59.00	59.08	59.14	59.35	59.84	59.18	59.05	58.99	58.60	58.67	59.79
Industrials	62.78	61.84	62.18	61.80	62.39	61.74	61.00	60.79	60.96	60.70	61.26	61.29	61.35	61.62	61.16	61.80
Information Technology	61.82	62.42	62.09	62.02	61.19	61.14	61.47	60.62	61.56	61.11	61.38	61.35	61.38	62.58	61.88	60.86
Materials	58.29	60.47	60.77	60.57	60.03	59.50	60.08	59.39	59.44	59.48	59.23	59.33	59.86	59.51	60.22	61.83
Real Estate	61.23	61.80	62.33	62.47	61.96	62.89	62.09	61.13	60.91	62.55	61.39	60.93	61.46	60.41	60.02	60.77
Utilities	58.27	60.48	59.38	61.30	61.65	61.52	60.64	61.17	60.77	61.82	60.44	61.26	60.37	60.42	61.22	61.52

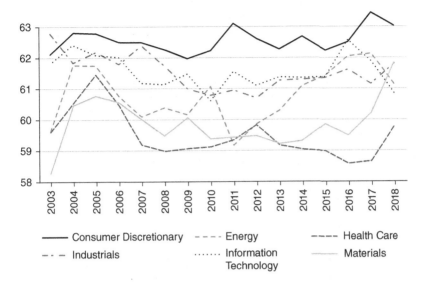

Figure 4.5 Time-series evolution of average CSR score of some economic sectors

sectors, thus verifying again the numbers on previously mentioned tables. The "Consumer Discretionary" sector presents the highest CSR score along with Information Technology sector. On the contrary, the "Materials" and "Health" sectors present the lowest average CSR score and thus seem to lag behind in terms of average social performance.

A similar conclusion can be reached if we observe the annual decomposition of the average CSR score per sector, as depicted in Table 4.6 and Figure 4.5. Health Care and Materials sectors all present a significant decrease on the average CSR score over the sample period. On the contrary, Information Technology and Consumer Discretionary sectors present an upward trend for the period, and both sectors score the highest numbers relative to the other sectors. Nevertheless, the most important increase on CSR was reported in the Energy sector, especially from 2011 until 2017, but still lagging behind relative to Consumer Discretionary and Information Technology sectors.

Conclusion

Corporate governance determines the principles, systems, rights, and interests by which large-scale companies, state-owned entities, or even nonprofit organizations are governed. It also defines the interests of groups that are involved or affected by the processes and practices of the above. European governance reform is at a crucial point. In the past few years, the EU has become one of the fast-changing environments in the field of corporate governance as a result not only of global factors and initiatives but also of European initiatives that aim to improve governance plans and competitiveness among European companies and organizations while at the same time bringing convergence to European governance schemes among European companies Given the heterogeneous European corporate landscape, the pursuit of effective governance is complex and challenging. EU actions show a consistent and significant effort to improve governance standards within the EU, taking into consideration existing differences and simultaneously aiming at avoiding future unnecessary risks to the European economy.

References

Aguilera, R. V., & Cuervo – Cazzura, A. (2004). Codes of good governance worldwide: What is the trigger. *Organizational Studies, 25*(3), 417–446.

Borio, C. (2005). Monetary and financial stability: So close and yet so far. *National Institute Economic Review, 192*(1).

Brunnermeier, M., Crockett, A., Goodhart, C. A. E., Persaud, A. D., & Shin, H. (2009). The fundamental principles of financial regulation. *Geneva Report on the World Economy, 11*.

Cai, L., Cui, J., & Jo, H. (2016). Corporate environmental responsibility and firm risk. *Journal of Business Ethics, 139*(3), 563–594.

Camilleri, M. A. (2017). *Corporate sustainability, social responsibility and environmental management: An introduction to theory and practice with case studies*. Cham, Switzerland: Springer International Publishing AG.

Charter Financial Analyst (CFA) Institute. (2016). *Corporate governance policy in the European Union. Position paper*. Retrieved from www.cfainstitute.org/-/media/documents/article/position-paper/corp-gov-policy-in-european-union-through-investor-lens.ashx

The Committee on the Financial Aspects of Corporate Governance. (1992). *Report (The Cadbury Report)*. London: Burgess Science Press. Retrieved January 10, 2021, from www.ecgi.org/codes/documents/cadbury.pdf

Dahlsrud, A. (2008). How corporate social responsibility is defined: An analysis of 37 definitions. *Corporate Social Responsibility and Environmental Management, 15*(1), 1–13.

de Larosière, J., Balcerowitz, L., Issing, O., Masera, R., Mc Carthy, C., Nyberg, L., Pérez, J., & Ruding, O. (2009). The high – level group on financial supervision in the EU- de Larosiere. Report. Brussels (February 25). Retrived from https://www.eiopa.europa.eu/sites/default/files/publications/pdfs/publication14527_en.pdf

down minimum requirements implementing the provisions of Directive 2007/36/EC of the European Parliament and of the Council as regards shareholder identification, the transmission of information and the facilitation of the exercise of shareholders rights (Text with EEA relevance.). Retrieved from https://eur-lex. europa.eu/legal-content/EN/TXT/?uri=celex%3A32018R1212

Dyduch, J., & Krasodomska, J. (2017). Determinants of corporate social responsibility disclosure: An empirical study of Polish listed companies. *Sustainability*, *9*, 1934.

European Commission. (2001). *European governance: A white paper.* COM(2001) 428. Retrieved January 10, 2021, from https://ec.europa.eu/commission/presscorner/detail/en/DOC_01_10

European Commission. (2003a). *Report from the commission on European governance.* Luxembourg: Office for Official Publications of the European Communities. Retrieved January 10, 2021, from https://ec.europa.eu/governance/docs/comm_rapport_en.pdf

European Commission. (2003b). *Modernising company law and enhancing corporate governance in the European Union – A plan to move forward.* Communication from the Commission to the Council and the European Parliament, COM-284 final, May 21. Brussels: European Commission.

European Commission. (2010a). *Corporate governance in financial institutions and remuneration policies.* Green Paper, COM(2010)284. Brussels: European Commission. Retrieved December 17, 2020, from https://eur-lex.europa.eu/LexUriServ/LexUriServ.do?uri=COM:2010:0284:FIN:EN:PDF.

European Commission. (2010b). *Audit policy: Lessons from the crisis.* Green Paper COM(2010) 561. Brussels: European Commission. Retrieved from https://eur-lex.europa.eu/legal-content/EN/TXT/?uri=CELEX%3A52010DC0561

European Commission. (2011). *The EU corporate governance framework.* Brussels, Belgium: Green Paper.

European Commission. (2012). *European company law and corporate governance – a modern legal framework for more engaged shareholders and sustainable companies.* Action Plan [COM(2012)740]. Brussels: European Commission. Retrieved December 17, 2020, from https://eur-lex.europa.eu/LexUriServ/LexUriServ.do?uri=COM:2012:0740:FIN:EN:PDF

European Commission. (2018). *Implementing regulation (EU) 2018/1212 of 3 September 2018 laying.* Brussels, Belgium.

European Commission. (2019a). *The European commission's priorities for 2019–2024.* Retrieved from https://ec.europa.eu/info/strategy/priorities-2019-2024_en

European Commission. (2019b). *Corporate social responsibility, responsible business conduct, and business & human rights: Overview of progress* (Commission Staff Working Paper, SWD (2019) 143). Brussels: European Commission. Retrieved September 23, 2020, from https://ec.europa.eu/transparency/regdoc/rep/10102/2019/EN/SWD-2019-143-F1-EN-MAIN-PART-1.PDF.

European Commission. (2020). *Sustainable corporate governance initiative.* [Ref.Ares(2020)4034032–30/07/2020]. Retrieved from https://ec.europa.eu/info/law/better-regulation/have-your-say/initiatives/12548-Sustainable-corporate-governance.

European Corporate Governance Institute. (2011). *European commission green papers on corporate governance and the ECGI agenda.* Brussels: Université Libre de Bruxelles.

European Union. (2011). *A renewed EU strategy 2011–2014 for corporate social responsibility*. Brussels: European Commission. Retrieved October 7, 2020, from http://ec.europa.eu/enterprise/newsroom/cf/_getdocument. cfm?doc_id=701

European Union. (2013a). Directive 2013/36/EU of the European Parliament and of the Council of 26 June 2013 on access to the activity of credit institutions and the prudential supervision of credit institutions and investment firms, OJ L 176. Retrieved February 17, 2018, from http://eur-lex.europa.eu/ legal- content/EN/TXT/?uri=celex%3A32013L0036

European Union. (2013b, June 27). Regulation No 575/2013 of the European Parliament and of the Council of 26 June 2013 on prudential requirements for credit institutions and investment firms and amending Regulation (EU) No 648/2012, OJ L 176, pp. 1–337. Retrieved February 17, 2018, from http://eur-lex. europa.eu/legal- content/en/TXT/?uri=celex%3A32013R0575

European Union. (2017). *Directive (EU) 2017/828 of the European parliament and of the council of 17 May 2017 amending Directive 2007/36/EC as regards the encouragement of long-term shareholder engagement* (Text with EEA relevance). Retrieved from https://eur-lex.europa.eu/legal-content/EN/ TXT/?uri=celex%3A32017L0828

Gunningham, N. (2009). Shaping corporate environmental performance: A review. *Environmental Policy and Governance, 19*(4), 215–231.

He, M., & Chen, J. (2009). Sustainable development and corporate environmental responsibility: Evidence from Chinese corporations. *Journal of Agricultural and Environmental Ethics, 22*(4), 323–339.

Hermes, N., Postma, T. J. B. M., & Zivkov, O. (2006). Corporate governance codes in the European Union: Are they driven by external or domestic forces? *International Journal of Managerial Finance, 2*(4), 280–301. https://doi. org/10.1108/17439130610705490.

Knopf, J., Kahlenborn, W., Hajduk, T., Weiss, D., Feil, M., & Fiedler, R. (2010). *Corporate social responsibility national public policies in the European Union*. Brussels: EU Commission.

Krenn, M. (2016). Convergence and divergence in corporate governance: An integrative institutional theory perspective. *Management Research Review, 39*(11), 1447–1471.

Kubíček, A., Štamfestová, P., & Strouhal, J. (2016). Cross-country analysis of corporate governance codes in the European Union. *Economics and Sociology, 9*(2), 319–337.

Lenssen, G., Gasparski, G., Rok, B., Lacy, P., & Eberhard-Harribey, L. (2006). Corporate social responsibility as a new paradigm in the European policy: How CSR comes to legitimate the European regulation process. *Corporate Governance, 6*(4), 358–368.

Matten, D., & Moon, J. (2005). A conceptual framework for understanding CSR. *Corporate Social Responsibility Across Europe*, 335–356.

Mazurkiewicz, P. (2004). Corporate environmental responsibility: Is a common CSR framework possible. *World Bank, 2*, 1–18.

Tumpel-Gugerell, G. (2009). *Beyond the turmoil: Rules, supervision and infrastructures*. SPIN 2009 Conference, Rome. Retrieved from www.ecb.int/press/ key/date/2009/html/sp090615.en.html

Van Marrewijk, M. (2003). Concepts and definitions of CSR and corporate sustainability: Between agency and communion. *Journal of Business Ethics*, 44(2–3), 95–105.

Wahba, H. (2008). Does the market value corporate environmental responsibility? An empirical examination. *Corporate Social Responsibility and Environmental Management*, 15(2), 89–99.

Weil, Gotshal & Manges LLP. (2002). In consultation with Easd – European association of securities dealers & Ecgn – European corporate governance network. In *Comparative study of corporate governance codes relevant to the European union and its member states*. Retrieved January 20, 2020, from https://ecgi.global/sites/default/files/codes/documents/comparative_study_eu_i_to_v_en.pdf

Part II

Corporate Governance and Corporate Social Responsibility in the EU

An Empirical Examination

5 The Role of the Board of Directors in Corporate Philanthropy

An Empirical Study of UK Insurance Firms

Zafeira Kastrinaki

Introduction

An increasing importance is being attached to the crucial role of corporate governance mechanisms, especially boards of directors, in establishing corporate social responsibility (CSR) practices. CSR has been noted as a development of good governance where firms with well-designed corporate governance systems are often found to be engaging in CSR activities (for a review, see Gillan, Andrew, & Laura, 2021). The board of directors as a core element of corporate governance has increasingly been recognized as having a critical impact on firms' strategy and performance in general (Johnson, Schnatterly, & Hill, 2013) and CSR in particular (Jain & Jamali, 2016). Indeed, scholars have explored the influence of board characteristics on CSR reporting and disclosure (Chan, Watson, & Woodliff, 2014), CSR performance (Hussain, Rigoni, & Orij, 2018; Shaukat, Qiu, & Trojanowski, 2016), and CSR engagement (Rao & Tilt, 2016; Briscoe & Gupta, 2016). However, empirical evidence about the effect of board composition on CSR is far from conclusive. For example, some studies have demonstrated a positive effect of board independence on CSR performance (Burke, Hoitash, & Hoitash, 2019), while others have showed a negative (Deckop, Merriman, & Gupta, 2006) or nonsignificant effect (Galbreath, 2018a). Also, the effect of female directors on CSR performance has been found to be positive by some studies (e.g., Hussain, Rigoni, & Orij, 2018), while others have reported a negative effect (Walls, Berrone, & Phan, 2012). While these studies emphasize the link between corporate governance and CSR, a comprehensive study of board attributes, including the vital role of the CEO, has remained relatively unexplored. Furthermore, scholars show an interest in the more general concept of CSR, while studies on corporate philanthropy, as a strand of CSR, are scarce.

Furthermore, over the last decade, there has been a marked shift in the UK and EU Codes of Corporate Governance toward the adoption of a model that is inclusive of stakeholders' interests and CSR. Indeed, the UK Corporate Governance Code has, in 2017, been subject to reform in

DOI: 10.4324/9781003152750-7

an attempt to better alight itself with international and EU policy trends relating to CSR (for a review, see Tsagas, 2020). The Codes prompt the board of directors to pay respect to the interests of other stakeholders and sustainable practices during decision-making processes. However, there is considerable heterogeneity in the decision-making processes by boards as many companies are moving away from prescribed models of governance, while others are adopting governance recommendation as a result of institutional pressures which can be costly and inefficient (Crespí-Cladera & Pascual-Fuster, 2014; Carroll, 1991; Gupta, Briscoe, & Hambrick, 2017).

As the scope of corporate governance has broadened to consider main stakeholders of the firm, it is important to examine whether board effectiveness also extends to the protection of all stakeholders' interests. We thus examine the relationship between a firm's board composition and its corporate philanthropic activities. Particular emphasis is placed on the role of CEO as the most influential decision maker on the board in making corporate community contributions and charitable decisions. Corporate philanthropic activities have a growing strategic and economic significance as they highlight the accountability of corporations to a variety of stakeholder groups (Adams, Hoejmose, & Kastrinaki, 2017; Brammer & Pavelin, 2005; Aguinis & Glavas, 2012) and may influence their perception about the firm.

The empirical analysis focuses on the UK insurance industry over the period 1999–2013 as CSR in this industry has acquired a much higher profile in the public media.

We use the stakeholder perspective to inform our discussion of whether boards that are effective in protecting shareholders' interests are also effective in responding to social concerns. Stakeholder theory can provide a useful basis for conducting corporate social performance research in the case of insurance firms with multiple stakeholders such as investors, policyholders, and industry regulators which have competing but overlapping economic and political goals.

This chapter is structured as follows. The next section develops research hypotheses. The third section outlines the research design, including description of the sample, empirical models, and the variables used. The fourth section presents empirical results, while the final section of the chapter discusses findings and concludes.

Hypotheses Development

Existing research on board effectiveness mostly takes a shareholder perspective in analyzing the effects of board characteristics such as size, composition, and structure on CSR. We review this literature and develop hypotheses using the stakeholder perspective to inform our discussion of whether CEO and several characteristics of the structure of the board of directors influence corporate charitable giving.

The CEO and CSR

The CEO is the most influential decision maker on the board and may dramatically change the strategic directions of a firm including decisions relating to CSR.

The relationship between a firm's CEO and its shareholders is a classic agency theory scenario where the CEO pursues his own self-interests even if this is costly to the owners of the firm. Under this perspective, the greater the degree of autonomy to make decisions retained by a CEO, the greater is the likelihood of weak governance. When the CEO possesses power over other board members, he can use such authority to make personal economic gains at the expense of shareholders' utility (Veprauskaitė & Adams, 2013; Morse, Nanda, & Seru, 2011). CEOs thus tend to overinvest in CSR in order to enjoy publicity and media exposure, which in turn enhances their personal reputation. Indeed, Jiraporn and Chintrakarn (2013) empirically show that there is a non-linear relationship between CEO power and CSR. An increase in CEO power leads to more CSR activities, but when the CEO consolidates his power to a certain threshold, he is so entrenched and invulnerable that he no longer views CSR as necessary.

Under the stakeholder theory, the CEO engages in CSR to resolve the conflicts among various groups of stakeholders. Since the CSR investment is not made for personal benefits, the CEO power is not expected to influence CSR activity. However, a CEO may pursue or discard CSR initiatives that reflect deeply held personal beliefs and choices (Gupta et al., 2017; Petrenko, Aime, Ridge, & Hill, 2016; Borghesi, Houston, & Naranjo, 2014). A powerful CEO could thus use their stronger influence over the board and greater access to firm resources to implement their CSR choices. Also, powerful CEOs may affect CSR activities by enhancing trust and motivating directors to offer advice and resources and provide vital information.

If the CEO is also the chairman of the board, this can increase the degree of CEO power on the board and the degree of decision-making autonomy held by the CEO (Combs, Ketchen, Perryman, & Donahue, 2007). CEO duality thus may increase the propensity of firms to engage in corporate philanthropy. Also, CEOs who have held office for longer have accumulated greater firm-specific and management-specific knowledge and experience and are more likely to have been involved in the appointment of other board members (Dedman, 2015) which adds to their power. Thus, we propose the following hypothesis:

H1a: *The CEO duality is positively related to corporate charitable giving.*

H1b: *The CEO tenure is positively related to corporate charitable giving.*

CEOs differ in their experiences and characteristics, and often this heterogeneity matters for corporate policies related to CSR (McCarthy, Oliver, & Song, 2017; Petrenko et al., 2016; Borghesi et al., 2014; Hemingway & Maclagan, 2004). CEOs with general skills that are transferable across firms or industries can move across firms more easily compared to CEOs with firm-specific skills that are valuable only within an organization (Custódio, Ferreira, & Matos, 2013). Thus, generalist CEOs make their long-term wealth less contingent on the future prosperity of the firm and may be reluctant to engage in projects with long-term payoffs. We therefore expect that generalist CEOs are less likely to engage in CSR activities because such activities require the slow, time-consuming process of improving firm–stakeholder relationships and the payoff is not immediate (Chen, Huang, Meyer-Doyle, & Mindruta, 2020; Kang, 2016). Thus, we propose the following hypothesis:

> *H2: A generalist CEO is negatively related to corporate charitable giving.*

Literature (Oh, Chang, & Cheng, 2016) shows that CEO career horizon may influence strategic decisions in general and decisions on CSR in particular. As CEO career horizon is determined by age (McClelland, Barker, & Oh, 2012; Davidson, Xie, & Ning, 2007), older CEOs are likely to have relatively shorter career horizons. Research (Aktas, Boone, Croci, & Signori, 2021) shows that CEOs with shorter career horizon tend to avoid risks and are less likely to make long-term-oriented decisions. Based on these arguments we propose that as CEOs are getting older they are less incentivized to engage in corporate charitable giving because such strategy is likely to be reimbursed after their incumbency.

> *H3: CEO age is negatively related to corporate charitable giving*

Independent Directors and CSR

Agency theory suggests that independent directors are more likely to effectively monitor decisions of the board because they are free from personal links with the firm (Fama & Jensen, 1983). However, empirical evidence provides mixed results regarding the effectiveness of independent directors on firm financial performance (Adams & Jiang, 2016; Armstrong, Core, & Guay, 2014; Harris & Raviv, 2008; Adams & Ferreira, 2007; Hardwick, Adams, & Zou, 2011). For example, some scholars (e.g., Volonté, 2015) argue that independent directors serve on a part time basis, so they are less likely to gain a thorough understanding of each firm, which may affect their effectiveness as monitors.

On the other hand, independent directors have an incentive to actively support greater corporate responsiveness to society's needs in an attempt to enhance the value of their reputational capital. Thus, independent outside directors could be more active in balancing the conflicting claims of different stakeholders by engaging in voluntary aspects of CSR such as corporate giving (Ben Barka & Dardour, 2015; Post, Rahman, & McQuillen, 2015; Ibrahim, Howard, & Angelidis, 2003). Therefore, the following hypothesis is put forward:

> *H4a: The proportion of independent directors on the board is positively related to corporate charitable giving.*

Furthermore, busy directors, defined as those who concurrently hold three or more directorships, have received attention in the academic literature. Busy directors are likely to have more experience and a wider network of contacts, which a growing body of literature (Field, Lowry, & Mkrtchyan, 2013; Masulis & Mobbs, 2011) suggests is quite valuable as it enhances the advising benefits of the directors. Firms that select busy directors may need particular director expertise and network ties more than director time (Field et al., 2013). The number of independent board seats a board director holds signals the quality of their reputation and denser networks which may be used to further themed alliances to influence CSR activities. Based on these observations we propose the following hypothesis:

> *H4b: The board busyness is positively related to corporate charitable giving.*

Board Gender Diversity and CSR

Board gender diversity refers to the proportion, number, or presence of women on the board of directors. The representation of female directors on the board may enhance diversity and contribute to an increase in the number of alternatives that are considered and influence the quality of boards' decision-making. An increasing number of studies examine the relationship between female board representation and CSR, suggesting at least three channels that may lead female directors to display a stronger commitment to CSR activities (Carter, Simkins, & Simpson, 2003).

First, diversity research suggests that the corporate decision-making process can benefit from boards with different perspectives and diverse demographic and social backgrounds (Estélyi & Nisar, 2016), which means that female directors bring experiences, skills, and information to the board that may help boards consider the implications of strategic decisions such as CSR for a wider range of corporate stakeholders (Galbreath, 2018b; Byron & Post, 2016). Second, social role theory treats gender as a source of social roles and expectations. Women are often expected to possess communal characteristics and behaviors such as being concerned and sympathetic to others' needs and the welfare of the broader society (Elsesser & Lever, 2011; Rosette & Tost, 2010). Driven thus by female directors' internal values and interests, female directors are more likely to promote CSR activities than their male counterparts (Adams & Funk, 2012). Third, a stakeholder theory perspective suggests that the female representation on boards may improve connections among a wider set of stakeholders (Fernandez, Koma, & Lee, 2018; Macaulay et al., 2018; Abdullah, 2014). Female directors are perceived to be more sensitive and behaviorally inclined to precautionary strategies, so they are more likely to exercise their duties incorporating a broader range of stakeholder interests (Adams & Funk, 2012; Brammer, Millington, & Pavelin, 2009).

Empirical research (Francoeur, Labelle, & Balti, 2019; Shoham, Almor, Lee, & Ahammad, 2017; Bear, Rahman, & Post, 2010) shows that a high proportion of females on boards influences CSR practices, signaling, thus, that such firms are governed more openly and address the concerns of multiple stakeholders in their strategic decision-making. Therefore, we hypothesize that female board representation enhances corporate charitable giving:

> H5: *The proportion of female directors on the board is positively related to corporate charitable giving.*

Executive Compensation and CSR

Research (Kim, Kim, & Park, 2020; Maas, 2018; Hong, Li, & Minor, 2016; Mahoney & Thorn, 2006) on executive compensation and CSR has yielded mixed findings, indicating that CSR may be positively or negatively related, or have no association, with executive compensation. We look at two key dimensions of executives' compensation, namely bonus plan and stock options.

Scholars (e.g. McGuire, Oehmichen, Wolff, & Hilgers, 2019; Mahoney & Thorn, 2006) report that as bonuses are contingent on short-term financial goals, CEOs give greater priority to short-term activities that can directly improve firms' financial performance and so enable the realization of bonus targets. This may be detrimental to the fulfillment and consideration of corporate philanthropy, which may not have such an obvious and immediate impact. Accordingly, we anticipate a negative association between CEO bonus plan and charitable giving. We propose the following hypothesis:

> H6: *The CEO bonus plan is negatively related to corporate charitable giving.*

Stock options are regarded as a form of long-term incentive compensation. CEOs and inside directors who receive stock options are more likely to have long-run horizons and take actions aiming at maximizing firm's long-run objectives. Insider-owner may wish to maximize their utility by focusing on firm's financial performance yet concomitantly reducing charitable giving on the grounds that it is a value-diluting indulgence (Brown, Helland, & Smith, 2006). Thus, we posit the following hypothesis:

> *H7a: The proportion of inside (CEOs and directors) ownership is negatively related to corporate charitable giving.*

However, if the capital markets recognize the advantage of investing in social objectives (Brooks & Oikonomou, 2018), which benefit the firm and society in the longer run, then the CEO and insider-owner's self-interest would benefit from the firm's pursuing of CSR. Nevertheless, if the goals of the board are to further social objectives, then CEOs and board directors' ownership may be used to align insiders' self-interest with CSR (Kolk & Perego, 2014). We thus propose the following alternative hypothesis:

> *H7b: The proportion of inside (CEOs and directors) ownership is positively related to corporate charitable giving.*

Business Experts and CSR

Board directors bring human and social capital to boards which may be crucial to achieving external links with significant stakeholders (Tian, Haleblian, & Rajagopalan, 2011; Gray & Nowland, 2013; Hillman & Dalziel, 2003; Gray & Nowland, 2013; Hillman & Dalziel, 2003). Business experts who have knowledge based on their prior executive experience in similar sectors may better detect threats and opportunities and be more likely to engage with stakeholders' needs and consequently be more proactive in engaging in CSR activities (Dass, Kini, Nanda, Onal, & Wang, 2014; Shropshire, 2010). Nikolova and Arsi (2017) also claim that "CSR cannot exist if individuals do not possess enough maturity and competence to act responsibly". Prior empirical literature (Ramon-Llorens, Garcia-Meca, & Pucheta-Martinez, 2019; Ben Barka & Dardour, 2015; Konrad, Steurer, Langer, & Martinuzzi, 2006) shows that boards with a higher proportion of business experts tend to be more effective in encouraging CSR reporting. Hence, we propose the following hypothesis:

> *H8: The proportion of business experts on the board is positively related to corporate charitable giving.*

Research Design

Empirical analysis focuses on the insurance industry and provides a "natural control" against the potentially confounding effects that can arise in cross-sectional industry studies of CSR (e.g., as a result of different managerial motives and environmental exigencies).[1] The UK's nonlife insurance industry is ranked third internationally (after the US and Japan) and comprises about 270 active insurance companies. The following sections describe the data, specify the empirical model, and, in Table 5.1, define the variables used in the empirical analysis.

Data

The data set covers 91 randomly selected UK insurance companies over 1999–2013. The sample constitutes roughly a third of nonlife insurance companies operating in the UK over our period of analysis and comprises a mix of firms of varying size, ownership structure, and product range. The time frame of our analysis coincides with the date from when CSR started to be of direct strategic interest to UK insurers. Financial and board level data were obtained from the companies' annual reports and accounts and industrial databases (e.g., FAME).

Dependent Variable

We treat charitable donations as the dependent variable of analysis. Corporate charitable donations are voluntary actions that exceed legal standards and anticipate public opinion, which is a dominant feature of the CSR literature (Lantos, 2001), and thus a good measure of CSR. Moreover, corporate donations in the UK tend to be made directly by companies (Brammer & Millington, 2004).

Independent Variables

We use a range of board-level variables to capture the variety and nuances of board composition and test our hypotheses. Details of the variables used in the empirical analysis are given in Table 5.1.

Control Variables

Prior studies (e.g., Brown et al., 2006; Brammer & Millington, 2004, 2008) indicate that in the context of examining the determinants of corporate donations, a number of firm-specific control variables are important. For this reason we control for (a) firm size (e.g., see Brammer & Millington, 2008); (b) ownership structure (e.g., see Adams & Hardwick, 1998); (c) profitability (e.g., see Brown et al., 2006); (d) leverage

Table 5.1 Definition of variables

VARIABLE		REPRESENTS	DEFINITION
Dependent variable	DON_{it}	Corporate Donations	Annual corporate donations
	$DONDUM_{it}$	Corporate Donations	Binary variable equal to 1 if an insurer has donated in time *t*, and 0 otherwise
Independent variables			
Corporate governance variables	IND_{it}	Independent (nonexecutive) directors	Percentage of independent directors to total board members
	$BOARDbusy_{it}$	Board Busyness	Percentage of independent on the board who hold ≥ 1.5 full-time equivalent positions
	$FEMALE_{it}$	Gender mix	Percentage of female directors to total board members
	$INSIDEown_{it}$	Insider ownership	Binary variable equal to 1 if an insurer has a managerial share ownership scheme, and 0 otherwise
	$BUSINESSexp_{it}$	Business experts' representation	Percentage of directors with prior executive experience in similar sectors to total board members
	$CEOdual_{it}$	CEO duality	A binary variable of 1 if the CEO is also the Chairman of the board, and 0 otherwise
	$CEOten$	CEO tenure	Number of years a CEO has been at the head of an insurance firm

(*Continued*)

Table 5.1 (Continued)

VARIABLE		REPRESENTS	DEFINITION
	CEOgen	CEO's skills and expertise (general versus firm specific)	A binary variable of 1 if the CEO's expertise is in economics, management, accounting, and finance, and 0 otherwise
	CEOage	CEO age	The age of a CEO (in years)
	$CEOown_{it}$	CEO incentive compensation (stock options)	A binary variable of 1 if the CEO owns >3% of shares in issue, and 0 otherwise
	CEObonus	CEO incentive compensation (bonus plan)	A binary variable of 1 if the CEO receives incentive compensation (e.g., bonus), and 0 otherwise
Firm-specific control variables	$SIZE_{it}$	Firm size	Total value of assets (inflation-adjusted)
	OWN_{it}	Ownership structure	Percentage of shares held by the top three shareholders to total shares in issue
	$PROFIT_{it}$	Profitability	Annual earnings before interest & taxes (millions) (inflation-adjusted)
	LEV_{it}	Leverage	Percentage of annual premiums written to total capital (equity + reserves) i.e., the premium-to-surplus (P-S) ratio
	AGE_{it}	Length of time an insurer has been operating	Number of years of operation

Note: Dummy variables are used where metric data were not available from public sources.

(e.g., see Webb & Pettigrew, 1999); and (e) firm age (e.g., see Godfrey, 2005). The motivation for including these control variables in our analysis can be summarized as follows: Firm size is likely to be positively associated with a firm's market profile and political exposure, thereby promoting CSR activities. The board, and in particular the CEO, is likely to have greater decision-making discretion over the CSR function in firms with widely held shareholdings than firms with a more closely held ownership structure. Given that CSR is invariably a discretionary investment, we expect the propensity of charitable giving to be greater in firms with low levels of leverage and so at a lower risk of financial distress/bankruptcy as well as in more profitable firms with greater levels of free cash flows. Finally, as a firm's resource relations with constituents develop over time, we expect CSR activities to be a positive function of a firm's age. Details of the control variables used in the empirical analysis are also given in Table 5.1.

Estimation

We model the charitable donation–boards relation in two separate regressions. We first estimate a random effects probit model by maximum likelihood to examine the determinants of the decision to donate or not. The error term is decomposed to capture unobservable effects (e.g., managerial CSR experience) on decision to donate (see, Greene, 2003). Second, we estimate a left-censored Tobit model to examine the determinants of the amount donated (see, Greene, 2003). Explanatory variables are described in Table 5.1.

To gauge the sensitivity of the explanatory variables to changes in the predicted probability of the corporate donation decision, the coefficient estimates in the probit model are transformed to represent the marginal effects evaluated at the means of the regressor variables computed from averaging individual observation responses (Hoetker, 2007). Similarly, marginal effects are also evaluated against median values given the skewed distribution of some variables (e.g., firm size) in the panel data set. The marginal effects for the dummy variables are calculated as the discrete change in the dependent variable as it changes from 0 to 1 (Greene, 2003).

Empirical Evidence

This section reports and discusses descriptive statistics for our sample and results of multivariate analysis.

Descriptive Statistics

Table 5.2 (Panels A and B) reports the descriptive statistics for our sample.

Furthermore, Table 5.2, Panel B, reports the statistical tests of mean differences in our explanatory variables. We conducted t-tests (for metric measured variables) and chi-square (χ^2) statistics (for categorical variables) to examine differences in the mean values for the firm and board characteristics of charitable donators and non-donators. Results show that statistically significant differences exist between the means of all our explanatory variables (at $p \leq 0.05$, two-tail, or better) except from CEO age and generalist CEO. These results hint strongly at firm and board effects in the decision to engage in corporate philanthropy.

Multivariate Analysis

Table 5.3, Panel A, reports results of the probit analysis. It presents three models beginning with the base-line Model 1, then adds in a stepwise manner board composition variables in Model 2 and CEO characteristics in Model 3.

The propensity of insurers to donate is positively related to the proportion of independent directors on the board (IND), the presence of female directors (FEMALE), and insiders' ownership (INSIDEown). These results are in line with existing literature (e.g., Brammer et al., 2009) and support the notion that independent (non-executives) and female directors tend to be more inclined to balance stakeholders' different interests and support CSR initiatives. It is interesting to note that insider ownership (INSIDEown) and CEO ownership (CEOown) have a statistically positive effect, while the CEO bonus schemes (CEObonus) has a statistically negative effect on charitable giving. This finding suggests that CEOs are likely to be disinclined to support corporate philanthropy if it reduces payoffs on their bonus plans, but the existence of ownership plans for board directors and CEO can promote CSR engagement and so enhance the value of their equity investment.

The presence of business experts on the board (BUSINESSexp) could positively influence charitable giving. However, business experts on the board have a statistically negative effect on corporate donations, which is consistent with the notion that business experts may focus on short-term profit maximization objectives. This may reflect a predominantly precautionary and self-interested approach to business strategy among business and finance experts.

Model 3 indicates that the corporate decision to engage in charitable giving is affected negatively by the CEO duality (CEOdual) and positively by the CEO tenure (CEOten). These findings suggest that when the CEO tenure increases and the CEO acquires slightly more power, he invests more in CSR. However, when the CEO gains substantially more power and enjoys a dual role of chairman and CEO, he tends to reduce CSR investments. Thus, private wealth maximization predominates over

Table 5.2 UK Insurers, 1999–2013: Descriptive statistics of explanatory variables

Panel A: Pooled (1999–2013) Variable	Mean	Median	Std. Dev.	Min	Max
DON	0.05	0.00	2.15	0.00	2.60
SIZE	997	54	3,727	1.8	31,220
OWN	0.63	0.69	0.29	0.00	1.00
LEV	1.18	1.11	0.25	0.53	3.85
PROFIT	52.45	2.79	256	−237	3,377
AGE	52.40	34.00	34.83	2.00	136
BSIZE	7.95	8.00	2.35	3.00	14.00
IND	0.55	0.55	0.12	0.00	0.82
BOARDbusy	0.36	0.34	0.28	0.00	0.65
FEMALE	0.03	0.00	0.07	0.00	0.40
BUSINESSexp	0.29	0.20	0.12	0.00	0.63
CEOten	3.71	3	2.30	1	18
CEOage	54	55	4.45	42	65

Panel B: Donators versus Non Donators Variable	Don. Mean	Non-Donators Mean	t /X^2 statistics
R(SIZE)	.64	.38	−15.83***
OWN	1.25	1.10	9.12***
LEV	1.25	1.11	−9.12***
R(PROFIT)	.62	.40	−12.95***
R(AGE)	.48	.52	2.45***
BSIZE	8	5	16.32***
IND	0.59	0.52	−8.82***
BOARDbusy	0.30	0.42	9.89***
FEMALE	0.04	0.01	−6.21***
BUSINESSexp	0.30	0.27	−4.60***
CEOten	4.10	3.50	−3.26***
CEOage	54	53	−0.24
INSIDEown			87.48***
CEOdual			5.21**
CEObonus			30.70***
CEOown			34.14***
CEOgen			0.12

Note: This table gives the summary statistics for the panel of UK insurers in our sample (1,133 firm/year cases). Continuous variables are measured in £ millions. We replace SIZE, PROFIT, and AGE with their rank-transformed equivalents R(SIZE), R(PROFIT), and R(AGE) to address the effects of extreme values. Definitions of the variables are given in Table 5.1. In Panel B, X^2 test is used to test the independence between categorical variables (INSIDEown, CEOdual, CEObonus, CEOown, CEOgen) and the incidence of donation. The t-test is used for all continuous variables. The statistical significance values *, **, *** denote statistical significance at the 10%, 5%, and 1% levels respectively (two-tail).

social philanthropy among very powerful CEOs. Other CEO characteristics, age (CEOage), general skills, and expertise (CEOgen) have no effect on charitable giving. Also, board busyness has no effect on charitable giving.

Furthermore, donation decision is positively related to the size (R(SIZE) and age (R(AGE) of insurers. Ownership concentration (OWN) is found to be negatively associated with the decision to give to charitable causes, in particular when board composition variables come into play (see Table 5.3, Model 2). The Hausman specification test (Hausman, 1978) was performed to test the validity of the random effects estimator. Results show that Hausman test did not reject the null hypothesis that unobservable firm-effects are serially uncorrelated with the explanatory variables, thereby supporting the random-effects specification. Unobserved firm-related heterogeneity (e.g., differences in managerial ability) in the random effects probit model was also controlled (Heckman, 1981).

Table 5.4 (Models 1 to 3) presents results of Tobit analysis. In accordance to the probit analysis, the Tobit results confirm that IND, FEMALE, and INSIDEown positively influence charitable giving, while BUSINESSexp is inversely related to the amount donated to charities. It is interesting to note that in practical economic terms 1% increase of IND on the board increases corporate charitable donations by between 2% and 7% as marginal effects reported in Table 5.4, Panel B suggest. Also, an 1% increase of FEMALE on the board increases amount of charitable giving by 14% to 18%.

Furthermore, INSIDEown is positively related to the financial amount donated as Models 2 and 3 of Table 5.4 show. However, the CEO's incentive compensation, stock option, or bonus plan seems not to have any effect on the amount of charitable giving. Also, CEOdual does not exert any influence on financial amount donated, but CEOten continues to have a positive effect on the level of charitable contributions. These findings suggest that contributing to charitable causes could benefit owner-directors and less entrenched CEOs. Deeply entrenched and powerful CEOs would only be interested in the strategic decision of whether to donate or not but not in the amount donated. Although CEOage does not affect the propensity to donate, it does have a negative effect on the amount donated.

Furthermore, firm size (R(SIZE)) positively influences the amount of charitable giving. Results are now stronger for concentrated ownership structure (OWN), which has a negative effect on amount donated in all three models (see Models 1 to 3, Table 5.4).

Finally, the explanatory power of our models in Tables 5.3 and 5.4 increases incrementally. This suggests that the incidence and propensity of corporate donations are influenced by not only the board composition but also CEO characteristics and conjointly with other firm-related factors.

Table 5.3 UK Insurers, 1999–2013: Estimates and marginal effects of the random-effects probit model

Panel A: Random-effects probit model estimates

	Model 1	Model 2	Model 3
R(SIZE)	6.08***	5.06***	6.76***
	(0.00)	(0.00)	(0.00)
OWN	–0.84*	–2.37***	0.84
	(0.08)	(0.00)	(0.30)
LEV	0.21***	0.53	0.80
	(0.00)	(0.23)	(0.54)
R(PROFIT)	0.34	0.37	–1.10
	(0.61)	(0.57)	(0.42)
R(AGE)	2.45***	2.86***	3.83***
	(0.00)	(0.00)	(0.00)
IND		2.63***	2.53*
		(0.01)	(0.08)
BOARDbusy		–0.11	–0.07
		(0.34)	(0.85)
FEMALE		5.05***	10.73***
		(0.01)	(0.01)
INSIDEown		3.02***	3.18***
		(0.00)	(0.00)
BUSINESSexp		–1.69***	–4.43**
		(0.16)	(0.02)
CEOdual			–2.32**
			(0.03)
CEOten			0.12*
			(0.08)
CEObonus			–3.85***
			(0.00)
CEOown			0.59*
			(0.10)
CEOage			–0.04
			(0.31)
CEOgen			–0.28
			(0.41)
CONSTANT	–5.27***	–5.79***	–5.11**
	(0.00)	(0.00)	(0.03)
Estimated *p*	0.97	0.92	0.94
Likelihood-ratio test of *p* = 0	806	679	506
X² (01)	(0.00)	(0.00)	(0.00)
(McFadden's) adjusted pseudo-R^2	5%	7%	22%
N	1024	1024	1024

(*Continued*)

Table 5.3 (Continued)

Panel B: Random-effects probit model marginal effects

	Model 1		Model 2		Model 3	
	at means	at medians	at means	at medians	at means	at medians
R(SIZE)	2.32	2.35	1.93	0.60	2.44	0.10
OWN	−0.32	−0.32	−0.91	−0.28	0.30	0.01
LEV	0.80	0.82	0.20	0.06	0.29	0.01
R(PROFIT)	0.13	0.13	0.14	0.04	−0.40	−0.01
R(AGE)	0.93	0.95	1.09	0.34	1.38	0.05
IND			1.01	0.31	0.91	0.03
BOARDbusy			−0.65	−0.32	−0.02	−0.01
FEMALE			1.94	0.60	3.87	0.15
INSIDEown			1.16	0.36	1.15	0.04
BUSINESSexp			−9.65	−0.20	−1.60	−0.06
CEOdual					−0.84	−0.03
CEOten					0.04	0.01
CEObonus					−1.39	−0.05
CEOown					0.21	0.01
CEOage					−0.01	−0.001
CEOgen					−0.10	−−0.001

Note: This table gives the results of the random-effects probit model (where the dependent dummy variable is the decision whether or not to donate to charitable causes – *DONDUM*). We replace *SIZE*, *PROFIT*, and *AGE* with their rank-transformed equivalents *R(SIZE)*, *R(PROFIT)*, and *R(AGE)* to address the effects of extreme values. BSIZE is excluded due to multicollinearity. Marginal effects represent discrete changes from 0 to 1. Values in parentheses refer to *p*-values; *, **, and *** indicate statistical significance at 10%, 5%, and 1% levels respectively. Significance levels are one-tail where a one-way direction is predicted and two-tail otherwise.

Table 5.4 UK Insurers, 1999–2013: Estimates and marginal effects of the Tobit model

Panel A: *Tobit model estimates*

	Model 1	Model 2	Model 3
R(SIZE)	0.25***	0.17***	0.12***
	(0.00)	(0.00)	(0.00)
OWN	−0.15***	−0.26***	−0.03**
	(0.00)	(0.00)	(0.02)
LEV	0.23***	0.18***	0.01
	(0.00)	(0.00)	(0.23)
R(PROFIT)	0.10**	0.06	−0.02
	(0.02)	(0.11)	(0.11)
R(AGE)	0.00	0.11***	0.02
	(0.99)	(0.01)	(0.16)
IND		0.22***	0.05*
		(0.00)	(0.07)
BOARDbusy		0.09	0.01
		(0.33)	(0.64)

	Model 1	Model 2	Model 3
FEMALE		0.53***	0.40***
		(0.00)	(0.00)
INSIDEown		0.21***	0.07***
		(0.00)	(0.00)
BUSINESSexp		−0.21***	−0.06**
		(0.01)	(0.03)
CEOdual			−0.02
			(0.12)
CEOten			0.01***
			(0.00)
CEObonus			−0.05
			(0.00)
CEOown			0.03
			(0.00)
CEOage			−0.01***
			(0.01)
CEOgen			−0.01
			(0.99)
CONSTANT	−0.43***	−0.46***	−0.01
	(0.00)	(0.00)	(0.17)
(McFadden's) adjusted pseudo-R^2	44%	65%	76%
N	497	497	497

Panel B: Tobit model marginal effects

	Model 1		Model 2		Model 3	
	at means for all obser-vations	at means for don>0	at means for all obser-vations	at means for don>0	at means for all obser-vations	at means for don>0
R(SIZE)	0.09	0.07	0.06	0.05	0.05	0.04
OWN	−0.05	−0.04	−0.09	−0.07	−0.02	−0.01
LEV	0.08	0.07	0.06	0.05	0.01	0.01
R(PROFIT)	0.04	0.03	0.02	0.02	−0.01	−0.01
R(AGE)	0.00	0.00	0.04	0.03	0.01	−.01
IND			0.07	0.06	0.02	0.02
BOARDbusy			0.02	0.02	0.01	0.01
FEMALE			0.18	0.15	0.19	0.14
INSIDEown			0.08	0.06	0.04	0.03
BUSINESSexp			−0.07	−0.06	−0.03	−0.02
CEOdual					−0.01	−0.01
CEOten					0.01	0.01
CEObonus					−0.03	−0.02

(Continued)

Table 5.4 (Continued)

	Model 1		Model 2		Model 3	
	at means for all obser-vations	*at means for don>0*	*at means for all obser-vations*	*at means for don>0*	*at means for all obser-vations*	*at means for don>0*
CEOown					0.02	0.01
CEOage					−0.001	−0.001
CEOgen					−0.001	−0.001

Note: This table gives the results of the Tobit model (where the dependent dummy variable is the financial amount donated to donate to charitable causes – DON). BSIZE is excluded due to multicollinearity. Marginal effects represent discrete changes from 0 to 1. We replace SIZE, PROFIT, and AGE with their rank-transformed equivalents R(SIZE), R(PROFIT), and R(AGE) to address the effects of extreme values. Values in parentheses refer to p-values; *, **, *** indicate statistical significance at 10%, 5%, and 1% levels respectively. Significance levels are one-tail where a one-way direction is predicted and two-tail otherwise.

Concluding Remarks

Taking a strategic stakeholder theory perspective and using UK nonlife insurance firms for the 14 years, 1999–2013, we investigate the internal determinants of corporate charitable giving, as a strand of CSR, namely the role of good corporate governance. We find that the proportion of independent directors on the board, the presence of female directors, and inside directors' ownership is positively related to the propensity to donate and the financial amount donated. These findings support the often-cited claim that independent directors and female directors on the board tend to be more inclined to balance stakeholders' different interests and support corporate philanthropy. Also, the positive impact of inside directors' ownership on charitable giving may imply that the boards are now interested in broadening firm's objectives to incorporate social concerns, so directors align self-interest with corporate giving.

Business experts on the board reduce the probability and the level of charitable giving. This result is not in line with the notion that business experts on the board are likely to be familiar with and thus inclined toward corporate philanthropy. This means that although potentially sympathetic to corporate philanthropy, business experts may in practice assign a higher strategic priority to financial performance issues that they do to discretionary matters such as charitable giving.

We also find that CEO power and bonus reduce the propensity of insurers to donate to charitable causes but have no effect on the amount donated. Yet CEO ownership tends to be positively related to charitable donations. CEO tenure, on the other hand, has a positive effect on corporate decisions to contribute to charitable causes as well as the extent of such CSR investment. CEO age as a proxy of career horizon does not exert any influence on the propensity of insurers to engage in corporate giving but is negatively related when it comes to decisions on financial amount donated. These observations show the primacy of self-interested objectives of CEOs over altruism and suggest that performance-related (ownership) compensation discourages (encourages) corporate philanthropy as it reduces (increases) CEOs' personal wealth position.

Our findings further imply that the strategic benefits of CSR investment in general, and charitable giving in particular, are likely to vary between firms depending on the different size, ownership structure, and corporate governance tools that might or might not exist. As a result, insights gleaned from our research suggest that managers, investors, and regulators should better focus on corporate governance quality as a way of increasing CSR activities. Also, to the extent that self-interested CEOs have an interest in pursuing their own agendas at the expense of a broader set of stakeholders, since companies are increasingly moving toward the stakeholder view of corporate governance, CSR-contingent compensation contracts can help align the interests of CEOs with those of the stakeholders (see also Ikram, Li, & Minor, 2019).

Note

1 See, for example, Godfrey, Hatch, and Hansen (2010)

References

Abdullah, S. N. (2014). The causes of gender diversity in Malaysian large firms. *Journal of Management and Governance, 18*, 1137–1159. https://doi.org/10.1007/s10997-013-9279-0

Adams, M., & Hardwick, P. (1998). An analysis of corporate donations: United Kingdom evidence. *Journal of Management Studies, 35*, 641–654.

Adams, M., Hoejmose, S., & Kastrinaki, Z. (2017). Corporate philanthropy and risk management: An investigation of reinsurance and charitable giving in insurance firms. *Business Ethics Quarterly, 27*(1), 1–37.

Adams, M., & Jiang, W. (2016). Do outside directors influence the financial performance of risk-trading firms? Evidence from the United Kingdom (UK) insurance industry. *Journal of Banking & Finance, 64*(C), 36–51.

Adams, R. B., & Ferreira, D. (2007). A theory of friendly boards. *The Journal of Finance, 62*, 217–250.

Adams, R. B., & Funk, P. (2012). Beyond the glass ceiling: Does gender matter? *Management Science, 58*, 219–235.

Aguinis, H., & Glavas, A. (2012). What we know and don't know about corporate social responsibility: A review and research agenda. *Journal of Management, 38*, 932–968.

Aktas, N., Boone, A., Croci, E., & Signori, A. (2021). Reductions in CEO career horizons and corporate policies. *Journal of Corporate Finance, 66*, 101862.

Armstrong, C. S., Core, J. E., & Guay, W. R. (2014). Do independent directors cause improvements in firm transparency? *Journal of Financial Economics, 113*, 383–403.

Bear, S., Rahman, N., & Post, C. (2010). The impact of board diversity and gender composition on corporate social responsibility and firm reputation. *Journal of Business Ethics, 97*, 207–221.

Ben Barka, H., & Dardour, A. (2015). Investigating the relationship between director's profile, board interlocks and corporate social responsibility. *Management Decision, 53*(3), 553–570.

Borghesi, R., Houston, J. F., & Naranjo, A. (2014). Corporate socially responsible investments: CEO altruism, reputation, and shareholder interests. *Journal of Corporate Finance, 26*, 164–181.

Brammer, S., & Millington, A. (2004). The development of corporate charitable contributions in the UK: A stakeholder analysis. *Journal of Management Studies, 41*, 1411–1434.

Brammer, S., & Millington, A. (2008). Does it pay to be different? An analysis of the relationship between corporate social and financial performance. *Strategic Management Journal, 29*, 1325–1343. https://doi.org/10.1002/smj.714

Brammer, S., Millington, A., & Pavelin, S. (2009). Corporate reputation and women on the board. *British Journal of Management, 20*, 17–29.

Brammer, S., & Pavelin, S. (2005). Corporate community contributions in the United Kingdom and the United States. *Journal of Business Ethics, 56*, 15–26.

Briscoe, F., & Gupta, A. (2016). Social activism in and around organizations. *Academy of Management Annals, 10*(1), 671–727.

Brooks, C., & Oikonomou, I. (2018). The effects of environmental, social and governance disclosures and performance on firm value: A review of the literature in accounting and finance. *The British Accounting Review, 50*(1), 1–15.

Brown, W. O., Helland, E., & Smith, J. K. (2006). Corporate philanthropic practices. *Journal of Corporate Finance, 12*(5), 855–877. https://doi.org/10.1016/j.jcorpfin.2006.02.001

Burke, J. J., Hoitash, R., & Hoitash, U. H. (2019). The heterogeneity of board-level sustainability committees and corporate social performance. *Journal of Business Ethics, 154*, 1161–1186.

Byron, K., & Post, C. (2016). Women on boards of directors and corporate social performance: A meta-analysis. *Corporate Governance: An International Review, 24*(4), 428–442.

Carroll, A. B. (1991). The pyramid of corporate social responsibility: Toward the moral management of organizational stakeholders. *Business Horizons, 34*(4), 39–48.

Carter, D., Simkins, B., & Simpson, G. (2003). Corporate governance, board diversity, and firm value. *Financial Review, 38*, 33–53.

Chan, M. C., Watson, J., & Woodliff, D. (2014). Corporate governance quality and CSR disclosures. *Journal of Business Ethics, 125*, 59–73. https://doi.org/10.1007/s10551-013-1887-8

Chen, G., Huang, S., Meyer-Doyle, P., & Mindruta, D. (2020). Generalist versus specialist CEOs and acquisitions: Two-sided matching and the impact of CEO characteristics on firm outcomes. *Strategic Management Journal*, 1–32.

Combs, J. G., Ketchen, D. J., Perryman, A. A., & Donahue, M. S. (2007). The moderating effects of CEO power on the board composition-firm performance relationship. *Journal of Management Studies, 44*(8), 1299–1323.

Crespí-Cladera, R., & Pascual-Fuster, B. (2014). Does the independence of independent directors matter? *Journal of Corporate Finance, 28,* 116–134.

Custódio C., Ferreira, M. A., & Matos, P. (2013). Generalists versus specialists: Lifetime work experience and chief executive officer pay. *Journal of Financial Economics, 108,* 471–492.

Dass, N., Kini, O., Nanda, V., Onal, B., & Wang, J. (2014). Board expertise: Do directors from related industries help bridge the information gap? *Review of Financial Studies, 27*(5), 1533–1592.

Davidson, W. N., Xie, B., & Ning, Y. (2007). The influence of executive age, career horizon and incentives on pre-turnover earnings management. *Journal of Management and Governance, 11,* 45–60.

Deckop, J. R., Merriman, K. K., & Gupta, S. (2006). The effects of CEO pay structure on corporate social performance. *Journal of Management, 32,* 329–342.

Dedman, E. (2015). CEO succession in the UK: An analysis of the effect of censuring the CEO-to-chair move in the combined code on corporate governance 2003. *The British Accounting Review, 48*(3), 359–378.

Elsesser, K. M., & Lever, J. (2011). Does gender bias against female leaders persist? Quantitative and qualitative data from a large-scale survey. *Human Relations, 64*(12), 1555–1578.

Estélyi, K. S., & Nisar, T. M. (2016). Diverse boards: Why do firms get foreign nationals on their boards? *Journal of Corporate Finance, 39,* 174–192.

Fama, E. F., & Jensen, M. C. (1983). Separation of ownership and control. *Journal of Law and Economics, 26,* 301–325.

Fernandez, S., Koma, S., & Lee, H. (2018). Establishing the link between representative bureaucracy and performance: The South African case. *Governance, 31,* 535–553. https://doi.org/10.1111/gove.12319

Field, L., Lowry, M., & Mkrtchyan, A. (2013). Are busy boards detrimental? *Journal of Financial Economics, 109,* 63–82.

Francoeur, C., Labelle, R., & Balti, S. (2019). To what extent do gender diverse boards enhance corporate social performance? *Journal of Business Ethics, 155,* 343–357.

Galbreath, J. (2018a). Do boards of directors influence corporate sustainable development? an attention-based analysis. *Business Strategy and the Environment, 27,* 742–756.

Galbreath, J. (2018b). Is board gender diversity linked to financial performance? The mediating mechanism of CSR. *Business & Society, 57,* 863–889.

Gillan, S. L., Andrew, K., & Laura, T. S. (2021). Firms and social responsibility: A review of ESG and CSR research in corporate finance. *Journal of Corporate Finance,* 101889.

Godfrey, P. C. (2005). The relationship between corporate philanthropy and shareholder wealth: A risk management perspective. *Academy of Management Review, 30,* 777–798.

Godfrey, P. C., Hatch, N. W., & Hansen, J. M. (2010). Toward a general theory of CSRs. The roles of beneficence, profitability, insurance, and industry heterogeneity. *Business and Society, 49,* 316–344.

Gray, S., & Nowland, J. (2013). Is prior director experience valuable? *Accounting Finance, 53*, 643–666.

Greene, W. H. (2003). *Econometric analysis.* New York: McGraw-Hill.

Gupta A., Briscoe, F., & Hambrick, D. C. (2017). Red, blue, and purple firms: Organizational political ideology and corporate social responsibility. *Strategic Management Journal, 38*(5), 1018–1040.

Hardwick, P., Adams, M., & Zou, H. (2011). Board characteristics and profit efficiency in the United Kingdom life insurance industry. *Journal of Business Finance and Accounting, 38*, 987–1015.

Harris, M., & Raviv, A. (2008). A theory of board control and size. *Review of Financial Studies, 21*, 1797–1832.

Hausman, J. A. (1978). Specification tests in Econometrics. *Econometrica, 46*, 1251–1271.

Heckman, J. (1981). Statistical models for discrete panel data. In C. Manski & D. McFadden (Eds.), *The structural analysis of discrete data.* Cambridge, MA: MIT Press.

Hemingway, C. A., & Maclagan, P. W. (2004). Managers' personal values as drivers of corporate social responsibility. *Journal of Business Ethics, 50*, 33–44.

Hillman, A. J., & Dalziel, T. (2003). Boards of directors and firm performance: Integrating agency and resource dependence perspectives. *Academy of Management Review, 28*(3), 383–396.

Hoetker, G. (2007). The use of logit and probit models in strategic management research: Critical issues. *Strategic Management Journal, 28*, 331–343.

Hong, B., Li, Z., & Minor, D. (2016). Corporate governance and executive compensation for corporate social responsibility. *Journal of Business Ethics, 136*, 199–213.

Hussain, N. U., Rigoni, R., & Orij, P. (2018). Corporate governance and sustainability performance: Analysis of triple bottom line performance. *Journal of Business Ethics, 149*, 411–432.

Ibrahim, N. A., Howard, D. P., & Angelidis, J. P. (2003). Board members in the service industry: An empirical examination of the relationship between corporate social responsibility orientation and directorial type. *Journal of Business Ethics, 47*(4), 393–401.

Ikram, A., Li, Z. F., & Minor, D. (2019). CSR-contingent executive compensation contracts. *Journal of Banking & Finance,* 105655.

Jain, T., & Jamali, D. (2016). The effect of corporate governance on corporate social responsibility. *Corporate Governance-an International Review, 45*, 102–123.

Jiraporn, P., & Chintrakarn, P. (2013). How do powerful CEOs view corporate social responsibility (CSR)? An empirical note. *Economics Letters, 119*(3), 344–347.

Johnson, S. G., Schnatterly, K., & Hill, A. D. (2013). Board composition beyond independence: Social capital, human capital, and demographics. *Journal of Management, 39*(1), 232–262. doi:10.1177/0149206312463938

Kang, J. (2016). Labor market evaluation versus legacy conservation: What factors determine retiring CEOs' decisions about long-term investment? *Strategic Management Journal, 37*, 389–405.

Kim, T., Kim, H. D., & Park, K. (2020). CEO inside debt holdings and CSR activities. *International Review of Economics & Finance, 70*, 508–529.

Kolk, A., & Perego, P. (2014). Sustainable bonuses: Sign of corporate responsibility or window dressing? *Journal of Business Ethics, 119*(1), 1–15.

Konrad, A., Steurer, R., Langer, M. E., & Martinuzzi, A. (2006). Empirical findings on business-society relations in Europe. *Journal of Business Ethics, 63*, 89–105.

Lantos, G. P. (2001). The boundaries of strategic corporate social responsibility. *Journal of Consumer Marketing, 18*(7), 595–632. https://doi.org/10.1108/07363760110410281

Maas, K. (2018). Do corporate social performance targets in executive compensation contribute to corporate social performance? *Journal of Business Ethics, 148*, 573–585.

Macaulay, C. D., Richard, O. C., Peng, M. W. et al. (2018). Alliance network centrality, board composition, and corporate social performance. *Journal of Business Ethics, 151*, 997–1008. https://doi.org/10.1007/s10551-017-3566-7

Mahoney, L. S., & Thorn, L. (2006). An examination of the structure of executive compensation and corporate social responsibility: A Canadian investigation. *Journal of Business Ethics, 69*, 149–162.

Masulis, R. W., & Mobbs, S. (2011). Are all inside directors the same? Evidence from the external directorship market. *Journal of Finance, 66*, 823–872.

McCarthy, S., Oliver, B., & Song, S. (2017). Corporate social responsibility and CEO confidence. *Journal of Banking and Finance, 75*, 280–291.

McClelland, P. L., Barker, V. L., & Oh, W. Y. (2012). CEO career horizon and tenure: Future performance implications under different contingencies. *Journal of Business Research, 65*, 1387–1393.

McGuire, J. Oehmichen, J., Wolff, M., & Hilgers, R. (2019). Do contracts make them care? The impact of CEO compensation design on corporate social performance. *Journal of Business Ethics, 157*(2), 375–390.

Morse, A., Nanda, V., & Seru, A. (2011). Are incentive contracts rigged by powerful CEOs? *The Journal of Finance, 66*, 1779–1821.

Nikolova, V., & Arsi, S. (2017). The stakeholder approach in corporate social responsibility. *Engineering Management, 3*(1), 24–35.

Oh, W.Y., Chang, Y. K., & Cheng, Z. (2016). When CEO career horizon problems matter for corporate social responsibility: The moderating roles of industry-level discretion and blockholder ownership. *Journal of Business Ethics, 133*, 279–291.

Petrenko, O. V., Aime, F., Ridge, J., & Hill, A. (2016). Corporate social responsibility or CEO narcissism? CSR motivations and organizational performance. *Strategic Management Journal, 37*(2), 262–279.

Post, C., Rahman, N., & McQuillen, C. (2015). From board composition to corporate environmental performance through sustainability-themed alliances. *Journal of Business Ethics, 130*(2), 423–435.

Ramon-Llorens, M. C., Garcia-Meca, E., & Pucheta-Martinez, M. C. (2019). The role of human and social board capital in driving CSR reporting. *Long Range Planning, 52*(6), 101846.

Rao, K., & Tilt, C. (2016). Board composition and corporate social responsibility: The role of diversity, gender, strategy and decision making. *Journal of Business Ethics, 138*(2), 327–347.

Rosette, A. S., & Tost, L. P. (2010). Agentic women and communal leadership: How role prescriptions confer advantage to top women leaders. *Journal of Applied Psychology, 95*(2), 221–235.

Shaukat, A., Qiu, Y., & Trojanowski, G. (2016). Board attributes, corporate social responsibility strategy, and corporate environmental and social performance. *Journal of Business Ethics, 35*(3), 569–585.

Shoham, A., Almor, T., Lee, S. M., & Ahammad, M. F. (2017). Encouraging environmental sustainability through gender: A micro-foundational approach using linguistic gender marking. *Journal of Organizational Behaviour, 38*, 1356–1379.

Shropshire, C. (2010). The role of the interlocking director and board receptivity in the diffusion of practices. *Academy of Management Review, 35*, 246–264.

Tian, J., Haleblian, J., & Rajagopalan, N. (2011). The effects of board human and social capital on investor reactions to new CEO selection. *Strategic Management Journal, 32*(7), 731–747.

Tsagas, G. (2020). A proposal for reform of EU member states' corporate governance codes in support of sustainability. *Sustainability, 12*(10), 4328. https://doi.org/10.3390/su12104328

Veprauskaitė, E., & Adams, M. (2013). Do powerful chief executives influence the financial performance of UK firms? *The British Accounting Review, 45*(3), 229–241.

Volonté, C. (2015). Boards: Independent and committed directors? *International Review of Law Economics, 41*, 25–37.

Walls, J. L., Berrone, P., & Phan, P. H. (2012). Corporate governance and environmental performance: Is there really a link? *Strategic Management Journal, 33*, 885–913.

Webb, D., & Pettigrew, A. (1999). The temporal development of strategy: Patterns in the U.K. insurance industry. *Organization Science, 10*, 601–621.

6 Corporate Social Responsibility, Corporate Sustainability, and Executive Compensation in the EU

The Role of CSR Committees

Panagiotis Dimitropoulos

Introduction

A sustainable corporate activity is one that is environmentally and socially warranted, is ethically piloted, abides to existing laws and regulations, and creates economic value (Brockett & Rezaee, 2012). Over the years corporate sustainability activities and relative sustainability reports have increased significantly, and CEOs and executives have been characterized as key players in sustainability activities and reports. Corporate sustainability offers long-term competitive advantages, enhances financial performance, and even contributes to the well-being of the society (Chang et al., 2017).

According to Berrone and Gomez-Mejia (2009), and Al-Shaer and Zaman (2019), corporate sustainability has been considered as a crucial corporate strategy that not only contributes to societal and environmental needs but also assists firms to survive in the long run (Mattingly & Berman, 2006; Callan & Thomas, 2014). The UNs principles for responsible investments, which were published in 2012 (UNPRI, 2012), was the first official document of a supranational organization that considered the association between corporate sustainability and executive compensation, since it provided guidance on how executives should be rewarded for achieving sustainable corporate goals (Al-Shaer & Zaman, 2019). Flammer, Hong, and Minor (2019) posit that the association between executive compensation and corporate social and environmental behavior can direct managerial efforts from short-term financial goals toward long-term sustainable goals, a fact that can contribute positively to corporate value enhancement and viability.

The relationship between executive compensation and corporate sustainability has been thoroughly examined in the literature, and there seems to be two main streams of thought trying to explain that relationship. Barnea and Rubin (2010) substantiated the overinvestment hypothesis (which is based on the agency theory of Jensen & Meckling, 1976), which proposes a positive association between sustainability

DOI: 10.4324/9781003152750-8

performance and executive compensation and dictates that sustainable (social and environmental) activities constitute a waste of scarce corporate resources if they do not contribute toward firm value maximization (Cai, Jo, & Pan, 2011). The second theory on this issue is the conflict-resolution hypothesis (based on stakeholder theory), which assumes a negative association between executive compensation and sustainability (Francoeur, Melis, Gaia, & Aresu, 2017). Also, Hoi, Wu, and Zhang (2019) argue that firms residing within areas of higher social capital tend to mitigate managerial rent extraction through CEO compensation, leading to lower levels of CEO payments.

Both sustainability activities and executive compensation are tightly connected to firms' governance structure as both are under the control of the board of directors. According to Al-Shaer and Zaman (2019), the establishment of a CSR-sustainability committee suggests that the company is dedicated to sustainable practices and has an active strategic stance toward its stakeholders. Berrone and Gomez-Mejia (2009) argue that the existence of such committees allows the board to effectively assess executive performance and consider this assessment on executive compensation. According to Winschel and Stawinoga (2019), the existence of a CSR committee enhances the integration and evaluation of environmental and social aspects of corporate strategy, which sometimes directly affect CEO compensation (Al-Shaer & Zaman, 2019; Chen & Wu, 2016). However, nothing comes without a cost. According to Adams, Ragunathan, and Tumarkin (2016) and Vafeas and Vlittis (2019), the enhanced delegation toward such committees may create barriers of communication within board members and further deteriorate efficient decision-making, thus increasing firm's agency costs.

The scope of this chapter is to examine how corporate sustainability performance impacts on executive compensation while considering the existence of a voluntary CSR-sustainability committee within the board of directors utilizing a sample of EU firms. Despite the fact that the EU legislated on corporate sustainability with the directive on sustainable development (EU, 2014) and provided guidance on corporate environmental and social behavior, limited research has been done on the topic, and so the current study responds to the calls for further research on the issue by other researchers (Camilleri, 2017) and adds to the growing literature on executive compensation and corporate sustainability.

First, we consider an aggregate sustainability measure (including both social and environmental activities), along with nine separate social and environmental performance sub-scores (Velte, 2019; Winschel & Stawinoga, 2019). Second, we have performed a cross-country study by including listed and unlisted corporations from 24 EU countries over a longer period of time (2003–2018) as proposed by Francoeur et al. (2017) and Beck, Friedl, and Schäfer (2020). Third, responding to the call by Winschel and Stawinoga (2019) and Kang (2017) we consider the existence of a voluntary CSR (sustainability) committee within the board of directors as a mechanism that is directly connected to sustainability performance but has been limitedly considered by previous studies, especially on its impact on executive compensation. Finally, as argued by Velte (2019), we aim to control for this bidirectional association by considering a GMM instrumental variables approach, propensity score matching, along with a system of simultaneous equations, thus providing more salient and robust inferences on the variables under study (Wintoki, Linck, & Netter, 2012).

Literature Review and Research Hypotheses

Executive compensation has been examined under different theoretical lenses offering diverse theoretical and empirical explanations. At first, the principal-agent theory proposed by Berle and Means (1932) and extended by Jensen and Meckling (1976) and Fama and Jensen (1983) is the main theoretical framework that tries to examine how executive compensation steers or is affected by sustainability activities and performance. The agency theory (which sets on its core the shareholder value maximization as the main goal) views executive compensation as a governance mechanism that contributes to the mitigation of corporate agency costs through the alignment of executives' and shareholders' interests (Winschel & Stawinoga, 2019). The second theoretical framework is the stakeholder theory, which assumes that the firm's CEO enters into a contractual relation with the firm's key stakeholders (beyond shareholders). This relationship directs CEOs to consider stakeholders' interests on firm's strategic decisions and allocate resources toward satisfying those interests (Hill & Jones, 1992).

Following the agency theory framework, Barnea and Rubin (2010) documented that executives try to build their reputation and image toward firm's shareholders and stakeholders but at their cost, so they tend to overinvest in sustainability-related activities. The improvement on executives' reputation will lead to enhanced career opportunities, bargaining power, and ultimately higher levels of compensation. Alternatively, CEOs who bear little cost for sustainability activities (due to lower ownership status) will be motivated to increase sustainability activities for gaining private rents (Karim, Lee, & Suh, 2018). Empirical evidence by Berrone and Gomez-Mejia (2009), Cordeiro and Sarkis (2008), and Milbourn (2003) indicate a positive association between executive compensation and firms' environmental (pollution control and reduction policies) and social performance. Similar evidence are provided by Karim et al. (2018) in the United States, since they concluded that CEOs equity-based compensation is positively associated to corporate social responsibility.

On the contrary, the stakeholder theory perspective proposes the opposite (negative) association between executive compensation and sustainability performance. According to Cai et al. (2011), the conflict-resolution hypothesis assumes that CSR contributes to the mitigation of conflicts between stakeholders, leading to a negative impact on executives' compensation. Firms with enhanced sustainability performance face lower levels of risk, leading to reduced compensation for their executives. Similarly, Hoi et al. (2019) suggest that CEOs within firms of enhanced social capital anticipate higher marginal costs from opportunistic behavior related to their compensation; thus, they are inclined to receive lower remuneration.

An alternative explanation is offered by Francoeur et al. (2017), who argue that firms interested on achieving sustainability goals may choose CEOs who are self-motivated and share common interests with the firm. Moreover, CEOs who are motivated by nonmonetary values may prefer to work for firms that achieve higher standards of social or sustainability performance, gaining intrinsic rewards working for them (Brekke & Nyborg, 2008; Francoeur et al., 2017). Therefore, under this assumption, highly sustainable firms are more likely to pay their CEOs less and their CEOs may accept such compensation because they are intrinsically rewarded and motivated.

Empirical evidence in different countries and time periods provided by Riahi-Belkaoui (1992), Hong, Li, and Minor (2016), Rekker, Benson, and Faff (2014), Francoeur et al. (2017), Hoi et al. (2019), and Cai et al. (2011) all indicate a negative impact of social and environmental performance on executive compensation, corroborating the arguments of the conflict-resolution (stakeholder theory) hypothesis (Moriarty, 2009). Thus, based on the this discussion we state the first research hypothesis in the following null form:

> H1: *Corporate sustainability performance has no impact on executive compensation.*

The establishment of independent board committees within the firm's corporate governance is an underresearched issue despite the fact that over the years such committees have increased within firms. The CSR-sustainability committee is an example of a voluntary type of board committees that are responsible for drafting, proposing, controlling, and evaluating the firm's sustainability (social or environmental) strategy and report accordingly to the board and stakeholders. The existence of such committee may have a differential impact on the association between executive compensation and sustainability performance.

At first, the creation of a voluntary committee provides several benefits to the operation of the board by performing both an advisory and a strategic function of the firm (Reeb & Upadhyay, 2010; Adams, 2003) yielding knowledge specialization turnover. According to Vafeas and

Vlittis (2019), this fact creates task efficiency benefits since it enhances the board's operating efficiency, overall task efficiency, and flexibility and provides managerial support toward day-to-day handling of affairs (Chen & Wu, 2016).

Specifically, the establishment of a voluntary-type sustainability committee can create significant pressure on the firm's sustainability commitment, and even in the case where the firm is managed by self-serving CEOs, the presence of a sustainability committee may urge them to integrate sustainability goals and performance on their agendas in order to avoid several costs related to noncompliance with sustainability rules and regulations (Kock, Santaló, & Diestre, 2012; Francoeur et al., 2017). Firms that have established such voluntary committees should be focused on employing CEOs who share the same sustainability vision, will be self-motivated on developing sustainability activities, and will be willing to behave as stewards of sustainable operation. Consequently, under the conflict-resolution hypothesis the existence of a voluntary sustainability committee on the board may further complement the negative association between executive compensation and sustainability performance.

However, there are several voices of opposition regarding the potential benefits of voluntary committees on the board. According to Chen and Wu (2016) and Vafeas and Vlittis (2019), such committees may increase information segregation costs and enhance information asymmetries between committee members, leading to inefficient dissemination of information and decision-making abilities. Also, Adams et al. (2016) posit that delegating operating tasks within such committees may lead to communication obstructions, a fact that creates significant agency costs. Finally, Alam, Chen, Giccotello, and Ryan (2014) posit that the status of the sustainability committee may signal the existence of two tiers of directorship that may impact CEOs recruitment and remuneration. Thus, following this discussion, the impact of sustainability committees on the association between corporate sustainability and executive compensation remains an open empirical question since it may have a moderating impact on the issue under study as well. Thus, we form the second research hypothesis in the null form as follows:

H2: The existence of a sustainability committee does not moderate the impact of corporate sustainability performance on executive compensation.

Data Selection Procedure and Research Design

In the current study we utilize a sample of corporations (both listed and unlisted) from 24 EU member countries over the period 2003–2018.

All financial, governance, social, and environmental responsibility data have been extracted from the Datastream database. The ESG scores are extracted from company reports and relevant publications, press releases, organizational reports, and other public forms of information. From a total of 6,56,734 firm-year observations, we excluded those firms without social and environmental score data for at least five consecutive years in order to avoid bias in the empirical results and also to facilitate the estimation of differenced and lagged variables. Furthermore, we excluded firms with incomplete financial, sustainability, and governance data and those that do not close their fiscal year in December. Also, financial services firms (such as banks and insurance companies) were excluded from the sample. In addition, we winsorized the upper and down 1% of the data distribution in order to mitigate the influence of significant outliers in the empirical analysis. After this procedure was completed, we ended up with a final sample of 1,21,154 firm-year observations. Table 6.1 presents the sample selection process in more detail.

In order to examine our research hypotheses we will evaluate panel regression models estimated with Generalized Least Squares (GLS) random effects. In order to select the random effect estimation compared to the fixed effect estimation, we performed the Breusch-Pagan Lagrange multiplier test for random effect. The test produced a highly significant statistic (Chi^2 428.77, $p < 0.00001$) indicating that the random effects estimation is appropriate. The functional form of the equations includes the average sustainability for each firm and year, where i denotes the firm, t the year, and e the error term. The model also includes year, industry, and country-fixed effects in order to capture any heterogeneity or influences in the data originating from firm-specific and country-specific

Table 6.1 Sample selection process

Description	Observations
For our sample selection we focused on EU firms covered by the ESG Datastream database over the period 2003–2018.	6,56,734
Firms with less than five years of consecutive ESG data (not continuous evaluation and coverage).	–3,05,447
Firms with incomplete financial, compensation and governance data.	–1,24,355
Available observations with complete ESG and financial data	2,26,932
Firms which do not close their fiscal year on December	–1,12,500
Winsorized the upper and down 1% of the data distribution	–2,250
Final sample	*1,12,182*

omitted variables that are time-invariant or sector-specific time-varying omitted factors:

$$
\begin{aligned}
LnCOMP_{it} = {} & a_0 + a_1 AV\_SUST_{it} + a_2 SIZE_{it} + a_3 LEV_{it} \\
& + a_4 ROA_{it} + a_5 GROWTH_{it} \\
& + a_6 BDSIZE_{it} + a_7 LISTED_{it} + Year\ F.E \\
& + Industry\ F.E. + Country\ F.E. + e_{it}
\end{aligned}
\tag{1}
$$

The dependent variable LnCOMP is the natural logarithm of executive total compensation in a given year (including cash and equity-type of compensation), as in Cai et al. (2011), Francoeur et al. (2017), and Hoi et al. (2019). AV_SUST denotes each company's annual average sustainability score, which is estimated by averaging nine (9) social and environmental performance sub-scores, including their CSR strategy, workforce, human rights protection, community involvement, shareholders protection, product responsibility, resource utilization, emission reduction, and environmental innovation. Following the discussion on the hypothesis development section, coefficient a_1 is expected to have a positive sign if the agency theory is valid or a negative sign under the conflict-resolution hypothesis. Moreover, in order to provide more salient inferences regarding the differential impact of each social and environmental performance sub-score on executive compensation, we will estimate the following random effect regression model including each sustainability performance sub-score in Model (1), along with the same control variables and with the year, sector, and country-fixed effects.

$$
\begin{aligned}
LnCOMP_{it} = {} & a_0 + a_1 EN\_INNOV_{it} + a_2 EMM_{it} + a_3 RES\_USE_{it} \\
& + a_4 STRAT_t + a_5 WORK_{it} \\
& + a_6 HUMAN_{it} + a_7 COMM_{it} + a_8 PROD_{it} \\
& + a_9 SHARE_{it} + a_{10} SIZE_{it} \\
& + a_{11} LEV_{it} + a_{12} ROA_{it} + a_{13} GROWTH_{it} \\
& + a_{14} BDSIZE_{it} + a_{15} LISTED_{it} \\
& + Year\ F.E + Industry\ F.E. + Country\ F.E. + u_{it}
\end{aligned}
\tag{2}
$$

The first three variables refer to environmental responsibility performance and the following six to social responsibility performance. EN_INNOV is the environmental innovation score, EMM denotes the company's emission reduction score, RES_USE indicates the firm's resource use score, STRAT denotes each company's CSR strategy score, WORK denotes the company's workforce score, HUMAN denotes the firm's human rights score, COMM is the company's community score, PROD is the firm's product responsibility score, and SHARE is the firm's shareholder score. All environmental and social responsibility scores range between zero (0) and 100, so the higher the score the more socially and environmentally responsible the firm is.

In addition, we have included in both models a set of control variables that have been proved significant determinants of executive compensation. SIZE is the natural logarithm of annual total assets capturing firm size. A positive relationship between firm size and executive compensation is expected since large firms are able to pay their executives more and also have the ability to attract the most competent executives. Beck et al. (2020), Gabaix and Landier (2008), and Frydman and Saks (2010) point that company size explains a significant part of the variation of executive compensation. Empirical evidence by Beck et al. (2020) concluded that executive compensation is positively affected by the level and growth of firm's size.

LEV is the ratio of total debt to total assets, and according to Francoeur et al. (2017), the firm's debt structure may influence its decision to use executive compensation as a mechanism to solve agency problems within the firm. Hence, a positive coefficient is expected on that variable. ROA is the ratio of return on assets capturing profitability. Cai et al. (2011) and Callan and Thomas (2014) indicate that profitability has a positive relationship to executive compensation because more profitable firms can pay their executives more. However, Francoeur et al. (2017) indicate a negative association, yet not statistically significant. GROWTH captures firms' growth opportunities and is estimated as the annual percentage change in sales revenues. Firms with growth potentials are more in need of highly skilled executives and so may tend to provide higher remuneration to them, thus a positive coefficient is expected on that variable.

We also control for the size of the board of directors (BDSIZE). Empirical evidence is inconclusive on the impact of board size on executive compensation since several studies consider that an optimal board size is not existent and so different sizes could have differential impact on executive compensation. Ozkan (2011) found that firms with a larger board size pay higher executive compensation because of problems with communication and coordination within larger boards. The results of most extant studies are consistent with this finding – that is, the larger the board size, the higher the executive compensation (Ozkan, 2011; Croci, Gonenc, & Ozkan, 2012; Van Essen, Heugens, Otten, & van Oosterhout, 2012; Schultz, Castelló, & Morsing, 2013). However, there is also a small number of studies that draw different conclusions. For example, Sheikh et al. (2018) found that board size has no effect on executive compensation, using data of Pakistan listed firms from 2005 to 2012. Also, empirical evidence by Cai et al. (2011) and Karim et al. (2018) provide a negative yet insignificant impact of board size on compensation, so we lack a clear prediction on the impact of that variable on executive compensation. Finally, LISTED is a dichotomous variable receiving unity (1) for listed corporations and zero (0) otherwise. Listed corporations tend to pay their executives higher compensation, thus a positive coefficient is expected on that variable.

Furthermore, for examining our second research hypothesis and whether the existence of a CSR-sustainability committee has a differential effect on the sustainability–compensation relation, Models (1) and (2) will be estimated after separating the sample firms between those that have established a voluntary sustainability (or CSR) committee and those that do not (a binary variable equals 1 denotes firms with sustainability committees and 0 otherwise). If the sign and significance of coefficient a_1 in Model (1) (and the respective coefficients of the nine components of AV_SUST) differs between the two subgroups, we can infer that the existence of a sustainability committee within the board has an effect on the relation between executive compensation and sustainability performance.

Empirical Results

Descriptive Statistics and Correlation Analysis

Table 6.2, Panel A, presents the descriptive statistics of the variables utilized in the regression models. First of all, the mean AV_SUST is 56.6 (with a standard deviation of 24.6), indicating that the sample firms have a satisfactory sustainability performance score. Also, the average LnCOMP is 15.9 (with a standard deviation of 1.57 where in monetary value is on average 8.3 million euro), which is above the average executive compensation in studies by Cai et al. (2011) and Francoeur et al. (2017). More than half of the sample firms have established a voluntary sustainability committee within the board (average SUST_COM is 0.55), and thus they incorporate sustainability issues on a strategic level within firm decisions and have been investing resources toward that direction. The sample firms are highly profitable (mean ROA 21.2), present significant growth opportunities (mean GROWTH at 58.9), and have on average 12 directors on the board. Finally, our sample firms seem to be highly leveraged since the average total debt covers almost 62% of total assets and almost 10% of them are listed in the stock market.

Table 6.2, Panel B, presents the descriptive statistics on the nine components of the AV_SUST variable in order to control for any differences between the determinants of corporate sustainability. The highest

Table 6.2 Panel A, Descriptive statistics of the sample variables

Variables	Mean	Standard deviation	Min	Max
LnCOMP	15.928	1.576	1.558	23.719
AV_SUST	56.618	24.668	0.450	99.838
SUST_COM	0.552	0.497	0	1
SIZE	20.496	2.848	2.302	30.311
LEV	0.627	0.098	0.006	0.908
ROA	21.281	48.257	−27.861	174.17
GROWTH	58.931	14.174	−69.711	409.07
BDSIZE	12.271	4.703	3	38
LISTED	0.095	0.293	0	1

Table 6.2 Panel B, Descriptive statistics of AV_SUST components

Variables	Mean	Standard deviation	Min	Max
EN_INNOV	61.335	25.959	0.202	99.919
EMM	65.916	26.190	0.161	99.920
RES_USE	66.541	25.732	0.081	99.844
STRAT	55.777	28.171	0.164	99.804
WORK	65.425	25.369	0.318	99.845
HUMAN	67.169	25.897	0.900	99.809
COMM	55.609	29.271	0.253	99.851
PROD	61.407	27.848	0.081	99.844
SHARE	50.389	28.721	0.450	99.838

Table 6.2 Panel C, LnCOMP and other controls based on AV_SUST ranked portfolios

Variables	P1 – High AV_SUST	P2 – Medium AV_SUST	P3 – Low AV_SUST	Difference (P1 – P3)	p-value
LnCOMP	15.902	15.846	16.059	−0.157*	0.001
SIZE	20.502	20.556	20.333	0.169*	0.001
LEV	4.356	5.536	4.989	−0.633*	0.024
ROA	26.164	10.100	4.242	21.922*	0.001
GROWTH	104.36	39.412	26.089	78.271*	0.001
BDSIZE	12.451	12.146	12.026	0.425	0.847

Note: Asterisks denote statistical significance at the 5% significance level at least.

average score is that of human rights protection score (HUMAN averages around 67.2) followed by resources use efficiency score (RES_USE averages around 66.5). Emission reduction (EMM) and workforce (WORK) scores are both averaging on 65, suggesting that those issues are important facets of corporate sustainability. On the other hand, shareholders (SHARE) and community (COMM) scores produced the smallest averages (50.3 and 55.6 respectively), indicating that those two are the least-performing issues on sample firms' agenda, without of course ignoring that none of the nine sub-scores was below 50. Consequently, sample firms seem to have a differentiated focus between various sustainability activities, and this verifies arguments by Velte (2019) that aggregate sustainability measures do not always provide the entire picture on corporate CSR and sustainability performance.

Table 6.2, Panel C, presents the differences between the main financial variables after separating firms within low, medium, and high AV_SUST performance groups in order to examine the extent to which sustainability performance impacts on executive compensation and other control variables. Following Suto and Takehara (2018), we performed a portfolio formation approach and estimated the average of the AV_SUST variable per year and country and assigned each firm as a low AV_SUST firm if its annual score is below the 1st quartile, high AV_SUST firms if their AV_SUST score is above the 3rd quartile, and all other firm observations lying between the 1st and 3rd quartiles as medium AV_SUST firms. The column under the title "difference" reports the average difference between the high AV_SUST portfolio firms and the low AV_SUST portfolio. The "*p*-value" column presents the corresponding probability values from estimating the Welch two-sample *t*-test and asterisks indicate statistical significance at least at the 5% significance level (Suto & Takehara, 2018). As we can see from the last column, high sustainability performing firms are characterized by statistically lower executive compensation and leverage but conversely highly sustainable firms are larger, more profitable, and with higher growth opportunities. These findings seem to corroborate arguments based on the conflict-resolution hypothesis that enhanced sustainability performing firms pay their executives less (Cai et al., 2011; Hoi et al., 2019).

Table 6.3 presents the Pearson correlation coefficients between the sample variables. The majority of the correlation coefficients are significant with economic meaning and are not very high, indicating the absence of multicollinearity on the data. The VIF estimation of the sample variables provided values that were far below the threshold of 5, indicating no multicollinearity. As we can see, LnCOMP is negatively associated with AV_SUST, corroborating the findings of Table 6.2, Panel C, and provides an initial indication regarding our first research hypothesis. Also, LnCOMP is positively correlated to board size, listing status, and the existence of a sustainability committee with the board while negatively and significantly associated with SIZE. Nevertheless, firms with higher sustainability performance tend to have a voluntary sustainability committee, are more profitable, and have larger board size. Also, more profitable firms are positively associated with AV_SUST and SIZE. Finally,

Table 6.3 Pearson correlation coefficients of sample variables

Variables	1	2	3	4	5	6	7	8
1. LnCOMP	1							
2. AV_SUST	-0.037	1						
3. SUST_COM	0.028	0.578	1					
4. SIZE	-0.025	-0.025	-0.038	1				
5. LEV	-0.015	-0.001	0.001	-0.046	1			
6. ROA	0.001	0.012	-0.004	0.127	-0.070	1		
7. GROWTH	0.003	0.001	0.003	0.001	-0.001	-0.001	1	
8. BDSIZE	0.083	0.064	0.037	0.073	0.001	0.063	0.004	1
9. LISTED	0.023	0.039	-0.001	-0.023	-0.002	0.006	-0.001	0.057

Note: Correlation coefficients in bold indicate statistical significance at least at the 5% significance level.

growth opportunities did not provide any significant correlation coefficients with AV_SUST and other control variables.

Regression Results

Table 6.4 presents the GLS random effects regression results of Model (1) for the full model estimation in the first column and after separating the firms between those that have established a sustainability committee and those that do not. First, the coefficient on AV_SUST produced a negative and highly significant coefficient (-0.003, $p < 0.001$) for the full sample estimation. The result is economically significant since a 1% increase in average sustainability performance leads to an almost 0.3% decrease in executive compensation, ceteris paribus. This finding rejects hypothesis H1 and corroborates the conflict-resolution hypothesis, which assumes that sustainability performance contributes to the mitigation of conflicts between stakeholders leading to a negative impact on executives' compensation. Also, this finding is in line with previous empirical evidence in the literature such as Riahi-Belkaoui (1992), Hong et al. (2016), Rekker et al. (2014), Francoeur et al. (2017), Hoi et al. (2019), and Cai et al.

Table 6.4 Regression results on the impact of AV_SUST on LnCOMP and the effect of the sustainability committee

Variables	Full sample	SUST_COM = 1	SUST_COM = 0
Constant	15.55***	15.276***	15.845***
	(12.89)	(7.25)	(6.79)
AV_SUST	-0.003***	-0.004***	-0.002
	(-4.12)	(-2.56)	(-1.40)
SIZE	0.005	0.016*	-0.004
	(0.91)	(1.81)	(-0.48)
LEV	-0.311***	-0.215**	-0.467***
	(-5.23)	(-2.40)	(-4.39)
ROA	-0.378***	-0.255*	-0.504***
	(-3.58)	(-1.77)	(-2.58)
GROWTH	0.004**	0.003	0.001
	(2.20)	(0.78)	(0.77)
BDSIZE	0.031***	0.042***	0.029***
	(8.69)	(7.06)	(4.78)
LISTED	0.009	0.014	0.008
	(0.78)	(1.09)	(0.96)
R^2	0.145	0.205	0.158
Wald-x^2	23.45***	12.75***	9.69***
Observations	112182	61924	50258

Note: *, **, *** indicate statistical significance at the 10%, 5%, and 1% significance level respectively; z-statistics in parenthesis.

(2011), indicating that the recognition of the firm's moral responsibilities toward its stakeholders leads managers to accept lower payments, less provocative remuneration, and other perks.

After decomposing our sample firms based on the existence of a sustainability committee in the board, we found that the negative impact of sustainability performance on executive compensation is significant only for firms with a voluntary sustainability committee. The coefficient on AV_SUST is negative and economically significant (-0.004, $p < 0.001$) and with a similar size relative to full sample estimation. This result leads us to reject hypothesis H2. The existence of a sustainability committee suggests that the firm is considering sustainability as a key strategic issue, which creates more room for developing sustainability activities on a voluntary basis. Thus, after accepting the conflict-resolution hypothesis, the existence of a voluntary sustainability committee on the board further complements the negative association between executive compensation and sustainability performance (Kock et al., 2012).

Referring to the control variables, SIZE produced a positive and statistically significant coefficient only for those firms with a voluntary sustainability committee (0.016, $p < 0.10$), so partly we can accept arguments in the literature that larger firms provide higher remuneration to their executives (Beck et al., 2020; Gabaix & Landier, 2008; Frydman & Saks, 2010; Cai et al., 2011). LEV produced negative and highly significant coefficients for firms both with and without a voluntary sustainability committee. This result suggests that highly leveraged firms provide lower remuneration to their executives as a way to deal with stakeholder concerns. This result is in line with findings by Karim et al. (2018). ROA also yielded a negative and significant coefficient for both subgroups of firms verifying evidence by Francoeur et al. (2017) and Karim et al. (2018). On the contrary, GROWTH produced a positive and significant coefficient only for the full sample estimation, indicating that firms with growth potentials are more in need for highly skilled executives and thus may tend to provide higher remuneration to their executives. Finally, the size of the board of directors (BDSIZE) also has a positive and significant impact on executive compensation since it produced positive and highly significant coefficients on all types of estimation. The result corroborates most relevant evidence on the literature (Ozkan, 2011; Croci et al., 2012; Van Essen et al., 2012; Schultz et al., 2013), suggesting that firms with a larger board size pay higher executive compensation.

Table 6.5 presents the panel GLS random effects estimation of Model (2) after decomposing sustainability performance on its nine sub-score variables relating to social and environmental performance. The control variables produced similar coefficients in size and significance relative to Table 6.4. As we can see, there is a significant variation among the various scores and between firms with and without sustainability committees.

Table 6.5 Regression results on the impact of AV_SUST components on LnCOMP and the effect of the sustainability committee

Variables	Full sample	SUST_COM = 1	SUST_COM = 0
Constant	15.912***	15.466***	16.427***
	(9.08)	(6.07)	(6.27)
EN_INNOV	-0.005***	-0.007***	-0.002
	(-6.31)	(-6.54)	(-1.44)
EMM	0.001	-0.002	0.002*
	(0.48)	(-1.42)	(1.71)
RES_USE	-0.001	0.001	-0.002
	(-0.78)	(0.87)	(-1.54)
STRAT	0.001	-0.002	0.002*
	(0.09)	(-1.31)	(1.84)
WORK	-0.008	0.001	-0.004***
	(-1.00)	(1.21)	(-3.25)
HUMAN	0.000	0.002	-0.001
	(0.47)	(1.42)	(-0.65)
COMM	-0.003***	-0.003***	0.002
	(-4.09)	(-3.07)	(1.61)
PROD	0.005	-0.001	-0.003**
	(0.68)	(-0.83)	(-2.17)
SHARE	-0.048***	-0.005***	-0.006***
	(-8.49)	(-5.43)	(-6.59)
SIZE	0.003	0.018*	-0.018
	(0.05)	(1.85)	(-1.66)
LEV	-0.341***	-0.250**	-0.461***
	(-4.52)	(-2.50)	(-4.06)
ROA	-0.325**	-0.275*	-0.441**
	(-2.55)	(-1.74)	(-2.18)
GROWTH	0.004*	0.003	0.001
	(1.72)	(0.60)	(0.76)
BDSIZE	0.035***	0.041***	0.026***
	(7.85)	(6.55)	(4.16)
LISTED	0.012	0.011	0.008
	(1.24)	(1.11)	(0.76)
R^2	0.321	0.430	0.350
Wald-x^2	18.59***	12.18***	10.05***
Observations	112182	61924	50258

Note: *, **, *** indicate statistical significance at the 10%, 5%, and 1% significance level respectively; z-statistics in parenthesis.

Environmental innovation score (EN_INNOV) and community score (COMM) both impact negatively on executive compensation, and that impact is significant only for firms with sustainability committees. This result verifies our previous evidence and discussion relating to conflict-resolution hypothesis. Also, shareholder score (SHARE) yields a negative coefficient, which is equally significant between the two subgroups of firms. Product responsibility score (PROD) and workforce scores (WORK) had negative and significant coefficients only for the subgroup of firms without a sustainability committee.

On the contrary, emission reduction score (EMM) and CSR strategy score (STRAT) produced positive but marginally significant coefficients and only for the group of firms without a voluntary sustainability committee. This result could be explained under the lens of the agency theory, which views executive compensation as a governance mechanism that contributes to the mitigation of corporate agency costs through the alignment of executives' and shareholders' interests. Our results on those two variables corroborate previous empirical evidence by Berrone and Gomez-Mejia (2009), Cordeiro and Sarkis (2008), and Milbourn (2003), indicating a positive association between executive compensation and firms' environmental (emission reduction policies) and social performance. So overall, the decomposition of sustainability performance sub-scores revealed a completely different picture regarding the impact of each environmental and social performance score on executive compensation, where some yield a positive impact while the majority of them yield a negative impact on the dependent variable. Thus, when researchers focus only on a single or aggregate measure of social or environmental performance without considering other sub-performance items, it may lead to inconclusive or misleading results (Velte, 2019; Winschel & Stawinoga, 2019).

Sensitivity Analysis

In our analysis so far we have controlled for various control variables and sustainability sub-scores on the regression models within a panel GLS random effects research design. Nevertheless, we cannot exclude the possibility that some omitted variables might affect the main empirical results (the negative impact of average sustainability performance on executive compensation may be the outcome of some unobservable characteristics). For this reason we followed the work by Cai et al. (2011), Hasan, Hoi, Wu, and Zhang (2020), and Karim et al. (2018), and we applied two different procedures for controlling for the endogenous relation between compensation and sustainability performance. The first is an instrumental variables approach using the generalized method of moments (GMM). Following Cai et al. (2011) we used the sector-median AV_SUST performance as an instrument since it fulfills both the relevancy condition and the exclusion restriction and has been proved to be a significant instrument in other studies as well. The selection of the GMM procedure over 2SLS was made because it allows to estimate efficient and consistent estimators under *i.i.d.* error terms (Baum, 2006). So in the first-stage regression we estimated firm-level AV_SUST for each year and industry, and the industry-median AV_SUST is used as the instrument on a regression having the average sustainability performance as the dependent variable and the rest of the control in Model (1) as the independent variables. The fitted values from the first stage were used in the second-stage regression, having LnCOMP as the dependent variable.

The relative results are presented in Table 6.6. As we can see, the instrument on the first-stage regression is highly significant, indicating that an increase on the industry-median sustainability performance contributes positively on firm-level sustainability performance. In order to check the validity of the instruments we performed the AR(1) test, which rejected the null hypothesis, suggesting that the instrument is valid for our research setting. Moreover, we performed the Hansen J-statistic of over-identifying restrictions, which was insignificant within conventional levels, suggesting that the instrument was completely exogenous. On the second-stage results we observed that AV_SUST again produced a negative and significant coefficient verifying results in Table 6.4 and rejects H1. Thus, our initial evidence remains robust after controlling for the endogenous relation between sustainability performance and executive compensation and is not driven by unobserved firm characteristics.

Table 6.6 GMM IV regression results on the impact of AV_SUST on LnCOMP

First-stage GMM results		Second-stage IV-GMM results	
Constant	4.372***	Constant	15.225***
	(8.58)		(22.41)
SIZE	0.276	AV_SUST	−0.014**
	(1.08)		(−2.03)
LEV	−2.332***	SIZE	0.074**
	(−2.75)		(2.24)
ROA	3.430**	LEV	−0.213
	(2.47)		(−0.52)
GROWTH	0.039	ROA	1.195
	(1.45)		(1.27)
BDSIZE	0.033***	GROWTH	0.011**
	(3.68)		(2.03)
Ind_Med_AV_SUST	0.041***	BDSIZE	0.036***
	(4.57)		(5.48)
LISTED	0.021*	LISTED	0.008
	(1.79)		(0.76)
R^2-adjusted	0.355	R^2	0.128
F-stat	129.21***	Wald-x^2	533.73***
Observations	112182	Observations	112182

Note: *, **, *** indicate statistical significance at the 10%, 5%, and 1% significance level respectively; t-statistics in parenthesis on the first-stage results (dependent variable AV_SUST); z-statistics in parenthesis on the IV-GMM results (dependent variable LnCOMP).

The second sensitivity testing involved propensity score-matching estimation of Model (1) following the process described by Caliendo and Kopeinig (2008) and Hasan et al. (2020). As we discussed previously in the descriptive analysis section, we ranked firms based on their annual AV_SUST score and the top-third quartile firms are characterized as the treatment group and the bottom-first quartile firms are the control group. For the treatment group of firms, we assigned a dummy variable HIGH_SUST equals to one (1) and zero (0) for the control group. In order to create the propensity score, we followed Hasan et al. (2020) and ran a probit regression having HIGH_SUST as the dependent variable, and the rest of the controls, as depicted in Model (1), except the country and year dummies, were the independent variables. Afterward, we matched (without replacement) each treatment firm in a given year with a unique control firm in the same year based on a difference of the predicted scores between the treatment group and the control group up to 1%. This procedure produced 8624 matched pairs where 4760 have established a sustainability committee and 3864 do not. Evidence is presented in Table 6.7, and as we see HIGH_SUST produced negative and significant coefficients on the full sample estimation and for those firms with a voluntary sustainability committee, thus rejecting again H1

Table 6.7 Propensity-score matching results (GLS random effects)

Variables	Full sample	SUST_COM = 1	SUST_COM = 0
Constant	14.877***	15.685***	15.744***
	(11.47)	(8.05)	(7.26)
High_AV_SUST	-0.014***	-0.021***	-0.001
	(-4.93)	(-3.15)	(-1.21)
SIZE	0.009**	0.019*	0.004
	(1.96)	(2.31)	(1.38)
LEV	-0.340***	-0.267***	-0.511***
	(-4.83)	(-2.80)	(-3.43)
ROA	-0.313***	-0.281**	-0.468***
	(-3.66)	(-2.19)	(-2.73)
GROWTH	0.002	0.002	0.001
	(1.54)	(0.96)	(0.52)
BDSIZE	0.040***	0.037***	0.024***
	(8.19)	(6.69)	(4.08)
LISTED	0.005	0.006	0.004
	(0.54)	(0.63)	(0.18)
R^2	0.174	0.256	0.166
Wald-x^2	26.22***	13.88***	10.07***
Observations	8624	4760	3864

Note: *, **, *** indicate statistical significance at the 10%, 5%, and 1% significance level respectively; z-statistics in parenthesis (dependent variable LnCOMP).

and H2, supporting the main inferences and conclusions drawn from Table 6.4.

In addition, we controlled for the possible bidirectional association between executive compensation and sustainability performance, following the arguments and evidence by Callan and Thomas (2014) and Al-Shaer and Zaman (2019). For this reason, we estimated a system of two equations using seemingly unrelated regression (SUR) having AV_SUST as the dependent variable and LnCOMP as the independent variable, and vice versa, in order to control for the concurrent determination of those variables. Empirical evidence is presented in Table 6.8, and as we see, LnCOMP has a negative impact on AV_SUST (-1.020, $p <$ 0.001) and at the same time AV_SUST impacts negatively on LnCOMP (-0.005, $p < 0.001$). Thus, there is a negative and significant bidirectional association between those variables. Also, the Breusch-Pagan test of independence is highly significant, indicating that the implementation

Table 6.8 SUR simultaneous equation results on the impact of AV_SUST on LnCOMP

Variables	Full model		
Equation 1 – Dep. Variable: AV_SUST	Coef.	z-stat	P>|z|
LnCOMP	−1.020***	−7.71	0.001
SIZE	−0.061	−0.83	0.406
LEV	−1.294*	−1.65	0.099
ROA	−1.590	−1.38	0.169
GROWTH	0.003**	2.21	0.027
BDSIZE	0.080*	1.73	0.084
LISTED	0.019*	1.80	0.070
Constant	7.385***	2.83	0.001
R-sq	0.180		
Chi² (*p*-value)	68.15*** (0.001)		
Equation 2 – Dep. Variable: LnCOMP	Coef.	z-stat	P>|z|
AV_SUST	−0.005***	−7.71	0.001
SIZE	0.005	0.95	0.344
LEV	−0.313***	−5.66	0.001
ROA	−0.381***	−4.68	0.001
GROWTH	0.004***	4.36	0.001
BDSIZE	0.031***	9.65	0.001
LISTED	0.006	0.84	0.401
Constant	15.69***	13.27	0.001
R-sq	0.132		
Chi² (*p*-value)	212.34*** (0.001)		
Breusch-Pagan test of independence	14.87***		
Chi² (*p*-value)	(0.001)		

Note: *, **, *** indicate statistical significance at the 10%, 5%, and 1% significance level respectively.

of the SUR method is more efficient than the separate estimation of the two equations.

Furthermore, Model (1) was re-estimated after substituting the average sustainability performance (AV_SUST) with the first principal component (using PCA analysis) from the nine sub-scores (SUST_PCA) utilizing the orthogonal method of extraction and particularly Varimax rotation. Untabulated results corroborated evidence in Table 6.4 documenting a negative impact of sustainability performance factor on executive compensation and especially for firms with sustainability committees. In addition, following Karim et al. (2018) we separated total compensation into cash and equity-based compensation and re-estimated Model (1), but results remain qualitatively similar. Also, following Cai et al. (2011) and Callan and Thomas (2014), we included annual differences of executive compensation and sustainability performance, one- and two-year lags of AV_SUST, and also controlled for the nonlinear impact of firm size on executive compensation by including a squared term of SIZE on Model (1). Empirical results remained qualitatively unchanged from those modifications relative to those in Table 6.4.

Finally, following evidence by Francoeur et al. (2017), we controlled for the impact of the firm's legal origin on the association between compensation and sustainability performance. Relative literature by La Porta, Lopez-de-Silanes, Shleifer, and Vishny (1998, 1999) suggests that code law firms are more stakeholder oriented, and this may motivate managers to engage in sustainability-related activities (Kim et al., 2017). On the contrary, firms from common-law countries are more shareholder-oriented, having as top priority the protection of investor rights, and this fact creates less incentives for managers to engage in sustainability-related activities. Model (1) was re-estimated after separating firms based on the legal origin of the country they are registered. Untabulated results indicated that sustainability performance has a negative and significant impact on executive compensation for both common and code law firms, so legal origin does not seem to have a differential impact on the main conclusions of our study.

Conclusions

We responded to call for more research in the discipline of corporate sustainability and compensation made by Velte (2019) Winschel and Stawinoga (2019) Al-Shaer and Zaman (2019), and Flammer et al. (2019), and so we tried to extend current literature on this topic.

The empirical findings corroborated the conflict-resolution hypothesis (Brekke & Nyborg, 2008; Francoeur et al., 2017) since we documented a negative and significant impact of sustainability performance on executive compensation. Moreover, this negative association is significantly manifested within firms characterized as having a more strategic focus toward sustainability performance through the establishment of a voluntary sustainability committee. Finally, the examination of social and environmental performance sub-scores proved to have a differential impact on executive compensation. Specifically, environmental innovation score (EN_INNOV) and community score (COMM) proved to have a negative impact on executive compensation but only for firms with sustainability committees, while on the contrary product responsibility score (PROD) and workforce scores (WORK) had a negative and significant impact on compensation only for the subgroup of firms without a sustainability committee.

The evidence of this study is likely to be of interest to corporations, investors, and regulators. Corporations and board of directors need to take into consideration the association between sustainability strategies and executive compensation in order to sufficiently incorporate such targets on their operations. Also, the insignificant impact of sustainability performance on compensation for firms without CSR committees may lead such firms to incorporate such committees on their board structures as a mechanism to deal with potential agency problems and better align and control managerial behavior. Similarly, boards could explicitly embrace the notion that sustainability performance remains a significant indicator of executives' fiduciary duties.

Also, investors could consider the findings of this study as a useful indication of lower agency conflicts and higher stakeholder orientation of sustainable firms. Managers in such firms could act as stewards focusing not only on shareholders' interests. This could decrease information asymmetries and firm risk or enhance financial transparency, leading to significant corporate growth in the future. Finally, regulators can promote the creation of sustainability committees so as to align sustainable strategies and performance with compensation. Nevertheless, future research can extend the findings of the current study by examining more extensively the moderating impact of other governance mechanisms relating to board structure, board committees, and ownership concentration on the association between executive compensation and sustainability performance. Also, it will be interesting to examine in more detail the association of compensation to the specific environmental and social performance scores, as those seem to have differential impact on the issue on hand.

References

Adams, R. (2003). *What do boards do? Board committee structures, ownership and firm performance* (Working paper). New York: Federal Reserve Bank of New York.

Adams, R., Ragunathan, B., & Tumarkin, R. (2016). *Death by committee? An analysis of delegation in corporate boards* (Working paper). University of New South Wales, Sydney, Australia.

Alam, Z., Chen, M., Giccotello, C., & Ryan, H. (2014). Does the location of directors matter? Information acquisition and board decisions. *Journal of Financial and Quantitative Analysis, 49*(1), 131–164.

Al-Shaer, H., & Zaman, M. (2019). CEO compensation and sustainability reporting assurance: Evidence from the UK. *Journal of Business Ethics, 158*, 233–252.

Barnea, A., & Rubin, A. (2010). Corporate social responsibility as a conflict between shareholders. *Journal of Business Ethics, 97*, 71–86.

Baum, C. F. (2006). *An introduction to econometrics using Stata.* College Station, TX: Stata Press Books, StataCorp LP.

Beck, D., Friedl, G., & Schäfer, P. (2020). Executive compensation in Germany. *Journal of Business Economics, 90*, 787–824.

Berle, A. A., & Means, G. C. (1932). *The modern corporation and private property.* New York: The Macmillan Company.

Berrone, P., & Gomez-Mejia, L. R. (2009). Environmental performance and executive compensation: An integrated agency-institutional perspective. *Academy of Management Journal, 52*(1), 103–126.

Brekke, K. A., & Nyborg, K. (2008). Attracting responsible employees: Green production as labor market screening. *Resource and Energy Economics, 30*(4), 509–526.

Brockett, A., & Rezaee, Z. (2012). *Corporate sustainability: Integrating performance and reporting.* Hoboken, NJ: John Wiley and Sons Inc.

Cai, Y., Jo, H., & Pan, C. (2011). Vice or virtue? The impact of corporate social responsibility on executive compensation. *Journal of Business Ethics, 104*, 159–173.

Caliendo, M., & Kopeinig, S. (2008). Some practical guidance for the implementation of propensity score matching. *Journal of Economic Surveys, 22*(1), 31–72.

Callan, S. J., & Thomas, J. M. (2014). Relating CEO compensation to social performance and financial performance: Does the measure of compensation matter? *Corporate Social Responsibility and Environmental Management, 21*, 202–227.

Camilleri, M. A. (2017). *Corporate sustainability, social responsibility and environmental management: An introduction to theory and practice with case studies.* Cham Switzerland: Springer International Publishing AG.

Chang, R.-D., Zuo, J., Zhao, Z.-Y., Zillante, G., Gan, X.-L., & Soebarto, V. (2017). Evolving theories of sustainability and firms: History, future directions and implications for renewable energy research. *Renewable and Sustainable Energy Reviews, 72*, 48–56.

Chen, K., & Wu, A. (2016). *The structure of board committees* (Working paper 17–032). Harvard Business School.

Cordeiro, J. J., & Sarkis, J. (2008). Does explicit contracting effectively link CEO compensation to environmental performance? *Business Strategy and the Environment, 17*(5), 304–317.

Croci, E., Gonenc, J., & Ozkan, N. (2012). CEO compensation, family control and institutional investors in continental Europe. *Journal of Banking and Finance, 36*, 3318–3335.

EU. (2014). *Non-financial reporting.* Retrieved January 2020, from http://ec.europa.eu/internal_market/accounting/nonfinancial_reporting/index_en.htm.

Fama, E., & Jensen, M. C. (1983). Separation of ownership and control. *Journal of Law and Economics, 26*(2), 301–325.

Flammer, C., Hong, B., & Minor, D. (2019). Corporate governance and the rise of integrating corporate social responsibility criteria in executive compensation: Effectiveness and implications for firm outcomes. *Strategic Management Journal, 40*, 1097–1122.

Francoeur, C., Melis, A., Gaia, S., & Aresu, S. (2017). Green or greed? An alternative look at CEO compensation and corporate environmental commitment. *Journal of Business Ethics, 140*, 439–453.

Frydman, C., & Saks, R. E. (2010). Executive compensation: A new view from a long-term perspective, 1936–2005. *Review of Financial Studies, 23*(5), 2099–2138.

Gabaix, X., & Landier, A. (2008). Why has CEO pay increased so much? *Quarterly Journal of Economics, 123*(1), 49–100.

Hasan, I., Hoi, C.-K., Wu, Q., & Zhang, H. (2020). Is social capital associated with corporate innovation? Evidence from publicly listed firms in the US. *Journal of Corporate Finance, 62*, 101623.

Hill, C., & Jones, T. (1992). Stakeholder-agency theory. *Journal of Management Studies, 29*(1), 131–154.

Hoi, C. K., Wu, Q., & Zhang, H. (2019). Does social capital mitigate agency problems? Evidence from chief executive officer (CEO) compensation. *Journal of Financial Economics, 133*, 498–519.

Hong, B., Li, Z., & Minor, D. (2016). Corporate governance and executive compensation for corporate social responsibility. *Journal of Business Ethics, 136*, 199–213.

Jensen, M., & Meckling, W. (1976). Theory of the firm: Managerial behavior, agency costs and ownership structure. *Journal of Financial Economics, 3*, 305–350.

Kang, J. (2017). Unobservable CEO characteristics and CEO compensation as correlated determinants of CSP. *Business and Society, 56*(3), 419–453.

Karim, K., Lee, E., & Suh, S. (2018). Corporate social responsibility and CEO compensation structure. *Advances in Accounting, 40*, 27–41.

Kim, H., Park, K., & Ryu, D. (2017). Corporate environmental responsibility: A legal origin perspective. *Journal of Business Ethics, 140*, 381–402.

Kock, C. J., Santaló, J., & Diestre, L. (2012). Corporate governance and the environment: What type of governance creates greener companies? *Journal of Management Studies, 49*(3), 492–514.

La Porta, R., Lopez-de-Silanes, F., Shleifer, A., & Vishny, R. (1998). Law and finance. *Journal of Political Economy, 106*, 1113–1155.

La Porta, R., Lopez-de-Silanes, F., Shleifer, A., & Vishny, R. (1999). The quality of government. *Journal of Law Economics and Organization, 15*, 222–279.

Mattingly, J., & Berman, S. (2006). Measurement of corporate social action: Discovering taxonomy in the Kinder Lydenburg Domini ratings data. *Business and Society, 45*(1), 20–44.

Milbourn, T. (2003). CEO reputation and stock-based compensation. *Journal of Financial Economics, 68*(2), 233–262.

Moriarty, J. (2009). How much compensation can CEOs permissibly accept? *Business Ethics Quarterly, 19*(2), 235–250.

Ozkan, N. (2011). CEO compensation and firm performance: An empirical investigation of UK panel data. *European Financial Management, 17*, 260–285.

Reeb, D., & Upadhyay, A. (2010). Subordinate board structures. *Journal of Corporate Finance, 16*(4), 469–486.

Rekker, S. A. C., Benson, K. L., & Faff, R. W. (2014). Corporate social responsibility, and CEO compensation revisited: Do disaggregation, market stress, gender matter? *Journal of Economics and Business, 72,* 84–103.

Riahi-Belkaoui, A. (1992). Executive compensation, organizational effectiveness, social performance and firm performance: An empirical investigation. *Journal of Business Finance and Accounting, 19*(1), 25–38.

Schultz, F., Castelló, I., & Morsing, M. (2013). The construction of corporate social responsibility in network societies: A communication view. *Journal of Business Ethics, 115,* 681–692.

Sheikh, M. F., Shah, S. Z. A., & Akbar, S. (2018). Firm performance, corporate governance and executive compensation in Pakistan. *Applied Economics, 50*(18), 2012–2027.

Suto, M., & Takehara, H. (2018). *Corporate social responsibility and corporate finance in Japan.* Singapore: Springer Nature.

United Nations Principles for Responsible Investment (UNPRI), 2012. United Nations Global Compact LEAD. (2012, June). *Integrating ESG issues into executive pay: Guidance for investors and companies.* Retrieved from www.unglobalcompact.org/docs/issues_doc/lead/ESG_Executive_Pay.pdf.

Vafeas, N., & Vlittis, A. (2019). Board executive committees, board decisions and firm value. *Journal of Corporate Finance, 58,* 43–63.

van Essen, M., Heugens, P., Otten, J., & van Oosterhout, J. (2012). An institution-based view of executive compensation: A multilevel meta-analytic test. *Journal of International Business Studies, 43,* 396–423.

Velte, P. (2019). Do CEO incentives and characteristics influence corporate social responsibility (CSR) and vice versa? A literature review. *Social Responsibility Journal.* doi:10.1108/SRJ-04-2019-0145

Winschel, J., & Stawinoga, M. (2019). Determinants and effects of sustainable CEO compensation: A structured literature review of empirical evidence. *Management Review Quarterly, 69,* 265–328.

Wintoki, M. B., Linck, J. S., & Netter, J. K. (2012). Endogeneity and the dynamics of international corporate governance. *Journal of Financial Economics, 105*(3), 581–606.

7 Corporate Governance and Company Leadership During a Time of Crisis

Duties, Responsibilities, and Liabilities of Directors in the UK

Niki Alexandrou

Corporate Governance Defined

Corporate governance has become a topic of broad public interest as governments have stepped up their support for corporates in times of crisis, while at the same time the power of institutional investors has increased and the impact of the business of corporates on society has grown. Yet, ideas about how corporates should be governed and whose interests they should have regard to vary widely. There is disagreement, for example, on such basic matters as the purpose of the corporate, the interests that it should have regard to, and the proper way to measure corporate performance. This chapter will address prevalent definitions, practices, and issues from a UK perspective.

Corporate governance is concerned with the supervisory oversight of a company or other organization within a framework of checks and balances, primarily in the areas of (i) responsible decision-making, (ii) effective internal control and risk management systems, (ii) accurate and timely disclosures, and (iv) stakeholder engagement. The purpose of corporate governance is to facilitate effective, entrepreneurial, and prudent management that can deliver the long-term success of the company. These areas of focus are to be distinguished from the day-to-day management of the business of a company carried out by the executive director team.

The OECD Principles of Corporate Governance, first published in 1999, state:

> Corporate governance involves a set of relationships between a company's management, its board, its shareholders and other stakeholders. Corporate governance also provides the structure through which the objectives of the company are set, and the means of attaining those objectives and monitoring performance are determined.
>
> (OECD, 1999)

DOI: 10.4324/9781003152750-9

In 2015, an updated version of these Principles was endorsed by the OECD Council and the G20 Leaders Summit (OECD, 2015). The OECD Principles have since become the international benchmark.

Since their inception, corporate governance rules have provided guidance to those who have a role in the process of developing good corporate governance and have supported policymakers in evaluating and improving the legal, regulatory, and institutional framework within which companies operate. Such rules are widely claimed to influence the efficient and effective operation of a company, to assist in ensuring transparency, and to support decision makers (particularly directors) to achieve specific goals and objectives, such as the long-term success of the company and delivery of sustainable value to its shareholders. Effective corporate governance processes also mitigate risks (such as the risks of corporate failure, damage to reputation or market failing).

However, the past few years have highlighted shortcomings in the area of corporate governance. A review of the financial crisis of 2008, for example, has revealed that significant weaknesses in the corporate governance of financial institutions played a role in the crisis (European Commission, 2012). Over time, corporate governance rules have evolved, been adapted, and broadened to take account of developments in the financial sphere and capital markets, the results of sociological studies on leadership and sustainability, and forces such as climate change, income inequality, digitalization, and rising populism throughout the world.

More recently, the Covid crisis has put whole industries under review by local governments discussing policies on how best to support them. With additional government support comes higher regulation; we are thus seeing regulators raising environmental standards and human rights to the level of strategic priority, with companies facing regulatory fines if they fail to deliver. Since 2008, there have been over 170 Environmental, Social, and Governance (ESG) related regulatory measures proposed globally – more than the previous six years combined (Medlock, 2020). This is reflective of a global trend toward greater ESG awareness and rising consumer pressure on companies and policymakers to ensure high standards in respect of their customers, employees, and the planet (Schmid, Gehra, Hefter, Seiler, & Meier, 2020). Many sets of rules on corporate governance now call for efforts to better align the activities of corporates with society's interest in building a more inclusive, equitable, and sustainable economy (Paine & Srinivasan, 2019).

As interest in sustainability increases, with environmental and social issues becoming more prominent during the Covid crisis, ESG issues now play an increasingly important role in activist investing. Since 2008 there has been a steady insurgence of activist shareholders using their equity stake in a corporate to put pressure on its management and influence how the company is run. Lipton (2020) reports that there are currently more than 100 activist hedge funds in operation with more than

US$100 billion of assets under management. As Gottfried and Dona-hue (2020) observe the Covid crisis likely allowed some to accumulate equity positions at advantageous levels, and it seems, as the crisis begins to recede, activism will return just as it did after the 2008 financial crisis.

During the Covid crisis we have seen several hedge funds beginning to focus on ESG issues. Reuters (2020) reports on one such example, that of activist investor Gianluca Ferrari, who is reportedly setting up a fund in 2021 to target companies lagging on ESG issues. The move follows strong growth in assets at traditional money managers, which seek to invest in companies with good performance on issues from carbon emissions and water usage to boardroom diversity. That left a gap for activist managers to seek for change at weaker companies in order to bring about more sustainable returns and share price gains. It is therefore critical that boards do not let their ESG standards slide and that they observe good practices in these areas (Breitinger, 2017).

In the UK, the first version of the Corporate Governance Code was published in 1992 by the Cadbury Committee. The latest version of the UK Corporate Governance Code (the *Code*) was published by the Financial Reporting Council in July 2018, and it remains the primary governance code in the UK (FRC, 2018). The Code applies to companies with a Premium listing of equity shares on the London Stock Exchange, regardless of whether they are incorporated in the UK or elsewhere. Other companies, such as those with a Standard listing of equity shares and companies admitted to trading on AIM, the London Stock Exchange's market for small and medium-size growth companies, may also choose to apply the Code or another available corporate governance code. The Code sets out good governance expectations in five key areas:

(a) Board leadership and company purpose.
(b) Division of responsibilities.
(c) Composition, succession and evaluation.
(d) Audit, risk and internal control.
(e) Remuneration.

In relation to each of these areas, the Code sets out a number of principles that emphasize the value of good corporate governance to long-term sustainable success, followed by more detailed provisions. The Code is to be applied on a "comply or explain" basis, so it does not set out a set of rigid rules. Full compliance with the Code is not mandatory, but where a company does not comply, it must disclose this fact in its annual report and provide a clear and meaningful explanation of its reasons for noncompliance.

As important as these matters may be, this chapter will focus principally on companies to which the Code applies and on the statutory rules behind the leadership principles of the Code (Section A – Leadership).

According to Section 1(A) of the Code: "A successful company is led by an effective and entrepreneurial board, whose role is to promote the long-term sustainable success of the company, generating value for shareholders and contributing to wider society." The principles set out in Section 1(A) highlight the board's responsibility to act, primarily, in the best interests of the company as a whole, distinct entity, and not in the interests of any particular part of its members – such as its shareholders, creditors, or any other category of stakeholders. This section further acknowledges that the company has obligation to generate value for its shareholders and contribute to the wider society.

Leadership Defined

The issue of what constitutes good leadership of a corporate is particularly contentious, with some authorities and markets supporting traditional models of corporate leadership prioritizing policies which aim at maximizing financial returns, and others giving primacy to a modern style of leadership prioritizing sustainability, innovation, growth, CSR, and stakeholder engagement.

The complex and evolving nature of leadership means that there is no universal definition. The word "leadership" has its origins in the Anglo-Saxon word for "path" or "road", suggesting that a leader is one who walks ahead of their team members or shows the way to fellow travelers (De Vries, 2006). This theme of leaders paving the way for others and making the achievement of common goals possible, is frequently used as a primary defining characteristic of leadership. However, in the past 20 years, models of leadership have evolved along with society's understanding of what leadership entails. These days, leadership is less about decisive action and precise design and more about putting together different solutions and approaches while maintaining a future-oriented perspective (Grayson, Coulter, & Lee, 2018).

Out of the main leadership theories prevalent among academics and researchers in the last 20 years, the high-impact leadership theory stands out. In defining high-impact leadership, this chapter draws extensively on the Cambridge Impact Leadership Model. "Informed by CISL's work with over 8,000 leaders across the world", the model describes the leadership needed in order to deliver value for business, society and the environment. The model shows that developing leadership across business results in leading change for a sustainable economy. Organizations that "cultivate purposeful, reflective leadership at all levels", as well as "embrace diverse and complementary strengths and approaches will enable leaders to align commercial success with the delivery of positive social and environmental outcomes" (CISL, 2018).

Given the systemic pressures around the world, leadership can no longer be viewed as the preserve of just a few individuals. Global trends and complex systems can have a significant impact on leadership. The rapid spread of globalization means that nations and individuals are more connected than ever before, and this has resulted in social systems that grow in increasingly complex ways. A single post on sexual harassment published on social media one day can spread into hundreds of local and international campaigns within weeks; and the nonperformance of a single collateralized bond can lead to the collapse of the entire housing markets of several nations within months. Similarly, policy changes, major technological advancements, and international trade also stimulate the development of new systems and ways of organizing business. The relationships between systems are more complex than before, and this calls for leaders who are capable of what leadership and organizational experts call "systems thinking"; viewing systems from a broad perspective that include seeing overall structures, patterns, and cycles in systems, rather than seeing only specific events in the system (Arnold & Wade, 2015).

The importance of systems thinking is particularly relevant when considering the VUCA (volatile, uncertain, complex, and ambiguous) nature of the world and how it affects business. The term "VUCA" originated in the military to describe the *volatility, uncertainty, complexity*, and *ambiguity* of the global context following the Cold War. Since then, the term has been used across a wide range of disciplines (including risk management, strategic thinking and leadership) to characterize the current environment and the leadership required to navigate it successfully (Giles, 2018).

The financial crisis of 2008 and the Covid crisis of 2020 have served to bring to the surface the many socioeconomic challenges faced by societies, companies, and organizations across the world (Schnick, Hobson, & Ibisch, 2017). In terms of leadership at the business level, VUCA describes the types of challenges that directors aiming to be high-impact leaders need to consider when reconsidering their approach to leadership. Directors often need to make decisions about complex, intertwined, systemic problems with no precedent on which to rely.

As businesses become more interconnected and dependent on others, they need to engage with an increasingly diverse group of stakeholders. Producers of primary goods, policymakers, investors, global clients, and nongovernmental organizations operating in a related industry could all have a role to play in the development of a particular business. Professor R. Edward Freeman (1984), the acknowledged father of the stakeholder approach, defines a stakeholder as "any group or individual who can affect or is affected by the achievement of the organisation's objectives". Friedman and Miles (2006) argue that "the organization itself should be thought of as a grouping of stakeholders and the purpose of the organization should be to manage their interests, needs and viewpoints". Nurturing and maintaining good relationships with both internal stakeholders (such as the board of directors, managers, employees and other members of the workforce) and external stakeholders (such as shareholders, the national government, the financial community, the local community, nongovernmental organizations, suppliers, partners and trade associations) have thus become of primary importance to the sustainability and growth of a business.

Stakeholder engagement during a time of financial distress can be a useful tool for directors to (i) understand and appreciate the challenges around them from different perspectives; (ii) make informed decisions on the basis of real-time data and needs; and (iii) manage risks. For high-impact leaders, innovation is also important when responding to the considerable challenges and opportunities that arise in the modern business environment. According to Jack Welch, former CEO of General Electric, "When the rate of change inside an institution becomes slower than the rate of change outside, the end is in sight. The only question is when." In other words, innovation can be a key factor not only in seizing opportunities for businesses but also in ensuring the long-term viability of a business.

Thinking like a high-impact leader means honing your leadership mindset. Developing the mindset necessary for leading change in complex systems (through coaching or otherwise) involves four main thinking skills: adopting a system thinking approach; understanding the VUCA nature of the world and its complications; being able to adapt and evolve thinking; and establishing short-term priorities and decisions with a view to the long term (CISL, 2018). As a result, directors called upon to make decisions must first consciously engage with themselves and develop their leadership skills. They also need to take into account an array of matters that could potentially have an impact on the well-being of the company and its business.

This chapter will approach leadership at the systemic and organizational (macro) level only through the lens of high-impact organizational leadership (organizations taking a leading role in society and leading an organization within the wider business sector). The chapter will discuss some of the challenges that directors, as leaders of corporates, are facing in the decision-making process, in the context of corporate governance rules and director's duties and liabilities under UK law. It will *not* deal with the director's decision-making process at the level of leadership development (how organizations align their internal priorities to develop leaders) or leaders developing organizations (leadership within a team).

Duties and Responsibilities of Directors

In the UK, the main statutory framework surrounding the duties of directors of public and private companies, and which incorporates certain corporate governance principles, is primarily set out in

(a) the Companies Act 2006 (**CA 2006**), which governs all companies registered in the UK; and
(b) the Insolvency Act 1986 (**IA 1986**), which governs company insolvency and winding up (including the winding up of companies that are solvent).

Under the CA 2006, directors of UK companies owe general statutory duties to

(a) act within the powers conferred by the company's constitution and only exercise powers for the purposes for which they are conferred;
(b) promote the success of the company for the benefit of its members (shareholders) as a whole;
(c) exercise independent judgment;
(d) exercise reasonable care, skill and diligence;
(e) avoid conflicts of interest;
(f) not accept benefits from third parties; and
(g) declare interests in (proposed) transactions or arrangements with the company.

The Introduction to the Code includes a statement specifying that nothing in it overrides or is intended as an interpretation of the statutory statement of directors' duties in the CA 2006 (FRC, 2018).

Directors also have potential liability under other legislation and common law (with many such claims overlapping with the above). For example, they could be disqualified as a director under the Directors Disqualification Act 1986 and may be ordered to pay compensation where their conduct has caused loss to creditors, including to particular creditors or classes of creditors.

For the purposes of this chapter, we will focus on directors' duties and potential liabilities in relation to companies in financial difficulty, particularly liability for failure to promote the success of the company and for wrongful trading, under

(a) section 172 CA 2006 (section 172 CA) (duty to promote the success of the company); and
(b) section 214 IA 1986 (section 214 IA) (wrongful trading provisions).

This chapter will not expressly address other statutory duties under the CA 2006 or the IA 1986 or other common law duties and will not address rules applicable in insolvency scenarios. The Companies (Miscellaneous Reporting) Regulations 2018 introduced new reporting requirements for financial years starting on or after 1 January 2019 on executive pay, corporate governance arrangements, and how directors are having regard to the matters in section 172(1) (a) to (f) CA 2006. As a result, as far as directors' duty and stakeholder engagement is concerned:

(a) large companies (public, quoted, and private) must include a statement, as part of their strategic report, describing how directors have had regard to the matters in section 172(1)(a) to (f) CA 2006. This means that they must report on how their directors have fulfilled their duty to promote the success of the company for the benefit of its members as a whole, having had regard (among other matters) to a number of considerations (including stakeholder considerations such as the interests of employees and the impact of the company's operations on the community and environment);

(b) companies with more than 250 UK employees must include a statement, as part of their directors' report, summarizing how directors have engaged with employees, how they have had regard to employee interests and the effect of that regard, including on the principal decisions taken by the company in the financial year being reported on; and

(c) large companies must include a statement, as part of their directors' report, summarizing how directors have had regard to the need to foster the company's business relationships with suppliers, customers and others, and the effect of that regard, including on the principal decisions taken by the company in the financial year being reported on.

The law does not distinguish between the duties and liabilities of executive and nonexecutive directors or shadow directors (broadly interpreted as people in accordance with whose directions or instructions the directors of the company are accustomed to act). All members of the board owe the same duties to the company. Each director owes their duties individually and must exercise reasonable care, skill, and diligence. In the exercise of those duties (and while the company is solvent), the directors must act in the way they consider in good faith would be most likely to promote the success of the company for the benefit of its members as a whole (see further below). In practice, a company's members are the general body of shareholders, and the shareholders thus generally have the power to ratify a breach of fiduciary duty by the directors. Upon the company becoming insolvent (or nearing insolvency or being threatened with insolvency), there are further interests to which directors should have regard. While their statutory duties are still owed to the company, directors in those situations must also consider the interests of the creditors of the company.

The Duty to Promote the Success of the Company

Section 172 CA requires a director "to act in the way he considers, in good faith, would be most likely to promote the success of the company for the benefit of its members as a whole". Courts and policymakers alike have acknowledged that company directors are in control of an entrepreneurial venture and that a degree of commercial risk-taking is a necessary part of earning a sufficient return on the capital invested (Daniels v Anderson, 1995).

However, in exercising this duty, directors must have regard to at least six factors set out in the CA 2006 which aim to import a strong notion of CSR into decision-making. These factors are, broadly,

(a) the likely long-term consequences of the decision;
(b) the interests of employees;
(c) the need to foster relationships with suppliers, customers, and others;
(d) the impact of the company's operations on the community and the environment;
(e) the desirability of the company maintaining a reputation for high standards of business conduct; and
(f) the need to act fairly as between the members of the company.

This is not an exhaustive list, and the six factors themselves are subsidiary to the overall duty to promote the success of the company. It should be noted that although there are other stakeholders referred to in section 172 CA, the duty to promote the success of the company is owed directly to the company and not to these additional stakeholders. As a result, shareholders and other third parties will normally only have a cause of action against the company, not against individual directors.

In looking at whether a director has fulfilled her section 172 CA duty, a 2008 case confirmed that the test is a subjective one – the question is whether the director honestly believed that her act or omission was in the interests of the company and the court will not consider that there has been a breach of the duty simply because, in the court's opinion, the particular exercise of the power was not to promote the success of the company. However, in that case the court noted that there is also an objective element – a breach will have occurred if it is established that the relevant exercise of the power is one which could not be considered by any reasonable director to be in the interests of the company (Re Southern Counties fresh Foods Limited, 2008). This view was supported by the comments of the High Court judge in the more recent *Fairford Water Ski Club* v Cohoon case (2020).

Duty to Creditors

The duty imposed by section 172 CA is displaced when the company nears insolvency or is threatened by insolvency – in which case directors have an obligation to have regard to the interests of creditors. The question as to what point the duty to creditors applies is critical, and directors need to be aware of it when taking decisions during a time of crisis. This matter was considered in a Court of Appeal decision, in the *LLC* v *Sequana* case (2019).

In the *Sequana* case, Lord Justice David Richards, with whom the other judges in the Court of Appeal agreed, looked at the various English and

Commonwealth authorities which are not consistent and use a variety of phrases to describe the appropriate test. He identified four potential answers:

(a) when the company is actually insolvent, on a cash flow or balance sheet basis;
(b) when the company is on the verge of insolvency or approaching insolvency;
(c) when the company is or is likely to become insolvent; or
(d) where there is a real, as opposed to a remote, risk of insolvency.

Lord Justice Richards took the view that there are differences in substance between these potential answers, and overall he favored the test in (c). In his view, the trigger as to when directors should start to consider the interests of creditors is when they know, or should know, that their company is or is likely to become insolvent, and in this context, "likely" means probable. He went on to say that where directors know or ought to know that the company is presently and actually insolvent, then it is at that point that creditors' interests should be treated as paramount.

Wrongful Trading Provisions

Interests of creditors are protected where a company is in financial distress by the English law regime against wrongful trading (under Section 214 IA 1986). Under Section 214 IA, if, in the course of an insolvent winding up or insolvent administration of a company, it appears that a person who is, or was, a director of the company knew or ought to have concluded at some point before the commencement of the liquidation or administration that there was *no reasonable prospect that the company would avoid going into insolvent liquidation or insolvent administration*, the liquidator or administrator of the company can seek a court declaration that the director make a contribution to the company's assets. Again, the standard of knowledge is to be applied having regard to a subjective and an objective test:

(a) the general knowledge, skill, and experience that may reasonably be expected of a person in the person's position; and
(b) the general knowledge, skill, and experience that that person has.

Under this test, directors are at risk of personal liability for wrongful trading at any time after they knew or ought to have known that the company could not avoid insolvent liquidation or insolvent administration. Identifying the precise point at which the financial position of the company means that insolvent liquidation or insolvent administration is effectively inevitable and the point at which the directors should have realized that this is the case is difficult in practice – for example, during periods of negotiation with creditors, identifying the point at which agreement may not be reached.

Liability only arises under section 214 IA if it is shown that the company is worse off as a result of the continuation of trading (Re Marini Ltd, 2003). Section 214(3) IA goes on to affirm that the court will not make an order for wrongful trading if, knowing there was no reasonable prospect that the company would avoid going into insolvent liquidation or insolvent administration, the director took every step with a view to minimizing the potential loss to the company's creditors as he ought to have taken.

The high risk of potential liabilities for directors of companies in financial difficulties is a source of an increasing number of mandates to restructuring advisors and legal counsels. As soon as directors are aware that a company is in financial difficulty, it is essential that they seek external advice independent of the company's advisers.

Directors' Liability

If directors breach their duties to the company, they may be personally liable to compensate the company for losses caused. They may also have to account for any profits made and pass those to the company, and they may have to restore company property. In addition, depending on the circumstances, the company may be able to terminate any contracts with, or involving, the director which have been entered into. Directors may also be removed from office, disqualified from acting as a director, and incur liabilities under other statutory and regulatory regimes as a result.

When the CA 2006 came into effect, it was thought possible that the risk of shareholder litigation against directors would increase because of the uncertainty in relation to how the statutory duty provisions would be interpreted, particularly in view of the possibility of shareholders suing directors in the company's name to recover loss that the company suffers as a result of the directors' negligence, default, breach of duty, or breach of trust. This right of action under the CA 2006, known as a "derivative claim", enables shareholders to bring claims if the company suffers loss as a result of the directors' negligence, default, breach of duty, or breach of trust.

Where shareholders do not want to bring proceedings against directors, they may choose to ratify breaches of directors' duties by ordinary resolution (although the votes of the relevant director and any connected person on that resolution must be disregarded). However, ratification is not always possible, including if the relevant act is unlawful or constitutes a fraud on the minority or on the company's creditors. For example, this might be because the conduct involves the payment of an unlawful dividend.

Under the CA 2006, if proceedings for negligence, default, breach of duty, or breach of trust are brought against a director, the court may relieve her, either wholly or partly, from her liability on such terms as the court thinks fit if it appears to the court that

(a) the director is, or may be, liable but has acted honestly and reasonably; and
(b) having regard to all the circumstances, the director ought fairly to be excused.

Measures Taken During the Covid Crisis

The director's potential personal liability for wrongful trading is often the trigger that leads to directors deciding to put a company into an insolvency process. The Covid crisis enhanced such risks and brought forward the need for some guidance for directors concerned that they could not be confident of companies avoiding insolvent liquidation due to restrictions on trading. In an unprecedented move by UK legislators, on 25 June 2020 the Corporate Insolvency and Governance Act (2020) (*CIGA*) received Royal Assent and temporarily limited the potential liability of directors for wrongful trading provisions under UK Insolvency Laws. Since the introduction of CIGA, similar measures have been introduced in other jurisdictions, including Australia and Singapore.

A key aim of the Act is to provide businesses with the flexibility and breathing space necessary to enable them to continue trading during the Covid crisis, and so the measures, some permanent and some temporary, are designed to help UK companies and other similar entities by easing the burden on businesses and helping them avoid insolvency during this period of economic uncertainty.

Under the initial temporary provisions (originally applicable from 1 March 2020 to 30 September 2020 – and then further extended to 30 April 2021, applicable to all companies (other than the excluded companies listed in the Schedules to the Act which include insurance companies, banks, public private partnership project companies and overseas companies)), in determining whether a director is liable to make a contribution to the assets of a company for wrongful trading, the courts had to "assume that the person is not responsible for any worsening of the financial position of the company or its creditors that occurs during the relevant period".

The Act, however, does not provide for a clear and blanket "suspension" of liability, and commentators are divided as to the extent of this protection. For instance, it seems unlikely that the court would continue to make that assumption if there is evidence that a director was responsible for losses in the Covid period as a result of fraud. There could also be compensation ordered for wrongful trading prior to, during, and after the Covid period, but where the liability would not include any worsening of the financial position or the company or its creditors during the Covid period.

Despite the debates on the precise scope of CIGA, it is widely acknowledged that the introduction of CIGA enabled businesses to continue to operate without creating additional risks for directors and encouraged companies to take advantage of the unprecedented financial support offered by the government to help support cash flow if the directors reasonably believed that doing so was in the best interests of the company and/or its creditors. Provided directors have properly evaluated and documented their decisions and they are reasonable in all the circumstances, the likelihood of liability for wrongful trading appears to be significantly reduced. While the changes to the wrongful trading provisions may provide some comfort to directors concerned about incurring additional credit or borrowing around this period, directors would still be expected to apply best practices. It should be anticipated that with the easing of the crisis, the risks of wrongful trading may increase as government support ceases to be available.

Good Practices (During a Crisis and Beyond)

There are several sources of guidance on good corporate governance and decision-making which are helpful for directors (including those issued by the Association of General Counsel and Company Secretaries of the FTSE 100, the ICSA Chartered Governance Institute and the Financial Regulation Council). The corporate governance and leadership principles referred to here would also be sensible points of reference for all directors looking to enrich their decision-making process pro-actively.

From a corporate governance and leadership perspective, to mitigate against risks, directors of companies in financial difficulty should, as a matter of good practice:

(c) identify their stakeholders, including their employees, suppliers, and other stakeholders, and keep records of how they have, for example, engaged with them to understand the issues to which they must have regard, so that they can report on these matters in their annual section 172(1) CA statement;

(d) hold regular full board meetings if the company is in financial difficulties and report the commercial decisions of the directors in full in the company's minutes;

(e) reach their commercial decisions at board meetings independently, on the basis of the financial and legal information and advice available to them;

(f) always have up-to-date financial information and be careful to monitor compliance with financial covenants contained in any arrangements with lenders. Directors should not wait for an event such as a creditor's claim, a winding up petition or administration application, or a failure to meet sales or cash flow forecasts to alert them to the fact the company is in financial difficulty;

(g) consider not only the company's balance sheet, and balance sheet solvency, but also the company's ability (current and expected) to pay its debts as they fall due: if the company cannot pay its debts as they fall due, or is likely to cease to be able to do so, this will increase the risk that a creditor may attempt to wind the company up: a liquidation may affect the likely realization proceeds achievable from the company's assets and thus its balance sheet solvency;

(h) take advice from an insolvency practitioner as soon as they are aware that there is no reasonable prospect of avoiding insolvent liquidation or insolvent administration, or fear that is the case;

(i) during a crisis, ensure that they monitor UK government advice that impacts their business and any new or amended UK government financial support that is made available. The best interests of the creditors of the company would be likely to be served by the company exploring the ability to obtain cash grants, loans, and other support from the government and its existing lenders. In the case of the Covid crisis in particular, directors ought to be formulating a plan for the exit from lockdown and general strategy going forward;

(j) at times of high scrutiny and difficult decision-making, refrain from entering into transactions that are not in the ordinary course of their business; minimize expenditure and outgoings and preserve cash as best as they can.

Case Studies

Introduction

In illustrating some of the main principles set out earlier, we will consider two case studies in particular. Each case study is based on a hypothetical (albeit perhaps common) scenario, and the approach to each is taken from the perspective of corporate governance, good leadership, and directors' duties under section 172 CA and section 214 IA. The legal analysis is illustrative only and shall by no means be interpreted as legal guidance or advice. Certain aspects of the legal analysis in each case derive from the views expressed in a recent FC publication by Andrew Thompson QC and Ben Griffiths of Erskine Chambers.

Case study 1: CJ is a director of a large UK company which manufactures and trades sports equipment. In recent months, the company has seen its profits slashed by 80%. This is primarily due to disruptions to their supply chain and factory operations caused by a pandemic affecting their country of operations. CJ has been serving as director for the last 12 years, she built this company and feels a great sense of duty towards shareholders, many of whom are her friends. She has a real vision for turning the company around with a new product line, and is hopeful that things will improve soon. Practically, CJ did not have much time to test this idea in the market and has little input from external stakeholders during the pandemic.

The company is currently in financial difficulty and struggling to pay the balance of an invoice for new equipment. The CFO of the company suggests that they prioritize this payment over all others, so that company's accounts can reflect revenues from such equipment (albeit prematurely). CJ is due to meet with the bank creditor of the company next month. The biggest loan of the company is due in a year's time and the company's bankers are anxious to ensure that the company will be able to meet its obligations. CJ cannot be certain. The latest balance sheet did not raise any immediate concerns but CJ foresees a likelihood that the company will not be able to meet interest payment obligations under existing financings by the end of the year. She can see how favorable accounts would be good news for everyone involved. She also suspects that the company may be in breach of financial covenants under these financings but did not have the opportunity to discuss this with the internal accountants yet.

CJ finds it difficult to assess the long-term effects on trading and scale of their financial risks (including the risk of ultimate insolvency), because the future is so uncertain. How should CJ behave? She usually bears the responsibility of all decisions made at board level so feels enormous pressure to put forward the right proposal for the future of the company.

(a) This is a common challenge for directors of businesses in financial distress, particularly where such directors feel personally vested in the company. During this period, CJ should focus on how to enhance corporate governance measures, particularly such measures dealing with:

i   Good decision-making and transparent procedures for reaching decisions at board level. CJ seems to bear the burden of decisions made at board level. It is the board responsibility to ensure that directors are adequately informed, appropriately qualified and impartial so that they can reach their commercial decisions at board meetings independently, on the basis of the financial and legal information and advice available to them. CJ's long engagement in his role could increase her sense of feeling personally vested in the company and could thus cloud her judgment. CJ should put conscious effort in maintaining a clear, impartial perspective based on facts. The board should also ensure that other directors are adequately impartial and all concerns are tabled and addressed accordingly.

ii   Closely monitoring financial performance of the company. CJ seems uncertain about the current position of the company and the likelihood of it being unable to meet its debt obligations as they fall due. She is also tempted to pursue questionable practices suggested by the company's CFO. Without taking into account the possibility of fraud, directors have the duty to question and always have up to date financial information and must ensure accurate, impartial financial reporting. Directors also need to be careful to monitor compliance with financial covenants contained in any financings of the company so that they are better placed to assess any risks. Decisions should not be made based solely on the company's balance sheet but also the company's ability (current and expected) to pay its debts as they fall due. If the company is likely to cease to be able to pay debts as they fall due, this will increase the risk that a creditor may attempt to wind the company up and may affect the likely realization proceeds achievable from the company's assets on liquidation.

iii Setting and aligning both short- and long-term goals and objectives; CJ has a vision for introducing a new product line but little feedback on such an idea. CJ should raise such issues at board level so that directors can address such areas and set specific, measurable goals, both short term and long term.

(b) From an organizational leadership perspective, a situation such as this would demand agile ways to adapt and develop in order to avoid insolvency. The question that every director is required to address in his or her role on a daily basis is "How can I use the tools that I have in my possession, to drive this company to long term success?" This question will now need to be examined with fresh insights and a growth mindset. In this exercise, directors should look to innovation and stakeholder engagement to support them in the decision-making process.

(c) CJ also seems to have limited input from external stakeholders during this time. To plan stakeholder engagement, directors will have to reexamine their engagement plan in light of latest developments. In identifying groups and people that are relevant to their business, they may now decide to include government agencies, medical suppliers and networks of support on which they have come to rely. *Business for Social Responsibility* (BSR, 2017) suggests four steps for planning stakeholder engagement: (i) identifying (ii) analyzing; (iii) mapping; and (iv) prioritizing (BSR, 2017).

(d) From a legal perspective, there is uncertainty as to when directors owe a duty to take into account creditors' interests under UK law. The potential liability would arise not from trading when the company is insolvent but from continuing to trade when there is no reasonable hope of restoring it to solvency. In a corporate rescue scenario, the company is technically insolvent at the time when its facilities are in default (and therefore payable on demand) and it enters into negotiations with its bankers. If all creditors were to demand repayment in full, the company would most likely be unable to repay. However, so long as there is a reasonable prospect of achieving a refinancing with the lenders under which the existing or new lenders will support the company, or an alternative source of funding can be negotiated, then the directors can properly continue to trade.

(e) If we were to apply the test in *LLC* v *Sequana* (2019), the directors would not be subject to the creditor duty unless they had concluded that insolvency is more likely than not. In a case of complete uncertainty, one might argue that the directors are not in a position to form any particular view, and thus cannot form such view. However, such an argument cannot be relied on safely. Uncertainty as to the future is rarely so complete that no view at all as to the scale of the risk of insolvency can be taken. In practice there is no precise point at which duties switch from being owed to creditors instead of shareholders. Rather, the directors would be best served to assume that the duties are owed to both stakeholder groups during that period of uncertainty.

(f) If directors remain reasonably confident that the company is not yet actually insolvent, they can behave as if insolvency is likely. Practically, this would mean focusing on the interests of the company as an entity and maximizing its assets, and refraining from distributions to shareholders. Adopting that precautionary approach in practice will protect creditors if things turn out badly. If things eventually turn out well and insolvency is avoided, their cautious strategy may even have enhanced the value of the company for shareholders and will not have harmed shareholders (save possibly by delaying their receipt of dividends).

Case study 2: DMC *is a company operating in hospitality and owning a large city hotel with 3 restaurants. The company has several core and noncore assets (primarily real estate) and low cash balances. In the last 5 years the company operated with low profit margins and limited growth. This year, the company was hit hard by the Covid crisis. During the crisis the company has scaled back operations, expenses and staffing and currently runs on a negative profit margin (–23%). Their industry peers were all affected in a similar way, however, a small minority of them opted to offer different services and divest noncore assets and have shifted their business models in anticipation of new trends in hospitality in the years ahead.*

Right before the Covid crisis, DMC were interested in developing their own line of bio fruit and vegetables for use in their restaurants as well as for trading for profit. DMC hold a permit to use a very large plot of land adjacent to one of their properties for these purposes and have secured financing by an international bank. Directors believe that this project is crucial to DMC survival. It would ensure the sustainability of all their hotel restaurants and would provide a new source of revenue. Admittedly, none of the directors of DMC has any experience in the bio agriculture sector. The manager of the food and beverage team, the manager of the events team, and the manager of corporate hospitality team do not seem to agree on the actual monetary value that the bio project will generate. The office of the local governor issued a statement in which they publicly supported the project as "an impressive project that will set a new national benchmark for sustainable agricultures and will greatly benefit the local community". This was good publicity, but it also attracted interest from an activist fund looking to invest in DMC.

Last week two bank creditors of DMC reached out to the CEO to inquire on DMC financial performance. They suggested entering into negotiations for a potential debt restructuring. The company has made use of all possible measures offered by the government to ease off the effects of the Covid *crisis and can currently pay its debts as they fall due, but the true long-term value of its business and assets is uncertain.*

Directors assess that they are currently solvent but they are not in a position to assess confidently if this position will change imminently. They are also having second thoughts about the bio project, should they obtain new financing and embark on such new project at this stage? How can such directors resolve that uncertainty? What should they do if they cannot?

(a) This is a common challenge for directors of asset-rich businesses facing financial distress. One of the options available to such businesses is to divest operations and thus generate a new stream of revenues.

(b) From a corporate governance perspective, directors should focus on how to enhance measures dealing with:

   i) ensuring transparency by decision makers during the decision-making process. DMC seems to have a complex operational structure with different managers engaged in the food and beverage area. This may not be optimal from an operational perspective. It could potentially add layers of uncertainty to the decision-making process and strip managers of accountability. Great care should be exercised in gathering accurate factual information, assessing the risks and analyzing the financial implications of the bio project. Directors must be open and transparent as to which they consider to be the key issues that they take into account and whose interests do they have regard to;

ii) ensuring that expert views are invited and assessed. This is particularly important here, given that DMC directors have no experience in the agriculture sector;

iii) ensuring good record keeping of the decision-making process, particularly with regard to internal discussions and minutes of board meetings involving resolutions; and

iv) mitigating risks, primarily by limiting expenditure, proactively managing their assets and operations, monitoring developments at national policy level and seeking to benefit from any relief measures available to them. Directors will need daily updated financial information in order to make the right decisions.

(c) During this period, directors should refrain from authorizing transactions that are not in the ordinary course of the company's business and minimize expenditure and outgoings and preserve cash as best as they can. Embarking on the bio project would involve both incurring new debt and developing a new line of business outside of DMC's ordinary course of business. Directors should first raise their concerns with the rest of the board with a view to taking immediate independent financial and accounting advice. Further credit should almost certainly not be incurred pending such advice.

(d) DMC has been invited to commence restructuring negotiations with two of its creditors. It is not uncommon for companies to be under pressure to take such action from creditors, who have no direct fiduciary duties to the company and may stand to benefit at the expense of others. Directors who are in this situation need to take independent advice.

(e) The bio project has received good public recognition for being beneficial to the environment and the local community. DMC directors may be encouraged by this and tempted to embark on the project without a proper assessment of the potential effects on the company. Would a positive environmental and social impact be sufficient to justify a shift in directors' obligation to act in the best interests of the company and its shareholders? There is no currently evidence to support this. While ESG measures should be taken into account, directors should keep a clear focus on their duty to the company as a whole, and the interests of shareholders in particular.

(f) DMC is also concerned by the interest shown by the activist fund. While there is no way for a company to completely protect against becoming a target, there are circumstances that attract activists. In the case of DMC, such circumstances could have been the profit warnings, the lack of agility compared to industry peers, the potential for noncore divestiture, and a board tenured too long and lacking nonexecutive industry specialists in a new area of operations. Companies can unlock shareholder value by donning an activist investor lens (Agrawal, Bhardwaj, & Jerry, 2020). In the case of DMC, directors should have acted early on to identify where investors could perceive hidden value; critically assess areas of vulnerability to activist attack; analyze growth and operating performance across all business units more closely; socialize areas for improvement with the board on a regular basis; and implement necessary changes.

(g) From a leadership perspective, directors should be mindful of the factors that drive their decisions and maintain a clear strategy as to how the situation is best managed. They should be in contact with key creditors, suppliers, shareholders and other stakeholders in order to develop a resolution plan.

(h) In many cases the question of whether the company has become actually insolvent will be answered by reference to its ability to pay its debts as they fall due (i.e., cash flow insolvency), rather than whether its assets, when properly valued, exceed its liabilities. Often cash flow insolvency is far easier to detect.

(i) From a legal perspective, the duties to shareholders and creditors would most likely overlap for a period. Once it becomes likely that the company is cash flow insolvent, directors will need to assess and decide whether it is in the best interests of creditors at this point to continue trading. Is there a viable plan to continue trading whilst minimizing losses to creditors and returning the company to solvency perhaps through a refinancing or restructuring process?

(j) If not, then the directors must consider appointing an administrator or liquidator. It is certainly likely that a decision to appoint an administrator or liquidator would reduce the value of the assets overnight because of the public perception of insolvency (which could result for example to a fire sale of assets at below market value), so it may be in the interests of creditors to hold off as long as possible before appointing an administrator or liquidator. A trading company would be worth more on a going concern basis that asset break up.

(k) An administrator would continue to trade the company for a period of time, but this is only possible under insolvency legislation where this would result in a rescue of the business, or if not possible, then a better return for creditors than could be achieved in a liquidation. A liquidator would cease trading the business and merely collect and sell its assets and effect distributions to its creditors on a pari passu basis. The value to shareholders will almost certainly be destroyed by such an appointment.

Summary: These case studies demonstrate the importance of long-term, cohesive corporate governance policies and leadership practices in all areas of the company. Complex internal structures, lack of independence and expertise by directors, lack of accountability at management level, lack of active asset management and insufficient information on a particular decision may have an adverse effect on the interests of the company in the long term. Seemingly minor or temporary shortcomings could have a severe impact on the viability of a company if not addressed at the outset. Directors ought to collect and process information at all times, with the aim to materially improve the prospects and governance of the business. Regardless of the options available to companies in distress under UK law, directors should remain mindful of their own obligations and liabilities throughout their tenure and remain proactive in obtaining expert advice where necessary.

Conclusion

Corporate governance, organizational leadership, and legislature are studied as three separate disciplines and are applied in a distinct context. Each of these three disciplines functions independently, supported by a long lineage of precedents and jurisprudence. Despite the different contexts in which they apply, principles of corporate governance, organizational leadership, and legislation have found a way to co-exist in modern codifications of good corporate governance in the UK. This chapter explains how leadership principles are applied in the UK Corporate Governance Code and, in turn, how corporate governance has been transposed into legislation relating to directors' duties and liabilities in the UK. It also demonstrates how such principles are influenced by statutory liability of directors in the UK and have the potential, when taken together, to offer practical support to directors in their role as decision makers during a time of crisis and beyond. In recent trends, corporate governance continues to evolve toward an environmental and social responsibility mandate. It will be interesting to see how new functions of corporate governance can be supported by leadership principles and statutory measures in the years ahead.

References

Agrawal, R., Bhardwaj, A., & Jerry, D. (2020, May). EY strategy and transactions: How the TMT sector can unlock value by adopting a shareholder-activist mindset. *EY*. Retrieved from www.ey.com/en_gl/strategy-transactions/tmt-sector-unlock-value-by-adopting-shareholder-activist-mindset

Arnold, R. D., & Wade, J. P. (2015). A definition of systems thinking: A systems approach. *Procedia Computer Science, 44, 669–678*. The International DOI Foundation. https://doi.org/10/106/j.procs.2015.03.050

Australian case of Daniels v Anderson [1995] 13 ACLC 614

Breitinger, D. (2017, August). What is shareholder activism and how should businesses respond? *World Economic Forum*. Retrieved from www.weforum.org/agenda/2017/08/ shareholder-activism-business-response-explainer/

BTI 2014 LLC v Sequana SA [2019] EWCA Civ 112

Business for Social Responsibility. (2017). *The healthy business stakeholder engagement guide*. Retrieved from https://healthybusiness.bsr.org/files/Healthy_Business_Stakeholder_ Engagement.pdf

Cambridge Institute for Sustainability Leadership (CISL). (2018). *Sailing from different harbours: G20 approaches to implementing the recommendations of the task force on climate-related financial disclosures*. Cambridge.

Corporate Insolvency and Governance Act (Coronavirus) (Suspension of Liability for Wrongful Trading and Extension of the Relevant Period) Regulations (2020) (SI 2020/1349))

COVID-19/directors' duties: Andrew Thompson QC and Ben Griffiths of Erskine Chambers consider advising directors in the current crisis and their duties and liabilities. News Release, 27 April 2020. Retrieved from: https://www.fromcounsel.com/corporate/ca/browse/2020-04-27/2020-04-29

De Vries, M. K. (2006). *The leadership mystique: Leading behavior in the human enterprise*. London: Financial Times and Prentice Hall.

European Commission. (2012). Communication from the commission to the European parliament, the council, the European economic and social committee and the committee of the regions action plan: European company law and corporate governance – a modern legal framework for more engaged shareholders and sustainable companies/COM/2012/0740 final

Fairford Water Ski Club Ltd v Cohoon [2020] EWHC 290

Financial Reporting Council. (2018). *The UK corporate governance code*. London: The Financial Reporting Council Limited.

Freeman, R. R. (1984). *Strategic management: A stakeholder approach*. Boston: Pitman Publishing Inc.

Friedman, A. L., & Miles, S. (2006). *Stakeholders: Theory and practice*. Oxford: Oxford University Press.

G20/OECD Principles of Corporate Governance OECD. (2015). *G20/OECD principles of corporate governance*. Paris: OECD Publishing.

Giles, S. (2018). How VUCA is reshaping the business environment, and what it means for innovation. *Forbes*. Retrieved from www.forbes.com/sites/sunnieg iles/2018/05/09/how-vuca-is-reshaping-the-business-environment-and-what-it-means-for-innovation/

Gottfried, K., & Donahue, S. (2020, April). *The impact of COVID-19 on shareholder activism. Harvard law school forum on corporate governance*. Retrieved from https://corpgov.law.harvard.edu/2020/04/12/the-impact-of-covid19-on-shareholder-activism

Grayson, D., Coulter, C., & Lee, M. (2018). *All in: The future of business leadership*. London and New York: Routledge.

Lipton, M. (2020, January). *Dealing with activist hedge funds and other activist investors. Harvard law school forum on corporate governance*. Retrieved from https://corpgov.law.harvard.edu/2020/01/20/dealing-with-activist-hedge-funds-and-other-activist-investors-3

Medlock, R. (2020, May). ESG regulations and their impact on advice. *Financial Adviser*. Retrieved from www.ftadviser.com/investments/2020/05/18/esg-regulations-and-their-impact-on-advice

OECD. (1999). *G20/OECD principles of corporate governance*. Paris: OECD Publishing. https://doi.org/10.1787/9789264236882-en

Paine, L. S., & Srinivasan, S. (2019, October). A guide to the big ideas and debates in corporate governance. *Harvard Business Review*. Retrieved from https://hbr.org/2019/10/a-guide-to-the-big-ideas-and-debates-in-corporate-governance

Re Marini Ltd (the liquidator of Marini Ltd v Dickenson and others) [2003] EWHC 334

Re Southern Counties Fresh Foods Limited ([2008] EWHC 2810)

Reuters. (2020, November). *ESG environment, exclusive: Activist investor Ferrari targets environment, social laggards with new fund by Simon Jessop*. Retrieved from www.reuters.com/article/idUSL8N2IB5CD

Schmid, C., Dr Gehra, B., Dr Hefter, K., Seiler, M., & Meier, F. (2020, November). *BCG whitepaper Switzerland's new rules on corporate responsibility: Taking ESG (Environmental, social and governance) The Boston consulting group*. Retrieved from BCG Whitepaper Switzerland's New Rules on Corporate Responsibility: Taking ESG (Environmental, Social and Governance) The Boston Consulting Group.

Schnick, A., Hobson, P. R., & Ibisch, P. L. (2017). Conservation and sustainable development in a VUCA world: The need for a systemic and ecosystem-based approach. *Ecosystem Health and Sustainability*, 3(4), 1–12. The International DOI Foundation. https//doi.org/10.1002/3hs2/1267

8 Corporate Governance and Business Ethics

Anna Kourtesopoulou

Introduction

While the world economy transforms, business ethics has grown into a major concern for companies maintaining a competitive advantage over other businesses. The concept of business ethics has evolved since the initial matter of the corporations back in the1960s. The triangle of business ethics includes ethics sensitivity, ethics incentives, and ethical behavior. Businesses have gradually broadened their concerns regarding social issues and causes within the environment and joint obligation. All these were influenced to a great extent by the new role of the consumer, since customers' global power can transform product purchase into a vote on multinational companies. Recognizing the vital role of the consumer in world business success, the continuing concern is the investigation on social impact attempt that builds real value (Serafeim, 2020).

According to the Institute of Business Ethics (IBE), the corporate governance ethical points of view in practical terms lie within the business board members by setting the example, the board structures and the processes be followed, as well as the business' purpose, strategy and vision achievement. Some other ethical aspects of directors' panel comprise internal control standards as business operation values and relevant monitoring and reporting procedures. Additionally, it has been noticed that the EU level policy is primarily focused on supporting and developing good governance using processes and procedures, rather than on establishing behavioral standards of ethics as a key element of a substantial board evaluation. Generally, as the European governance practices rely on soft law instruments, the boards are responsible, without obligation, to define the value which will lead the company activities (Casson, 2013; Noti, Mucciarelli, Angelici, Pozza, & Pillinini, 2020).

There is an increasing concern that companies' social behavior estimated to maximize shareholder value. Businesses react to unprecedented pressure from consumers, communities, investors, and governments by acting in a socially responsible manner, including engagements to sustainability, community health and welfare, as well as reliance on unethical

DOI: 10.4324/9781003152750-10

labor practices. However, many leaders face controversies on incorporating socially and environmentally beneficial practices into core business strategy (Dassel & Wang, 2016). It appears that corporate leaders are uncertain of the extent the social efforts impact on their business and financial performance. Due to the Covid-19 spread, it is difficult to ignore the existence of varying consequences and organizations' need for a new management model to sustain operations under such crisis conditions. During global financial collapses, those firms that were considered more social responsible appeared with reduced defeatist stock returns than their opponents (Serafeim, 2020; Torre, Mango, Cafaro, & Leo, 2020).

The global economy's central focus is company sustainability, a condition of corporate long-term resilience and multiple stakeholders flexible management, world unpredictabilities, financial crashes –caused by a pandemic, social controversy, or a climate change catastrophic impact. For organizational accountability and ethical attitude, crucial foundations are provided globally through international protocols, taking into account EU policy initiatives. In this context, this section contributes to

i   build a perception of the state of key initiatives and standards on CSR, considering its characteristics as a world governance mechanism within business ethics;
ii promote the development of research to advance theoretical and practical knowledge on the European CSR, governance, and business ethics;
iii participate creatively in the debate on the impact of CSR and governance on organizational performance on the grounds of stakeholder theory and management.

Key Initiatives and Standards on CSR as a Global Governance Mechanism within Business Ethics

Concepts linked to business ethics, corporate governance, and social responsibility are treated in different ways in management and business ethics literature, notwithstanding the fact that these concepts have some common characteristics and are interrelated. This section presents a review of recent literature on CSR and the role of governance in business ethics.

Several theories are proposed on CSR, some focusing on stakeholder theory and others on corporate accomplishments. An equivalent term of CSR is responsible business conduct (RBC), which includes all those business efforts of maximizing society and environmental benefits and minimizing risks and costs in their own companies. One major principle of CSR is the obligation to a wider board of stakeholders' addendum and self-reinforcement. Within CSR notion, corporations are expected to act within a moral good or normative behavior, while gaining higher outcome from the socially responsible initiatives. A more strategic view of applying CSR is provided by a modified approach model introduced by Jurgens, Berthon, Papania, and Shabbir (2010). In their B2B marketing model for creating and supervising, from a managerial perspective, stakeholder relationships, there are four core steps: (1) determine important interested parties, (2) identify stakeholder groups' objectives and needs, (3) create policies and behaviors needed to fit with stakeholders' expectations, and (4) observe stakeholder objectives fulfillment response. This model assists in corporations' internal practices improvement and external stakeholders' relationships.

By viewing the CSR normative stakeholder theory proposal, authors suggested that CSR is a subset of business ethics. Within this concept, business practices are responsible toward their identified stakeholders and, broadly speaking, to the environment of which it is a subset. Therefore, as determined by financial disclosure, within the environmental ecosystem, economic criteria alone cannot be the ground for the connection between the firm and its stakeholders. The cause of this issue, it is suggested that other business operational procedures, such as politics, corporate governance, and proactive outreach to key stakeholders, must be used by firms to combine with the ethical standards of a company.

Overall, the perception of socially responsible corporation differs among countries as businesses employ several instruments to disclose their CSR principles with regard to their environmental and social impacts. Recent theoretical developments, namely the Sustainable and Responsible Investment (SRI), have revealed and recorded accurately long-term returns for investors, and aid the society by effecting companies' behavior. SRI is an extended approach that combines fundamental analysis of Environmental, Social, and Governance (ESG) criteria. Key parameters that determine European policymakers' work, such as Eurosif, are transparent, long-term, and sustainable investments. Globally, this evaluation process obtains trust in investment decisions and is a widely used strategy by SRI investors, with most of them having vast policy documentation (Eurosif, 2018).

At the same time, broader concepts, in particular the Triple Bottom Line (TBL), corporate governance, and accountability, have arisen. A consequence of the situation is that regulatory bodies, such as OECD, support the implementation of good corporate governance practices, demanding that companies adopt corporate governance principles. Based on the six G20/OECD Principles (OECD, 2015, 2019), an effective corporate governance framework needs to foster transparency, recognition of stakeholders' rights, boards' accountability, and encourage enterprise and market confidence through their practices. This framework also outlines the need for fair treatment and protection of shareholders' rights, integrity, and ethical behavior of directors and executives and builds sustainable long-term value throughout investors, stock markets, and other intermediaries. Another critical principle of effective corporate governance is the intelligibility of the company's financial reporting and other disclosures about corporate performance. Specifically, corporate reporting should be timely and credible. The dynamic role of regulatory frameworks in risk management and remuneration policy and in their contribution to the global financial crisis has already been pointed out (OECD 2019).

The most distinguished and fundamental models within corporate governance are the Anglo-Saxon and continental European. In these, tangible differences exist in their main characteristics, such as goals, policy frameworks, board responsibilities, shareholders' rights, and ownership and control. Stakeholders' value maximization approach is the center of the continental European model since shareholders are firm members with high amounts of shares. Therefore, it is mainly based on an internal control process, focusing on strategic shareholders such as banks (Ahmad & Omar, 2016). A more comprehensive description of the comparison of these two models of corporate governance can be found in Koslowski (2009), who focuses on the capital market function. While in the European model the participation of stakeholder groups has an active role in shaping the corporate governance, in the case of the American, capital market is a principal determining factor. Moreover, European models excel on strategies oriented to workers incentives and company investments plan on labor. Such strategies include employees' participation in decision-making and advisory boards, ensuring that ideal decisions are applied for the enterprise and any possible shirking of the employees is prevented.

Another distinguished difference between the two corporate governance models concerns the firm's purpose as well as the legal and ethical principles acquired from it. Obviously, company purpose is the central cause and principle for its accomplishment and shaping economic, cultural, and moral values into business activities. From this point of view, the European participatory model of corporate governance is more inclusive, underlining that the multipurpose value of shareholder interests plays a decisive role. Within the Anglo-Saxon, shareholder primacy is concerned to be the only, or at least the primary, purpose of the corporation, with the rest of the objectives concerning either the stakeholders' relationships and their management input in corporate profitability and growth, or functional ones such as monitoring the progress of company projects (Koslowski, 2009; Susnienė & Sargūnas, 2011).

Part of this cooperation and shareholders participatory role can be explained by the audit committee concept, which emerges the preventing arguments of interests that can be encountered for executive directors, and at the same time guaranteeing the integrity of business judgment. According to its wide function, an audit committee is expected to have an active role into financial records, external auditor designation, risk assessment, and internal control. Overall, it is well-known the audit committee's essential role in European countries, with single or dual board corporate governance system. Nevertheless, the European Commission addresses the need for adapting and tailoring its own European corporate governance perspective, but lacking in the international level set standards (Collier & Zaman, 2005).

Theoretical and Practical Knowledge on the CSR, and Governance and Business Ethics within Europe

A CSR strategy has been developed in Europe in accordance with international guidelines and principles on business and human rights, such as the United Nations (UN) Global Compact (UNGC); the UN Guiding Principles on Business and Human Rights (UNGP; ISO 26000 Guidance on Social Responsibility; ILO Tripartite Declaration of Principles concerning Multinational Enterprises on Social Policy; Task Force on Climate-related Financial Disclosures (TCFD); and the OECD Guidelines for Multinational Enterprises. The main intention of those international guidelines is to establish common fundamentals for responsible business conduct and promote best practice across Europe (European Commission, 2019).

The CSR Europe provides useful tools and guidelines for an impactful business approach sustainability, like the stakeholder dialogue. During this dialogue process, a company could build a clear framework of action and successful reaction to change, strengthening its CSR and business approach, while improving its reputation among stakeholders. Another useful tool is the materiality assessment which aims to find and examine possible Environmental, Social, and Governance (ESG) matters influencing business and stakeholders' performance. CSR Europe also developed the responsible and transparent tax behavior service, with activities tailored to any company's tax situation and maturity level. Additionally, it has perfected the Grievance Management Assessment (GMA) as an implementation tool for essential building block for human rights due diligence practice. This last assessment helps to recognize high-risk areas and possible systematic mistakes in company's activity (CSR Europe, 2020).

ESG valuation framework concludes some enterprise's operational standards that will awake investor's decisions on promising and sustainable investments. ESG issues take into account environmental criteria such as CO_2 footprint for energy companies and water scarcity. Also, consider social factors such as relationship management of staff, suppliers, clients, and communities and governance issues like executive compensation, audits, internal management mechanisms, and Board accountability (CFA Institute, 2015). Broadly, ESG is a multistakeholder notion underling the aforementioned three distinguished performance pillars. In the comprehensive analysis of examining the market valuation of ESG performance, Nekhili, Boukadhaba, and Nagati (2020; Nordberg, 2008) concluded that employee representation on directors board decreases ESG performance. Precisely, firms with staff shareholder board agents appeared with higher ESG outcomes in the case of environmental and governance performance. Furthermore, those firms having employee board agents were confidently and remarkably associated only with social efficiency. To date, several studies have assessed the efficacy of company's commitment to ESG, providing support for receiving greater amount of reputation among investors (Ding, Ferreira, & Wongchoti, 2016) and more positive reaction of the stock market and gaining investors better understanding and engagement in the enterprise's long-term strategy rather than short-term profits (De Lucia, Pazienza, & Bartlett, 2020; Serafeim, 2020; Goel & Ramanathan, 2014).

Working environment behavior transparency reports have been required more often from companies. The UK, Denmark, and France have recommended legislation on company's reports in Europe, while in the same area level-regulation on nonfinancial disclosure is affiliated. Corporate transparency expectations include a statement in the annual or in a distinct environmental sustainability report, communal and staff interests, esteem human rights, prevent corruption and subornation issues. For a complete and spherical view of a company's financial or nonfinancial details, Integrated Reporting (IR) is used. Business and policymakers in their effort to increase the pace of transformation toward a Sustainable Europe 2030 support that EU policies and regulations should be part of an integrated approach, including accompanying measures and capacity-building activities (CSR Europe, 2020).

The IR framework is considered as a holistic approach of promoting the vital importance of value creation of all stakeholders and communicating this information strategically. Under this IR becomes a defining factor in establishing rigorous and effective governance practices in the public and private business sectors. IR is about a new corporate reporting system and philosophy of doing business which focuses on the ability of an organization to create value and represented by nonfinancial aspects (IIRC, 2021). As mentioned in the CSRforALL project (2016), as far as transparency and reporting are concerned, there are a number of movements, such as the Global Reporting Initiative (GRI), the UN Guiding Principles Reporting Framework, and the UN Communication on Progress (COP). BMW and Novartis use Sustainable Value Report (SVR) and GRI to report on their environmental and social performance.

In the case of ethics valuation, the company's usual common procedure is the Impact Assessment (IA). IA is a process of recognizing the results of a recent or future action (impact prediction/forecasting) and communal significance examination of those impacts (impact evaluation). According to the International Association for Impact Assessment (IAIA), the important ethical factor in the impact assessment process is that it ensures integrity, eliminates bias, and respects the human rights involved in relevant influential decisions. For this reason, the essential first step is the evaluation of the effectiveness of equity-related initiatives from multiple perspectives. Another important ethical aspect is the avoidance of interference of the professional's beliefs, cultural preferences, or private interests. Furthermore, considering the future generation, it is noteworthy to look for sustainable and fair or impartial results from people's actions, which may affect the environment and social functions. Another crucial consideration is the human rights protection by refusing bias during the analysis of a potential project or plan in order to justify a predetermined result (Fuggle, 2012).

The major concerns in the implementation of IA regarding ethics are procedural equity, equal treatment, justice, work responsibilities, and rights. These elements are considered within the moral rules, fundamentals, and patterns that rule human conduct and when ethical unpredictability occurs are controlled by sensitivity analysis (Lawrence, 2013). Companies' practices regarding ethics included moral analysis and valuation of their economic applications and movements at the economic system level, the organizational and the intra-organizational (microeconomic). A determinant factor of their business ethics is also the diversity in the way organizations govern their operations with regard to their relationships with various stakeholders.

Within the CSR framework ethical responsibility is about corporations' expectation to act responsibly, with accuracy and fairness, even if this is not part of the legal framework. Therefore, the central point to the entire ethical responsibilities discipline is the concept of what is socially anticipated, except economic and legal expectations. By looking into European and US CSR policies, diversity is highlighted. For example, in the American context emphasis is on corporate policies locally, whereas in Europe there is a high level of taxation and the existence of important welfare state provisions for local public functions. There are two main CSR forms, with the first being the explicit, referring to corporate policies, program, and strategies in voluntary base. The second is the implicit, which refers to the country's formal and informal organizations through which the corporations' duties for society's matters are concurred and dealt by companies. With reference to the implicit form, CSR usually comprises a number of values, standards, and rules, which mostly cause compulsory demands for enterprises (Zimmerli, Richter, & Holzinger, 2007).

Despite the adoption of the Transparency Directive and International Financial Reporting Standards (IFRS) by the EU, several EU members did not follow an attitude close to partner governance and ethics. As far as ethics and governance protections to their particular factors, the adaptation level of European countries was relying on their own technical, cultural, and political procedures. However, this diversity in relation to alternations could be a contributing factor to the standardization and improvement of the EU's directives (Williams & Seguí-Mas, 2010).

According to the IFC (2015), four key corporate governance challenges for Europe have emerged: (1) finding the right blend of regulation and soft law, (2) boilerplating, meaning the commonly provided information in many European listed companies' annual reports, (3) weak explanations referring to the absence of explanation in case of a company's deviation from the national regulations of corporate governance, and (4) finding the right blend of national and regional regulation.

Impact of CSR and Governance to Organizational Performance on the Grounds of Stakeholder Theory and Management

While the scrutinizing of CSR research has been completed, only few researchers are able to draw on any systematic research into the corporate motives for social behavior. For instance, Campbell (2007) argued that healthy economic conditions of the corporations affect positively their social responsible activation. Another important issue is the opportunities for institutionalized dialogue among firms and their stakeholders, within the claim of the global economic system reformation of being more socially conscious.

The effectiveness of the ethical systems design technique has been exemplified in a report by Filabi and Haidt (2017). Considering the three-level analysis of personal, organizational, and governmental, ethical systems design can support growth in terms of building a good reputation, avoiding illegal conduct and their accompanied extreme costs, and financially rewarding through attracting high-value employees. The improvement of income equality can be illustrated briefly by taking into consideration stakeholder aspects and without focusing only on short-term profits; therefore, businesses motivations should focus on generating high value and avoiding lack of equality.

It is now understood that motivational aspects are crucial in firms' commitment to CSR. It is suggested that utilitarianism is a great motivator since firms expect to gain profits and increase investment returns and sales growth with the aid of CSR strategy and practices. Other promises of CSR are the improvement in the satisfaction levels of stakeholders' behavioral norms as well as the corporation's identity. It assists businesses to be proactive and aim for a positive impact on society (Forte, 2013).

From a sample analysis of 46 public firms in Europe (Torre, Mango, Cafaro, & Leo, 2020), results revealed that both concepts, CSR and business ethics, are of great importance in small medium enterprises. There is also a distinction between voluntariness and compliance of what must and should be applied. For example, sustainability of a business was less voluntary and had a more operational and formal orientation. Another important finding was that CSR and business ethics should not be considered as equivalent concepts because both have different macro and micro focuses. Social responsibility committed to the environment and the broader world, whereas business ethics are more concerned with behaviors and actions. As for the shareholder value, small business owners recognize that it is key to engage in CSR, which leads to shareholder value (Fassin, Rossem, & Buelens, 2011).

Another important finding is that socially responsible investment (SRI) funds increasingly appear as a well-known business investment chance, since investors have become increasingly aware that those corporations meet high ethical and social patterns. Consequently, those funds to enterprises with an increased focus to governance, social and environmental control, lead to better risk-adjusted returns by reducing possibilities for assets diversification (Renneboog, Horst, & Zhang, 2008). Another critical ethical tool is the Enterprise Risk Management (ERM) framework, which portrays an organization's ethics, its strategy and the way it performs. The main concept of this particular framework is based on a risk governance ethical maturity scale, where ethical conformation includes a holistic ethical system. Under this holistic notion, there is alignment of risk management roles and duties to organizational jurisdictions and liabilities. Furthermore, risk management is part of enterprise management and is seen with high coherence and ethics in all areas. In order for corporations to pay attention from confrontation to a better reciprocating risk-based ethical method, they have to address governance structure challenges and adopt a set of guidelines that help companies implement ERM (Demidenko & McNutt, 2010).

Another useful conceptual framework on sustainability accounting is the Task Force on Climate-related Financial Disclosures (TCFD), which includes performance metrics on environmental, social, and human capital. In 2017, almost 30 of the largest 80 European companies have already started to align their corporate statements by reporting all four core TCFD elements, drawn mainly from oil and gas, agriculture, and automobiles sectors. However, the results of disclosures demonstrated a wide range in the quality of integrated report approaches. Interestingly, companies focused more on the risks and opportunities possibly emerged from climate change affecting the business and not the opposite (TCFD, 2017).

Since ethical choices and practices are considered a key ingredient of success in business, the way business deals with externalities, which cause market failures, illustrates clearly the consequences of ethical and unethical behaviors in corporations. Although there are different empirical methods of evaluation in order to assess the value of an externality, there is still no focus on critical human or community resources protection. With respect to this weakness, recent evidence suggests that the existing sustainability performance frameworks lack the capacity to measure the absence of positive effects of companies' functions on the ecosystem and community (Nikolaou, Tsalis, & Evangelinos, 2019). An explanation of this is given by Joannidès (2019), who mentioned that social and green accounting usually is based on nonpositive externalities, such as costs for stakeholders and natural resources. Besides this, most of the time the recognition of negative externalities is eclectic.

Recognizing that externalities are a feature of market economics, as well as a component of continuous discussions among companies and communities about the type of business-associated duties of liability, corporations are required to pay attention to the way of externalities reporting. However, effectiveness of sustainability reporting relies on the possibility if stakeholders treat these reports as origins of data regarding externalities. Meanwhile, corporation members are requiring higher levels of noneconomic data updates within business reporting. There is an opportunity through innovative reporting for a company, to convert those externalities in financial internalities by providing advantageous, inclusive, and comparative data on externalities (Druckman, 2018; Unerman, Bebbington, & O'dwyer, 2018).

The literature pertaining to the TBL framework strongly suggests that companies operating within a social acceptance level need to consider seriously their strategy adaptation. It is crucial to align not only their strategy single based on legislation but also with the stakeholder needs and expectations. Ethical acknowledgment of stakeholder claims is generally assumed to have a crucial part in the success of organizations in the current and future environment (Castelló, & Lozano, 2011; Darnall, Seol, & Sarkis, 2009; Gray, 2010).

Therefore, it is not of high importance to know what encourages professional accountants' ethics and how their acceptance level of the responsibility acts in the public interest. One major motive is released from their central role within the organization in producing and diffusing relevant information for decision-making. In parallel, management accountants are expected to comply with fundamental ethical principles in order to decide what is right or wrong. However, in their dealing with ethical issues, sometimes they face ethical dilemmas expressed as a result of uncertainty to share particular information or not (Joannidès, 2019).

One of the main responsibilities of the directors' board is that they are responsible for observing corporate risk. The Global Risk Perception Survey for 2017–2019 (World Economic Forum, 2019) outcome was influenced in the sector of environmental concerns, as it is supported by the World Economic Forum. Most of the company's investors appraise nonfinancial execution as environmental performance relying on corporate revelation (EY, 2020).

Another significant finding is related with the beneficial role of corporate governance on brand value. Very critical components of corporate governance were found to be trust and ethics, acting as value drivers rather than a set of fiscal rules and procedures. These two factors, trust and ethics, are considered necessary since they introduce virtues of desirable values that influence the organization's everyday operations and contribute to building sustainable relationships (Tuan, 2014). Consistent with Tuan's (2014) standpoint, there is research evidence that customers value as equally important business ethics and social responsibility. However, this is only a first impression since the majority of consumers seemed to not identify the different constructs of business and CSR. Indeed, the results of an exploratory study (Ferrell, Harrison, Ferrell, & Hair, 2019) provide new insights related to business ethics' superior influence on consumer attitudes toward the brand value than CSR activities. In terms of practice, corporations should create a high-priority strategy to identify those positive ethical behaviors and communicate to customers in order to support positive brand attitudes.

More importantly, business is argued that need to establish a corporate culture in order to make their ethics programs effective. Webley and Werner (2008) provide some practical dimensions of shaping and maintaining a strong corporate culture, such as the necessity of agreement on explicit core values and the establishment of relevant and compliant behavior to each organizational member code of ethics. Additional ways of building an effective ethical culture is through providing training on standards and awareness of the expectations raising programs. Further techniques of fostering high-quality ethics and compliance programs are the reward systems, a workplace where employees feel comfort speaking up, and procedural justice (Deloitte, 2015).

Discussion

The initial objective of this chapter was to identify corporations' key initiatives on adapting CSR practices as well as pointing out the connection of CSR with their governance and business ethics performance. In terms of CSR practices, maximizing society and environmental benefits appeared as a strong motivator for enterprises in their effort to meet social responsibility. In light of this shift, businesses have gradually broadened their concerns regarding social issues and causes within the environment and joint obligation. Nowadays, companies try to make effective views their value, especially the intangible value, by building a sustainability-oriented brand. A possible explanation for this might be the changing role of the consumer, who seemed to affect in a great level corporations' greater sustainable awareness and prioritizing as an essential part of their practices. Obviously, there are also expectations and pressure from investors' point of view for more sustainable and responsible investments.

In recent years, nonfinancial business reporting is receiving wider acceptance globally. As already mentioned, a number of international and European initiatives are available to organizations to encourage environmental and social consciousness, such as ESG criteria, TCFD, GMA, IFRS, GRI framework, and the adoption of the EU Directive 2014/95/EU. The number of companies willing to provide voluntary information on nonfinancial key performance indicators and communicate this information strategically is continuously increasing. This new evaluation process obtains trust in investment decisions, while improving the company's reputation among stakeholders. This may be considered a promising aspect of more ethical business practices in future, since the boards are responsible, without obligation, to define the value which will lead the company's activities. It can thus be suggested that business reaction to consumers, communities, investors, and governmental pressure for acting in a socially responsible manner might lead to adapting more ethical corporate standards. Consistent with the literature, business leadership in order to improve its ethical behaviors and actions should take into greater consideration stakeholder aspects and avoid focusing only on short-term profits. Additionally, since risk management is part of enterprise management and appeared to be highly related to ethics, it is suggested for corporations to alternate their risk-based ethical method by addressing governance structure challenges and adopting a set of guidelines that help companies implement effectively the Enterprise Risk Management (ERM) framework. Furthermore, the implementation of a systematic impact assessment of investment proposals grants more sustainable results in case of preventing negative environmental impacts while at the same time maximizing local socioeconomic returns.

By reviewing the European Commission's CSR strategy, various guidelines and principles have been developed aiming to establish common fundamentals of responsible business growth. In parallel, considering the participatory nature of the European corporate governance model, CSR is a critical contributing factor to build sustainable long-term relationships with stakeholders. On this basis, the European model is more inclusive in its nature. Despite the availability of various international frameworks and recommendations on sustainability performance, the lack of capacity to measure the absence of positive effects of companies' functions on the ecosystem and community has been noticed. This finding provides a potential mechanism for innovative reporting for a company in order to convert externalities into financial internalities by providing advantageous, inclusive, and comparative data on externalities.

Ethical acknowledgment of stakeholder claims is generally assumed to have a crucial part in the success of organizations in the current and future environment. This conclusion follows from the fact that business ethics' superior influence is on consumer attitudes toward the brand value than CSR activities. Strategies to enhance positive brand attitudes might raise the need for setting a high business priority identifying positive ethical behaviors and communicating to customers. To develop a full picture of the powerful role of business ethics, additional studies are needed that explore this influence on consumer attitudes toward the brand value. Another possible area of future research would be to investigate why corporations choose to behave morally by pointing out their most important motives/incentives. Another question of future research to investigate various ethical dilemmas that management accountants sometimes face, as a result of uncertainty to share particular information or not. Regardless, future research could continue to explore the critical role of trust and ethics components of corporate governance acting as a value driver.

References

Ahmad, S., & Omar, R. (2016). Basic corporate governance models: A systematic review. *International Journal of Law and Management*, *58*(1), 73–107.

Campbell, J. L. (2007). Why would corporations behave in socially responsible ways? An institutional theory of corporate social responsibility. *Academy of Management Review*, *32*, 946–967. https://doi.org/10.5465/amr.2007.25275684

Casson, J. (2013). A review of the ethical aspects of corporate governance regulation and guidance in the EU. *Occasional Paper*, *8*, 1–44.

Castelló, I., & Lozano, J. M. (2011). Searching for new forms of legitimacy through corporate responsibility rhetoric. *Journal of Business Ethics*, *100*, 11–29.

CFA Institute. (2015). *Environmental, social, and governance issues in investing. A guide for investment professionals*. Retrieved from www.cfainstitute.org/-/media/documents/article/position-paper/esg-issues-in-investing-a-guide-for-investment-professionals.ashx

Collier, P., & Zaman, M. (2005). Convergence in European corporate governance: The audit committee concept. *Corporate Governance: An International Review*, *13*(6), 753–768.

CSR Europe. (2020). *The European pact for sustainable industry: Making the green deal a success* (CSR Europe White Paper 2020). Retrieved from https://static1.squarespace.com/static/5df776f6866c14507f2df68a/t/5f91ab8f19bc811d73d086b2/1603382174412/CSR+Europe+White+Paper+2020.pdf

CSRforALL. (2016). *Corporate social responsibility for all project. Sustainability reporting handbook for employers' organisations*. Retrieved from www.csrforall.eu/en/icerik/publications/CSRforAll-010216.pdf

Darnall, N., Seol, I., & Sarkis, J. (2009). Perceived stakeholder influences and organizations' use of environmental audits. *Accounting, Organizations and Society*, *34*(2), 170–187.

Dassel, K., & Wang, X. (2016). *Social purpose and value creation. The business returns of social impact*. Misk, Belarus: Deloitte Consulting LLP.

Deloitte. (2015). *Building world-class ethics and compliance programs: Making a good program great. Five ingredients for your program*. Deloitte Development LLC. Retrieved from https://www2.deloitte.com/content/dam/Deloitte/no/Documents/risk/Buildin world-class-ethics-and-compliance-programs.pdf

Demidenko, E., & McNutt, P. (2010). The ethics of enterprise risk management as a key component of corporate governance. *International Journal of Social Economics*, 37(10), 802–815. https://doi.org/10.1108/03068291011070462

De Lucia, C., Pazienza, P., & Bartlett, M. (2020). Does good ESG lead to better financial performances by firms? Machine learning and logistic regression models of public enterprises in Europe. *Sustainability*, 12(13), 5317.

Ding, D. K., Ferreira, C., & Wongchoti, U. (2016). Does it pay to be different? Relative CSR and its impact on firm value. *International Review of Financial Analysis*, 47, 86–98.

Druckman, P. (2018). 'Corporate reporting and accounting for externalities': A practitioner view. *Accounting and Business Research*, 48(5), 523–524.

European Commission. (2019). *Corporate social responsibility, responsible business conduct, and business & human rights: Overview of progress*. Brussels. Retrieved from https://ec.europa.eu/transparency/regdoc/rep/10102/2019/EN/SWD-2019-143-F1-EN-MAIN-PART-1.PDF

Eurosif. (2018). *Sustainable development goals (SDGs) for SRI investors*. Retrieved from www.eurosif.org/wp-content/uploads/2018/01/Eurosif-SDGs-brochure.pdf

EY. (2020). *How can climate change disclosures protect reputation and value?* Retrieved from www.ey.com/en_gl/climate-change-sustainability-services/how-can-climate-change-disclosures-protect-reputation-and-value

Fassin, Y., Van Rossem, A., & Buelens, M. (2011). Small-business owner-managers' perceptions of business ethics and CSR-related concepts. *Journal of Business Ethics*, 98(3), 425–453.

Ferrell, O. C., Harrison, D. E., Ferrell, L., & Hair, J. F. (2019). Business ethics, corporate social responsibility, and brand attitudes: An exploratory study. *Journal of Business Research*, 95, 491–501.

Filabi, A., & Haidt, J. (2017). Ethical systems design: What smart leaders are using to improve their organizations (and the world). *World Economic Forum*. Retrieved from www.weforum.org/agenda/2017/01/ethical-systems-design-what-smart-leaders-are-using-to-improve-their-organizations-and-the-world/

Forte, A. (2013). Corporate social responsibility in the United States and Europe: How important is it? The future of corporate social responsibility. *International Business & Economics Research Journal (IBER)*, 12(7), 815–824.

Fuggle, R. (2012). *Ethics. International association for impact assessment*. Fargo. Retrieved from www.iaia.org/uploads/pdf/Fastips_2%20Ethics.pdf

Goel, M., & Ramanathan, M. P. E. (2014). Business ethics and corporate social responsibility – is there a dividing line? *Procedia Economics and Finance*, 11, 49–59.

Gray, R. (2010). Is accounting for sustainability actually accounting for sustainability . . . and how would we know? An exploration of narratives of organisations and the planet. *Accounting, Organizations and Society*, 35(1), 47–62.

International Finance Corporation. (2015). *A guide to corporate governance practices in the European Union*. International Finance Corporation. Retrieved from www.ifc.org/wps/wcm/connect/506d49a2-3763-4fe4 a7835d58e37b8906/CG_Practices_in_EU_Guide.pdf?MOD=AJPERES&CVID=kNmxTtG

International Integrated Reporting Council – IIRC. (2021). *The international <IR> framework*. Retrieved from https://integratedreporting.org/wp-content/uploads/2021/01/InternationalIntegratedReportingFramework.pdf

Joannidès, V. (2019). *Strategic management accounting, volume III: Aligning ethics, social performance and governance.* Switzerland: Springer Nature.

Jurgens, M., Berthon, P., Papania, L., & Shabbir, H. A. (2010). Stakeholder theory and practice in Europe and North America: The key to success lies in a marketing approach. *Industrial Marketing Management, 39*(5), 769–775. https://doi.org/10.1016/j.indmarman.2010.02.016

Koslowski, P. (2009). The ethics of corporate governance. A continental European perspective. *International Journal of Law and Management, 51*(1), 27–34.

Lawrence, D. P. (2013). *Impact assessment: Practical solutions to recurrent problems and contemporary challenges.* Hoboken, NJ: John Wiley & Sons. Retrieved from http://site.ebrary.com/id/10716717.

Nekhili, M., Boukadhaba, A., & Nagati, H. (2020). The ESG – financial performance relationship: Does the type of employee board representation matter? *Corporate Governance: An International Review,* 1–28.

Nikolaou, I. E., Tsalis, T. A., & Evangelinos, K. I. (2019). A framework to measure corporate sustainability performance: A strong sustainability-based view of firm. *Sustainable Production and Consumption, 18,* 1–18.

Nordberg, D. (2008). The ethics of corporate governance. *Journal of General Management, 33*(4), 35–52.

Noti, K., Mucciarelli, F. M., Angelici, C., Pozza, V., & Pillinini, M. (2020). *Corporate social responsibility (CSR) and its implementation into EU company law.* European Union. Retrieved from www.europarl.europa.eu/RegData/etudes/STUD/2020/658541/IPOL_STU(2020)658541_EN.pdf

OECD. (2015). *G20/OECD principles of corporate governance.* Paris: OECD Publishing. Retrieved from http://dx.doi.org/10.1787/9789264236882-en

OECD. (2019). *OECD corporate governance factbook 2019.* Retrieved from www.oecd.org/corporate/corporate-governance-factbook.htm

Renneboog, L., Ter Horst, J., & Zhang, C. (2008). Socially responsible investments: Institutional aspects, performance, and investor behavior. *Journal of Banking & Finance, 32*(9), 1723–1742. https://doi.org/10.1016/j.jbankfin.2007.12.039

Serafeim, G. (2020, September–October). Social-impact efforts that create real value. They must be woven into your strategy and differentiate your company. *Harvard Business Review, 98*(5), 37–48.

Susnienė, D., & Sargūnas, G. (2011). *Stakeholder management paradoxes from the perspective of normative, descriptive and instrumental approach.* Proceedings of 4th international Conference changes in social and business environment. Kaunas University of Technology: Panevėžys Institute.

TCFD. (2017). *Final report. Recommendations of the task force on climate-related financial disclosures.* Retrieved from https://assets.bbhub.io/company/sites/60/2020/10/FINAL-2017-TCFD-Report-11052018.pdf

Torre, M. L., Mango, F., Cafaro, A., & Leo, S. (2020). Does the ESG index affect stock return? Evidence from the Eurostoxx 50. *Sustainability, 12*(16), 6387.

Tuan, L. T. (2014). Corporate governance and brand performance. *Management Research Review, 37*(1), 45–68.

Unerman, J., Bebbington, J., & O'dwyer, B. (2018). Corporate reporting and accounting for externalities. *Accounting and Business Research, 48*(5), 497–522.

Webley, S., & Werner, A. (2008). Corporate codes of ethics: Necessary but not sufficient. *Business Ethics: A European Review, 17*(4), 405–415.

Williams, C. C., & Seguí-Mas, E. (2010). Corporate governance and business ethics in the European Union: A cluster analysis. *Journal of Global Responsibility, 1*(1), 98–126.

World Economic Forum. (2019). *The Global Risks Report 2019* (14th ed.). Geneva, Switzerland.

Zimmerli, W. C., Richter, K., & Holzinger, M. (2007). *Corporate ethics and corporate governance*. Switzerland: Springer.

9 Corporate Social Responsibility and Corporate Financial Performance in the EU

Panagiotis Dimitropoulos

Introduction

The external effects of enterprises have attracted more and more attention over the years, and corporate social responsibility (CSR) research has become a hot topic in today's academic community. Since Sheldon (1924) has put forward the theory of CSR, the difference between theoretical and empirical research conclusions has always restricted the development of theory and practice, until Freeman (1984) proposed an equivalent in a broad definition. He believed that the stakeholders were individuals or groups who could influence the attainment of objectives, and this provides a theoretical foundation and framework for the study of CSR. Carroll (1991) proposed the CSP model of CSR, which set the direction for the development of CSR theory and CSR practice, and entered a new stage of CSR theory development. In the stakeholder theory, Freeman (1984) believed that in daily business activities, companies should not only be responsible for the interests of corporate shareholders but also consider the benefits of corporate employees, consumers, and other groups. People realize that companies not only need to evaluate finances, but the evaluation of social responsibility is even more critical. Kraft and Hage (1990), Brammer and Millington (2008) reported that CSR would first reflect in its CFP, and the quality of financial performance will further affect its degree of fulfilling social responsibilities.

Early research on the CSR–Corporate Financial Performance (CFP) relationship was mainly conducted in North America and some developed countries in Europe. European companies play a significant role in the development of the EU region and economy and have expanded their operations worldwide. Due to the immediacy of EU companies' information dissemination, their performance of social responsibility will be more quickly reflected on their CFP, and the quality of CFP will further affect the degree of their performance of social responsibility.

So far, for the study of the relationship between CSR and CFP, scholars have continuously improved their research methods. However, due to the inconsistency of specific concepts and research methods, previous

DOI: 10.4324/9781003152750-11

studies did not produce consistent results. At the same time, some developed countries have set up specialized CSR assessment agencies and attached more importance to fulfilling social responsibility. However, in some European countries, companies do not realize the importance of CSR. Hence, studying the relationship between CSR and CFP of European firms is very important for providing new insights and more decisive inferences on that association. Although the research on the relationship between CSR and CFP is relatively abundant in European and American countries, earlier empirical studies examined CSR actions within a one-dimensional way, despite the fact that many researchers argue about the multidimensional nature of CSR (Clarkson, 1995; Godfrey & Hatch, 2007; Waddock & Graves, 1997). According to Clarkson (1995), the multidimensional nature of CSR can be better approached by stakeholder theory, which considers how companies handle their relationship with key stakeholders.

The scope of this chapter is to examine the impact of CSR performance on the financial performance of the firms (CFP). We aim to add a significant gap on the literature as argued by Chen, Ngniatedema, and Li (2018) by covering a large multi-country sample of listed European firms over a long period of time and also by considering the bidirectional association between CSR and CFP.

CSR–CFP Association and Testable Hypothesis

Sheldon (1924) pointed out that (from the perspective of corporate managers) the obligation to fulfill social responsibility is inherent in managerial behavior and so CSR contains moral factors. Bowen (1953) had a more explicit discussion of CSR. He thought that the decisions made by businessmen in the business process have a more significant impact on employment, economic prosperity, and commercial growth rate. Both Sheldon (1924) and Bowen and Johnson (1953) studied CSR from the individual level of the business operator. With the in-depth study of CSR in academia, the research perspective has been extended to the level of corporate organization. Davis (1967) pointed out that CSR is related to the whole society and associated influences. Since the ownership and control of modern enterprises are separated, their management responsibility must be clear. If an enterprise wants to grow in the long run, CSR should match the strength of the enterprise. CSR should emphasize the impact of corporate behavior on the entire industry and society, rather than one-sided consideration of the personal action of the operator.

Carroll (1991), based on the four-part model proposed in 1972, expanded this idea into a "social responsibility pyramid" model. This model has the most significant impact on the relevant theories of CSR. He subdivided CSR from four aspects, namely economic, legal, ethical, and philanthropic, to reflect the previous definition of CSR. When these four dimensions are used to describe CSR, they are not independent of each other, of which economic responsibility is the most important, legal responsibility is the primary criterion, ethical responsibility is expected by the public, and philanthropic responsibility is freely determined by the company. This model has a massive impact on the study of CSR and is widely cited by academia.

Schwartz and Carroll (2003) extended the three-domain model based on the pyramid model. The three-domain model intersects the relationship between the levels of the pyramid and better explains the classification of CSR. In the past two decades, academic research on the definition of CSR has tended to describe it from different dimensions. Dahlsrud (2008) collected 37 definitions of CSR and found that more researchers identify five characteristics that describe CSR: those of shareholders, social, economic, charity, and the environment. Still, to better define CSR, it is necessary to consider the political, economic, cultural, and business management strategies of the company. Jackson and Apostolakou (2010) believed that different institutional backgrounds would affect CSR, so various policymakers and stakeholder groups have different definitions of CSR, which explains the diversity of meanings of CSR to a certain extent.

Goll and Rasheed (2004) focused their research on CSR at the individual level. They believed that the decision-making layer within the company intentionally created the fulfilment of CSR. Zu and Song's (2009) research showed that in the era of rapid global economic development, many companies are committed to integrating CSR into their business activities, and company executives should respond to the social responsibility demands of various stakeholders. According to the different impacts of CSR on corporate risks, Mishra and Modi (2013) divided CSR into two types: positive CSR and negative CSR. Girerd-Potin, Jimenez-Garcès, and Louvet (2014) stressed that CSR could be evaluated from three aspects: corporate stakeholders (suppliers, employees and users), social stakeholders (society and environment), financial stakeholders (creditors and shareholders). Blowfield and Frynas (2005) believed that CSR behaviors are complicated, and companies need to be responsible to all stakeholders, integrating responsibilities to multiple entities, which are mainly manifested in responsibilities to the economy, ethics, and regulations.

Freeman (1984) proposed the stakeholder theory that supports that good CSR will lead to good CFP. Generally, companies with good CSR can improve overall operational efficiency. For example, companies provide employees with the right treatment and benefits, which can attract more excellent employees and ultimately bring better CFP. Russo and Fouts (1997) pointed out that due to compliance with environmental regulations, environmentally friendly companies are expected to obtain higher profit margins, while increasing the operating stage rate can also reduce costs. Ruf, Muralidhar, Brown, Janney, and Paul (2001) argue that the company should take the initiative to undertake social responsibility activities since it exerts positive changes on sales growth rate. Waddock and Graves (1997) pointed out that the importance that companies attach to social relations may result in the reduction of favorable tax regulations or local regulations, thereby enabling companies to reduce operating costs, expand markets, and increase productivity. Kacperczyk (2009) believed that changes in the company's views on the environment, diversity, and social relations have a positive impact on market-based long-term financing. Garay and Font (2012) found that the core competitive advantages and compliance of stakeholders have a more significant effect on CFP and social responsibility information than altruism. Companies need to implement CSR activities further to gain a more significant competitive advantage.

Similar conclusions are provided by Moskowitz (1972), Preston and O'Bannon (1997), Simpson and Kohers (2002), Ahmed, Islam, and Hasan (2012), and Oeyono, Samy, and Bampton (2011). Similarly, Inoue and Lee (2011) have studied the relationship between the CSR and CFP in the tourism industry and suggested that good social responsibility performance can effectively enhance the profitability of an enterprise, thereby effectively increasing the level of financial returns. Also, Karagiorgos (2010) selected listed energy companies for empirical research and concluded that CSR is positively associated to CFP. Similarly, Stellner, Klein, and Zwergel (2015) reached similar conclusions, arguing that CSR performing firms gain increased legitimacy and support toward their operations from their stakeholders, a fact that leads to higher customer loyalty, improved reputation, and financial performance (revenues and profits).

However, there is a significant number of studies on the literature arguing for a negative impact of CSR on financial performance. According to Friedman (1970), corporate managers have the responsibility to bring maximum profits to shareholders, and if the owners and managers of the company, as agents of shareholders, engage in nonprofit activities, then it would result in decline in profits in the future. Therefore, managers' attention to people's interests other than investors will eventually reduce the welfare of shareholders. Research by Suto and Takehara (2018) demonstrated that investors did not provide an apparent response to the social responsibility of the company disclosed in the company annual report, and they have a negative attitude toward the federal government's spending on CSR. The investment of social capital causes the stock price of the company to fall. This punishment is not direct but reflected in the stock price.

Zheng (2006) believed that in the course of business operations, enterprises should take various measures to reduce their operating costs to achieve improvement in their competitiveness. Preston and O'Bannon (1997), based on the manager's opportunity hypothesis, believed that when managers are concerned about their interests and their remuneration is related to the CFP, they will reduce social responsibility expenditures on the company. Also, Brammer, Brooks, and Pavelin (2006) used the stock return rate to assess the financial performance of a company and found that companies that fulfill their social responsibilities well have a low stock return rate, which leads to a negative correlation between the two. Similarly, Makni (2009) concluded that the investment in environmental responsibility leads to a negative impact on financial performance, and investors reacted negatively to social responsibility in order to avoid more capital investment.

Nevertheless, there are some studies on the literature which provide evidence of a nonsignificant association between CSR and CFP. McWilliams and Siegel (2001) analyzed the KLD data and the average annual value of companies from 1991 to 1996 and they found that there is no significant correlation between CSR and CFP. However, since the implementation of related responsibilities increases the expenditure of the company, it causes the operating pressure of the company to rise and hinders the profitability of the company. Similarly, analyzing the world's top 500 companies Inoue and Lee (2011) adopted the KLD index dataset to divide the social responsibility stakeholders of the company into five different dimensions, and separately evaluated the relevant responsibility systems and analyze the indicators in specific evaluations. The research showed that CSR-CFP do not indicate a positive correlation, nor a negative correlation. Ahmed, Islam, and Hasan (2012) used content analysis to measure CSR and uses sales net profit indicators to measure financial performance, and finally, find no significant correlation between the two through research.

Similarly, Becchetti and Trovato (2011), Aras, Aybars, and Kutlu (2010), Liu and Kong (2006), Reverte, Gomez-Melero, and Cegarra-Navarro (2016), Bidhari, Salim, Aisjah, and Java (2013) and Sadeghi, Arabsalehi, and Hamavandi (2016) all examined the impact of CSR on financial performance within different countries and sectors and concluded that there is no statistically significant relationship between CSR and CFP. There are two main reasons for the nonsignificant relationship between CSR and CFP. First, there is an inevitable argument for the definition and analysis of the relevant responsibilities of the company based on the lack of proper and systematic academic justification and grounding. Second, in the current market system, CSR lacks a unified implementation evaluation standard. Therefore, various researchers use different analysis methods to analyze different CSR studies, and various research conclusions will appear.

At present, the stakeholder theory has become the mainstream idea for studying the relationship between CSR and CFP. According to the stakeholder theory, CSR will have a positive impact on CFP. First of all, an enterprise actively fulfilling its social responsibilities will send a positive signal to stakeholders, showing that it is trustworthy, so as to obtain the support of all stakeholders, and then realize the sustainable development of the enterprise and improve its financial performance. Secondly, Suto and Takehara (2018) documented that when corporation in CSR activities within their daily operations, corporate reputation will improve CFP through market feedback, strengthening its reputation, gain more loyal consumers, improve employee work efficiency, obtain government support, thereby creating more business value, enhancing the company's financial status, and achieving maximized benefits. So, following the above-mentioned discussion, the main (and alternative) research hypotheses are formed as followed:

H1a: The CSR performance has a positive impact on CFP.
H1b: The CSR performance has a negative impact on CFP.

Data Selection and Research Design

Data Selection Procedure

The current chapter utilizes a sample of corporations (both listed and unlisted) from 23 EU-member countries over the period 2003–2018. Financial and social responsibility data have been collected from Datastream database. We excluded those firms without social score data for at least five consecutive years in order to avoid bias in the empirical results and also to facilitate the estimation of differenced variables. Also, firms operating within the financial sector were excluded from the sample due to their specific financial and accounting characteristics. Furthermore, firms with incomplete financial data and those that do not close their fiscal year on December were excluded. In addition, the upper and down 1% of the data distribution was winsorized for mitigating the influence of outliers in the empirical analysis. After this procedure was finalized, the final sample summed up to 67074 firm-year observations.

Research Design

In order to examine the validity of the research hypothesis we will take into consideration the bidirectional association between CSR and CFP. Following Testa and D'Amato (2017), profitable firms can have more resources available to invest in CSR activities, which may increase their reputation to the market and improve their image toward their stakeholders leading to higher financial performance. The simultaneity is possible on the examination between CSR financial performance and vice versa (Chen et al., 2018). In order to control for the potential impact of endogeneity we will estimate a system of seemingly unrelated regressions (SUR). The functional form of the system of equations includes the average annual CSR score for each firm and year estimated as the annual average of the ESG workforce score, community score, human rights score, product responsibility score and CSR strategy score, where i denotes the firm and t the year and e is the error term:

$$CSR_{it} = a_0 + a_1 ROE_{it} + a_2 SIZE_{it} + a_3 DUAL_{it} + a_4 BDSIZE_{it}$$
$$+ a_5 CSR\_COM_{it} + Year\ F.E$$
$$+ Industry\ F.E. + Country\ F.E. + e_{it} \qquad (1)$$

$$ROE_{it} = a_0 + a_1 CSR_{it} + a_2 SIZE_{it} + a_3 DUAL_{it} + a_4 BDSIZE_{it}$$
$$+ a_5 CSR\_COM_{it} + Year\ F.E$$
$$+ Industry\ F.E. + Country\ F.E. + u_{it} \qquad (2)$$

CSR is the firms' annual average of the aforementioned five scores. The CSR score ranges between zero (0) and 100, so the higher the score, the more socially responsible and efficient is the firm. ROE is return on equity and is measured as the ratio of net income before tax to common equity. We expect a positive coefficient in this variable thus H1a will be accepted. If the CSR variable produces also a positive and significant coefficient, this will verify the bidirectional association between CER and CFP. SIZE is the natural logarithm of total assets and captures firm size. DUAL is a dummy variable taking unity (1) if the CEO serves also as the board chairman, and zero (0) otherwise. BDSIZE is the number of directors serving on the board. Finally, CER_COM is a dummy variable taking unity (1) if the firm has established a social responsibility (or sustainability) committee and zero (0) otherwise.

Empirical Results

Descriptive Statistics and Correlations

Table 9.1 presents the descriptive statistics of the variables utilized in the regression models. First of all, the mean CSR is 61.07 (with a standard deviation of 19.93), indicating that the sample firms have a relatively significant social performance score. The sample firms are highly profitable (mean ROE 79.53) and have a large size of total assets. Finally, 71.7% of our sample firms have a CEO who also serves as the board chairman, boards on average include 12 members, and the 55% of our sample firms have established a social responsibility committee. Table 9.2 presents the Pearson correlation coefficients between the sample variables. The variance inflation factor (VIF) values suggest that multicollinearity is not a problem with our data. As we can see, CSR is positively associated with ROE but not statistically significant, while it is negatively and

Table 9.1 Descriptive statistics of the sample variables

Variables	Mean	Standard deviation	Min	Max
CSR	61.077	19.931	5.244	98.077
ROE	79.537	34.821	-33.315	118.315
SIZE	20.496	2.848	2.302	30.311
DUAL	0.717	0.450	0.000	1.000
BDSIZE	12.271	4.703	1	38
CSR_COM	0.552	0.497	0.000	1.000

Table 9.2 Pearson correlation coefficients of sample variables

Variables	ROE	CSR	SIZE	BDSIZE	DUAL	CSR_ COM
ROE	1					
CSR	0.002	1				
SIZE	0.056	-0.004	1			
BDSIZE	0.017	0.060	0.073	1		
DUAL	-0.004	-0.067	-0.081	-0.125	1	
CSR_COM	-0.005	0.563	-0.038	0.037	-0.015	1

Note: Correlation coefficients in bold indicate statistical significance at least at the 5% significance level.

significantly associated with CEO duality, suggesting that firms with a CEO serving as board chairman are associated with lower CSR performance. Nevertheless, firms with larger boards, especially those with a social responsibility committee, tend to perform better on the CSR score.

Regression Results

Table 9.3 presents the regression results from the SUR estimation of Models (1) and (2). The Breusch-Pagan test of independence is statistically significant at the 1% level suggesting that the SUR estimation provides informational value beyond that produced by estimating the relative models separately. The estimation of equation (1) produced a positive and significant coefficient of ROE on CSR suggesting that more profitable firms are associated with higher CSR performance (Giannarakis, 2014; Syed & Butt, 2017). Also, the estimation of equation (2) produced a positive and significant coefficient on the CSR variable, indicating that CSR has a positive impact on CFP. This result corroborates our main research hypothesis (H1a) and verifies previous arguments by Jiang, Xue,

Table 9.3 Regression results on the bidirectional association between CSR and CFP

Variables			
Equation 1 – Dep. Variable: CSR	Coef.	z-stat	P>|z|
ROE	0.017**	2.10	0.036
SIZE	0.053**	2.43	0.015
DUAL	-2.361***	-16.68	0.001
BDSIZE	0.117***	8.77	0.001
CSR_COM	22.818***	179.72	0.001
Constant	47.720***	94.65	0.001
R-sq	0.329		
Chi² (*p*-value)	329.59*** (0.001)		
Equation 2 – Dep. Variable: ROE	Coef.	z-stat	P>|z|
CSR	3.851***	2.10	0.036
SIZE	33.725***	3.27	0.001
DUAL	3.920	0.06	0.954
BDSIZE	19.397***	3.05	0.002
CSR_COM	-204.32***	-2.79	0.005
Constant	-94.527***	-3.71	0.001
R-sq	0.198		
Chi² (*p*-value)	30.80*** (0.001)		
Breusch-Pagan test of independence	8.981**		
Chi² (*p*-value)	(0.001)		

Note: **, *** indicate statistical significance at the 5% and 1% significance levels respectively; z-statistics in parenthesis.

and Xue (2018), Chen et al. (2018) and Fiadrino, Devalle, and Cantino (2019). Also, we verify the bidirectional association between CSR and CFP, confirming that profitable firms also present higher CSR performance and vice versa.

Regarding the rest of the control variables, larger firms proved to be more profitable, corroborating empirical evidence by Orlitzky (2001) and Dimitropoulos and Tsagkanos (2012) documenting that larger firms can take advantage of economies of scale in their operations and can exert greater control on their external stakeholders and resources, leading to enhanced financial performance. BDSIZE produced a positive and significant coefficient, while on the contrary DUAL produced a positive yet insignificant coefficient. These findings verify analogous evidence by Mitchell (2005) on CEO duality and its impact on CFP. Finally, the existence of a CSR sustainability committee (CSR_COM) produced highly significant but negative coefficient. This result corroborates arguments and evidence by Chen et al. (2018) regarding the impact of CSR activities and initiatives on CFP.

Sensitivity Analysis

Several sensitivity tests have been performed for examining the robustness of the main findings. At first, we considered the impact of endogeneity since it is an important issue that has been raised by several studies (Testa & D'Amato, 2017; Chen et al., 2018; Suto & Takehara, 2018). For this reason, we estimated Models (1) and (2) using the GMM method. In this case, we selected two instrumental variables, a dummy variable COMMON receiving (1) if the firm is based on a common law country and (0) otherwise, and the firm's listing status dummy receiving (1) if the firm is listed in the stock market and (0) otherwise (Monteiro & Aibar-Guzmán, 2010). The Anderson-Rubin test was used for testing the relevance of the instruments (Baum, 2006). The Anderson-Rubin test produced a chi-square value of 67.44 ($p > \chi^2 = 0.0001$) indicating that our instruments are relevant and valid for our research setting. Empirical results on the GMM estimation yielded qualitatively similar results relative on those presented on Table 9.3.

In order to further verify the rigourness and soundness of the conclusions of this chapter, we replaced the return on equity (ROE) with the return on total assets (ROA) and re-estimated Models (1) and (2). Also, SIZE was estimated using the natural logarithm of revenues and the number of employees. All those estimations produced similar results, leaving main inferences unaffected. Moreover, we introduced additional controls like leverage and growth opportunities on Models (1) and (2) but the results still provide support on H1a.

Conclusion

Social responsibility research has focused on the impact that CSR activities have on financial performance (CFP). Empirical evidence provide different views and results regarding the impact of corporate social performance on financial profitability (Clarkson, 1995; Jones & Wicks, 1999; McWilliams, Siegel, & Wright, 2006). The majority of evidence point that CSR activities contribute to improved stakeholder relationships, which in turn enhance financial profitability and competitive advantages (Jiang et al., 2018). The aim of this chapter was to examine the impact of CSR activities on the financial performance of corporations originating from 23 EU countries over the period 2003–2018.

Empirical results indicated that CSR leads to enhanced financial performance, verifying existing studies by Jiang et al. (2018), Chen et al. (2018) and Fiadrino et al. (2019). Also, our evidence supports arguments in the literature regarding the bidirectional association between CSR and CFP (Testa & D'Amato, 2017). Our evidence confirm that profitable firms are associated with improved CSR performance. In turn higher

CSR performance contributes to enhance CFP which feeds back to higher social investments and CSR performance. The empirical results remain robust after several sensitivity tests regarding the definition of the independent variables and after controlling for the impact of endogeneity.

The relationship between CSR and CFP is abundantly researched. However, because companies are involved in several sectors, and because the EU region lacks behind in terms of CSR, there are fewer researches on European companies, especially the research theory on empirical methods is even more lacking. This article can make up for this shortcoming and enrich the theoretical research on CSR-CFP association. This chapter considers a significant amount of European firms as the research object to conduct an in-depth analysis of the relationship between CSR and CFP and promote the vigorous development of Europe's social responsibility focus and performance. The pertinence and timeliness of research is an aspect that the current theory is hugely lacking. At the same time, this article can help European companies to realize the relationship between their CSR and CFP, thereby improving their sense of social responsibility. Finally, based on the research in this chapter, it can enhance the company's concept of CSR and help the company develop better and improve CFP.

From a research process and research outcomes perspective, this article has the following limitations: First, this article sets five control variables based on literature, but many indicators affect CFP. Therefore, this may affect the rigourness of the conclusion of this article. Furthermore, reliable future research can further improve and enhance the control variables, so as to more rigorously demonstrate the relationship between CSR and CFP, and draw more sound conclusions.

Secondly, the collection of data and the determination of variables are not complete and innovative. As an empirical analysis, data is an essential factor in ensuring the quality of the empirical analysis. In the empirical analysis, this chapter mainly selects some corporations that are large in size. Relevant data from small or medium sized corporations within the EU could further enhance the analysis in this chapter and provide more salient inferences regarding the impact of CSR on CFP within different size-classes. Finally, it will be also interesting to consider how and if the current Covid-19 pandemic (as an exogenous shock to several economic sectors) has affected or even changed the association between CSR and CFP.

References

Ahmed, S. U., Islam, Z. M., & Hasan, I. (2012). Corporate social responsibility and financial performance linkage: Evidence from the banking sector of Bangladesh. *Journal of Organizational Management*, 1(1), 14–21.

Aras, G., Aybars, A., & Kutlu, O. (2010). Managing corporate performance: Investigating the relationship between corporate social responsibility and financial performance in emerging markets. *International Journal of Productivity and Performance management, 59*(3), 229–254.

Baum, C. F. (2006). *An introduction to econometrics using Stata.* College Station, TX: Stata Press Books, StataCorp LP.

Becchetti, L., & Trovato, G. (2011). Corporate social responsibility and firm efficiency: A latent class stochastic frontier analysis. *Journal of Productivity Analysis, 36*(3), 231–246.

Bidhari, S. C., Salim, U., Aisjah, S., & Java, E. (2013). Effect of corporate social responsibility information disclosure on financial performance and firm value in banking industry listed at Indonesia stock exchange. *European Journal of Business and Management, 5*(18), 39–46.

Blowfield, M., & Frynas, J. G. (2005). Editorial Setting new agendas: Critical perspectives on corporate social responsibility in the developing world. *International Affairs, 81*(3), 499–513.

Bowen, H. R. (1953). *Social responsibility of the businessman.* University of Iowa Press, Iowa, US.

Brammer, S., Brooks, C., & Pavelin, S. (2006). Corporate social performance and stock returns: UK evidence from disaggregate measures. *Financial Management, 35*(3), 97–116.

Brammer, S., & Millington, A. (2008). Does it pay to be different? An analysis of the relationship between corporate social and financial performance. *Strategic Management Journal, 29*(12), 1325–1343.

Carroll, A. B. (1991). The pyramid of corporate social responsibility: Toward the moral management of organizational stakeholders. *Business Horizons, 34*(4), 39–48.

Chen, F., Ngniatedema, T., & Li, S. (2018). A cross-country comparison of green initiatives, green performance and financial performance. *Management Decision, 56*(5), 1008–1032.

Clarkson, M. B. E. (1995). A stakeholder framework for analyzing and evaluating corporate social performance. *Academy of Management Review, 20*(1), 92–117.

Dahlsrud, A. (2008). How corporate social responsibility is defined: An analysis of 37 definitions. *Corporate Social Responsibility and Environmental Management, 15*(1), 1–13.

Davis, K. (1967). Understanding the social responsibility puzzle. *Business Horizons, 10*(4), 45–50.

Dimitropoulos, P. E., & Tsagkanos, A. (2012). Financial performance and corporate governance in the European football industry. *International Journal of Sport Finance, 7*(4), 280–308.

Fiadrino, S., Devalle, A., & Cantino, V. (2019). Corporate governance and financial performance for engaging socially and environmentally responsible practices. *Social Responsibility Journal, 15*(2), 171–185.

Freeman, R. E. (1984). *Strategic management: A stakeholder approach.* Boston: Pitman.

Friedman, M. (1970). A Friedman doctrine: The social responsibility of business is to increase its profits. *The New York Times Magazine, 13*(1970), 32–33.

Garay, L., & Font, X. (2012). Doing good to do well? Corporate social responsibility reasons, practices and impacts in small and medium accommodation enterprises. *International Journal of Hospitality Management*, *31*(2), 329–337.

Giannarakis, G. (2014). Corporate governance, and financial characteristic effects on the extent of corporate social responsibility disclosure. *Social Responsibility Journal*, *10*(4), 569–590.

Girerd-Potin, I., Jimenez-Garcès, S., & Louvet, P. (2014). Which dimensions of social responsibility concern financial investors? *Journal of Business Ethics*, *121*(4), 559–576.

Godfrey, P. C., & Hatch, N. W. (2007). Researching corporate social responsibility: An agenda for the 21st century. *Journal of Business Ethics*, *70*(1), 87–98.

Goll, I., & Rasheed, A. A. (2004). The moderating effect of environmental munificence and dynamism on the relationship between discretionary social responsibility and firm performance. *Journal of Business Ethics*, *49*(1), 41–54.

Inoue, Y., & Lee, S. (2011). Effects of different dimensions of corporate social responsibility on corporate financial performance in tourism-related industries. *Tourism Management*, *32*(4), 790–804.

Jackson, G., & Apostolakou, A. (2010). Corporate social responsibility in Western Europe: An institutional mirror or substitute? *Journal of Business Ethics*, *94*(3), 371–394.

Jiang, Y., Xue, X., & Xue, W. (2018). Proactive corporate environmental responsibility and financial performance: Evidence from Chinese energy enterprises. *Sustainability*, *10*, 964.

Jones, T., & Wicks, A. (1999). Convergent stakeholder theory. *Academy of Management Review*, *24*, 208–221.

Kacperczyk, A. (2009). With greater power comes greater responsibility? Takeover protection and corporate attention to stakeholders. *Strategic Management Journal*, *30*, 261–285.

Karagiorgos, T. (2010). Corporate social responsibility and financial performance: An empirical analysis on Greek companies. *European Research Studies Journal*, *13*(4), 85–108.

Kraft, K. L., & Hage, J. (1990). Strategy, social responsibility and implementation. *Journal of Business Ethics*, *9*(1), 11–19.

Liu, C., & Kong, X. (2006). An empirical study of social responsibility accounting information disclosure: Empirical data from the shanghai stock exchange from 2002 to 2004. *Accounting Research*, *10*, 36–43.

Makni, R., Francoeur, C., & Bellavance, F. (2009). Causality between corporate social performance and financial performance: Evidence from Canadian firms. *Journal of Business Ethics*, *89*(3), 409.

McWilliams, A., & Siegel, D. (2001). Corporate social responsibility: A theory of the firm perspective. *Academy of Management Review*, *26*(1), 117–127.

McWilliams, A., Siegel, D., & Wright, P. M. (2006). Guest editor's introduction. Corporate social responsibility: Strategic implications. *Journal of Management Studies*, *43*(1), 1–18.

Mishra, S., & Modi, S. B. (2013). Positive and negative corporate social responsibility, financial leverage, and idiosyncratic risk. *Journal of Business Ethics*, *117*(2), 431–448.

Mitchell, L. (2005). Structural roles, CEOs and the missing link in corporate governance. *Brooklyn Law Review*, *70*, 1313–1368.

Monteiro, S., & Aibar-Guzmán, B. (2010). Determinants of environmental disclosure in the annual reports of large companies operating in Portugal. *Corporate Social Responsibility and Environmental Management, 17*, 185–204.

Moskowitz, M. (1972). Choosing socially responsible stocks. *Business and Society Review, 1*(1), 71–75.

Oeyono, J., Samy, M., & Bampton, R. (2011). An examination of corporate social responsibility and financial performance. *Journal of Global Responsibility, 2*(1), 100–112.

Orlitzky, M. (2001). Does firm size confound the relationship between corporate social performance and firm financial performance? *Journal of Business Ethics, 33*, 167–180.

Preston, L. E., & O'Bannon, D. P. (1997). The corporate social-financial performance relationship: A typology and analysis. *Business & Society, 36*(4), 419–429.

Reverte, C., Gomez-Melero, E., & Cegarra-Navarro, J. G. (2016). The influence of corporate social responsibility practices on organisational performance: Evidence from eco-responsible Spanish firms. *Journal of Cleaner Production, 112*, 2870–2884.

Ruf, B. M., Muralidhar, K., Brown, R. M., Janney, J. J., & Paul, K. (2001). An empirical investigation of the relationship between change in corporate social performance and financial performance: A stakeholder theory perspective. *Journal of Business Ethics, 32*(2), 143–156.

Russo, M., & Fouts, P. (1997). A resource-based perspective on corporate environmental performance. *Academy of Management Journal, 40*(3), 54–559.

Sadeghi, G., Arabsalehi, M., & Hamavandi, M. (2016). Impact of corporate social performance on financial performance of manufacturing companies (IMC) listed on the Tehran stock exchange. *International Journal of Law and Management, 58*(6), 634–659.

Schwartz, M. S., & Carroll, A. B. (2003). Corporate social responsibility: A three-domain approach. *Business Ethics Quarterly, 13*(4), 503–530.

Sheldon, O. (1924). *The philosophy of management.* Boston: Pitman.

Simpson, W. G., & Kohers, T. (2002). The link between corporate social and financial performance: Evidence from the banking industry. *Journal of Business Ethics, 35*(2), 97–109.

Stellner, C., Klein, C., & Zwergel, B. (2015). Corporate social responsibility and Eurozone corporate bonds: The moderating role of country sustainability. *Journal of Banking & Finance, 59*, 538–549.

Suto, M., & Takehara, H. (2018). *Corporate social responsibility and corporate finance in Japan.* Singapore: Springer Nature.

Syed, M. A., & Butt, S. A. (2017). Financial and non-financial determinants of corporate social responsibility: Empirical evidence from Pakistan. *Social Responsibility Journal, 13*(4), 780–797.

Testa, M., & D'Amato, A. (2017). Corporate environmental responsibility and financial performance: Does bidirectional causality work? Empirical evidence from the manufacturing industry. *Social Responsibility Journal, 13*(2), 221–234.

Waddock, S. A., & Graves, S. B. (1997). The corporate social performance-financial performance link. *Strategic management Journal, 18*(4), 303–310.

Zheng, L. I. (2006). A study on relation of corporate social responsibility and corporate value: Empirical evidence from shanghai securities exchange. *China Industrial Economy*, 2, 77–83.

Zu, L., & Song, L. (2009). Determinants of managerial values on corporate social responsibility: Evidence from China. *Journal of Business Ethics*, 88(1), 105–117.

Part III

Managerial Aspects of CSR and Governance in the EU

10 Corporate Social Responsibility, Governance, and Gender Diversity

Oana – Antonia Colibășanu

An Evolutionary Parallel in Literature Review: Corporate Social Responsibility, Corporate Governance, and Gender Studies

Almost a century has passed since the public debate between Adolf A. Berle Jr. and E. Merrick Dodd Jr., two American lawyers who were trying to respond to the question "whom are corporations accountable?", establishing the foundation for the discussion on what we call today "corporate social responsibility". Berle argued that the corporation should be held accountable only to shareholders, while Dodd argued that corporations needed to be accountable to both their shareholders and the society in which corporations operated. (Bratton & Wachter, 2008). In the 1950s, Howard Bowen launched the discussion on the "obligations of businessmen to pursue those policies, to make those decisions or to follow those lines of action which are desirable in terms of the objectives and values of our society" in his book titled *The Social Responsibilities of the Bussinessman*, formally introducing the term "social responsibility" for corporations' management (Bowen, 1953, p. 6). In the 1960s and the 1970s, authors like Keith Davis, who defined social responsibility as "business decisions and actions taken for reasons at least partially beyond the firm's direct economic or technical interest" (Davis, 1960, p. 70), but also Peter Drucker and Adolf Berle pointed out that corporate responsibility is synced with the expectations society has of businesses – and if corporations do not act to meet those expectations, society will push for government to intervene to its favor, by imposing new regulation. Indeed, since the 1970s, the state has started shaping regulation concerning the environment, consumer protection, or worker safety.

As that happened, companies began considering corporate responsibility to be a way to maximize profits for shareholders "within the rules of the game". This became known as the "shareholder primacy" view, a take that has been increasingly criticized as the broader vision of corporate social responsibility (CSR) was developed, during the late 1980s and early1990s (Hansmann & Kraakman, 2001).

DOI: 10.4324/9781003152750-13

The relation between CSR and profitability has increasingly become more complex as studies focused on executive perceptions of CSR and the business practice started to include mechanisms of voluntary reporting on corporate codes of conduct and sustainability reports (Carroll, 1999). It is interesting that as the idea of "social responsible investing" increased substantially and as management shifted to note and include CSR practices, the concept of corporate governance became an important one between academics, regulators, executives, and investors. Even if the issue with governance had begun with the beginning of corporations and dated back to Hudson's Bay Company, the Levant Company, and other such chartered companies existing in the sixteenth and the seventeenth centuries, it was in the 1970s that the concept really got fashionable for everyone to discuss about, again.

Both corporate governance and the responsibility that corporations had to society (CSR) became topics of great importance due to the fact that corporations were growing rapidly in the 1970s, especially in the United States, which were experiencing a strong economic growth, and in Western Europe, which had recovered its economy after World War II and was also beginning to grow.

Before the 1970s, companies were focused mostly on the business profitability and its internal management. After the end of World War II, most companies were of small and medium size and most of the owners were also the firm managers. In the 1960s, as businesses grew, managers were those running them, with shareholders following, even if they were still closely involved with the business. As corporations developed and became listed on the markets, the US Securities and Exchange Commission (SEC) brought the matter of corporate governance to the forefront, after the case of Pen Central Corporation filing for bankruptcy and further investigations made the Commission bring proceedings against directors and executives for misrepresenting the company's financial condition (Price, 2018). The term "corporate governance" first appeared in the US Federal Register in 1976. It is then that the SEC asked the New York Stock Exchange to require each listed corporation to have an outside audit, done by independent board directors. Formal governmental regulations regarding corporate governance have referred to the good conduct of financial affairs, leaving mostly the relationship between the society and the business world to be regulated by the markets.

However, as CSR has increasingly become a topic and corporations reported on their practices in the area on a voluntary basis, corporate governance has in fact transformed in response to a range of internal factors or external social pressures (Aguinis & Glavas, 2012; Gill, 2008; Kagan, Thornton, & Gunningham, 2003). While the 2008 financial crisis has brought new regulatory reforms meant to promote financial stability in the United States (the 2010 Dodd-Frank Wall Street Reform and Consumer Act) and the world, focusing on best practices for corporate government practices – to assure transparency, accountability, compliance, and efficiency – the area of sustainability practices remained voluntary.

Corporate governance mechanisms that cover the area of corporate sustainable responsibility are self-regulating codes of conduct, the implementation of CSR board committees, the establishment of business ethics rules, and the supply chain assurance, requiring suppliers to use international business norms and standards of human rights, labor protection, and social responsibility (Gill, 2008). All these are meant to ensure that the corporation voluntarily adopts a number of socially important issues that refer to labor, human rights, and the environment.

The practice of implementing all these mechanisms has started to become visible since the 1990s, as international trade and investment was increasing and transnational companies were opening offices and were starting operations in developing countries across the globe. Research done into the way these mechanisms work for increasing sustainability has underlined the fact that they are just façade improvements when they are not accompanied by significant organizational change (Schanzenbach & Sitkoff, 2019). Corporate governance has evolved as societies evolved. While most corporations have their home in developed countries, their transformation has been considered a symbol of modernization, while their investments abroad worked for influencing actors across the developing countries, which were also seeking growth and modernization.

Perhaps not coincidentally, as modern states evolved, pressed by social development, the research area of gender studies was institutionalized in the same time that the academic and business community started talking about corporate responsibility, and corporate governance became a prominent topic for everyone – in the 1970s. John Money is credited with the invention of the term "gender" in 1955 to describe the "social enactment of the sexual roles", formalizing the idea of the masculine and feminine social roles, while noting that sex (male or female) doesn't guarantee the gender role, considering the flexibility that's built into the "sex-gender system" (Halberstam, 2014). In 1972, Paul Money and Anke A. Ehrhard, with the publication of their book *Man and Woman; Boy and Girl* introduce gender studies into cultural studies. Indeed, gender is never isolated from other conditions that refer to someone's social position in the world – such as citizenship status, life experiences, region of origin, race or access to resources. Therefore, along with women's studies of which it emerged from (Wiegman, 2013), gender studies have become indispensable for discussing social development.

Approaches to both topics – corporate social responsibility (CSR) and gender studies have since become more diverse, even if not necessarily interconnected. While "shareholder primacy view" gained dominance in the United States until the late twentieth century, the academic literature continued to work on alternative theories and models (Ciepley, 2013, p. 142).

As business practice developed to include self-reporting mechanisms, such as corporate codes of conduct or as corporations adopted nonbinding standards from international organizations and NGOs, academic research on the topic of CSR has developed under at least three fields of social sciences: business management, business ethics and legal studies. In the beginning of the twenty-first century, research has started focusing more on answering the questions related to the "business case" for CSR, apart from ethical reasoning. This has shifted debates from CSR to a new concept: environmental, social and governance practices (ESG) implemented by corporations, part of a complex toolkit to mitigate both financial and nonfinancial risk and meant to bring portfolio performance or, in simplistic terms – profit (Gadinis & Miazad, 2019). In implementing such practices, the modern corporation would treat sustainability both as an internal and an external goal – usually coordinating CSR with ESG practices for achieving best outcomes on its actions (Sjåfjell, 2019).

The developments and research pertaining to the gender studies' domain, which are relevant for the business field, have mainly focused on a) the manner in which the feminist movements around the world have strengthened (or not) capitalism and the market economy (Connel, 2005) and b) on the way that gender has become a change factor within the corporations' management structures and governance style (Raworth, 2017, pp. 276–278). The latter is directly linked with the way corporations choose to implement their CSR (or their ESG) policies and establish their governance rules. The question on whether gender can be an agent for changing the way businesses make progress toward sustainability is currently pushing for a discussion on both internal management systems and the areas tackled by CSR strategies implemented by corporations.

This is fundamentally related to the importance gender studies are given within the environment that the corporations function. Judith Lorber (2006), in her article titled "Shifting Paradigms and Challenging Categories" identified several key paradigms' shifts in sociology that regard the gender question and, ultimately, influence the way businesses act. First, it is currently acknowledged that gender is "an organizing principle of the overall social order in modern societies", while the second is that gender and sexuality, in what regards behavioral aspects of personal identity is socially constructed. The third and the fourth paradigm shifts Lorber brought forth relate to the power and social control gender gains in society, considering that feminist social science has devised methodology that allowed and promoted the "standpoint of oppressed and repressed women throughout the world" (Lorber, 2006, p. 449). Her thesis looks into the way society considers women – and whether or not they are regarded to be a subordinated class, when looking into the social order of any place and when establishing how gender studies have effectively influenced local sociology – and therefore the environment where companies, along with other organizations are functioning.

In the same time, research on women in managerial positions has also grown in depth and importance, as businesses expanded their markets globally. In general, the existing literature acknowledges that there is a shortage of women in senior leadership positions around the world, while research has shown that having women in such influencing positions leads to noteworthy organizational benefits (Haynes, 2008; Wicks, Gilbert, &Freeman, 1994). The cultural background matters, meaning that the number of women in management positions differs from country to country but it is still less than that of men in similar positions, even if globally and generally, in all countries women represent the majority of both undergraduates and graduates in business administration and law. (OECD, 2019) In the same time, while there is a lot of statistical data available and empirical research done so far, the area of women in leadership and cross cultural management remains a fertile ground (Bullough, Moore, & Kalafatoglu, 2017) for further exploration and new research, precisely due to the application of findings and new theories into corporate governance and strategic areas, considering the social changes, including those sustained through the influence that (political) discussion on gender issues is having overall and the way society evolves.

Research on management, including international management has increasingly referred to gender issues under the vast areas of cross cultural management and diversity studies. Such research usually has the topic of feminism and gender equality issues treated similarly to that of racism and ethnicity. In this sense, while there is clear consideration of the topic of gender equality, it is also admitted that it is really one of the most vulnerable elements of society, no matter the country. It is also usual that less developed countries have less research on the area considering the economic realities (Bullough et al., 2017) – much of the discussion involving gender equality in business management refers to transnationals and businesses that have developed economies for home countries, even if such companies are welcoming local expertise when they go abroad. Accessing real businesswomen and aspiring businesswomen for research purposes is much more difficult in countries characterized by low gender equality, or conflict zones, even if such figures exist. In the same time, cross-cultural research, involving studies on topics related to gender and women in business in multiple countries is more difficult and more expensive, which explains why this is an area that could and should get more attention in the future.

While awareness of gender as a central feature of society has become more widespread, so has awareness of the need to increase the women's participation in the day-to-day business management and generally, in corporate management. In fact, considering research done by Paola Paoloni and Paola Demartini (2016) in between 2005–2015 to outline leading issues and themes on the topics, considering only two key journals ("Gender, Work and Organisation" and "Gender in Management"), "corporate governance" was the topic to capture most attention, followed by "discrimination" in the workplace and "differences between man and women". This points to one of the major questions to be answered next, which refers to understanding the role of women participation in the decision-making process when it comes to corporate governance in general and to CSR actions in particular. To establish the foundations for answering such a research question, we need to look into the existing research regarding the potential for women participation in management translate into a "factor for change". Psychologically, considering the perceptions of severity of potential outcomes, women tend to focus on long term and less risky actions (Harris, Jenkins, & Glaser, 2006), which could actually mean a shift toward a new agenda for corporations, one that includes sustainable matters.

Positive Change Correlations in Sustainable Transformations

Changing the Business World for Social Sustainability

The primary function of the corporation is to serve its goal and serve the interests of its shareholders (or its investors), which usually translates into the maximization of their returns or the corporation's profitability rate. Businesses are shaped by law, economics and politics. The concept encompassing sustainable business and finance is linked to the idea that 'doing good' – that is to have a positive effect on the environment and the society in general, will help the business profits as well.

Sustainability refers to people's attitude and their perception – therefore, sustainable attitude starts from within the corporation and is only enforced by the overall proposed strategy. It is the human resource in particular that needs to play a role in both demanding and implementing sustainable business goals. This is why the environment in which the company operates also plays a role – the community's culture, its education is playing an important role, considering the kind of expectations the human resource (potential or existing employees) have.

Available research by McKinsey, conducted through surveying more than 3,000 employees in transnational companies over the globe, each year between 2014–2017 has pointed to several elements being needed for motivating them to adopt a sustainable mindset, in other words be wary about the environment and the society that they work into (Bonini & Swartz, 2014). First, sustainable goals need to be in alignment with the company's goals, missions, or values and perceived as such by the workforce. The second motivation factor refers to continuous building of the company's reputation – even more-so, considering that a good corporate reputation with regard to sustainability is increasingly important for attracting good quality workforce (Story, Castanheira, & Hartig, 2016).

The third motivational factor refers to meeting the customers' expectations while only the fourth factor refers to the corporation's profitability and even then, it regards the long-term development of the firm, considering the motivation factor refers to ensuring the find and development of new growth opportunities. In the same time, a cooperation approach across industries, between suppliers and consumers, which is primarily meant to increase supply chains' efficiency (and therefore regards the firm's profitability first and foremost) is also one way to increase the corporate's (and industry's) sustainability (Bové & Swartz, 2016).

Sustainability practices help for the firms to establish a good reputation while they are synced with the overall growth strategy. This is the spirit of the article Michael Porter and Mark Kramer (2011): they explain that these practices are only "at the margin" of what businesses can do and, by themselves cannot achieve success. In fact, they point out that the more that corporations adopted such practices, they were also affected by a reputational side-effect where they're blamed for particular social failures because there was no focus on sustainability related practices earlier and the fixes come "rather late". This is why, they argue, companies must take the lead in bringing businesses and society back together by "moving beyond trade-offs", effectively focusing on the shared value that they can both create (Porter & Kramer, 2011). In doing so, corporations are considering the societal need to be central in their activity – which pushes them away from recognizing conventional economic needs only and takes them to admit social harms or social problems as causes for supplementary internal costs for them. In this sense, corporations need to become increasingly holistic in defining their markets, as the markets have a sense of sustainable needs.

Indeed, there is evidence that sustainability practices have converged over time with the regular marketing and PR practices, and what is more, have even become "business as usual" for those who have initiated them (Ioannou & Serafeim, 2019). More, it has become increasingly important for corporations to prove they are pursuing sustainability practices, not only for their clients but also for their investors (and potential investors). During the last decade, we have seen a surge on the monitoring of corporations' activities – for instance, the consultancy group MSCI keeps detailed information on more than 3,000 companies and has developed the so called "ESG ratings" to measure corporations' long-term resilience to environment, social and governance risks. That is to measure the efficiency of those practices such companies employ to support their sustainable business goals (Zadeh & Serafeim, 2018). There are still limits to how such information can be used by investors in a technical manner. Considering the lack of standardization of reporting on sustainability practices, (Zadeh & Serafeim, 2018, p. 92) there is still room for improvement on getting them to a level that they're effectively used. However, they are influencing the investment decision-making in a subjective, perceptive manner, considering that once in the group of the monitored corporations on ESG rating, the market, which is both suppliers and consumers, is reactive to any move that refers to sustainable practices pursued.

Ioannou and Serafeim (2019) investigated the MSCI dataset and found that while sustainable practices converge in time, they are not just a strategic differentiator for corporations pursuing them, but more of a strategic need, considering everyone else in the industry is pursuing such practices. More, they pointed out that those practices that show a higher level of convergence across industries are associated with practices that were first adopted by the industry market leader (Ioannou & Serafeim, 2019). Their conclusion focuses on the strategic characteristic of sustainable practices. Considering those upon which businesses converge over time to be "common practices", their research and analysis found that they are not contributing to a market value or profitability increase for the specific businesses in question. Instead, the strategic sustainable measures – those adopted by companies and that can't be matched by competitors – are creating value and increase profits as they create competitive advantages. In this sense, in order to grow, companies need to focus on finding their strategy with regard to sustainable practices. That not only increases their ESG ratings but, as Porter and Kramer (2006, 2011) put it, brings companies together with society, serving the societal needs instead of pure economic needs. Considering the strategic dimension of sustainable practice, the idea of implementing sustainable strategies for growth and development makes sense. In this light we need to look at what produces organizational change for corporate governance to be able to report it under CSR practices and increase its ESG ratings.

Organizational Change – Modernizing Corporate Governance

All businesses will undergo transformations in order to remain viable for the market. Change may refer to onboarding new employees, growing departments or even considering merging with other companies. In light of current discussion of companies needing to become sustainable, considering the external forces pushing toward the company bettering its relationship to society by responding to societal needs more than to the market's needs, we need to first examine what areas of the organization may serve such purpose.

Considering sustainability to be a strategic asset to the company's value, the modernization of corporate governance includes strategic organizational change. This process refers to the actions in which a company alters at least one major component of the organization such as its culture, its infrastructure or its internal processes. While regular organizational change can be adaptive, focusing on modest iterations, strategic organizational change is transformative and vast (Stobierski, 2020;

Voigt, 2009). Such changes take a substantial time and energy to enact and need to be closely monitored by the change management in order to make sure it creates the wanted shift in mission and strategy.

The "factors of change" coming from society and pushing toward a needed strategic organizational change are the existing "meta-regulation" that arises from institutional investors, from regulators, from nongovernmental organizations (NGOs) or other groups that measure, guide or monitor the corporation's performance and conduct. All this generates an area of "soft law" that links to the so called "industry standards" and which refers to particular ratings or rankings the company needs to achieve (Hall & Huber, 2019). Prominent frameworks that include standards needed to obey on topics such as human capital, environment or social impact are the UN Global Compact (UNGC), the Global Reporting Initiative (GRI) Standards and the Organization for Economic Cooperation and Development (OECD) Guidelines for Multinational Enterprises.

For organizational change management, it is important to understand the resolution needed to be reached, through implemented changes. In the case of "more sustainability", there are no real measurements, even if ESG ratings do push for some idea of corporate performance evaluation. While there is no uniform reporting and audit on nonfinancial reporting on sustainable practices (Harper & Ho, 2016), there are several jurisdictions of the world that are considering mandatory some sustainability disclosures. For example, the European Union Directive on the Disclosure of Non-Financial and Diversity Information asks for companies to report on their CSR practices and ESG data while the United Kingdom Companies act contains similar regulations in the stakeholder disclosure provision (Fisch, 2019). In the same time, the United Nations' Principles for Responsible Investment promote institutional investor engagement with portfolio firms around ESG performance (Harper & Ho, 2016).

Considering the push for companies to become more active in answering societal needs, investors and asset managers are using ESG data in assessing risk and managing their investments and to that goal, they are using ratings given by private, independent providers like MSCI, Sustainalytics, ISS and RepRisk. However, the third-party providers on ESG ratings do not provide consistent data that investors can work with. (Kotsantonis & Serafeim, 2019). However, all providers have two major indicators that they seek to measure and that refer to the way the corporation is organized: transparency practices and human resource diversity – which generally refers to gender equality and cultural aspects if the company works in a multinational or multiethnic environment. Even so, their varying methodologies produce conflicting ratings which are, in the end, subject to human biases (Doyle, 2018).

Considering the ESG investing is "essentially unregulated market" (Brakman, Reiser, & Tucker, 2019) and that factors that relate to the environment, social issues and governance are not clearly known, the only guideline points toward the existing commonalities in reporting. There might be no singular system that allows a customized approach to CSR and ESG, but transparency and diversity point to the areas where organizational change might be needed, whenever a corporation needs to show increased compliance with regard to sustainability (Grosser, 2011). Of the two, transparency refers to objective reporting and it is the easier to pinpoint and monitor. Diversity, referring to employee rights and gender equality is more difficult to grasp. This is where recent attempts of regulations have failed, while there is the common view that increasing gender equality is effectively improving ESG and generally, corporate governance ratings.

Sustainable Change for Organizational Governance – Is Gender a Factor?

It is important to note that companies mostly address and refer to gender equality in the context of addressing diversity. Even if diversity may mean more than that for some corporations nowadays – including different ethnicities and cultures, especially if we are talking about transnational corporations, it is mostly that, by implementing diversity measures, corporations seek a balance between males and females within the organization.

In discussing gender as a factor of change for the organization, and further, for the society, we need to consider two main subjects of reference. First, if we consider "shareholder primacy" to describe what went wrong with corporations not working for a sustainable society, we need to consider the way gender diversity as an internal corporate policy could positively change its working mode. Second, we need to look if the implemented policies of gender diversity make us see corporations differently – or not.

Existing literature points out that the predominance of males in decision-making jobs in business and finance is due to the values brought in by the very foundational economic theories for the sector, considering that males have had historically a de facto dominance over the public debate. Therefore, the values upon which traditional management was built upon are men's values and the lack of women in executive positions are a consequence of our male-dominated history, as are the norms, the rules and even the legislation that are guiding corporations (Prügl, 2012, pp. 21–35). There are several strategies that would change the reality of male dominated corporations, proposed by feminist studies.

First, there is the "liberal individualism" or "women empowerment" strategy which essentially argues that, for women to succeed into a male-dominated area, it is essential to teach them to learn and adapt to the environment. This kind of strategy involves having women know the existing rules and play by them – not changing the rules, but eventually changing their own personalities to fit the rules, if necessary (Grosser & Moon, 2017, p. 323). This goes counter to the idea that anything would change in terms of corporate's reality and its general management system, considering the same rules will apply and by similar actors. Organizationally, it will all remain the same and gender diversity would only be measured by the name and not by the essence.

Another way to go under the "liberal individualist" strategy for "women empowerment" refers to identify certain personality characteristics and value them for "feminine traits" and value them – the so-called "value feminine" strategy. Such traits would then either be made equal or even more valuable than males' specific characteristics: for example, a woman is a better communicator than a man as communication is a feminine characteristic. While such stereotypes might exist, supporting them through the corporation organizational structures has the potential to reinforce differences between genders, even if it might be to the advantage of women (Bellstrom, 2016; Profeta, 2017). This would very much support the idea of "gendered organization" even if the values upon human resources' management might not necessarily be male-related values, but incline toward female-related values. If such a strategy is adopted inside an organization, it is usual that women (and men) are assigned specific roles. It might be that through such a strategy, women are indeed empowered and have better access to jobs that they might not have access to otherwise, but it doesn't mean that while such a human resource strategy is implemented, the overall management rules of the organization are getting better, and the organization is becoming more sustainable for the environment it lives in. This strategy, however, has helped organizations fix their gender balance problems as it is instrumental for their diversity goals – on paper, at least.

The next strategy for achieving gender equality within the corporations refers to the structural change imposed by existing industry norms or even existing legislation with regard to the number of females employed within the organization – the so-called "stewardship rules". This strategy is called "liberal structuralism" and it is meant to influence not only the organization's governance system, but also the investor behavior. Similarly, and notably, this is a strategy that is also helping corporations adopt CSR practices (Grosser & Moon, 2017, p. 329). By reporting requirements concerning these practices as well as improvements made to allow women in decision-making positions, companies show accountability and compliance with externally imposed norms. An example for such strategy is given by the push for more gender-balanced corporate boards, although such a strategy is limited by the business case argument (Sjåfjell, 2014), considering that in most cases, such improvements begin by implementing a "value the feminine" strategy, which means that the organization is not necessarily more sustainable in the end.

However, if imposed by the law, such measures as promoting more women on corporate boards may eventually work for increasing the number of women that have a role in the decision-making process, but only if applied in due time and not immediately, considering the qualifications needed for being board members. This is the case of Norway, which is one of the most egalitarian countries in the world – and, as Sjåfjell (2014) writes in her article "Gender Diversity in the Boardroom and Its Impacts", even in such a country the idea was met with strong opposition considering the business cases and the needed professional expertise for being part of an executive board. In fact, the EU Parliament tried mirroring Norway's idea and failed meeting the Council's votes for a Directive on increasing the number of women on boards precisely due to the divisive countries' views on the matter (EU, 2012, 2015, 2017). The EU leaders in the Council feared that imposing such a regulation to corporations could create a conflict atmosphere between the business environment and the regulators, taking the specificities of each industries and the impossibility to generalize, not knowing the qualifications needed and existing in each business field in the European Union.

The other problem with structural liberalism is that, through regulation, changes may become symbolic. Corporations could indeed report changes made in the right direction because they must, but they don't necessarily address systemic reforms needed for the actual corporate government restructuring that would be needed for improving overall sustainability. A growing consciousness of elements that address gender equality amongst decision makers for instance may facilitate increased corporate sustainability if such elements are enforced on managerial levels and general production in general – in other words, in those areas where the company is not reporting on similar topics, but where changes are needed for sustainability to be achieved. (Villiers & Mähönen, 2015, pp. 184–189). Reporting works for measuring change, as long as it is done on substance.

The fourth strategy that has the goal of achieving gender equality builds upon the third and aims at creating substance by making small but deep cultural changes within the organization with the objective of also improving efficiency. In effect, the strategy has dual objectives and therefore addresses improving the corporation's governance through the idea of improving performance, while advantageously using gender equality. The problem such strategy may trigger during the implementation refers to the fact that, while gender equality is one of its major goals, the economic performance may be prioritized and may be perceived as superior to gender equality and therefore, the latter might slip away (Meyerson & Kolb, 2009, p. 557).

Another strategy that refers to organizational structural reforms is that of separatism (Sjåfjell & Fannon, 2018) – in the sense that the organization is renouncing the idea of achieving both profitability and supporting gender diversity and, instead, goes into social entrepreneurship for a separate line of business, testing it as an alternative for the status quo. Social entrepreneurship is however, not new – but mirrors the traditional "cooperative" that's the oldest form of economic organization (Bibby, 2014). Policy initiatives referring to the development of social entrepreneurship as well as the provisional adoption of the model by companies (even if for specific objectives or business lines), may indeed bring forth ideas on how to do business in a different way and therefore change the status quo organizational patterns. However, if they don't succeed in putting together the good practices needed for the eventual reform of the corporation (Baumfield, 2018), even if they do focus gender equality for a goal, they will remain a marginal attempt or a marketing sideshow that may aim to distract from the reality of a non-reforming, conservatory environment of the traditional corporation.

In effect, gender can be an agent for change if the environment that the company works into supports the idea of corporate transformation so that sustainable goals are achieved. This refers to theories like the ethic of care or social justice (Ang, 2018) but also to legal measures that support social sustainable goals (Sjåfjell & Richardson, 2015) be implemented or be supported for implementation by informal social behavior. The employment and the promotion of females into decision-making roles do not guarantee by itself change. It may, in fact sustain the idea of gendered society in making it more female than male, while male culture which stands at the foundation of what we call "shareholder primacy" culture is enforced.

It is the conditions that allow both men and women to act as free agents of change that matter – it is those external forces that come from the society that push for the need of organizational change meant to achieve sustainable goals. While patriarchal society that allows and supports the idea of women to be discriminated against has a negative impact on corporate social behavior, a matriarchal society that is guided by profit and similar rules is giving the same negative outcomes. This makes the case for the dilution (if not the eradication) of gendered society – which can only work if there is pressure coming from the market and a certain consciousness that the current working model of the corporation is unsustainable. Existing literature underlines the idea of a comprehensive approach being needed for a better and deeper understanding of the meaning of social sustainability so that norms, rules and legislation could be shaped according to the needs. As that takes shape, sustainable practices, which include those that support the idea of gender equality and the fight against discrimination remain voluntary for corporations and other organizations functioning within the society.

The Case of the European Union

The European corporate landscape is heterogeneous – politically and legally. It includes different ownership structures and different approaches to governance. Therefore, the European Union has not established a set of rules for corporate governance and there is no uniform code that could be implemented, considering the corporate law and codes of governance come under the individual member states. Instead, the EU has adopted a principles-based policy at the EU level with the goal of improving standards of corporate governance, considering the overall goal of promoting economic growth and reducing market inefficiencies.

Since 2000, the EU has had a predictable and slow approach in what regards its policy toward European corporate governance. The policy-making process typically starts with the commissioning of studies, continues with the transformation of the studies into consultative "Green Papers" which are then turned into "Action Plans". Then, the "Action Plans" can lead to the adoption of specific laws (at the national level), Directives or Recommendations. The process can span multiple years.

There are several topics that EU has addressed when it comes to corporate governance: enhancing corporate transparency, protecting shareholder rights, enhancing board effectiveness and building shareholder engagement and stewardship. For all, the emphasis was primarily put on "comply-or-explain" approach, which ultimately was giving the corporation the possibility of voluntary implementing recommendations issued by the EU policymakers.

After the financial crisis of 2008, which was believed to have been caused also because of the corporate governance failures, the European Parliament increased its role in the debate on European corporate governance. It has advocated for enhanced employee rights, gender diversity and building greater awareness of environmental, ethical and social problems affecting corporations. The Commission has remained focused – but increased its attention and monitoring, on the "shareholder primacy" issue. One of the outcomes of these changes in the attitude of the EU institutions was the issuance of the Capital Requirements Directive IV, (in 2013), which is capping bonus awards for bank executives among other prescriptions.

Another outcome is the Corporate Governance Action Plan issued by the EU in 2012 which is the Commission's most recent assessment of the corporate governance challenges faced in Europe. The Plan proposes 14 initiatives that refer to corporate law and governance in general, many of which are focused on increasing transparency through enhanced disclosure and address corporate law harmonization. Granular recommendations on board composition and diversity, time commitment, matters such as fiduciary duty, shareholder engagement and board evaluation can also be found mentioned in the document. The European Parliament adopted an update of the Shareholder's Directive Law in 2017 (SRD II) which is meant to improve transparency of shareholder engagement.

All these steps are meant to harmonize formal regulation that refers to corporate governance.

However, general disparities between government standards of the member states slowed down the process of issuing common legislation – for instance, measures of the SRD II come from a Green Paper issued in 2011 and the law was passed only six years later, in 2017. More, such disparities relate to existing infrastructure across the EU – it is often more practical and easier for a country like Germany than for a country like Slovakia or Romania to implement corporate governance measures adopted at the EU level.

Although the response to the 2008 financial crisis was focused on specific corrections aimed at increased transparency, the EU continues to promote a system that is based on responsible and accountable boards that are elected and report to shareholders. From this perspective, the EU is supportive of shareholders' rights, while it tries to regulate areas that refer to sustainable practices of corporate governance.

In fact, the European Commission proposed a Directive on Gender Balance on Boards in November 2012. However, as the initiative is blocked since 2015, the EU has so far failed to address through legislation the imbalance between men and women in corporations' boards. The EU Parliament strongly supported the legislative action in this area and adopted a favorable position on the Directive in 2013, but consensus was not reached at EU Council level, despite consensus across the EU in favor of taking measures to improve gender balance on company boards. Still, the matter remains high on the priorities list for the European Commission, considering the new EU Gender Equality Strategy 2020–2025, adopted on the 5th of March 2020.

This is not by chance. The EU is one of the major global actors in promoting gender equality. The origins of the EU gender equality policy lie in the article 119 of the Treaty of Rome, adopted in 1957, obliging the member states to "ensure the application of the principle of equal pay for equal work" (Hoskyns, 1996, p. 14). Consequently, all member states regulate equality through antidiscrimination legislation or through the labor code (Selanec & Senden, 2011, p. 16).

The European Union is also one of the most vocal and earliest promoters for sustainability. The concept appears in the Treaty on the European Union (signed in Maastricht in 1992 and entering into force in 1993) as there are several articles emphasizing the need for sustainable development. Indeed, the text also mirrors developments in international law, where sustainable development had started to become increasingly important and sustainability had slowly started (since the 70s) to become a general principle of international law (Segger, 2009). Even if the EU is considered to have been a supporter of liberal structuralism, considering its slow policymaking process, it is however at the forefront regarding sustainability measures, by putting the promotion of peace and the well-being of its people at the center of the EU values (Boyd, 2012; Sjåfjell, 2015).

The EU has developed a strong record of efforts to promote social sustainability and labor standards in international trade and is the only international organization that doesn't discuss corporate sustainability as corporate governance only, but rather under the umbrella of corporate social responsibility. In 2006, the European Commission launched the European Alliance for CSR and in 2011 published the first CSR Strategy for the EU where it defined CSR as the "responsibility of enterprises for their impacts upon society". This new definition required the integration, at the companies' level, of "social, environmental, ethical, human rights and consumer concerns into their business operations and core strategy". In 2014, the EU has issued a reporting directive which critics suggest is insufficient considering that the member states are not strongly following it.

In November 2020, after the issuance of a new Action Plan in 2018 and lacking an updated text for a CSR Strategy, a new Study on CSR and its implementation into EU Company law was published. It references problems occurred during the first months of the Covid-19 pandemic and addresses the limitations that the 2014 Directive has had. Conclusions refer to the fact that the business focus on sustainability should be included in the corporate governance rules across the European Union and specific legislative acts would follow to implement such plans, after public consultations are finished.

This approach to promoting corporate sustainability may work only if the EU legislators recognize the deeper systemic issues that are currently contributing to the unsustainable state we are in. With one of the most conservatory European states now no longer a member of the EU, the shareholder primacy approach will lose terrain while the EU progressive legislators will gain terrain, supporting the EU Commission in implementing the Green Deal also through a new CSR Strategy and new norms. All this will be done, however, while considering the impact that the current Covid-19 pandemic has over the economy in general and over the business operations in particular.

Conclusions: The Post-pandemic (European) Sustainable Transformations

The Covid-19 pandemic of 2020 has put forth the European dependence on international supply chains. More, it has challenged the European member states resilience and the European Union resilience, considering many companies operating in Europe were dependent on imports coming from other countries – they were dependent on the well-functioning of international supply chains. This proved to be of incremental importance during the first months of the pandemic, when most countries had imposed lockdown measures and the medical and pharmaceutical sectors were among the first ones to be hard hit by delays in supply and delivery to the end-users.

Later on, as the pandemic continued throughout 2020, the world has gone through a transformative process. Digitization increased in importance. While the initial disruptions of the supply chains were corrected, companies had to adapt to a new world where working from home became a new normal until the pandemic is over. Online education replaced classes for kids, which forced parents go into more than their primary roles as educators – most needed to support their young children learn technology and maintain their focus. This has pushed for a rapid organizational change within the corporate world: both externally and internally. While new solutions were implemented for goods and services delivery, the corporations' human resource departments were faced with new pressures.

Such transformative forces will clearly change the way we know corporate governance to have been so far. Not only everything went digital, including board meetings (which posed new security pressures on the IT departments, for sure), but, depending on their business sector, corporations also had to change their business logic. All these rapid changes have surely affected corporate governance and have had and will have an impact on their corporate sustainability strategies.

In fact, in the study the EU Commission published in November 2020, it is acknowledged that the CSR will likely be redefined in the post-pandemic times and such redefinition is yet unknown (EU, 2020, p. 13). What is certain is that corporations will need to continue to attract talented human resource and therefore, one of the consequences of the pandemic is that while resilience must thrive, the corporation's foresight function into *the purpose* of the human resource in pursuing work or consuming specific products becomes ever more important for the corporation's future. A corporation needs to understand both the incentives for its employees to continue working as well as its consumers' social needs.

In effect, the pandemic raises a number of issues with regard to corporate governance and CSR. First, sustainability is to remain one of the core elements for development, considering the increased demand for sustainable initiatives during the pandemic (Norton, 2021). Second, the human rights issues will remain key for corporate governance – this includes making sure the workers' rights and gender equality remain respected, which are also key for sustainability practices. Third, CSR may go beyond making sure social and environmental protective measures are taken by the companies: considering the effect that the supply chain disruptions have had on citizens, the EU wonders if the corporations should engage in protecting their consumers from such disruptions and carefully choose among international suppliers (EU, 2020, p. 11). More, the question is asked on whether authorities have a role in making sure corporates meet resilience standards, at least in what regards critical, strategic domains such as the health and pharmaceutical sectors. While, in this case, sustainability measures may translate into protectionism, it is to be seen if the post-pandemic world has the government and the regulators increase their role into pushing companies to have a certain behavior or whether it is – again – the society that needs to press for sustainable change. However, a different CSR and corporate governance are to be shaped, soon.

References

Aguinis, H., & Glavas, A. (2012). What we know and don't know about corporate social responsibility: A review and research agenda. *Journal of Management, 38*(4), 932–968.

Ang, Y. S. (2018). Exploring spatial justice and the ethic of care in corporations and group governance. In B. Sjåfjell & I. L. Fannon (Eds.), *Creating corporate sustainability. Gender as an agent for change* (University of Oslo Faculty of Law Research Paper No. 2018–14). Cambridge University Press. Retrieved February 19, 2021, from https://ssrn.com/abstract=3179444

Baumfield, V. S. (2018). How change happens: The benefit corporation in the United States and considerations for Australia. In B. Sjåfjell & I. L. Fannon (Eds.), *Creating corporate sustainability. Gender as an agent for change* (University of Oslo Faculty of Law Research Paper No. 2018–13). Cambridge University Press. Retrieved February 19, 2021, from https://ssrn.com/abstract=3179442

Bellstrom, K. (2016). Sheryl Sandberg: These are the biggest obstacles for women trying to lean in. *Forbes.* Retrieved January 28, 2021, from https://fortune.com/2016/09/27/sheryl-sandberg-women-in-the-workplace/

Bibby, A. (2014). Co-operatives are an inherently more sustainable form of business. *The Guardian.* Retrieved February 26, 2021, from www.theguardian.com/social-enterprise-network/2014/mar/11/co-op-business-sustainability

Bonini, S., & Swartz, S. (2014). *Profits with purpose: How organizing for sustainability can benefit the bottom line.* Retrieved February 22, 2021, from www.mckinsey.com/~/media/McKinsey/Business%20Functions/Sustainability/Our%20Insights/Profits%20with%20purpose/Profits%20with%20Purpose.ashx

Bové, A. T., & Swartz, S. (2016). *Sustainability in supply chains.* Retrieved February 10, 2021, from www.mckinsey.com/business-functions/sustainability/our-insights/starting-at-the-source-sustainability-in-supply-chains

Bowen, H. E. (1953). *Social responsibilities of the businessman.* New York: Harper & Row.

Boyd, D. R. (2012). *The constitutional right to a healthy environment' (2012) environment magazine.* Retrieved January 18, 2021, from www.environmentmagazine.org/Archives/Back%20Issues/2012/July-August%202012/constitutional-rights-full.html

Brakman Reiser, D., & Tucker, A. (2019). *Buyer beware: The paradox of ESG & passive ESG funds.* Retrieved February 18, 2021, from https://ssrn.com/abstract=3440768

Bratton, W. W., & Wachter, M. L. (2008). In shareholder primacy's corporatist origins: Adolf Berle and the modern corporation. *Journal of Corporation Law, 34*, 99–152.

Bullough, A., Moore, F., & Kalafatoglu, T. (2017). *Research on women in international business and management: Then, now, and next.* Forthcoming in

Cross Cultural and Strategic Management, Special Issue on Gender in International Business and Management. Retrieved February 24, 2021, from https://ssrn.com/abstract=2926139

Carroll, A. B. (1999). Corporate social responsibility: Evolution of a definitional construct. *Business & Society, 38*(3), 268–295. Retrieved February 7, 2021, from https://journals.sagepub.com/doi/10.1177/000765039903800303

Ciepley, D. (2013). Beyond public and private: Toward a political theory of the corporation. *The American Political Science Review, 107*(1), 139–158. doi:10.2307/23357761

Connell, R. (2005). Change among the gatekeepers: Men, masculinities, and gender equality in the global arena. *In Signs, 30*(3), 1801–1825. doi:10.1086/427525

Davis, K. (1960). Can business afford to ignore social responsibilities? *California Management Review, 2,* 70–76.

Doyle, T. M. (2018). *Ratings that don't rate: The subjective world of ESG ratings agencies.* American Council for Capital Formation. Retrieved February 10, 2021, from http://accfcorpgov.org/wpcontent/uploads/2018/07/ACCF_Rating sesGReport.pdf

EU. (2012). *Corporate government action plan 2012.* Brussels, Belgium. Retrieved January 5, 2021, from https://eur-lex.europa.eu/legal-content/EN/ALL/?uri=CELEX%3A52012DC0740

EU. (2015). *Gender balance on boards.* Brussels, Belgium. Retrieved January 5, 2021, from www.europarl.europa.eu/legislative-train/theme-area-of-justice-and-fundamental-rights/file-gender-balance-on-boards

EU. (2017). *EU is stuck half way to achieving gender equality, MEPs say.* Retrieved February 10, 2021, from www.europarl.europa.eu/news/en/press-room/20170308IPR65678/eu-is-stuck-half-way-to-achieving-gender-equality-meps-say

EU. (2018). *2018 Report on equality between men and women.* Brussels, Belgium. Retrieved January 5, 2021, from https://op.europa.eu/en/publication-detail/-/publication/950dce57-6222-11e8-ab9c-01aa75ed71a1

EU. (2020). *Corporate social responsibility (CSR) and its implementation in EU law.* Retrieved January 6, 2021, from www.europarl.europa.eu/RegData/etudes/STUD/2020/658541/IPOL_STU(2020)658541_EN.pdf

Fisch, J. E. (2019). Making sustainability disclosure sustainable. *Georgetown Law Journal, 107,* 923–966. Retrieved February 17, 2021, from https://papers.ssrn.com/sol3/papers.cfm?abstract_id=3233053

Gadinis, S., & Miazad, A. (2019). *Sustainability in corporate law* (Working paper). Retrieved February 18, 2021, from https://ssrn.com/abstract=3441375

Gill, A. (2008). Corporate governance as social responsibility: A research agenda. *Berkeley Journal of International Law, 26,* 452–478.

Grosser, K. (2011). *Corporate social responsibility, gender equality and organizational change: A feminist perspective* (PhD thesis). University of Nottingham. Retrieved January 5, 2021, from http://eprints.nottingham.ac.uk/12138/

Grosser, K., & Moon, J. (2017). CSR and feminist organization studies: Towards an integrated theorization for the analysis of gender issues. *Journal of Business Ethics.* Retrieved February 1, 2021, from https://research.cbs.dk/en/publications/csr-and-feminist-organization-studies-towards-an-integrated-theor

Halberstam, J. (2014). Gender. In B. Burgett & G. Hendler (Eds.), *Keywords for American cultural studies* (2nd ed., pp. 116–118). New York University Press. Retrieved February 28, 2021, from www.jstor.org/stable/j.ctt1287j69.33

Hall, J. A., & Huber, B. M (2019). ESG in the US: Current state of play and key considerations for issuers. In *The international comparative legal guide to: Corporate governance 2019* (12th ed., pp. 23–30). Retrieved February 17, 2021, from www.briefinggovernance.com/2019/07/esg-in-the-us-current-state-of-play-and-key-considerations-for-issuers/

Hansmann, H., & Kraakman, R. (2001). The end of history for corporate law. *Georgetown Law Journal, 89*, 439–469.

Harper Ho, V. (2016). Risk-related activism: The business case for monitoring nonfinancial risk. *Journal of Corporation Law, 41*, 647–704. Retrieved February 17, 2021, from https://papers.ssrn.com/sol3/papers.cfm?abstract_id=2478121

Harris, C. R., Jenkins, M., & Glaser, D. (2006). Why do women take fewer risks than men? *Judgment and Decision Making, 1*(1), 48–63. Retrieved January 20, 2021, from http://journal.sjdm.org/jdm06016.pdf

Haynes, K. (2008). Moving the gender agenda or stirring chicken's entrails? Where next for feminist methodologies in accounting? *Accounting, Auditing & Accountability Journal, 21*, 539–555.

Hoskyns, C. (1996). The European union and the women within: An overview of women's rights policy. In R. A. Elman (Ed.), *Sexual politics and the European union: The new feminist challenge* (pp. 14–23). New York: Berghahn Books.

Ioannou, I., & Serafeim, G. (2019). *Yes, sustainability can be a strategy* (Harvard Business School Accounting & Management Unit Working Paper No. 19–065). Retrieved January 28, 2021, from https://hbr.org/2019/02/yes-sustainability-can-be-a-strategy

Kagan, R. A., Thornton, D., & Gunningham, N. (2003). Explaining corporate environmental performance: How does regulation matter? *Law & Society Review, 37*(1), 51–90.

Kotsantonis, S., & Serafeim, G. (2019, Spring). Four things no one will tell you about ESG data. *Journal of Applied Corporate Finance, 31*(2), 50–58. Retrieved February 10, 2021, from https://papers.ssrn.com/sol3/papers.cfm?abstract_id=3420297

Lorber, J. (2006). Shifting paradigms and challenging categories. *Social Problems, 53*(4), 448–453. doi:10.1525/sp.2006.53.4.448

Meyerson, D., & Kolb, D. (2009). *Moving out of the 'armchair': Developing a framework to bridge the gap between feminist theory and practice.* doi:10.1007/978-3-531-91387-2_13. Retrieved January 7, 2021, from www.researchgate.net/publication/301990046_Moving_Out_of_the_%27Armchair%27_Developing_a_Framework_to_Bridge_the_Gap_Between_Feminist_Theory_and_Practice

Norton, L. (2021). *MSCI says growth in ESG outpaces its traditional index business.* Barrons. Retrieved February 25, 2021, from www.barrons.com/articles/msci-says-growth-in-esg-outpaces-its-traditional-index-business-51614041864

OECD. (2019). *Gender differences in university graduates by fields of study.* Retrieved February 20, 2021, from www.oecd.org/els/CO3_2_Gender_differences_in_university_graduates.pdf

Paoloni, P., & Demartini, P. (2016). Women in management: Perspectives on a decade of research (2005–2015). In *Nature*. Retrieved February 20, 2021, from www.nature.com/articles/palcomms201694

Porter, M. E., & Kramer, M. R. (2006). Strategy and society: The link between competitive advantage and corporate social responsibility. *Harvard Business Review*, *84*(12). Retrieved February 10, 2021, from https://hbr.org/2006/12/strategy-and-society-the-link-between-competitive-advantage-and-corporate-social-responsibility

Porter, M. E., & Kramer, M. R. (2011). Creating shared value. *Harvard Business Review*. Retrieved January 18, 2011, from https://hbr.org/2011/01/the-big-idea-creating-shared-value

Price, N. J. (2018). *What is the history of corporate governance and how has it changed?* Retrieved February 18, 2021, from https://insights.diligent.com/corporate-governance/what-is-the-history-of-corporate-governance-and-how-has-it-changed

Profeta, P. (2017). *Gender equality in decision-making positions: The efficiency gains*. Bocconi University, Milan. Retrieved February 17, 2021, from www.intereconomics.eu/contents/year/2017/number/1/article/gender-equality-in-decision-making-positions-the-efficiency-gains.html

Prügl, E. (2012). *If Lehman brothers had been Lehman Sisters. . .*, Gender and myth in the aftermath of the financial crisis. *International Political Sociology*, *6*(1), 21–35.

Raworth, K. (2017). *Doughnut economics: Seven ways to think like a 21st-century economist*. London: Cornerstone.

Schanzenbach, M. M., & Sitkoff, R. H. (2019). The law and economics of environmental, social, and governance investing by a fiduciary. *Stanford Law Review*. Retrieved January 26, 2021, from https://papers.ssrn.com/sol3/papers.cfm?abstract_id=3244665.

Segger, C. (2009). Sustainable development in international law. In P. Birnie, A. Boyle, & C. Redgwell (Eds.), *International law and the environment* (3rd ed., pp. 125–127). Oxford: Oxford University Press.

Selanec, G., & Senden, L. (2011). *Positive action measures to ensure full equality in practice between men and women including on company boards*. European Commission, European Network of Legal Experts in the Field of Gender Equality. Retrieved January 5, 2021, from https://op.europa.eu/en/publication-detail/-/publication/6b4179c6-13e5-406f-b30e-048804d1bea3

Sjåfjell, B. (2014). Gender diversity in the boardroom and its impacts: Is the example of Norway a way forward? *Deakin Law Review*, *25*. Retrieved February 10, 2021, from https://core.ac.uk/reader/229689280

Sjåfjell, B. (2015). The legal significance of article 11 TFEU for EU institutions and member states. In B. Sjåfjell & A. Wiesbrock (Eds.), *The greening of European business under EU law: Taking article 11 TFEU seriously*. London and New York: Routledge. Retrieved February 16, 2021, from https://ssrn.com/abstract=2530006

Sjåfjell, B. (2019). *Theories of the firm: What they are good for and what they are really bad at*. Retrieved February 21, 2021, from https://ssrn.com/abstract=3461603

Sjåfjell, B., & Fannon, L. I. (2018). Corporate sustainability: Gender as an agent for change? In B. Sjåfjell & I. L. Fannon (Eds.), *Creating corporate sustainability. Gender as an agent for change* (University of Oslo Faculty of Law Research Paper No. 2018–18, Nordic & European Company Law Working

Paper No. 19–12). Cambridge University Press. Retrieved January 7, 2021, from https://ssrn.com/abstract=3179450

Sjåfjell, B., & Richardson, B. J., (2015). The future of company law and sustainability. In B. Sjåfjell & B. J. Richardson (Eds.), *Company law and sustainability: Legal barriers and opportunities* (University of Oslo Faculty of Law Research Paper No. 2015–34). Cambridge University Press. Retrieved January 5, 2021, from https://ssrn.com/abstract=2663341

Stobierski, T. (2020). *Organizational change: What it is and why it is important.* Retrieved February 11, 2021, from https://online.hbs.edu/blog/post/organizational-change-management

Story, J., Castanheira, F., & Hartig, S. (2016). Corporate social responsibility and organizational attractiveness: Implications for talent management. *Social Responsibility Journal, 12*(3), 484–505. doi:10.1108/SRJ-07-2015-0095. Retrieved January 10, 2021, from www.emerald.com/insight/content/doi/10.1108/SRJ-07-2015-0095/full/html

Villiers, C., & Mähönen, J. (2015). Accounting, auditing, and reporting: Supporting or obstructing the sustainable companies objective? In B. Sjåfjell & B. J. Richardson (Eds.), *Company law and sustainability: Legal barriers and opportunities.* Cambridge University Press. Retrieved February 12, 2021, from www.jus.uio.no/ifp/english/research/projects/sustainable-companies/news/scnfr-cch.pdf

Voigt, C. (2009). *Sustainable development as a principle of integration in international law. Resolving potential conflicts between climate measures and WTO law.* Leiden: Martinus Nijhoff Publishers. Retrieved January 5, 2021, from https://brill.com/view/title/15079

Wicks, A., Gilbert, D. J., &Freeman, E. (1994). A feminist reinterpretation of the stakeholder concept. *Business Ethics Quarterly, 4,* 475–497.

Wiegman, R. (2013). Wishful thinking. *Feminist Formations, 25*(3), 202–213. Retrieved February 20, 2021, from www.jstor.org/stable/43860718

Zadeh, A. A., & Serafeim, G. (2018). Why and how investors use ESG information: Evidence from a global survey. *Financial Analysts Journal, 74*(3), 87–103. doi:10.2469/faj.v74.n3.2

11 Corporate Social Responsibility, Media, and Communication

Panagiota Antonopoulou

The Levels of the Pyramid

This original work aims to depict the relationship between media–CSR–entrepreneurship–society within the European environment in the form of a conceptual pyramid: At the top of the pyramid is the CSR European culture with primarily moral but also economic, political, and ideological dimensions. This culture is linked to the Ethics in Entrepreneurship and the social dividend return, but it often degrades to the level of the marketing events in order to attract publicity and the interest by the media. The media is on the next level of the pyramid; it is the voice and a vehicle of this culture, a key pillar in CSR activity, which to a large or short degree replaces the State's active participation in the society affairs. The media itself is an industry that should operate under specific rules and obligations for social responsibility. The role of the media in the promotion and dissemination of CSR culture is not always positive; it often imposes on CSR the rules of marketing "imaging" and often sterilizes it of its social content and intervenes throughout its entire range of operations: its organization, management, morals, and aesthetics.

On the next level is the political environment in the strict sense of establishing a framework of principles and rules in which the socioeconomic relations need to develop within the context of the "State" coordinate, but also in the broader sense of the dominant ideology that is formatted within the institutional coordinates of the European governance. Immediately below, and just one level above the base of the pyramid is the European entrepreneurship, which is both the consumer and the provider to the European CSR culture. Finally, at the base of the pyramid is the society, which is the final recipient and beneficiary of the European CSR culture.

The European CSR Culture

At the top of the pyramid, as mentioned earlier, is the CSR European culture with the economic, political, ideological, educational, and social

DOI: 10.4324/9781003152750-14

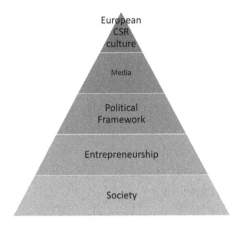

Figure 11.1 The CSR conceptual pyramid

dimensions. Both the economic and the moral factors are the dominant dimensions that have been studied by major researchers from the fields of economics and social sciences. For many years there was a weakness about establishing a precise definition of CSR. Over time, the Corporate Social Responsibility (CSR) has been described as "the commitment to the well-being of local communities through selective business practices" (Kotler & Lee, 2005), "a process of continuous improvement, an investment, not a cost" (Palazzi & Starcher, 2006), "a branding tool" (Breitbarth & Harris, 2007), "a public relations technique" (Capriotti & Moreno, 2007; Huertas & Capriotti, 2008), and in other ways. The European Commission has defined CSR as "the responsibility of enterprises for their impact on society and, therefore, it should be company led". Generally, the context of CSR is linked to the Ethics in Entrepreneurship; an ethical company treats its customers and employees honestly and also acts as a good citizen within the community in which it operates.

CSR has been interpreted through various versions with direct or indirect impacts on business: first, at social focus, reflecting the relationship between businesses and society but also environment when focusing on the contribution of businesses to the natural environment. In addition, researchers focused on the economic aspect while referring to the socioeconomic aspects of a business, including stakeholders. Meanwhile, the definitions of CSR may vary depending on who promotes them and why, and also the maturity of the market. Analyzing CSR practices in different countries and different markets as media may provide essential elements in identifying whether CSR is similarly understood and practiced around the world (Adi, Grigore, & Crowther, 2015). According to the Commission, the companies can become socially responsible by integrating social, environmental, ethical, consumer, and human rights concerns into their business strategy and operations following the law. Public authorities play a supporting role through voluntary policy measures and, where necessary, complementary regulation. In practice, in order to be considered socially responsible, a company must fulfill all the financial obligations (income – profit and compensation on all liabilities), legal obligations (compliance with laws and regulations), ethics (according to the code of conduct and business ethics), and the charitable responsibilities by returning a profit to society (Carroll, 1991).

CSR is generally based on principles and values that characterize the culture of every society: the interest and the respect about people, the environmental protection, and the improvement of living standards and quality of life. As European culture suggests, modern businesses and organizations have to focus their attention not only on their shareholders, clients, and employees but also on their "contributors" while emphasizing in sensitive social groups, environment, sports, and culture. According to that, CSR can be seen as a variety of strategic planning and practical actions where the businesses have as target to rotate their corporate interest from the "stockholders" to the "contributors" (Nguyen, 2010). As Werther and Chandler (as cited in Chong, 2007) pointed out, the "contributors" can be divided in three categories:

- Organizational contributors (individuals or groups of the business which have direct interest for business actions or the path that the company follows).
- Financial contributors (clients, banks, lenders, and suppliers).
- Governmental or nongovernmental organizations, law area, communities, and physical environment.

The actions that are used in order for businesses to rotate their focus from the area of "stockholders" to the "contributors" are directly connected with the type of the organization, the communication targets, the needs for its branding purposes, the communication acts of the company and its competitors (Huertas & Capriotti, 2008). Consequently, businesses and organizations are setting CSR through different strategies as they may differ in (a) capacity (level of employees and suppliers), (b) area of service, (c) years of operation, (d) location, (e) place of operation for the company and its competitors (Hokkanen & Timpe, 2009). For the accomplishment of CSR, media are playing a vital role, as described here.

The Role of the Media

For the researching area, focusing on media is a "key" for understanding the modern culture of society but also the CSR of businesses. Media can be seen through four significant affairs: media are constituting the basic path for publication and projection of each CSR action. Meanwhile, they offer back to the socially responsible companies a series of benefits as fame and enhanced business status, brand awareness within the society, and positive framework for contributors.

Media also constitute a part of modern business industry, which has obligations regarding the success or failure of the social benefit. They have the power to address their messages to large audiences of citizens who may participate in social acts as supporters or volunteers. Many European media groups have already established special organizations for that cause. Meanwhile, media have access and equipment to support acts as tele-marathons.

Media are also the cornerstone of the social good that information constitutes. They are a significant ground for CSR researchers as they have the obligation to act in a deontological way securing notions as democracy, pluralism, and credibility for the production and distribution of news.

Media also are educating public and shaping a common ground of citizens in order to move forward to a huge challenge of the twenty-first century: improve the life quality of the earth and its habitants while protecting the future needs. Across the European Union, media are called to contribute to certain acts in order for individuals to:

• Protect and stop damaging the physical environment
• Build and support a solid society by boosting justice
• Build a strong and solid economy.

Furthermore, it is vital to note that CSR as "business strategic opportunity" (Lewis, 2003; Werther & Chandler, 2006) also included its communication: Social sensitive businesses always target their act publications that they complete, but acts also have social utility when published and are broadly accessible. Also, CSR actions have to be applied to certain rules as far as their communication is concerned:

• The object of the act should be clearly published
• The act has to be easy to notice
• The act has to be addressed to the right audience
• Correct communication tools have to be applied
• The act has to provoke the positive reaction of the individuals

Lasswell' s model (1948) also can be applied to CSR as "Who, says What, in Which Channel, to Whom, with What effect". The element of "who" is addressed to the right of the supported individuals to have a solid knowledge toward the organization or the company that runs each CSR. There should not be any gap for nonrelevant companies or organizations to be presented as the main objects of the act.

With characterizing "what", we shape the content of the act and how it serves the presenting social needs. The "Channel" is noted for the media that help with the publication of the acts while serving the CSR in a deontological way. The element of "who" describes the society of the social group that is helped but also the broader audience that can see or read about the CSR acts not only at the business level but also at the individual level. With the "effect" we describe the way that audiences understand the CSR actions and the final culture that those movements shape.

Furthermore, CSR acts are aiming to attract the attention and motivate the audience in order to raise their interest for a specific topic. In order for that to be accomplished the specification of the targets is significant. While shaping the targets, the choosing of the main audience will be determined. With that, the CSR will be easily calculated as far as the results are concerned. Also, the main audience has to be examined not only for individuals but also as a major civilian movement. Individuals' elements may differ according to personalities, social positions, and other personal details as gender, age, education, and social and financial status. Major audiences may differ according to social groups.

Based on the above, there is a close cooperation between the entrepreneurship and the media in the field of CSR; the media are the main channel of communication between companies and society. The entrepreneurship communicates its CSR activities through the media, while the media perform its own debt for CSR by promoting the CSR culture to the sector of its readers-listeners-viewers. On a primary level the media contribute to the formation of CSR culture by Semiotic codes; the Signifiers are the codes that we "read" on the written or audiovisual texts while the Signifies are the ideas or meanings being expressed by these signifiers. On the one hand, the media influence the society on CSR culture in the forms of denotations (the literal meanings of the visual, auditory and tactile signs) and connotations (the secondary, cultural meanings of the signs); on the other hand, citizens understand and assimilate the messages of the media according to both their personal recruiters and the collective recruiters of the societies and/or individual social groups to which they belong. At this level an ideological relationship and a symbolic interactionism among the media, the entrepreneurship, and the society in the field of CSR develops; the media is the mediator of CSR culture between entrepreneurship and society, and vice versa, but also the media itself is a vehicle of dominant CSR culture.

On a second level the media is examined as a major part of socialization and culture. Whether we are referring to the traditional (old) media (printed Press, radio, broadcast TV, cable and satellite TV) or to the New media (digital and mobile), the media industry is a cornerstone of knowledge and information for all the social classes, regardless of income, race, or gender. On the European market both the private and the state-owned public media operate under private-economic criteria with a free-market organizational and operating structure.

The media industry nevertheless differs from any other field of business as the news as a "product" is a vital element of society and democracy (Keane, 1991) – that is why the moral and sustainable media are crucial for the equilibrium of the society (Dillon, 2010). Throughout the last years, media companies in Europe, but also worldwide, faced a variety of challenging problems that cost them corporate earnings, employees, status, and credibility. The increase in internet usage affected the traditional media such as television and newspapers, while the constant trap of fake news and clickbait articles seems to alienate the users from mainstream websites. There is also a huge impact of the coronavirus outbreak on media consumption, as noted here. In the European media industry, where the majority of news are provided for free via television, radio, and Internet, the companies have to build strong strategy plans toward their competitiveness and sustainability and also for ethical thinking in a professional environment.

The modern business models for media need to be based on the following factors: (a) the usage of new technologies through knowledge assets and knowledge capital, (b) the utilization of European digital environment of transmission and delivery of information and entertainment programs, (c) the skills development of media employees through modern business models, (d) the adaptation of media regarding the race, the gender, the age, and the financial status of the users, and, last but not least, the interdependent relation between media and society. In this field the CSR toolbox offers particular useful tools for the adaptation of European media to specific strategy plans in order to have the desired sustainability, a moral nature, and a vital advantage against financial and other risks.

The Social Responsibility of the media includes the obligation to present and promote the actions of socially responsible entrepreneurship, the obligation to an ethic-operating framework (journalistic and recreational ethics) of media itself, and finally the obligation of media to plan its own responsible actions. The first obligation is achieved by promoting the socially responsible actions of the other companies. However, the choice of actions that are presented by the media is often linked to advertising purposes and other marketing activities (Antonopoulou, 2008). In this case, the media chose to promote popular companies, which are strong advertising clients of the media. The perception that divides entrepreneurship into "popular", that is, promoted, and "unpopular", which don't interest the media, is a parameter for modern culture of CSR with significant impact on its social and organizational content. One serious consequence relates to both the society and the public authorities that often receive selective targeted and "filtered" information from the media, which distances them from a rational assessment of entrepreneurship.

People often become passive recipients of the CSR culture chosen by the media on commercial and business criteria or even on criteria that service the selfish goals of the media owners. The fact, moreover, that only one "speed", namely that of the popular entrepreneurship, which attracts the spotlight and the interest of the media, automatically creates conditions for the unequal treatment of entrepreneurship problems. In these cases the voice of the "non-high-profile" either does not reach the decision-makers or arrives as a powerless, weak, and, therefore, ineffective voice.

Conversely, the "high-profile" category has the forum and the ability to apply pressure on the State to satisfy its demands. The way in which CSR culture is handled by the media often leads to the creation of an "elite" of socially responsible companies that are continually presented in the media; it creates centers of power in entrepreneurship and through these centers attains privileged access to the centers of political power. The formation of this "entrepreneurship elite" differs from the "inferior entrepreneurship" that have limited or nonexistent access to the centers of political decision-making. Sometimes this separation extends also to the opportunities for CSR actions. The media often develops a "star system", which, on the one hand, "recycles" persons and identities that prevent the smooth emergence of new participants or new leaders in the field of CSR and, on the other hand, uses CSR actions for advertising purposes (Antonopoulou, 2008).

The second obligation is connected with the previous one as the best antidote to distortion is about an ethic-operating framework for media. The European Federation of Journalists (EFJ) hosted an online webinar on 11 January 2021 to talk about the new age of journalism. Three members of the European Parliament, Petra Kammerevert, Ramona Strugariu, and Alexandra Geese, Deputy Head of Unit (DG Connect) Audrius Perkauskas and four consortium members discussed and exchanged respective insights and best practices. Summing up the journalistic standards must be adhered to in order to regain the trust to media, EFJ General Secretary Ricardo Gutierrez underlined the obligation to quality, strong, and ethical journalism, media literacy for all, media pluralism, and, above all, a policy of increased transparency of those in power. He also underlined that journalists, too, have to be more transparent in their work. As mentioned, the ongoing challenges for the future are:

- making media councils better known to the public;
- helping to restore confidence in the media by pushing them to respect ethical principles;
- helping to create new media councils where they do not yet exist.

Finally, the third obligation of the media, which is connected with the previous ones, is to organize or participate in CSR actions. Many

European media are very active in this field. Public media across Europe interact with entrepreneurship CSR actions, as the government funding shall be used with the maximum return for the society. Meanwhile, many private media are also acting in the same level with establishing NGO's especially for certain CSR moves. BBC is undoubtedly the leader of the CSR actions across media as at the beginning of the millennium started a relevant organization chart with the below acts:

- Waste and recycling department responsible for the unused films and tapes and other consumables
- Relevant department for saving energy and water for the needs of the organization
- Transportation department, which is responsible for the environmental-friendly transportations of the 25.000 employees and the thousands of suppliers.
- Suppliers department which decides who are the associates that are respect the environmental politics and using environmental friendly procedures for their products.

According to its Annual Report for 2019–2020 the BBC was committed to the duty to help the society understand and engage with the world by providing impartial news to its audience, to show the most creative, highest quality and distinctive output and services continued, to support learning for all people regardless of their age, to serve and represent the diverse communities of all of the nations and regions in the country, to reflect the United Kingdom's culture and values to the world, to support a creative environmental for the economy. The basic perception of the CSR concept from BBC includes the participation of the active citizens. For example, through the annual report BBC emphasizes on the huge support that it receives from public regarding the CSR acts. For season 2019–2020 many million pounds were concentrated from CSR actions which were later distributed to weaker social groups and organization not only in UK but also all over the globe. According to BBC the cooperation with other organizations that help the national good and prosperity is a kind of duty. Through 2019, it had more than 350 corporations with larger or smaller culture organizations of the UK. Regarding the Ecology area, BBC commenced the Our Planet section where issues about environment where published and broadcasted. Furthermore, BBC has adopted the position that an ethical company acts as a good citizen within the community in which it operates but also treats its customers and employees honestly so emphasizes on company governance and social targets that are set from the Board of the company. BBD has always been an excellent "pilot" for the CSR functions that a media organization can perform.

The Political Framework for the CSR Communication and Media in Europe

The political environment in the strictest sense implies the creation of a framework of principles and rules within which the socio-economic relations in the context of the State factor are developed and in the broader sense the dominant ideology that is formed within the political system's institutional coordinates. More specifically, it is the political environment, in its strictest sense, that establishes the rules and principles for the development and the function of CSR, as well as the media's operating framework (Antonopoulou, 2008). In its broad sense, the political environment is both the transmitter and the receiver of the CSR's ideological functions. At the present time there is intense mobility worldwide for the preparation or improvement of National Corporate Social Responsibility Strategy Plans. In Europe, this mobility is more intense. National CSR projects, such as those of Denmark, Italy, Finland, Ireland and Germany, deserve special attention as they reflect the positive points of approach of Civil Society Organizations in these countries' CSR issues. The common goal of the aforementioned National CSR Plans is to consolidate the vanguard of companies for responsible (sustainable) development with the active involvement of the State. The main pillars of the Plans are to enhance transparency, the adoption of CSR by public bodies and its promotion through their activities, raising the social awareness of businesses, citizens and local communities, and supporting business development and implementation of CSR actions.

Additional issues addressed by some of the National Plans are the protection of the environment (and in particular the effects of climate change), the strengthening of human rights in business, its link to competitiveness, prosperity and justice. An additional opportunity is the adaptation of European countries to the EU "Europe 2020" Strategy, which many Member States have already done. The Europe 2020 Strategy describes the ways in which the European Union can emerge stronger from the current crisis and build an inclusive and sustainable environment, with key components of high levels of employment and productivity, environmentally friendly and climate-friendly energy supply and strong social cohesion.

It is a big bet for Europe to be able to implement these axes by using tools and policies that will encourage voluntary business activities and initiatives, which will be complemented by traditional regulatory structures and channels. The European countries have a number of tools for this purpose. The use of Communication and Information tools (information campaigns, training activities, seminars, conferences) is extremely important. Other tools are the following:

i   Legislative/regulatory tools (laws, directives)
ii Economic tools (tax exemptions, subsidies)

iii   Awareness and education tools
iv   Networking tools (networks of stakeholders, promotion of dialogue and cooperation, etc.).

There is no doubt that the maximum result will be achieved by the combination of the tools above. CSR Communication in Europe is being studied within the context of general European communication policy. In the last years there is a strong interest of the European Parliament about media and Communication issues.

In the Report on journalism and new media – creating a public sphere in Europe (2010/2015) the European Parliament "*asks the European Audiovisual Observatory and the Commission, via Eurostat, to monitor EU news broadcasting by public and private service networks in the Member States, at national, regional and local level, with a view to facilitating best practice, and to report their findings regularly to Parliament; also suggests that the European Audiovisual Observatory publish regular surveys of the coverage of EU affairs in the electronic media, looking at content devoted specifically to EU affairs as well as content including references to EU affairs, and calls on the Commission to conduct a regular analysis of the way in which new media are contributing to the creation of a European public sphere*". The European Parliament also believes that "*civil society organizations have an important role to play in the European debate; takes the view that their role should be enhanced by means of targeted cooperation projects in the public communication sphere*".

The misinformation through digital platforms is a big problem that permanently bothers the Commission but nowadays the problem has been increased on the occasion of Covid-19. On July 2020 the Commission launched a public consultation on the Digital Services Act, a landmark package announced in the Commission's digital strategy "Shaping Europe's Digital Future". The consultation sleeked to gather views, evidence and data from people, businesses, online platforms, academics, civil society and all interested parties. On December 2020 the Commission proposed an ambitious reform of the digital space, a comprehensive set of new rules for all digital services, including social media, online market places, and other online platforms that operate in the European Union: the Digital Services Act and the Digital Markets Act. In 2021 a modern rulebook across the single market will foster innovation, growth and competitiveness and will provide users with new, better and reliable online services. It will also support the scaling up of smaller platforms, small and medium-sized enterprises, and start-ups, providing them with easy access to customers across the whole single market while lowering compliance costs.

Influences to the Entrepreneurship

CSR actions are beneficial for the modern entrepreneurship for many different reasons. In fact, a variety of factors seem to interact in order to spread the CSR culture in the European and entrepreneurship. According to Palazzi and Starcher (1997), the globalization is the most fundamental factor. Globalization connects distant societies and diffuses power relations to the main continents and regions of the world (Held & McGrew, 1999). Other factors are the increasing competition, the rapid technological change and the shift from an industrial economy to a knowledge-based economy. These factors are essentially pushing adopting a more responsible corporate tactics. In addition, demographic change, environmental challenges and changing value systems create the conditions for achievement and competitiveness (Palazzi & Starcher, 1997). Finally, factors such as risk and reputation management, the protection of human capital, compliance with consumer requirements and avoidance of control, "force" companies to join the adoption of corporate social responsibility programs (Toohey, 2009). In this globalized context, the publicity of business actions and results through transparent procedures is vital for all stakeholders in the business. Into the European framework the companies are able to strengthening their CSR and business approach, while improving its reputation amongst stakeholders. Involving the direct and indirect stakeholders, such as customers, suppliers, distributors, and peers, allow them to develop and implement an impactful Corporate Sustainability and Responsibility (CSR) strategy.

It is a basic principle that a Stakeholder Dialogue is the best approach to directly influence the companies' management, decision-making process, performance, and accountability. CSR Europe is the leading European business network for Corporate Sustainability and Responsibility. It aims to support over 10,000 enterprises at local, European and global level. CSR Europe support businesses and industry sectors in their transformation and collaboration toward practical solutions and sustainable growth. In 2021, its portfolio of services was expanded in order to support not only companies but also industry federations to be sustainable.

In this context European companies not only owe to take strong initiatives for CSR acts but also to publish the results of these actions. A Code of Conduct, which includes voluntary rules on the principles and values that frame the operation of the company and its relations with stakeholders is necessary for any publicity action. The Annual CSR Report is the most common way to communicate the corporate results. Companies owe to present their own approach to CSR and analyze their activities in relation to the three main dimensions of CSR that is the social, the economic and environmental one. The writing of the Annual Social Report is considered to be a positive element in the overall image of the company and its publication is mandatory in some European countries.

Other common ways of publishing CSR practices to stakeholders are the following:

- The Thematic Reports about the CSR actions of the company different fields.
- The Press Releases for the information of journalists.

The News Releases for the information of internal audiences. It concerns all the actions that the company implements in order to communicate within its internal environment, the feasible social responsibility programs (intranet, corporate magazines and newspapers, staff meetings, etc.).

- Information by Internet, especially by the use of the corporate website and social media.
- Infotainment; publicity of CSR practices via an entertainment program.
- Chat and digital events. No visitors are required to travel so manpower, time, money, natural resources are saved. Virtual events maintain events, lectures and presentations that can be re-screened later. Their scope increases and the organizer makes better and faster amortization.
- Events and Marketing Actions linked to a social purpose. Companies have financial resources for charity or social purposes, while achieving their business goals.
- Awards to other companies for their CSR achievements as well as discriminations that other companies award to the particular company for its CSR activity.

The Society

The society is the final recipient of the European CSR culture. It has a triple capacity: it is simultaneously the vehicle of the CSR culture; consumer of the CSR actions; and finally, the "product" that CSR leaders "sell" to the media in order to gain publicity. The people participate in this process, not only as individuals but as members of social groups with particular ideologies, social perceptions, life styles, expectations, etc.; while their involvement with CSR actions also classifies them into other narrower or broader social groups not only as volunteers in CSR actions but also as beneficiaries of CSR actions or as customers of companies leading CSR culture. Within this perspective CSR actions constitute a structure for socializing the individual.

People often participate in media CSR in an additional way; as Citizen Journalists. The term "Citizen Journalism" refers to the production and distribution of news material by citizen-nonprofessional journalists who produce news material of their interest using New media and in particular social media. This material is usually distributed both through blogs or social media and professional media. Leading News Networks use visual and written texts produced by citizens since the beginning of twenty-first century. On December 2006, Time magazine created an emblematic front page, proclaimed "You" as the person of the year. It depicted a computer with the slogan "Yes, you. You control the Information Age. Welcome to your world".

At the same year Reuters and Yahoo! invited the public for cooperation in the field of photography. Since then, citizen journalism is been widely used not only in order to cover emergencies but also to highlight issues affecting local communities and people who have limited or non-existent access to the centers of political decision-making. Indicatively, BBC is licensed by the British government to exploit the potential of this particular way of producing news, Current TV (co-owner is the former US Vice President Al Gore) provides a program that is largely shaped by viewers from the visual and news material they produce, CNN has created the section iReport, etc. In this way, the professional media offer the opportunity to the citizens to highlight the problems that concern them and to seek solutions in collaboration with them.

This form of news material production differs from professional journalism but often precedes it, especially in emergencies, and provides the professional media with primary visual and audio material. J.D. Lasica (2008) defines Citizen Journalism as a journalists and public co-configuration through comments, photos, personal websites and video clips. Citizen journalists is an 'active audience' that promote the need for self-expression, solidarity and coordination for social purposes. The basic idea of "citizen journalism" is that the total knowledge and strength of citizens is greater than that of journalists (Gillmor, 2004).

It is obvious however that Citizen Journalism has not only positive effects on media CSR but also negative ones. Fake news, racism, hate speech, violence are only a few of them. The Leading News Networks have created internal structures for content moderation in order to avoid the negative effects. Content moderation refers to the practice of listening, escalating and responding to inappropriate print, audiovisual and digital content including reviews, tweets, blog or forum comments, videos and photos. It is however extremely doubtful that the small media organizations have create equally effective structures, so a further cooperation between the journalists' unions and the Commission is definitely needed in this area. It is important for all the European media to adopt a set of rules, which define what is acceptable and what is not, and to create internal structures for content moderation.

At the Time of the Coronavirus

The coronavirus pandemic that directly affected media companies in all aspects (news, organizational, management, financial, labor) has also changed their CSR area. In fact, the pandemic affected the content of CSR that media organize but also their social responsibility as it is strongly connected with their obligation for pluralistic and transparent information. As far as the content of media CSR is concerned, the interest has shifted into more direct and urgent social needs that were generated from the pandemic for social communities that were hurt from the coronavirus. Taking that into consideration, public media in Europe contributed to the education of students during the lockdown (and also the pause of real time lessons in schools) through special educative programs. Meanwhile, several TV Channels, through CSR actions supported vital areas as described below: The two public channels of Germany, ARD and ZDF, accepted to contribute the 50% of the cost for each production in order to support TV producers.

The European Broadcasting Union (EBU) which is the world's leading alliance of public service media (PSM) established a Women's Sport Expert Group as part of its commitment to make women's sport a standard fixture of the sports media landscape in order to increase the volume and coverage of women's sport while ensuring fair portrayal. EBU also organized the first annual event supporting women across all levels of music, by dedicating airtime to play musical – or related content – exclusively by women to coincide with UNESCO's International Women's Day on 8 March. 400 public service media radio broadcasters from over 40 countries took part as our Music Exchange provided ready-to-broadcast material showcasing women artists including interviews, operas and rarely performed pieces.

In addition, the main problem that is connected with media service and the media product is criticized and analyzed by the European Commission also. An effect, which has been strongly highlighted by the EU, is about the growing deprivation of Press Freedom. At the launch of its 2020 annual report on 29 April 2020, the Council of Europe (CoE) Platform for the Protection of Journalists voiced its concern that the "a fresh assault on media freedom amid the Covid-19 pandemic has worsened an already gloomy outlook". The Commission directly denounces the efforts of various governments to restrict press freedom under the guise of the pandemic by indicating:

> The media freedom crisis has further exposed systemic weaknesses in a number of countries, where governments and world leaders appear to have used the situation as an opportunity to implement a further crackdown on media freedom under the pretence of a concern for national security.

Usually the Commission does not use harsh expressions to describe a problem but in this case its highlights are very sharp; "in some cases, intense information suppression, narrative control and disinformation campaigns – often carried out in conjunction with highly visible, staged global health assistance – seem to be aimed at covering up government failures and conveying the message that authoritarian nationalism is the most viable answer to the pandemic, as well as that societies must choose between freedom and security".

As there is a large increase of the number of subscribers to audio-visual service channels, Commission requested the Member States to extend specific audiovisual rules to video-sharing platforms, as well as to audiovisual content shared on specific media and adopt settings for audiovisual content in all its forms of projection and reproduction. On December 2020 Commission presented a European Democracy Action Plan that *"goes hand in hand with the Media and Audiovisual Action Plan, which aims to help the sector recover and make the most of the digital transformation"*. The Commission proposed for 2021 the close co-operation with Member States "through a structured dialogue and provide a sustainable funding for projects on legal and practical assistance to journalists in the EU and elsewhere". It was also announced that further measures would be put forward to support media pluralism and to strengthen transparency of media ownership and state advertising, among others, through the new media Ownership Monitor.

According to that, EBU announced in March 2021, an initiative of 10 European public TV Channels that set a time frame until July 2021. Its target is to accomplish "a solid gain against misleading information and the hate or dividing speech through social media". Those 10 major public channels will share digital news content (articles, videos, etc.) through a digital platform, where the content will directly be translated in several languages through innovative tools and procedures. This "innovative" digital alliance will allow "public media to eliminate language boundaries and distribute to their audience credible information, produced from other European cooperators" as described in EBU announcement. Text and content will be based on mutual European values and interests and will offer a cross Europe point of view on top relevant and important issues. Covid-19 pandemic, climate change and migrant flow will shape a significant part of channel's news. In this initiative, German (BR-ARD), French – France Televisions, Belgian (RTBF), Spanish (RTVE), Finnish (YLE), Irish (RTE), Italian (RAI), Portuguese (RTP) and Swiss (SWI swissinfo.ch) but also French – German ARTE are contributing. The program is funded with "the support of EU" that is given after a "successful test period in which 14 major public media brands delivered 120.000 articles, available for eight months.

Conclusions

It is explained above that the media are a key pillar in CSR activity and to a large or a short degree replaces the State's active participation in the society's affairs. Media are responsible for certain aspects toward the organization, the service and the execution of CSR actions. Media also process itself performs important ideological, moral-educational, political, aesthetic and economic functions.

In this base a three-step model is used here to describe the media attitudes on CSR:

1   The one-dimensional model of actions was first established by Thurston (1928) and defines that an act is correlated with one feeling or an evaluation of a certain aspect. The media responsibilities for CSR actions as described through law and deontology is directly connected with this model. In addition a "healthy" media organization can face CSR actions as conditio sine qua non subject for its sustainability.

2   The two-dimensional model was pointed out from Allport (1954) to describe the correlation of an aspect with a feeling or an evaluation and the readiness for social activity on it. Media groups are usually willing to support popular CSR actions in order to strength their own social profile as well. This model also describes the emotional aspects of a CSR action.

3   The three-dimensional model was established by Rosenberg and Hovland (1960). According to that an action may be described from cognitive, emotional and behavioral aspects. These three areas transform the actions into a thoughtful and full of emotion proceeding (Hogg & Vaughan, 2010). This model identifies a more modern perception of the CSR moves while it includes the total acts of initiatives that executives can follow in order to enforce the relationships among companies, society and "cooperators". Regarding the "cooperators" the emphasis is given:

    a) To the teams that the company relies on for its existence
    b) to the teams or the individuals that affect or being affected for the completion of business goals (Hunger & Wheelen, 2003).

In the first category the media audience may be categorized as readers, viewers, listeners and users (but also the society in general) meanwhile employees, suppliers and Media activities are a subcategory for the second category (b). Regarding the three-dimensional model many European media companies organize or participate into CSR actions as sponsors. Those acts emphasize on Environment, Life Quality, Culture and also the support of the weaker social groups. Nevertheless in many cases there is a falsification and a commercialization of the CSR activity in the European environment and this is not without consequences for CSR culture. Often, a fair critique on media may be observed as they tend to present CSR actions in exchange with a significant advertisement deal or to shift the human pain and dignity to a show.

The gamble and the responsibility for European Governance is to remove these distortions, wherever they appear, by preparing and implementing a framework of institutional integrity that will govern the operation of CSR on businesses and its promotion by the media.

References

Adi, A., Grigore, G., & Crowther, D. (2015). *Corporate social responsibility in the digital age.* Bingley, UK: Emerald Publishing Limited.

Allport, G. (1954). *The nature of prejudice.* Cambridge, MA: Addison-Wesley Pub. Co.

Antonopoulou, P. (2008). *Αθλητισμός, Πολιτική και ΜΜΕ.* Athens. Drakopoulou Publications.

Breitbarth, T., & Harris, P. (2007). *Conceptualising the role of corporate social responsibility in professional football.* Paper presented at the Australian and New Zealand Marketing Academy (ANZMAC) Conference, December 3–5, Dunedin, New Zealand.

Capriotti, P., & Moreno, A. (2007). Corporate citizenship and public relations: The importance and interactivity of social responsibility issues on corporate websites. *Public Relations Review, 33*(1), 84–91.

Carroll, A. B. (1991). The pyramid of corporate social responsibility: Toward the moral management of organizational Stakeholders. *Business Horizons, 34*(4), 39–48.

Chong, M. (2007). The role of internal communication and training in infusing corporate values and delivering brand promise: Singapore Airlines' experience. *Corporate Reputation Review, 10,* 201–212.

Dillon, M. (2010). *Introduction to sociological theory.* Chichester, UK: Wiley-Blackwell.

Gillmor, D. (2004). *We the media: Grassroots journalism by the people, for the people.* California, U.S. O' Reilly Media, Inc.

Held, D., & McGrew, A. (1999). *Global transformations: Politics, economics and culture.* Stanford, CA: Stanford University Press.

Hogg, M., & Vaughan, G. (2010). *Κοινωνική Ψυχολογία (Social psychology).* Athens: Gutenberg.

Hokkanen, A-M., & Timpe, T. (2009). *Corporate social responsibility (CSR) and contract manufacturing: Exploring the management structures and processes of ethical sourcing practices.* Retrieved March 2021, from https://gupea.ub.gu.se/bitstream/2077/20871/1/gupea_2077_20871_1.pdf.

Huertas, A., & Capriotti, P. (2008). *Using corporate social responsibility as a public relations tool in a local community.* Paper presented at the XXII Annual Congress AEDEM, July 18–20, Salamanca, Spain.

Hunger, J. D., & Wheelen, T. L. (2003). *Essentials of strategic management* (3rd ed.). Upper Saddle River, NJ: Prentice Hall.

Keane, J. (1991). *The media and democracy.* Cambridge: Polity Press.

Kotler, P., & Lee, N. (2005). *Corporate social responsibility: Doing the most good for your company and your cause.* Hoboken, NJ: John Wiley & Sons, Inc.

Lasica, J. D. (2008). *Civic engagement on the move: How mobile media can serve the public good hardcover.* Washington: Published by the Aspen Institute.

Lasswell, H. (1948). *The structure and function of communication in society. The communication of ideas.* New York: Institute for Religious and Social Studies.

Lewis, S. (2003). Reputation and corporate responsibility. *Journal of Communication Management*, 7(4), 356–364. Retrieved January 2021, from www.research gate.net/publication/235291001_Reputation_and_Corporate_Responsibility

Nguyen, S. (2010). *Influence of perceived shared corporate social orientation of employees and volunteers with sport organizations on attitudinal outcomes.* Retrieved January 2021, from https://www.researchgate.net/publication/254672548_Influence_Of_Perceived_Shared_Corporate_Social_Orientation_Of_Employees_And_Volunteers_With_Sport_Organizations_On_Attitudinal_Outcomes

Palazzi, M., & Starcher, G. (1997). *Corporate social responsibility and business success.* Paper presented at the AIESEC Global Theme Conference, May 6, Basle, Switzerland.

Palazzi, M., & Starcher, G. (2006). *Corporate social responsibility and business success.* Retrieved April 12, 2021, from http://centreonphilanthropy.com/files/kb_articles/1269270655EBBF%20Corporate%20Responsibility%20and%20Business%20Success.pdf

Rosenberg, M. J., & Hovland, C. I. (1960). Cognitive, affective and behavioral components of attitudes. In M. J. Rosenberg & C. I. Hovland (Eds.), *Attitude organization and change: An analysis of consistency among attitude components.* New Haven: Yale University Press.

Thurston, L. L. (1928). Attitudes can be measured. *The American Journal of Sociology*, 33(4), 529–554.

Toohey, K. (2009). *Challenges and opportunities for the Olympic movement in the next decades – The corporate social responsibility.* Retrieved December 2020, from https://library.olympic.org/Default/doc/SYRACUSE/161841/challenges-and-opportunities-for-the-olympic-movement-in-the-next-decades-the-corporate-social-respo.

Werther, W., & Chandler, D. (2006). *Strategic corporation social responsibility.* London: Sage Publications.

Websites

https://ec.europa.eu/growth/industry/sustainability/corporate-social-responsibility_en.

https://ec.europa.eu/info/strategy/priorities-2019-2024/europe-fit-digital-age/shaping-europe-digital-future_en.

www.europarl.europa.eu/RegData/etudes/BRIE/2020/651905/EPRS_BRI(2020)651905_EN.pdf

www.europarl.europa.eu/doceo/document/A-7-2010-0223_EN.html

www.csreurope.org/our-network-1

https://europeanjournalists.org/blog/2021/01/12/takeaways-from-online-webinar-media-councils-in-the-digital-age-how-to-regain-trust-and-ethics-in-journalism.

www.bbc.co.uk/mediacentre/latestnews/2020/bbc-annual-report-2019-20

www.coe.int/en/web/media-freedom/the-platform

www.digitalnewsreport.org/

www.ebu.ch/news/2021/01/ten-public-service-broadcasters-join-an-ebu-initiative-to-give-audiences-access-to-trusted-news-from-across-europe.

https://opentextbc.ca/mediastudies101/back-matter/glossary.

12 Corporate Social Responsibility, Governance, and Sport Marketing: An International Review

John Douvis and Vaios Kyriakis

Introduction

Sport and the sport industry are going through a period of crisis. The change of paradigms brought about by the social changes in the twentieth century has created many problems in sport, which are also inherited in the twenty-first century (Digel, 2010; Forster, 2006; Jalonen, 2016). Forster (2006) has pointed out that Global Sport Organizations (GSO) maintained their monopoly and authority status over sport governance, as well as all the structures originally designed for amateur sport to enter the new era. Using this monopoly as revenue device became the source of later problems. Digel (2010) mentioned the market ideology phenomenon which is also imposed on sport, the economization and globalization of sport, the consequences of sport as a type of lifestyle, the inequalities in education and available time, and the environmental problems that arose. In addition, Hakala (2015) and Kokoulina, Simina, and Tatarova (2019) reported on contemporary problems of modern sports which include doping, political influence, corruption, commercialization and discrimination, violence, hooliganism, nationalism, cheating, and fraud. These negative and challenging issues are events which are linked to and affect the prestige and image of sport as an institution, but also the credibility and integrity of sport organizations worldwide. According to the research of Kokoulina et al. (2019), "the existence of these problems shows the lack of legal and moral regulation in sports" (p. 213). In Lindsey's (2016) work, governance is defined as a reference "to issues of social coordination and the nature of patterns of rule" (p. 802). Therefore, governance in sport should include aspects of legal and ethical regulation of problems in matters of social coordination and rules of behavior relating to the sport and society by adopting practices that contribute to good governance for the benefit of sport and those whom it is offered for.

Sport has a mass appeal on the population because of its social character and its status as a social institution (see Smith & Westerbeek, 2007). Also, it composes a multiverse industry thus creating a worldwide sports market of millions of dollars in worth annually. The sport

DOI: 10.4324/9781003152750-15

industry should strive for the good, the betterment of society and the world through social activities and policies, instead of just using its size and monopoly power as a revenue device. Hence, the concept of Sports Corporate Social Responsibility (CSR) is a suitable framework for this purpose (PricewaterhouseCoopers, 2015, 2016, 2017, 2018, 2019).

In the business world the concept of CSR represents an effort to alleviate the damage that has been made because of a company's operations (Gardner & Nichols, 2017). In sport businesses, the corporate world has chosen the CSR concept as a vehicle for the implementation of activities, initiatives, or programs in the form of cause-related marketing, CSR-linked sponsorships, and so on. Anagnostopoulos (2011) reports that "the sport field has not been immune to this development" and "Corporate social responsibility (CSR) is increasingly important to business, including professional team sport organizations" (Anagnostopoulos, Byers, & Shilbury, 2014 p. 259). In recent years, famous sport clubs, like Barcelona, Manchester United, and so on, in Europe and around the world, have created and owned foundations in order to fulfill social obligations by forming partnerships and alliances in the social arena (Al-Daaja & Szabados, 2018; Anagnostopoulos, Gillooly, Cook, Parganas, & Chadwick, 2017; Baena, 2018). Also, Global Sport Governing Bodies (IOC, FIFA, UEFA, etc.) choose to dedicate units and staff responsible with social issues to promote their own policies in relation to the development of the sport they represent and their social developmental goals (Athanasopoulou, Douvis, & Kyriakis, 2011; Bradish & Cronin, 2009). However, there are cases where the integration of CSR in sports governance is viewed with skepticism as scandals come into light (Dowling, Robinson, & Washington, 2013; Kulczycki, Pfister, & Koenigstorfer, 2018; Levermore, 2010; Walker, Heere, Parent, & Drane, 2010; Woods & Stokes, 2019).

In this respect, social responsibility becomes an interwoven concept in the governance of sport, and an important aspect of governance in maintaining GSOs' and professional sport teams' credibility and institutional license to operate on behalf of the global society. After all, it is impossible for an institution governed by tarnished structures and facing scandals and problems worldwide to serve its original humanitarian and social purposes. The solution lies in sport policy, designed to include Good Governance and CSR (Auweele, 2010) in order to promote integrity in sport. Corporate Governance and CSR are two related and interwoven business concepts that are deeply embedded in business practices. Both Corporate Governance and CSR focus on the ethical practices in the business and the responsiveness of an organization to its stakeholders and the environment in which it operates. Corporate Governance and CSR result in better image of an organization and directly affect the performance of an organization. Further, it is worthwhile to mention that CSR is based on the concept of self-governance, which is related to external legal and regulatory mechanism, whereas Corporate Governance is a widest control mechanism within which a company takes its management decisions. Furthermore, the objectives and benefits of CSR and Corporate Governance with respect to marketing are similar in nature: (a) establishing strong brand reputation of the company, (b) making substantial improvement in its relationship with various stakeholders, (c) contributing to the development of the region and the society around its area of operation, (d) addressing the concerns of its various stakeholders in a balanced way so as to maintaining a strong market position. This chapter is an international review and a reference to the practices of the concept of CSR utilized in the governance of professional sports and international sport organizations, since it spots on issues with respect to various marketing aspects.

Aspects of CSR and Cause-Related Marketing in Sport

As Aurélien and Bayle (2017) have declared:

> [M]ultifaceted in its concept, corporate social responsibility (CSR) is viewed and applied differently in different countries. A general, definition of this concept could include economic, legal, ethical and discretionary expectations that society has of organizations at a given point in time.
>
> (p. 534)

Auweele (2010) refers to Sport CSR as the "inclusion of needs and objectives of the societal context in which sports organizations are operating". Furthermore, Babiak (2010) reports that CSR represents behaviors that have strategic importance for the majority of the companies. Other authors (Babiak, 2010; Gardner & Nichols, 2017) have considered CSR as a company's commitment to minimize or reduce the potentially harmful impacts of its operations on society and maximize its long-term beneficial impact. Walzel and Robertson (2016) explain that "the field of CSR developed out of the management field of Corporate Social Performance (CSP) – i.e., how well an organization performs alongside with its social obligation" (p. 199). In this sense, there is a reciprocal relationship between the sport industry society itself, in which sport organizations are obligated to return to society some of the so-called "good" that they have received (Ballouli & Brown, 2012).

For many researchers, corporate social responsibility, cause-related sport marketing, and CSR-linked sponsorships are tools for business in the sport industry. There are many references in the literature that CSR practices can have effects on brand love (Baena, 2018), or that CSR activity impacts on a club's brand image (Blumrodt, Desbordes, & Bodin, 2013).

There is also evidence that when CSR guides sport branding initiatives and sponsorship partnerships, increased levels of brand capitalization can appear. Similarly, there are certain dimensions of CSR that impact on a sport firm's value (Dimitropoulos & Vrondou, 2015). There is also evidence that cause campaigns supported by sport teams can result in increased sales for the benefit of charitable institutions (Nichols & Gardner, 2017) and that charitable giving as CSR would affect a professional sport team's financial performance (CFP) (Inoue, Kent, & Lee, 2011). Cause-related sport marketing programs also impact on key business stakeholders such as consumers (Irwin, Lachowetz, & Clark, 2010). Sport consumers around the world are likely to adopt and support any social cause endorsed by sports celebrities and teams, when it is advocated at an international level through sports events marketing networks (Arora, Grewal, & Singh, 2019).

Perceptual Variables as Factor in CSR

Perceptual variables are a strong factor that appears in many research studies throughout the literature of corporate social responsibility in the sport industry. Akman and Mishra (2017) mentioned Venkatesh's (2000) view, that perceptual variables are also associated and have significant influence on intentions. Additionally, in the explanation of "Attitudes" in the context of Ajzen's and Fishbein and Ajzen, theories of behavior, Cunningham and Kwon (2003), explicitly noted that ". . . if a person perceives that there are positive outcomes resulting from an activity, then his or her attitude towards performing that behavior is likely to be positive" (p. 129).

Perceptions have been examined among several demographic categories such as that of sports consumers, customers of sports leagues or professional sports teams, fans and spectators, sports communities but also sports executives and sponsorship managers. In sports marketing, perceptions of fans about the functions of sport (psychological well-being, self-expression, pride-in-place, social integration) can be used for segmentation purposes (Grove, Dorsch, & Hopkins, 2012). McDonald and Oates (2006) noted the importance of consumer perceptions which is well established in the literature (see: p. 161). In their research about consumers' behavior and marketing strategies, regarding Sustainability, McDonald & Oates made clear that different outlooks exist in how activities are perceived by groups of individuals. As they explicitly stated, "Activities are perceived so differently by individuals that it is difficult to implement a general marketing strategy to encourage such activities" (see: McDonald & Oates, 2006, p. 168). Holbrook (1981) suggested that perceptions about characteristics or attributes [of a product], have an intervening role when modeling consumers' preferences. Therefore, we can treat perceptions as intervening variables which ". . . can serve to explain the effects of product features on evaluative judgments. Thus, intervening perceptions help explicate affective responses that might otherwise be more difficult to understand" (see: Holbrook, 1981, p. 24). Sargeant, West, and Ford (2001) addressed the perceptual determinants (variables) that impacts on donors' giving behavior. They argued that a set of perceptions provide donors with the capacity to control their behavior in terms of alternative choices and level of support (see: p. 408). Thus, it is suggested (Paek, Morse, Hutchinson, & Lim, 2020) that "Sport marketers should consider what perceptions of sport fans can serve as a springboard for enhancing their relationships with sport teams and incorporate this information into their marketing strategies" (p. 11).

Perceptions and Cause-Related Marketing (CRM)

Perceptions play the role of mediator or moderator in a set of different effects and outcomes, depending on the type of research and the sporting context in which the research is conducted. In this way, *perceptions around CSR* in the sports industry have been studied in the context of international sporting events such as the Olympic Games or the FIFA Soccer World Cup, professional sports teams and league authorities, sports organizations, and even educational organizations. It is clear that there is research interest in the role that perceptions play regarding CSR activities in the sports industry.

Many leagues and teams use cause-related marketing practices as a way of "giving back" to their communities (Roy & Graeff, 2003). Due to the unique characteristics of the sport industry, the participation of sport teams and organizations in cause-related marketing activities is viewed as an expected activity (Roy, 2011). Also, Roy (2011) argued that ". . . cause-related marketing is not just a type of sponsorship but also a key tactic for a firm to implement its social responsibility strategy" (p. 21). In the core of this tactic is the association of an organization with a good cause, in part for charitable purpose and somewhat to serve certain corporate interests (K.T. Kim, Kwak, & Kim, 2010). In an extended way, cause-related marketing is a cooperation with a charity or a charitable foundation and can be defined as a strategic positioning and marketing tool which aims to provide a link for the company or the brand with an appropriate social cause or issue. The intention is to produce common benefits for both parties in this relationship. Also, this kind of relationship is under the umbrella of CSR with strong emphasis on marketing objectives, as a strategy out of many for profit improvement and reputation building (Joo, Koo, & Fink, 2016).

Consumers' perception of a sports team's cause-related marketing initiatives have been explored in the context of spectator sports. K. T. Kim et al. (2010) developed a model that incorporated perceived cause-related marketing (CRM), attitudes toward the team, and intentions to re-attend a game. They have found that the *spectators' perceptions* about the team's CRM motives did not produce a diverse effect on attitude and behavioral intention. However, consumers' attitude toward the team was a mediator for re-attendance intentions as a CRM effect.

CRM Cause Fit Perception Effects

A traditional way to drive public support for a good cause but also at the same time to transform this support into leads for both team, sponsor, and the supported cause is the cause-related marketing practice. Responses to cause-related programs in professional sports leagues depend on the congruence or the fit between the sponsor and the supported cause. Fans' support for such like programs is depending on the relationship between that congruence and the *perceived sincerity* of the sponsor. A study by Roy (2011) amongst a sample of 186 students, revealed that *perceived sincerity* was significantly more positive where linkages of congruence between sponsor and cause existed.

The imagery displayed during a campaign for a good cause supported by a professional sports team might have a controversial effect. Nichols, Cobbs, and Raska (2016) examined the role of a league-cause fit, *fans' perceptions* about the team's cause-related sport marketing (CRSM) *sincerity*, and intentions to support a campaign for war veterans. The research suggests that exposing fans to "hometown" team imagery during the campaign despite the high *league-cause fit perceptions*, can cause potential criticism effects since it might be perceived as a less sincere CRSM effort. A more neutral imagery context can help the team to achieve better overall responses from the fans.

Perceived altruism of CRM campaigns in sports was explored by Joo et al. (2016). Amongst a sample of 124 subjects and contingent on their team identification level (lower vs. higher identifiers), results revealed that *perceived altruism* can wield an impact on consumers' change in attitude toward the team. In addition, the effect of perceived altruism on consumers' responses also mediated by their attitudes toward the CRM campaign.

Perceptions and CSR-linked Sponsorships Effects

Sponsoring of an event is a common marketing tool today. As Uhrich, Koenigstorfer, and Groeppel-Klein (2014) reported, some of the possible outcomes include an increased brand awareness, brand image and a positive association of sponsor with the event. It is also noted that many brands and sponsors tried and succeed to leverage their sponsorship activities by linking them with their CSR initiatives. Some of the latest examples include FIFA's official partnerships with Adidas and Coca-Cola during the World Cup in South Africa (Flöter, Benkenstein, & Uhrich,

2016; Uhrich et al., 2014). According to Flöter et al. (2016) the linkage of a sponsorship with CSR activities is called CSR-linked sponsorship and represent an opportunity for the sponsors of a mega event to express their corporate goodwill but also to gain benefits for their brands. Moreover, as Uhrich et al. (2014) found, in the context of commercialized sport events, when a sponsor chose to link its sponsorship activity with CSR issues it led to improved brand evaluations (i.e., credibility and attitudes) because a CSR-linked sponsorship adds social meaning to it.

CSR-linked sponsorships to international sporting events are a well-established corporate practice. In this context, Lacey, Close, and Finney (2010) collected 1636 responses in field surveys from attendees of an international sporting event, to examine the role that CSR and the *perceived sponsor's commitment* to it plays in event sponsorship effectiveness. Given the fact that attendees were knowledgeable about the sponsor's products, the perception of the sponsor as socially responsible had an effect on attendees' intentions to purchase the sponsor's products. Perception of higher levels of social responsibility amongst local attendees of a sporting event can generate a higher level of social impact.

According to their research between 458 local participants of a sporting event, Inoue and Havard (2014) pointed out that there is a link between the creation of social impact and business returns with the *attendees' perceptions* about the level of the event's social responsibility, which is likely to elicit support for the event itself and their sponsors.

Besides consumers and their perceptions about the CSR of sponsors and sports teams or organizations, sponsorship managers alike have their own perceptions about sport-related corporate social responsibility (S-CSR) sponsorships. Djaballah, Hautbois, and Desbordes (2017) analyzed the strategic sensemaking process and *managers' perceptions* about S-CSR from 23 corporations involved in sport CSR partnerships. Among other results, it became able to identify that sponsorship managers are with ambiguity in their interpretive process about their perceptions of what links sports properties with CSR. Such an "eccentricity" might obfuscate them from the reasoning for a better understanding of multiple possibilities of CSR's leverage.

Habitzreuter and Koenigstorfer (2018) investigated the influence of environmental CSR-linked sponsorship of mega sports events on consumers' attitudes toward the sponsors. Using the regulatory fit theory as a research framework, it is noticed that depending on the fit of *perceived motives* (perceived philanthropy-driven motives) a reinforcement on consumers' attitudes can occur toward the sponsor.

Another study from Mamo, James, and Andrew (2019) about *consumers' perception* around sponsors' sport-related CSR activities explored the issues of potential impacts on sponsor image, consumers' attitudes toward the sponsor but also to the sponsored sports property. Within a sample of individual persons from the US and 12 other countries, it became evident that what matters is the extent of consumers' awareness on the information (sponsorship information, sponsorship, and CSR-related information) that is available around an organization's sport-related CSR. That kind and extent of information lead to increased influence on *consumer perceptions* around the image of the sponsor but also to a positive attitude toward the sponsor.

Demirel (2020) sought if there is a link between sponsoring a professional sports team and *consumers' CSR perceptions* about the sponsoring brand. Factors that might evoke *consumers' perceptions* about the brand and the subsequent responses have also been explored. Demirel realized that what induces *consumers' perceptions* toward the sponsoring brand is the sponsorship fit. Consumers' social responsibility perceptions operate like an underlying process which drives the effect of sponsorship fit and arouses consumers' behavioral intentions toward the brand that sponsors the team. As a practical implication, it is noted, that the key predictor for CSR perceptions is *consumers' perceived fit* between the sponsoring brand and the sponsored sports team. This is what creates the brand's image as a socially responsible one.

Perceptions and Corporate Social Responsibility

Most of the literature on CSR perceptions in the sport industry concerns consumers, fans, spectators, and other groups in the field of professional sports and professional teams-organizations. Another smaller part also refers to CSR executives' perceptions at the corporate level and the level of sports organizations, but little is known about perceptions existing among students who are trained to become future executives in the developing field of sports. In this vein, Mallen, Bradish, and MacLean (2008) explored the perceptions of CSR and the principle of corporate citizenship (CC) in sport management classes. They sought to determine if the curriculum of sport management programs in a North American University addresses issues such as CSR and also if the classes taught within the curriculum, prepare students to be the corporate citizens for the sports industry of tomorrow. The study indicates that *sports students perceive* the sports industry as "good but not great" regarding CSR practices. The faculty also indicated that despite the fact that the principles of CSR and CC are evident in the curriculum, more effort is needed for those principles to be incorporated in the sport management pedagogy system.

Additionally, Park (2010) in another survey, in the context of education among Korean college students, examined their *perceptions toward a sports team's image*, and how this image can be altered due to the team's social responsibility activities. A sample of 245 male and female college students from three different Universities of a metropolitan area participated in the study. The perception of a sports team's social responsibility and image was significantly different among male and female students.

Male students had better knowledge than female students both about social responsibility activities and the sport itself. Moreover, the different type of a students' grade level (freshman, sophomore, junior, senior) and different level of sports participation had significant variations in their perceptions. CSR programs can be very crucial in shaping or altering the image of professional sport team players, especially in harsh times.

Professional sports organizations are also engaged in CSR initiatives. Giannoulakis and Drayer (2009) studied *individuals' perceptions* about "NBA Cares" CSR campaign in a period where the National Basketball Association (NBA) was surrounded with an increased controversy". Indeed, they found that the specific campaign had an increasing influence on participants' opinions regarding the image of NBA athletes.

Lacey and Kennett-Hensel (2010) collected field survey data from a large number of NBA customers during the 2007–2008 season. In their effort to depict links between *customers' perceptions* regarding the performance of CSR of an NBA team and the possible strength of their relationships, it was found that when a sports team invests in the participation of CSR, rewards can accumulate over the period of a business cycle. Also, engagement in CSR facilitates relationships through trust and commitment, which in turn helps further in forging desirable customer behaviors.

A great amount of how professionals in the sports industry define CSR relies upon how CSR is perceived. With a mixed-method approach, Sheth and Babiak (2010) explored the *perceptions of 27 sports executives* (community-relation directors and team owners) about CSR, since the way you define a concept determines the way you apply it in practice. It was found that sports executives placed different amounts of emphases on different CSR elements, while focusing mostly on philanthropic activities and ethical behaviors. Furthermore, sports executives view CSR as imperative for the strategy in their organizations which is also good for sport business.

Alonso and O'Shea (2012) explored the *consumers'/fans' CSR perceptions* about sports organizations and their role in the broader community. Within a sample of 2107 individuals, they have studied two variables that impact consumers/fans' responses: level of fandom and club affiliation which can elicit different responses from sport consumers/fans. Accordingly, as the authors report, sports organizations can be a "support network" or "social anchor" within the surrounding communities by going forward with activities like youth mentoring, sports participation promotion, and community outreach. Engagement with such activities can help sports organizations to preserve and reinforce their community relations.

A past study from Park, Moon, and Won (2012) examined the impacts of sports *fans' perception* regarding CSR activity and its relationship with the team's *perceived reciprocity*. Data analysis of 265 fans' responses from a Korean professional baseball team revealed that activity in the social responsibility domain had a significant impact on how fans perceive the reciprocity of their team. Additionally, the level of fans' identification with the team moderated the relationship between perceived CSR and perceived reciprocity. Once more, Park and Park (2013) explored CSR activity of professional sports teams as changes in sports fans' *perception of the reciprocity* and their behaviors toward their team (loyalty and revisit intentions). They have explored such a relationship amongst a sample of 241 fans from a professional baseball team. Data analysis revealed that CSR activity had a positive effect on *fans' perception* of reciprocity and on team loyalty but had no effect on revisit intentions. However, *fans' reciprocity perception* was the one that affected both their loyalty to the team and their revisit intentions.

Perceptions of corporate social responsibility (CSR) also play a role in the decision-making process of potential donors. Ko, Rhee, Kim, and Kim (2014) developed a model to examine the relationships between perceived CSR, commitment, and donation intentions. Using a large sample of 644 donors from a college booster club in the United States, they drew from the findings that perceptions around CSR activities had a significant influence on trust and commitment as far as the club is concerned. Potential donors' behavior also altered due to CSR perceptions and the variables of trust and commitment played a mediating role in that direction.

Consumers' responses to corporate social responsibility (CSR) in the sports marketing context are governed by *consumers' perceptions of a firm's CSR*. As Ibrahim and Almarshed (2014) realized, by conducting a field survey with 399 consumers, perceptions can exert significant gravity on consumers' commitment, identification, and trust but also can significantly affect their purchase intentions.

During a Korean professional soccer game, 380 spectators participated in a study about the effect that *perceived CSR engagement* of the host team might possibly have on their attitudes and intentions to re-attend a game of the sports team. Also, in this study, K. T. Kim, Kwak, and Babiak (2015) examined the differences that might exist between men and women regarding the aforementioned effect. Indeed, the perceptions of the team's CSR engagement found to yield a significant effect on spectators' intention to re-attend a team's game but also found that the mediator of this effect was the attitudes toward the professional team. Most intriguing, according to authors, was the finding that the CSR effect on team attitude was greater for male spectators.

In China, Liu, Wilson, Plumley, and Chen (2019) attempted to analyze fans' perceptions around corporate social responsibility (CSR) activities of a professional football club, based on a sample of 451 home team fans. They determined the impact of perceived CSR performance upon fans' intentions to support their team. The factors that were found to be predictive of fans' behavior were the CSR activities directed to consumers and employees' issues, community development, and youth education. These types of CSR activities are significant predictors of fans' intentions such as repeated purchases, word of mouth, and merchandise consumption. A less predictive factor to fans' patronage intentions was charitable CSR activity which also can affect merchandise consumption intentions only.

International sports organizations are also engaged in corporate social responsibility initiatives. This is true also for the International Olympic Committee (IOC). Within this NGO setting, Walker, Heere, Parent, and Drane (2010) examined the mediating influence of organizational motives from the scope of *consumers' perceptions*. During the Olympic games of Beijing in China, data were collected from consumers of the Games to access their *perception of IOC's CSR initiatives*. In the case that consumers perceived and judged the CSR initiatives as value-driven, their response was positive. In contrast, the researchers received negative responses in the case that efforts were perceived as a pure strategy for the accomplishment of the organizational goals. In those judgments, the consumer's awareness was a mediator. The attribution of these activities as value-driven or strategy-driven had also effects on consumers, regarding their patronage intentions and perceived reputation around the organization.

Sports are played not only in the sports fields and arenas but also in the lottery industry. Consumers of this kind of sports products, have also witnessed CSR activity. Li, Zhang, Mao, and Min (2012) examined 4980 participants regarding their perceptions of CSR in China's sports lottery industry and the impact of *perceived CSR* on their consumption behavior. Regulatory and addiction prevention, as well as product development responsibility of China's sports lottery administration, were the two factors associated with *participants' perceptions* and had an effect on their consumption behavior in terms of the amount of expenditure, the frequency of purchasing, and time commitment to the lottery products.

In a regional study that examined corporate social responsibility (CSR) evaluation issues of Greek professional sports organizations, the participating sport marketing *executives expressed the perception* that a barrier to CSR assessment is the intangible nature of CSR, due to which it is not always easy to assess and evaluate the effectiveness of CSR activities (Douvis, Kyriakis, Kriemadis, and Vrondou, 2015; Kim et al., 2018).

Expectations and *perceptions of CSR* initiatives might impact the quality of the relationship between a team and its fan base. To explore this issue Lacey and Kennett-Hensel (2016), in the context of the National Basketball Association (NBA), collected survey data over the period of three consecutive seasons. The results indicated that whenever fans expect their team to demonstrate its socially responsible face, and when these expectations closely match (fit) the team's CSR perceived practices, then the combined impact of these conditions improves the quality of relationships between fans and sports teams.

The perceived fit between a team and its CSR initiatives was examined by J.K. Kim, Overton, Hull, and Choi (2018). The study sought to explore how the aforementioned relationship could shape MLB team consumers' intentions to support these CSR initiatives. They conclude that perceptions that customers hold about the fit between the team and CSR initiatives can have a positive impact on consumers' patronage intentions.

In their efforts to engage in CSR initiatives, sports organizations come into partnerships with other organizations from different sectors, public, private, and nonprofit (S. P. Lee, Heinze, & Lu, 2018). In this case perception about portfolio warmth and competence of partnering organizations contribute and strengthen the predisposition of the public to donate to the cause supported by a sport organization. The notion of cause fit and response efficacy of partnership organizations is mediating the effect of the above-mentioned perceptions.

Fan-perceived team variables like emotion, pride, and attachment and their relationship to CSR of professional baseball teams in Seoul have established by the work of Kim and Kim (2016) They have found that, within an effective sample of 367 spectators, a professional sports club's CSR activity has a significant impact on the fan-perceived team emotion, pride, and attachment.

Sports fans have their own specific mechanisms on how they perceive a sports teams and this can lead up to an enhanced sense of pride, greater identification with the team, and regional attachment (Chang, Ko, Connaughton, & Kang, 2016). Gender differences can also act as a mediator to the outcomes. Their research results amongst 317 participants' responses indicates that a fan's pride is an important mediator for the relationship between his/her perceptions about corporate social responsibility and the subsequent identification with the team. The perception of corporate social responsibility, both in men and women also is an important indicator for enhancing the pride of team sports fans.

The way that recipients of corporate social responsibility (CSR) campaigns perceive the motives of the initiative can have an impact on important outcomes variables of the CSR. Kulczycki and Koenigstorfer (2016) looked at moderators of this relationship in the context of professional football teams. In a city residents' sample of 444, outcome variables such as the team's CSR perception, attitude toward the team, and behavioral intentions, were tested against residents' perception about the motives behind the CSR campaign.

Using two CSR-specific factors (local versus distant CSR activities and first-division versus third-division team) results revealed that when residents perceived CSR motives as philanthropy-driven, the effect of CSR on the outcome variables was more positive for the first division than the third division team. Also, in first division teams, distant CSR activities appeared to impact the outcome variables in contrast with the local CSR activities.

In a case study, Davies and Moyo (2017) explored at the community level the members' perceptions about a corporate social responsibility program of a Town's professional football club in South Africa. In this case, it was found that the corporate social responsibility program was clearly perceived by the community members, addressing a number of issues and problems that the community was facing. Also, the implementation of this corporate social responsibility program created a consensus among member stakeholders, that the relationship between the community and the team was mutually perceived as a two-way affiliation and was a mutually beneficial relationship of trust and loyal support for the professional team.

Professional football consumers' perceptions about corporate social responsibility (CSR) activities can operate as predictors of behavioral loyalty, according to a research between 634 sport customers conducted by Inoue, Funk, and McDonald (2017). However, as the authors further explained, behavioral loyalty cannot be predicted as a direct result of CSR initiatives. Specifically, behavioral loyalty found to be "contingent upon specific psychological states activated by consumers' perceptions of such initiatives" and it is mediated by involvement and commitment.

The Role of Intentions in Consumer Behavior

A person's intention to participate in an activity is subject on one's attitudes and subjective norms according to Ajzen and Fishbein (1975) and Ajzen's (1985, 1991) theories as reported by Cunningham and Kwon (2003). These theories that were constructed to explain a person's behavior toward a given activity, were used by Cunningham & Kwon to understand consumers' intentions in attending a sport event. They have predicted and confirmed that components like attitudes and subjective norms are antecedents of intentions. Moreover, they cite that when a person's perceptions about the outcome of an activity is positive it is most likely to perform with positive attitude and participate or support the proposed activity. As such, this relationship between intentions and their antecedents, becomes extremely meaningful and useful in CSR and CRM activity in the sport sector. As Ajzen (1991) quoted, "Intentions are assumed to capture the motivational factors that influence behavior; they are indicators of how hard are willing to try, of how much effort that they are planning to exert, in order to perform the behavior" (Cunningham & Kwon, 2003, p. 132).

Also, as they explain, the intention antecedent "Subjective norms" refers to the social expectations a person has from "significant others" to engage or not to engage in a given activity. Placing sport organizations and the governance bodies in the role of "significant others" for the sport fans in general, we can infer that when a sport organization meets the subjective norms (social expectations) by engaging in CSR activity, sports' consumers participation and support are facilitated. Additionally, they have quoted Sutton, McDonald, Milne, and Cimperman (1997) that ". . . a team's community involvement can be used as a strategy to foster more positive attitudes toward the team". In that vein, a community involvement as CSR strategy should be put forward as an aspect of CSR in Sport Governance.

Akman and Mishra (2017) mentioned that individuals who are responsible for the consequences of their actions, tend to make decisions related to ethical issues. In the ethical consumption context, intentions play a significant role however, there is a gap between intention and behavior. Carrington, Neville, and Whitwell (2014) noted that ethical concerns are prioritized over other concerns and that not all concerns are of equal salience. Carrington and colleagues also indicate that despite sustainability's importance, it is difficult to redirect the global population to adopt sustainable practices in our society. This means for the Governance of sports, that CSR activity toward sustainability should take in consideration that intention – behavior gap.

Intention has significant contribution in consumers' decisions regarding their purchases. Moreover, their awareness about CSR activities can positively influence their purchase intention (K.-H. Lee & Shin, 2010). CSR practices can be used to develop relationship quality with organizations' various stakeholders in order to satisfy their needs and stimulate their intentions toward the organization. In the sport field, sport organizations can use CSR and CRM and similar activities to develop and sustain bonds with their fans, from a sport consumer behavior viewpoint. As (Paek, Morse, Hutchinson, & Lim, 2020) reported on sport consumption behavior intention, ". . . the major intentional aspects of sport consumer behaviors include attendance, sports media consumption and, licensed merchandise consumption" (p. 4). Governance in sports should account on CSR practices to create or built relationship quality with fan bases at any organizational level (grassroots, amateur, professional).

CSR as a Gate Revenue Stream

Gau, Huang, Chen, and Naylor (2019) explored fans' knowledge about a Team's Social Responsibility (TSR) and their intentions associated with TSR, in the context of Chinese Professional Baseball League amongst a sample of 520 in Taiwan. Psychographic factors like values, sport involvement and team identification, were positively related to TSR-linked *intentions such as watch future games.*

Social media are used widely to communicate a team's CSR efforts to individual fans. J. K. Kim, Ott, Hull, and Choi (2017) studied the impact on attitudes and behavioral intentions of exposure to CSR messages, stemming from different information sources and different type of CSR activities, in the context of MBL. A halo effect was observed on individual attitudes and purchase or consumption intentions, as an indirect effect, given that activities are perceived as sincere. In terms of direct effects, *attendance* and word of mouth communication intentions, were also observed.

Cause related marketing (CSR) can have an effect on re-attendance intentions of spectator sport consumers, which is mediated through the attitude toward the team. According to K. T. Kim et al. (2010) perceived motives of a team's CRM effort have no significant impact on sport spectators regarding their attitude toward the team and hence their behavioral intention.

Gender has a moderating role on attitude and re-attendance intentions toward a professional sport team and its perceived CSR engagement (K. T. Kim et al., 2015). Kim and colleagues explored those differences among a sample of 380 spectators at a professional soccer game.

Fans' intention to revisit or re-attend at the sportscape of an event, seems to be connected with CSR activity of professional sport teams. Park and Park (2013) in the context of professional baseball, collected data from 241 spectators to test if there is a causal relationship between the above. CSR activity alone had no positive effect on fans' intentions to revisit, but combined with their perceptions about the teams' reciprocity, CSR was found to have a positive effect on intentions mediated by team loyalty.

Patronage and Word-of-Mouth (WoM) Intentions as CSR Outcome

Walker and Kent (2009) explored consumers' reactions to CSR in the sport industry in terms of patronage intentions. Using a sample of 297 NFL fans, they observed two types of patronage intentions that CSR impacts upon. Attitudes about an organization's CSR initiative impacts on consumers' evaluations and hence their intentions. CSR was a significant predictor of *word of mouth (WoM)* and merchandise consumption behaviors.

Magnusen, Hong, and Mondello (2011) studied a sample of 207 NBA spectators on how professional athletes' political skills and proactive influence tactics influence a sport organization's CSR reputation and hence sport consumers' intentions to become advocates of the organization through *word of mouth communication*. They found that athletes' political skill leads to inspirational appeal, which in turn haw direct effect on CSR reputation and sport consumer advocacy intentions.

The players' strike due to labor disputes between a league and the players' association can be considered as an anti-social behavior. Kim,

Goldsmith, Walker, and Drane (2014) explored how corporate social responsibility activities, especially donations, by the NHL during the lockout impacted on organizational credibility and affected fans' *patronage intentions*.

According to Kim et al. (2017) in their study on MLB, word of mouth *communication* was found to be directly affected when social media are used to communicate a team's CSR effort. Moreover, in a later study within a sample of 207 subjects Kim, Byon, Song, and Kim (2018) examined the impact of the congruence between an MLB league and its initiatives (CSR fit) on consumers' *patronage intentions*. They found that consumers' intentions to support a team's CSR activities are related to their public perceptions about CSR fit. Regardless the perceived nature of a team's CSR efforts as value driven or strategic driven, *patronage intentions* to the team remain untouched.

The perceived performance in certain areas of CSR can have impact on fans. Liu, Wilson, Plumley, and Chen (2019) studied 451 football fans of professional teams and found that performance of CSR activities to consumers and employees, community development and youth education can predict their *patronage intentions* such as repeat purchase, *word of mouth (WoM)* and merchandise consumption.

Organizational social responsibility in the context of nonprofit membership associations, like sport clubs, has the ability to engage members in voluntering, membership loyalty and *word of mouth behavior*. Misener, Morrison, Shier, and Babiak (2020) studied 735 members of seven grassroots associations in Ontario Canada. They found that the awareness of the socially responsible activities has a direct effect on members' intentions to become and stay involved with their club and to speak with positive words about their club to others (i.e., *word of mouth*).

Purchase Intentions Due to CSR and CRM-Linked Sport Sponsorships

During a telephone survey back in 2003, Roy and Graeff realized that sport consumers' purchase intention is less influenced by a team's cause related marketing campaign, despite their high expectations from professional athletes and teams to be involved in their local communities.

Irwin, Lachowetz, Cornwell, and Clark (2003) examined 442 spectators during a sporting event, which was associated with a nonprofit organization through a cause related marketing activity. They found not only consumers' (event spectators) attitudes and beliefs to be impacted but also their *intentions to purchase* products of the sponsoring the cause company.

Similarly, Bakhshandeh, Jalali Farahani, and Sajjadi (2016) in the context of Iranian professional football league, examined team CSR activities on fans intentions within a sample of 384 fans. They revealed a significant effect of CSR activity which was translated into *purchase intentions* regarding sponsors products.

In a mass participation event (Pink Ribbon Love Marathon) in Seoul, Sung and Lee (2016) collected responses of 650 females in their effort to explain the benefits of charitable sport events and how this contributes to the corresponding *purchase intentions* of participants. They found that there is a relationship between participants perception about the Event and their intentions to *patronage the sponsors* of the Event. The image of the sponsor (Corporate Image) was partial mediator in the above relationship.

Sport sponsorship can be used to promote sustainable activities and socially responsible companies. In a study Melovic, Rogic, Cerovic Smolovic, Dudic, and Gregus (2019) examined the impact of sponsorship perceptions and attitudes of sport team fans on their *purchase decisions*. A sport sponsorship that supports sustainable practices and promote socially responsible companies is a mean to educate the sport fan base, create a loyal base and influence *the intentions* to buy from sponsors (Lindsey, 2016).

CSR-linked sport sponsorships creates a halo effect that protects a company's service when this service might fail to deliver. Daehwan, Kim, Ko, Lee, and Kim (2019) through a scenario-based research, explored how a CSR-linked sport sponsorship can create attribution patterns among consumers in the incident of a service failure. Those attributes can influence consumers' attitudes toward a company involved in a CSR-linked sponsorship and thus lead to *re-purchase intentions*.

Other Types of Intentions as Outcome of CSR and CRM

Green stadium initiatives (GSI) can impact on donation intentions. Jin, Mao, Zhang, and Walker (2011) used the theory of reasoned action (TRA) to explore how the beliefs, attitudes, subjective and perceived behavioral control can impact on *donors' intentions* at a collegiate athletic context among a sample of 186 university students. Accordingly, educational, and promotional programs need to be developed in order to enhance beliefs, attitudes and supportive norms that impact *intentions to donate*.

College Athletic Departments rely at online fundraising platforms to solicit donations in order to generate revenues, which in turn cover operating expenses. Hwang, Kihl, and Inoue (2020) explored how CSR initiatives can influence fans' online *donation intentions*. The provided information about these CSR initiatives affects positively e-satisfaction which in turn is a predictor of the *donation intentions* among the fans of the college team. However, the effect is mediated by the fan-athletic department identification level.

Corporate Social Marketing Initiatives can urge and influence sport consumers toward voluntary behavior and stimulate intention to act in an environmentally responsible manner (*recycling intentions*). Inoue and Kent (2012a) examined the responses of participants during professional sport team games and found that environmental credibility of the team can influence the *intentions of sport consumers to recycle*, especially among those with less involvement in environmental issues.

Moreover, similar outcomes can derive from CSR environmental initiatives. There is a special underlying process that motivates and induces the consumers of a sport team to engage in pro-environmental behavior. As Inoue and Kent (2012b) explains, based on the Kelman's internalization perspective, a team's environmental practices can increase the internalization of team's value by its consumers. This internalization process is the key between a team's environmental practices and its consumers' behavioral intentions, such as support for the team's environmental initiative and *intention to demonstrate a pro-environmental* behavior daily in their lives.

Conclusion

CSR programs can be crucial for shaping the image of professional sport teams, players, sponsors and organizations, especially in harsh times. CSR is imperative for every organization's strategy, including the sport business world too. Engagement with such activities can help sport organizations preserve and reinforce their community relations. Community involvement can be used as a strategy to foster more positive attitudes toward the sport organization. Hence, community involvement as a CSR strategy should be put forward as an aspect of CSR in Sport Governance.

CSR adds social meaning to a brand, a sponsor and a sport property, in its sponsorship form or as a support action for a good cause. CSR efforts in the sport context, should challenge perceptual variables such as awareness to sensitize fans, engage them in a good cause, and thus enhance-evoke quality relationships with the sport organizations and the brands around them. Consumers' perceptions of such initiatives activate specific psychological states that lead to behavioral loyalty of fans and sport consumers. When consumers perceive and judge CSR initiatives as value-driven, then their response is positive.

Perceptions about the congruence or the fit between a CSR activity and the sport organization, help consumers regenerate the brand's image as a socially responsible one. Perceptions around a CSR activity, its fit or sincerity, and the motives behind it, drive fans' and consumers' intentions to participate and support the cause, the team, and the partnering organizations or sponsors of the initiative. This relationship between intentions and their antecedents, becomes significant and valuable in any CSR and CRM activity taking place in the sport sector. Intentions are indicators of how hard one is willing to try and how much effort one is planning to exert to perform a behavior. They play a significant role however, since there is a gap between intention and behavior. Intentions have a significant contribution to sport consumers' decisions regarding their purchases. With respect to governance in sports, CSR activity toward sustainability should consider this intention-behavior gap.

Bearing in mind all the above considerations, governance in sport should account for CSR practices to build and optimize the relationship quality between sport organizations, sponsors and their respective fan bases at any organizational level (grassroots, amateur, professional).

References

Ajzen, I. (1985). From intentions to actions: A theory of planned behavior. In *Action control* (pp. 11–39). Berlin, Heidelberg: Springer.

Ajzen, I. (1991). The theory of planned behavior. *Organizational Behavior and Human Decision Processes, 50*(2), 179–211.

Ajzen, I., & Fishbein, M. (1975). A Bayesian analysis of attribution processes. *Psychological Bulletin, 82*(2), 261.

Akman, I., & Mishra, A. (2017). Factors influencing consumer intention in social commerce adoption. *Information Technology & People, 30*(2), 356–370. doi:10.1108/ITP-01-2016-0006

Al-Daaja, Y., & Szabados, G. N. (2018). The current state of CSR in the football clubs of the professional football league in Jordan. *Applied Studies in Agribusiness and Commerce, 12*(3–4), 21–30. doi:10.19041/apstract/2018/3-4/3

Alonso, A. D., & O'Shea, M. (2012). "You only get back what you put in": Perceptions of professional sport organizations as community anchors. *Community Development, 43*(5), 656–676. doi:10.1080/15575330.2011.645048

Anagnostopoulos, C., Byers, T., & Shilbury, D. (2014). Corporate social responsibility in professional team sport organisations: Towards a theory of decision-making. *European Sport Management Quarterly, 14*(3), 259–281. doi:10.108 0/16184742.2014.897736

Anagnostopoulos, C., & Clements, N. (2011). Corporate social responsibility in sport: Towards a context-intensive and sector-specific empirical examination (pp. 15–16). Cologne, Germany: European Association for Sport Management (EASM).

Anagnostopoulos, C., Gillooly, L., Cook, D., Parganas, P., & Chadwick, S. (2017). Stakeholder communication in 140 characters or less: A study of community sport foundations. *VOLUNTAS: International Journal of Voluntary and Nonprofit Organizations, 28*(5), 2224–2250. doi:10.1007/s11266-016-9802-4

Arora, N., Grewal, B., & Singh, G. (2019). Sports social responsibility: Exploring the unexplored with a global perspective. *IUP Journal of Marketing Management, 18*(1), 7–22.

Athanasopoulou, P., Douvis, J., & Kyriakis, V. (2011). Corporate social responsibility (CSR) in sports: Antecedents and consequences. *African Journal of Hospitality, Tourism and Leisure, 1*(4), 1–11.

Aurélien, F., & Bayle, E. (2017). *Inter-country differences in CSR practices: A cross national comparison between the French and UK professional sport sectors* (pp. 534–535). Cologne, Germany: European Association for Sport Management (EASM).

Auweele, Y. V. (2010). Challenging modern sports' moral deficit: Towards fair trade Corporate Social Responsibility and good governance in sport. *Journal of Community and Health Sciences, 5*(2), 45–53.

Babiak, K. (2010). The role and relevance of corporate social responsibility in sport: A view from the top. *Journal of Management & Organization, 16*(4), 528–549. doi:10.1017/S1833367200001917

Baena, V. (2018). The importance of CSR practices carried out by sport teams and its influence on brand love: The real madrid foundation. *Social Responsibility Journal, 14*(1), 61–79. doi:10.1108/SRJ-11-2016-0205

Bakhshandeh, H., Jalali Farahani, M., & Sajjadi, S. N. (2016). Fan reaction to the club's social responsibility: A case study of selected team of Iran's football pro league. *Research in Sport Management and Motor Behaviour, 6*(11), 51–62.

Ballouli, K., & Brown, B. (2012). Social responsibility in sport: What is it worth? In *Association of marketing theory and practice proceedings* (p. 44). Georgia: Georgia Southern University.

Blumrodt, J., Desbordes, M., & Bodin, D. (2013). Professional football clubs and corporate social responsibility. *Sport, Business and Management: An International Journal, 3*(3), 205–225. doi:10.1108/SBM-04-2011-0050

Bradish, C., & Cronin, J. J. (2009). Corporate social responsibility in sport. *Journal of Sport Management, 23*(6), 691–697. doi:10.1123/jsm.23.6.691

Carrington, M. J., Neville, B. A., & Whitwell, G. J. (2014). Lost in translation: Exploring the ethical consumer intention – behavior gap. *Journal of Business Research, 67*(1), 2759–2767. doi:10.1016/j.jbusres.2012.09.022

Chang, M. J., Ko, Y. J., Connaughton, D. P., & Kang, J.-H. (2016). The effects of perceived CSR, pride, team identification, and regional attachment: The moderating effect of gender. *Journal of Sport & Tourism, 20*(2), 145–159. doi:10.1080/14775085.2016.1193822

Cunningham, G. B., & Kwon, H. (2003). The theory of planned behaviour and intentions to attend a sport event. *Sport Management Review, 6*(2), 127–145. doi:10.1016/S1441-3523(03)70056-4

Davies, S. E., & Moyo, T. (2017). Community perceptions of a CSR programme: A case study of a professional football club. *Corporate Ownership and Control, 14*(3), 197–203. doi:10.22495/cocv14i3c1art5

Demirel, A. (2020). CSR in sport sponsorship consumers' perceptions of a sponsoring brand's CSR. *International Journal of Sports Marketing and Sponsorship, 21*(2), 371–388. doi:10.1108/IJSMS-09-2019-0108

Digel, H. (2010). Perspectives of sport in a global world. *Procedia Social and Behavioral Sciences, 2*(5), 6719–6728. doi:10.1016/j.sbspro.2010.05.018

Dimitropoulos, P. E., & Vrondou, O. (2015, 12). Corporate social responsibility and firm value in the sport recreation sector: A review. *Business Management and Strategy, 6*(2), 28–43. doi:10.5296/bms.v6i2.8542

Djaballah, M., Hautbois, C., & Desbordes, M. (2017). Sponsors' CSR strategies in sport: A sensemaking approach of corporations established in France. *Sport Management Review, 20*(2), 211–225. doi:10.1016/j.smr.2016.07.002

Douvis, J., Kyriakis, V., Kriemadis, A., & Vrondou, O. (2015). Corporate social responsibility (CSR) effectiveness in the Greek professional sport context.

International Journal of Sport Management, Recreation & Tourism, 17, 37–45. doi:10.5199/ijsmart-1791-874X-17c

Dowling, M., Robinson, L., & Washington, M. (2013). Taking advantage of the London 2012 Olympic games: Corporate social responsibility through sport partnerships. *European Sport Management Quarterly, 13*(3), 269–292. doi:10.1080/16184742.2013.774039

Flöter, T., Benkenstein, M., & Uhrich, S. (2016, 4). Communicating CSR-linked sponsorship: Examining the influence of three different types of message sources. *Sport Management Review, 19*(2), 146–156. doi:10.1016/j.smr.2015.05.005

Forster, J. (2006). Global sports organisations and their governance. *Corporate Governance: The International Journal of Business in Society, 6*(1), 72–83. doi:10.1108/14720700610649481

Gardner, J., & Nichols, B. S. (2017). Disruptive cause-related marketing in professional sports: The case of Devon still and the cincinnati Bengals. In *Creating marketing magic and innovative future marketing trends. Developments in marketing science: Proceedings of the academy of marketing science* (pp. 989–990). Cham: Springer. doi:10.1007/978-3-319-45596-9_183

Gau, L.-S., Huang, J.-C., Chen, M.-I., & Naylor, M. (2019, 9). Team social responsibility embedded in correlates of universalism values, sport involvement, and team identification for sustainable management in sporting settings. *Sustainability, 11*(19), 5416. doi:10.3390/su11195416

Giannoulakis, C., & Drayer, J. (2009, 12). "Thugs" versus "good guys": The impact of NBA cares on player image. *European Sport Management Quarterly, 9*(4), 453–468. doi:10.1080/16184740903331796

Grove, S. J., Dorsch, M. J., & Hopkins, C. D. (2012). Assessing the longitudinal robustness of spectators' perceptions of the functions of sport: Implications for sport marketers, *20*(1), 23–38. doi:10.2753/MTP1069-6679200102

Habitzreuter, A. M., & Koenigstorfer, J. (2018). The impact of environmental CSR-linked sport sponsorship on attitude toward the sponsor depending on regulatory fit. *Journal of Business Research, 20*(1). doi:10.2753/MTP1069-6679200102

Hakala, U. (2015). Sport-based CSR – A tool in building a better society? In *CSR communication conference (CSRCOM)* (pp. 217–220). Ljubljana: Faculty of Social Sciences, University of Ljubljana.

Holbrook, M. B. (1981). Integrating compositional and decompositional analyses to represent the intervening role of perceptions in evaluative judgments. *Journal of Marketing Research, 18*(1), 13–28. doi:10.1177/002224378101800102

Hwang, G., Kihl, L. A., & Inoue, Y. (2020). Corporate social responsibility and college sports fans' online donations. *International Journal of Sports Marketing and Sponsorship, 21*(4), 597–616. doi:10.1108/IJSMS-07-2019-0079

Ibrahim, H., & Almarshed, S. O. (2014). Sporting event as a corporate social responsibility strategy. *Procedia Economics and Finance, 11*, 3–14. doi:10.1016/S2212-5671(14)00170-1

Inoue, Y., & Havard, C. T. (2014). Determinants and consequences of the perceived social impact of a sport event. *Journal of Sport Management, 28*(3), 295–310. doi:10.1123/jsm.2013-0136

Inoue, Y., Funk, D. C., & McDonald, H. (2017). Predicting behavioral loyalty through corporate social responsibility: The mediating role of involvement and commitment. *Journal of Business Research, 75,* 46–56. doi:10.1016/j. jbusres.2017.02.005

Inoue, Y., & Kent, A. (2012a). Investigating the role of corporate credibility in corporate social marketing: A case study of environmental initiatives by professional sport organizations. *Sport Management Review, 15*(3), 330–344. doi:10.1016/j.smr.2011.12.002

Inoue, Y., & Kent, A. (2012b). Sport teams as promoters of pro-environmental behavior: An empirical study. *Journal of Sport Management, 26*(5), 417–432. doi:10.1123/jsm.26.5.417

Inoue, Y., Kent, A., & Lee, S. (2011). CSR and the bottom line: Analyzing the link between CSR and financial performance for professional teams. *Journal of Sport Management, 25*(6), 531–549. doi:10.1123/jsm.25.6.531

Irwin, R. L., Lachowetz, T., & Clark, J. (2010). Cause-related sport marketing: Can this marketing strategy affect company decision-makers? *Journal of Management & Organization, 16*(4), 550–556. doi:10.5172/jmo.2010.16.4.550

Irwin, R. L., Lachowetz, T., Cornwell, T. B., & Clark, J. S. (2003). Cause-related sport sponsorship: An assessment of spectator beliefs, attitudes, and behavioral intentions. *Sport Marketing Quarterly, 12*(3), 131–139.

Jalonen, H. (2016). Responsible business through sport: A balance between pursuing esteem and avoiding disesteem. *Organisational Studies and Innovation Review, 2*(1), 1–7.

Jin, L., Mao, L. L., Zhang, J. J., & Walker, M. B. (2011). Impact of green stadium initiatives on donor intentions toward an intercollegiate athletic programme. *International Journal of Sport Management and Marketing, 10*(1/2), 121–141. doi:10.1504/IJSMM.2011.043620

Joo, S., Koo, J., & Fink, J. S. (2016). Cause-related marketing in sports: The power of altruism. *European Sport Management Quarterly, 16*(3), 316–340. doi:10.1080/16184742.2016.1143854

Kim, D., Goldsmith, A., Walker, M., & Drane, D. (2014). Does the social behavior of a high-profile sport league matter? *Journal of Contemporary Athletics, 8*(2), 65–65.

Kim, D., Ko, Y., Lee, J. L., & Kim, Y. C. (2019). The impact of CSR-linked sport sponsorship on consumers' reactions to service failures. *International Journal of Sports Marketing and Sponsorship, 21*(1), 70–90. doi:10.1108/ IJSMS-01-2019-0011

Kim, D.-W., & Kim, C.-H. (2016). Influence of a professional sports club's corporate social responsibility activity on fan-perceived team emotion, team pride and team attachment. *Korean Journal of Sports Science, 25*(2), 743–754. Retrieved from www.dbpia.co.kr/journal/articleDetail?nodeId=NODE07050516#

Kim, J. K., Ott, H. K., Hull, K., & Choi, M. (2017). Double play! Examining the relationship between MLB's corporate social responsibility and sport spectators' behavioral intentions. *International Journal of Sport Communication, 10*(4), 508–530. doi:10.1123/ijsc.2017-0081

Kim, J. K., Overton, H., Hull, K., & Choi, M. (2018). Examining public perceptions of CSR in sport. *Corporate Communications: An International Journal, 23*(4), 629–647. doi:10.1108/CCIJ-05-2018-0060

Kim, K. A., Byon, K. K., Song, H., & Kim, K. (2018). Internal contributions to initiating corporate social responsibility in sport organizations. *Management Decision, 56*(8), 1804–1817. doi:10.1108/MD-04-2017-0369

Kim, K. T., Kwak, D. H., & Babiak, K. (2015). Gender differences on the effect of CSR engagement on team attitude and loyalty: A case study of a professional soccer club in Korea. *International Journal of Sport Management and Marketing, 16*(1/2), 92–111. doi:10.1504/IJSMM.2015.074918

Kim, K. T., Kwak, D. H., & Kim, Y. K. (2010). The impact of cause-related marketing (CRM) in spectator sport. *Journal of Management & Organization, 16*(4), 515–527. doi:10.5172/jmo.2010.16.4.515

Ko, Y. J., Rhee, Y. C., Kim, Y. K., & Kim, T. (2014). Perceived corporate social responsibility and donor behavior in college athletics: The mediating effects of trust and commitment. *Sport Marketing Quarterly, 23*(2), 73–82.

Kokoulina, O., Simina, T., & Tatarova, S. (2019). Problems and challenges of modern sports. *Journal of Physical Education and Sport, 19*(1), 208–213. doi:10.7752/jpes.2019.s1031

Kulczycki, W., & Koenigstorfer, J. (2016). Doing good in the right place: City residents' evaluations of professional football teams' local (vs. distant) corporate social responsibility activities. *European Sport Management Quarterly, 16*(4), 502–524. doi:10.1080/16184742.2016.1164736

Kulczycki, W., Pfister, B., & Koenigstorfer, J. (2018). Adverse effects when partnering for corporate social responsibility in the context of FIFA world cup sponsorship. *Journal of Global Sport Management, 5*(4), 367–386. doi:10.10 80/24704067.2018.1537680

Lacey, R., Close, A. G., & Finney, R. Z. (2010). The pivotal roles of product knowledge and corporate social responsibility in event sponsorship effectiveness. *Journal of Business Research, 63*(11), 1222–1228. doi:10.1016/j. jbusres.2009.11.001

Lacey, R., & Kennett-Hensel, P. A. (2010). Longitudinal effects of corporate social responsibility on customer relationships. *Journal of Business Ethics, 97*, 581–597. doi:10.1007/s10551-010-0526-x

Lacey, R., & Kennett-Hensel, P. A. (2016). How expectations and perceptions of corporate social responsibility impact NBA fan relationships. *Sport Marketing Quarterly, 25*, 21–33.

Lee, K.-H., & Shin, D. (2010). Consumers' responses to CSR activities: The linkage between increased awareness and purchase intention. *Public Relations Review, 36*(2), 193–195. doi:10.1016/j.pubrev.2009.10.014

Lee, S. P., Heinze, K., & Lu, L. D. (2018). Warmth, competence, and willingness to donate: How perceptions of partner organizations affect support of corporate social responsibility initiatives in professional sport. *Journal of Sport and Social Issues, 42*(1), 23–48. doi:10.1177/0193723517731876

Levermore, R. (2010). CSR for development through sport: Examining its potential and limitations. *Third World Quarterly, 31*(2), 223–241. doi:10.1080/01436591003711967

Li, H., Zhang, J. J., Mao, L. L., & Min, S. D. (2012). Assessing corporate social responsibility in China's sports lottery administration and its influence on consumption behavior. *Journal of Gambling Studies, 28*, 515–540. doi:10.1007/ s10899-011-9270-0

Lindsey, I. (2016). Governance in sport-for-development: Problems and possibilities of (not) learning from international development. *International Review for the Sociology of Sport, 52*(7), 801–818. doi:10.1177/1012690215623460

Liu, D., Wilson, R., Plumley, D., & Chen, X. (2019). Perceived corporate social responsibility performance in professional football and its impact on fan-based patronage intentions. *International Journal of Sports Marketing and Sponsorship, 20*(2), 353–370. doi:10.1108/IJSMS-06-2018-0059

Magnusen, M. J., Hong, S., & Mondello, M. (2011). Social effectiveness and sport personnel: The impact of athlete political skill and influence tactics on sport organisation CSR reputation and consumer advocacy intentions. *International Journal of Sport Management and Marketing, 10*(1/2), 61–82. doi:10.1504/ IJSMM.2011.043619

Mallen, C., Bradish, C. L., & MacLean, J. (2008). Are we teaching corporate citizens? Examining corporate social responsibility and sport management pedagogy. *International Journal of Sport Management and Marketing, 4*(2/3), 204–204. doi:10.1504/IJSMM.2008.018649

Mamo, Y., James, J. D., & Andrew, D. P. (2019, 1). Consumer perceptions of sport sponsor's corporate social responsibility activities. *Journal of Global Sport Management,* 1–23. doi:10.1080/24704067.2018.1561207

McDonald, S., & Oates, C. J. (2006). Sustainability: Consumer perceptions and marketing strategies. *Business Strategy and the Environment, 14*(3), 157–170. doi:10.1002/bse.524

Melovic, B., Rogic, S., Cerovic Smolovic, J., Dudic, B., & Gregus, M. (2019). The impact of sport sponsorship perceptions and attitudes on purchasing decision of fans as consumers – Relevance for promotion of corporate social responsibility and sustainable practices. *Sustainability, 11*(22), 6389. doi:10.3390/ su11226389

Misener, K., Morrison, K., Shier, M., & Babiak, K. (2020). The influence of organizational social responsibility on involvement behavior in community sport membership associations. *Non-profit Management and Leadership, 30*(4), 591–611. doi:10.1002/nml.21406

Nichols, B. S., Cobbs, J., & Raska, D. (2016). Featuring the hometown team in cause-related sports marketing: A cautionary tale for league-wide advertising campaigns. *Sport Marketing Quarterly, 25*(4), 212–226.

Nichols, B. S., & Gardner, J. (2017). Corporate reputation and cause-related marketing in professional sports: The case of Devon still and the cincinnati Bengals. *Sport Marketing Quarterly, 26*(3), 168–175.

Paek, B., Morse, A., Hutchinson, S., & Lim, C. H. (2020). Examining the relationship for sport motives, relationship quality, and sport consumption intention. *Sport Management Review.* doi:10.1016/j.smr.2020.04.003

Park, C.-B. (2010). A study on the effects of sports team's social responsibility activity on their team image. *Korean Journal of Sport Science, 19*(4), 189–198. Retrieved from www.dbpia.co.kr/journal/articleDetail?nodeId=NODE01562511#

Park, J. K., & Park, S. Y. (2013). A study on analysis of relationships between corporate social responsibility of professional baseball team, fan perception of reciprocity and fan behavior. *Journal of Sport and Leisure Studies, 54*(1), 399–410. Retrieved from www.dbpia.co.kr/journal/articleDetail?nodeId=N ODE06245928#

Park, S. Y., Moon, G. W., & Won, Y. S. (2012). The impacts of sports fan's perceived reciprocity on corporate social responsibility of the professional baseball team: Moderating effect of fan identification. *Journal of Sport and Leisure*

Studies, 49(1), 167–177. Retrieved from www.dbpia.co.kr/journal/articleDeta il?nodeId=NODE06245541#

PricewaterhouseCoopers. (2015). *PwC sports outlook, at the gate and beyond: Outlook for the sports market in North America through 2019*. PwC. Retrieved from www.pwc.com/us/en/industry/entertainment-media/publications/assets/ pwc-sports-outlook-north-america-2015.pdf

PricewaterhouseCoopers. (2016). *PwC sports outlook, at the gate and beyond: Outlook for the sports market in North America through 2020*. PwC. Retrieved from www.pwc.ch/en/publications/2017/pwc_sports_outlook_north_america_ 2016.pdf

PricewaterhouseCoopers. (2017). *PwC sports outlook, at the gate and beyond: Outlook for the sports market in North America through 2021*. PwC. Retrieved from www.pwc.com/us/en/industry/entertainment-media/publications/assets/ pwc-sports-outlook-2017.pdf

PricewaterhouseCoopers. (2018). *Sports industry, lost in transition? PwC's sports survey 2018*. PwC. Retrieved from https://library.olympic.org/Default/ doc/SYRACUSE/176566/sports-industry-lost-in-transition-pwc-s-sports-survey-2018?_lg=en-GB

PricewaterhouseCoopers. (2019). *At the gate and beyond: PwC outlook for the sports market in North America through 2023*. PwC. Retrieved from www. pwc.com/us/en/industries/tmt/assets/pwc-sports-outlook-2019.pdf

Roy, D. P. (2011). Impact of congruence in cause marketing campaigns for professional sport organisations. *International Journal of Sport Management and Marketing*, 10(1/2), 21–34. doi:10.1504/IJSMM.2011.043614

Roy, D. P., & Graeff, T. R. (2003). Consumer attitudes toward cause-related marketing activities in professional sports. *Sport Marketing Quarterly*, 12(3), 163–172.

Sargeant, A., West, D. C., & Ford, J. (2001). The role of perceptions in predicting donor value. *Journal of Marketing Management*, 17(3/4), 407–428. doi:10.1362/0267257012652131

Sheth, H., & Babiak, K. M. (2010). Beyond the game: Perceptions and practices of corporate social responsibility in the professional sport industry. *Journal of Business Ethics*, 91, 433–450. doi:10.1007/s10551-009-0094-0

Smith, A. C., & Westerbeek, H. M. (2007). Sport as a vehicle for deploying corporate social responsibility. *Journal of Corporate Citizenship*, 25(1), 43–54.

Sung, M., & Lee, W.-Y. (2016). What makes an effective CSR program? An analysis of the constructs of a cause-related participant sport sponsorship event. *International Journal of Sports Marketing and Sponsorship*, 17(1), 56–77. doi:10.1108/IJSMS-02-2016-004

Sutton, W. A., McDonald, M. A., Milne, G. R., & Cimperman, J. (1997). Creating and fostering fan identification in professional sports. *Sport Marketing Quarterly*, 6, 15–22.

Uhrich, S., Koenigstorfer, J., & Groeppel-Klein, A. (2014). Leveraging sponsorship with corporate social responsibility. *Journal of Business Research*, 67(9), 2023–2029. doi:10.1016/j.jbusres.2013.10.008

Venkatesh, V. (2000). Determinants of perceived ease of use: Integrating control, intrinsic motivation, and emotion into the technology acceptance model. *Information Systems Research*, 11(4), 342–365.

Walker, M., Heere, B., Parent, M. M., & Drane, D. (2010). Social responsibility and the Olympic Games: The mediating role of consumer attributions. *Journal of Business Ethics*, *95*, 659–680. doi:10.1007/s10551-010-0445-x

Walker, M., & Kent, A. (2009). Do fans care? Assessing the influence of corporate social responsibility on consumer attitudes in the sport industry. *Journal of Sport Management*, *23*(6), 743–769. doi:10.1123/jsm.23.6.743

Walzel, S., & Robertson, J. (2016). *Corporate? Social? Responsibility? In sport: Stepping back, to move forward* (p. 199). Cologne, Germany: European Association for Sport Management (EASM).

Woods, C. L., & Stokes, A. Q. (2019). 'For the game, for the world': An analysis of FIFA's CSR initiatives. *Public Relations Inquiry*, *8*(1), 49–85. doi:10.1177/2046147X18804286

13 Corporate Social Responsibility and Volunteering

Christina Tsagdi and Ethan Strigas

Introduction

This statement has been coined by Aristotle and – in a way – summarizes the very nature of volunteering:

> Human, as a social being by nature, is happy only when he maintains substantial, deep relationships with other people.
>
> (Aristotle, *Politics*)

Investing in volunteering by public organizations, different levels of government, corporations and/or nonprofit organizations is an invaluable investment in social cohesion. Consequently, to exploit its value and social impact, participation in volunteer activities "requires" full recognition; recognition among volunteers creates an urge for participation, meaningful involvement and contribution to the common good, which – in turn – creates a noticeable social capital. In addition, volunteering is a resource for economic growth, a path to employment and social integration and a mechanism for improving cohesion. Volunteering is also a process for the reduction of the social, financial, and environmental inequalities (European Youth Forum, 2007).

To promote the mentality of participation, personal development, and active citizenship, individuals should be given access to voluntary activities and be strongly encouraged to participate. Furthermore, volunteers need to be empowered with the rights that accompany their participation in voluntary activities. Volunteering needs a dynamic and favorable environment to flourish. The full and effective implementation of the rights and obligations has the potential to improve working conditions for volunteers, strengthen their motives, and enhance their satisfaction levels (European Youth Forum, 2007).

Defining the Terms "Volunteer" and "Volunteering"

The *Cambridge Dictionary* defines the term *volunteer* as "a person who does something, especially helping other people, willingly and without being forced or paid to do it".

DOI: 10.4324/9781003152750-16

In addition, the most current definition of *volunteering* in Australia, as it was announced in 2015 by Volunteering Australia (the national body for volunteering), was that "Volunteering is time willingly given for the common good and without financial gain" (https://govolunteer.com.au/legal/definition-of-volunteering).

The term "volunteering" includes both formal volunteering (acts that take place within formal organizations in a structured way) and informal volunteering (it takes place outside the context of a formal organization and involves actions of individuals that are not organized/directed by a formal organization) (https://govolunteer.com.au/legal/definition-of-volunteering).

Defining Corporate Social Responsibility

Corporate social responsibility (CSR) is an evolving term that does not have a precise definition or generally acceptable criteria developed yet. According to Kotler and Lee (2005), CSR can be defined as a corporation's commitment to improve social welfare through voluntary commitment of sound business practices and the contribution of corporate resources. Today, most stakeholders have high expectations from profitable corporations; executives in all ranks and staff are required to develop long-term strategies to promote the profile of a good corporate citizen. This can be achieved through social responsibility business practices that are socially responsible, such as *company volunteering*.

The term *corporate social responsibility* refers to the actions of companies aiming to contribute to the environment and other "popular" social-related issues. An alternative definition promotes CSR as the strategic choice of a company to enhance its viability by undertaking its responsibilities to its stakeholders, to its customers, and to society at large (Afridi et al., 2020; Brammer et al., 2007).

The modern approach to CSR strategy implementation also involves active voluntary involvement of the company's human resources. The main objective is to cultivate a culture of volunteerism for employees. The active employee participation contributes to the voluntary action being taken and usually has a substantial effect: it strengthens the company intervention in addressing social, educational, political, welfare, environmental, or other problems. Furthermore, it enhances the atmosphere of cooperation between employees, increases productivity, and creates – at the same time – a better corporate image within the society these corporations do business and strive (El Akremi, Gond, Swaen, De Roeck, & Igalens, 2018; Ellen, Mohr, & Webb, 2000).

Businesses must reciprocate a portion of their profits back to society. CSR is the voluntary commitment of a corporation to strategies that address social, ethical, educational, and environmental concerns. These strategies are materialized through actions that contribute to sustainable development, social solidarity, while they built a relationship of trust among the company, its employees, the local community, and associated stakeholders.

Who Cares about Corporate Social Responsibility?

CSR is of interest to all of us because it reflects the basic principles of the society in which we live.

- CSR interests businesses which through responsible business practices can improve their economic, environmental, and social impact.
- Employees may have a strong interest because participating in CSR projects ensures a creative and rewarding work environment.
- It is of interest to consumers that are interested in quality products and services.
- It is of interest to local communities that strive to coexist with businesses who share ethical values and educational, environmental, economic, and social concerns.
- It is of interest to investors, who believe that responsible business behaviors support businesses in the long run and need to be encouraged.
- It interests all people, wherever they live, who expect companies based in Europe to behave in accordance with European values and principles wherever they operate.
- Finally, our children and future generations are interested; they demand to live in a world that respects people and nature.

CSR can often be confused with the term *social marketing* because both terms refer to the promotion of environmental and social issues. However, social marketing is a subcategory of CSR and, more specifically, a kind of initiative CSR initiative in promoting the social action of a company. The broader concept of CSR aims to create a climate in which entrepreneurs are respected, not only because they generate profits, but also for their proper contribution and response to contemporary social challenges (Basil et al., 2009; Bendapudi et al., 1996; Carroll, 1999).

What Is Corporate Volunteering?

According to Kenn Allen, corporate volunteering is "any effort by the employer to encourage and support volunteering in society, using its employees for the implementation of voluntary work" (Allen, 2012; Clary, Snyder, Ridge, & Copeland, 1998; Quirk, 1998). But "any effort" by an employer to encourage and support volunteering in society is a general concept and open to misinterpretations. In fact, companies in corporate volunteering are into mechanisms for implementing CSR actions and therefore need what corporate volunteering is. Sanchez-Hernandez and Gallardo-Vázquez (2013) support that corporate volunteering is the long-term and planned involvement of the company in the sustainable development of society through programs and actions implemented by employees and friends of the company.

On the same page is the definition of corporate volunteering provided by Clary and Snyder (1991), who argued that "corporate volunteering is a form of non-spontaneous assistance offers new perspectives beyond traditional forms of assistance to society, such as donation of a sum of money to an NGO or a charity". Therefore, corporate volunteering can be an integral part of the corporate community strategy and company liability. It is the process through which the company actively engages its employees with the overall CSR strategy. In this way, workers do not remain mere spectators in monitoring the implementation of the CSR strategy but are actively involved in its implementation (Brenner, 2010; Briggs, Peterson, & Gregory, 2010; Wilson, 2012).

The definition of corporate volunteering demonstrates the need for a reciprocal relationship between employees, business, and the society. Basic condition for planning and implementing successful corporate volunteering actions is to ensure that there are concrete benefits, for the business, the employees, and the society. For this reason, it is important that corporate volunteering actions follow some basic principles, which allow their effective implementation.

Basic Principles of Corporate Volunteering for CSR Actions

For the effective and successful implementation of CSR actions through the use of corporate volunteering, the following seven basic principles should be considered:

1 *Identification:* The corporation should recognize and appreciate the substantial benefits for the company when using volunteerism to promote CSR goals and strategies.

2 *Planning:* In order to reap the benefits mentioned earlier, the corporation should prepare and implement a volunteer management plan that takes into consideration the needs, motives, and time availability of the participating employees. Adequate resources should be allocated to implement all necessary actions, including rewards and program evaluation.

3 *Organizational Commitment:* In order for the volunteer program to be effective, the leadership of the corporation needs to show its strong commitment to the development and implementation of the program. Strong commitment sends a clear message not only to the employees participating but also to other social stakeholders.

4 *Employee Commitment:* For a volunteer program to be successful, employee participants should demonstrate high levels of commitment.

These levels are influenced by recognition strategies and action on behalf of the corporate management.

5   *Goals:* The corporation should develop S.M.A.R.T goals (specific, measurable, achievable, relevant, and time-limited) for its volunteer program that create a "fertile ground" for the program to grow and produce the desired benefits.

6   *Collaborations:* The corporation should develop a plan of collaboration with other public and/or private sector organizations toward the implementation of the proposed volunteer programs. These collaborations will multiply the effects of the volunteering programs and will impact not only the corporation but also society at large.

7   *Communication:* The corporation should develop sound channels of communication between all stakeholders of the volunteer program in order to ensure the quality of the coordinated action and timely conflict resolution of all problems that may arise.

Maximizing Involvement

The Benefits of Corporate Volunteering for Society-at-Large

A well-designed and strategically focused CSR project has the potential to offer a number of substantial benefits to the society within the organization operates (CSR Hellas, 2014; Deloitte Development, 2017; Dolnicar, Gruny, & Randle, 2007; Holroyd & Silver, 2001; Wei, Donthu, & Bernhardt, 2012; Zhang, Wang, & Jia, 2020). Some of these benefits are described here:

*   Direct and indirect benefits, resulted from CSR projects, impact positively local communities (usually where the corporation conducts its business) but also society at large (large businesses that operate throughout a nation or internationally).
*   Corporate volunteer programs embedded in CSR strategies give local citizens unique opportunities to get involved in projects that expose them to various social causes. This exposure and participation make them more sensitive to social problems and, as a result, more determined to help finding solutions.
*   In addition, the participation of locals in the planning phase of a voluntary action provides them with the opportunity to become co-creators of that action since they are recognized by the corporation as a vital stakeholder of the CSR strategy.
*   Corporate volunteer programs contribute significantly to the creation of a "generation" of active citizens who have a strong sense of humanity, increased desire for social contribution, and are equipped with knowledge, abilities and skills that make them a very desirable group to work with. As the number of active citizens who volunteer

time, skills, and abilities increases, society-at-large also "recruits" the skilled human resources needed to address social problems that government alone cannot address with its scarce resources.

The Benefits of Corporate Volunteering for the Company and Its Shareholders

CSR strategies and projects that utilize corporate volunteering result in substantial benefits for the corporation and its shareholders. More specifically, the corporation:

- Demonstrates a sense of social responsibility and respect of its commitments to society-at-large.
- Attracts better and well-qualified employees. Various business studies suggest that generations, such the Millennials, who are in the process of searching for a fitting work environment, are very sensitive of social and environmental problems. Therefore, they tend to affiliate with companies that are actively involved in addressing those issues through their business practices. Corporate volunteering programs embedded in CSR strategies, for that reason, are an essential criterion for selecting a company as an employer. According to recent research, more than half of university graduates prefer to work for organizations that offer corporate volunteering programs that are in line with their own needs, desires and wants for social activism. Furthermore, research also reveals that recent graduates are willing to work even at lower wages if the corporation demonstrates sensitivity to social causes and has an active CSR strategy (Deloitte Development, 2017; Madison, Ward, & Royalty, 2012).
- Improves internal communication because employees who also volunteer time and services in their company program develop new channels of communication with other employees/volunteers during the implementation phase of the program. Many times, and through these volunteer opportunities, employees have many opportunities to meet with each other and develop and/or even improve interpersonal relationships and collaboration, which in turn has a positive impact on the day-to-day operations within the organization.
- Builds company awareness within the markets the company operates, positions the company as a socially responsible one in the mind of consumers, and/or controls for damages if the company find itself amid a controversy, or a negative for its image situation.
- Improves chances to attract capital based on its social responsibility image: The systematic implementation of a sound, well-designed CSR strategy that promotes internal volunteer programs, the corporate social impact increases enabling the creation of sought after,

nonfinancial, business outcomes. These outcomes can be used to attract additional capital as an increasing number of financial institutions, venture capitalists and angel investors make financial decisions based on nonfinancial outcomes, such as the recognizability of the company as a socially responsible one (Karl, Peluchette, & Hall, 2008).

• Creates an organizational culture that promotes the spirit of altruism, diversity and inclusion, as well as values that currently gain a great momentum within society. In a fast-pacing world, it is extremely important for a company to take a leadership position in actions that serve the overall good.

The Benefits of Corporate Volunteering for Employees

Finally, through the implementation of corporate volunteer programs, benefits also accrue for the employees who participate in them as volunteers. More specifically (CSR Hellas, 2014; Deloitte Development, 2017; Paço, 2013; CSR Hellas, 2014; De Gilder, Schuyt, & Breedijk, 2005; Dolnicar & Randle, 2004; Pajo & Lee, 2011; Peloza & Hassay, 2006):

• Participation in corporate volunteer programs enhances employee productivity, commitment, and loyalty to the company. Through their participation, employees form convictions that the company cares for both its employees and society-at-large. In addition, this participation is proven to better the working environment and – as it was mentioned earlier – to increase staff productivity and trust to the firm.
• Volunteering through a company-designed program enables employees to acquire new knowledge, abilities, skills, and develop competencies that are useful for their professional development. Leadership style, group dynamics, emotional intelligence, teamwork, and creativity are some of the personality benefits that result through active participation in corporate-designed programs.
• Employees have the potential to develop, strengthen, or renew relationships with colleagues, while they boost their personal levels of confidence and self-esteem.
• Finally, the development of social skills and voluntary consciousness for participating corporate volunteers are two benefits that cannot be ignored, especially because they lead to the development of active citizens. Governments around the world consider the development of active citizenship as a top priority for the twenty-first century.

Barriers to Involvement

Recently, a growing number of researchers and practitioners in many disciplines closely examine volunteerism and actual volunteer programs in order to learn more about the undisputed benefits of volunteering for individuals, regardless their demographic characteristics and psychographic preferences (Dury et al., 2015; Willems & Dury, 2017). Research on motives and incentive schemes for participation in volunteer programs have also been extensively studied (Strigas, 2003; Gómez & Fernández, 2017). However, an important gap in the literature still exists, and mainly concerns the degree of attractiveness of volunteering to potential volunteers. Studies tend to focus on the positive aspects of volunteering and underestimate potential negative effects (Hustinx, Cnaan, & Handy, 2010; Strigas & Jackson, 2003). Potential barriers to volunteering are reported in a small number of studies and have been grouped to two main categories: personal factors and organization-related factors. Personal factors that influence volunteers in a potentially negative way are usually work or family related (e.g., demanding work schedule, lack of free/leisure time, increased family responsibilities, lack of support, single-parent families that place the burden on one parent). Organization-related factors usually relate to the volunteer experience itself; unfulfilled expectations, lack of volunteer support in the field, ignorance of volunteer motives and lack of incentives, learning experiences, and/or recognition usually have a very negative impact on volunteer decision-making process to continue with that specific organization, and/or totally withdraw from participating in volunteer programs in the future (Haski-Leventhal & Bargal, 2008; Hustinx, 2010; Willems et al., 2012).

Although there is research that sheds light on both motives to participate in voluntary activities and reasons to withdraw, it seems that we all know very little why people decide not to volunteer at all (Gazley & Dignam, 2008). Knowledge in this area could help volunteer organizations and policymakers in the nonprofit and public sector to identify and enforce viable solutions to this problem. Starting from identifying the differences (in terms of motives, demographic characteristics and psychographic preferences), organizations could use that data to form highly sophisticated volunteer programs that have a greater appeal to a larger group of individuals in society.

Conclusions

CSR strategy is a great vehicle for introducing corporate volunteering programs to the corporate world. In order for that to happen, and in an attempt to involve as many employees as possible, regardless of their status within the company, organizational objectives such as "sustainable," "facilitating," "diverse," "inclusive," "human centered" organization need to be developed, agreed among shareholders, and communicated to present (but also retired) employees.

Conceptual frameworks regarding CSR have historically been examined from the perspective of outsourcing sustainable development. As a result, they focus on variables that thrive outside the corporate activity. Nevertheless, CSR strategies, tactics and practices have been influenced not only by investors, suppliers, consumers, and the various levels of government, but also by employees, who are instrumental to the discussions about the impact and the consequences of CSR policies and practices (Aguilera, Rupp, Williams, & Ganapathi, 2007; Aguinis & Glavas, 2012).

The analysis of the *Employee Volunteering in Europe* has shown that, although there has been an adequate number of developed volunteer networks, there is still a long way to go before employee volunteering receives the appropriate recognition and support among corporate employers, but also employers in the public and voluntary sector as well. The other difficulty is the lack of substantial research on employee volunteering, which is an obstacle in the development of good corporate policies and best practices.

Since the benefits for participating in corporate volunteer programs are substantial for all employees but also society-at-large, corporations should consider their embedment in their CSR strategies. Administration should design and implement volunteer programs that are aligned with employee values, interests, and motivations, and encourage their participation by offering the necessary incentives, such as material rewards, performance appraisals, and reward points in the promotion process. Management should also make a sincere effort to communicate opportunities to volunteer time, skills, and expertise using an array of channels such as internal reports, training sessions, and company social events. It is critical that management provides feedback to employees on how their volunteer contributions and the overall corporate volunteer program impacted beneficiaries' lives.

Also, volunteer experiences at the early stages of life (e.g., parent-child volunteer participation) are an important predictor of future human behavior because individuals, who have experienced volunteerism in any form, are more likely to restart volunteering compared to individuals who have never volunteered before in their lifetime. Furthermore, earlier volunteer experiences are related to a higher awareness and appreciation of the benefits of volunteering. So, it is crucial for the government, school districts, and nonprofit organizations to realize that giving individuals many opportunities to start volunteering (as early as possible) will create the awareness and appreciation that is needed for later decisions to volunteer.

References

Afridi, S., Afsar, B., Shahjehan, A., Rehman, Z., Haider, M., & Ullah, M. (2020). Perceived corporate social responsibility, and innovative work behavior: The role of employee volunteerism and authenticity. *Corporate Social Responsibility and Environmental Management*, 27(4), 1–13.

Aguilera, R., Rupp, D., Williams, C., & Ganapathi, J. (2007). Putting the S back in corporate social responsibility: A multilevel theory of social change in organizations. *Academy of Management Review*, 32(3), 836–863.

Aguinis, H., & Glavas, A. (2012). What we know and do not know about corporate social responsibility: A review and research agenda. *Journal of Management*, 38(4), 932–968.

Allen, K. (2012). The big tent. The corporate volunteering in the global age. Retrieved April 3, 2019, from http://iave.org/iavewp/wp-content/uploads/2015/04/The-Big-Tent-2012.pdf

Ana Cláudia Nave Arminda do Paço. (2013). *Corporate volunteering: An analysis of volunteers*. Madrid, Spain: Asociación Española de Contabilidad y Administración de Empresas (AECA). Responsabilidad Social Corporativa Interna. Delimitación Conceptual e Información; Documentos AECA, Serie Responsabilidad Social Corporativa, 2016.

Basil, D., Runte, M., Easwaramoorthy, M., & Barr, C. (2009). Company support for employee volunteering: A national survey of companies in Canada. *Journal of Business Ethics*, 85(2), 387–398.

Bendapudi, N., Singh, S., & Bendapudi, V. (1996). Enhancing helping behavior: An integrative framework for promotion planning. *Journal of Marketing*, 60(3), 33–49.

Brammer, S., Millington, A., & Rayton, B. (2007). The contribution of corporate social responsibility to organizational commitment. *International Journal of Human Resource Management*,18(10), 1701–1719.

Brenner, B. (2010). Instituting employee volunteer programs as part of employee benefit plans yields tangible business benefits. *Journal of Financial Service Professionals*, 32–35.

Briggs, E., Peterson, M., & Gregory, G. (2010). Toward a better understanding of volunteering for nonprofit organizations: Explaining volunteers' pro-social attitudes. *Journal of Macromarketing*, 30(1), 61–76.

Carroll, A. (1999). Corporate social responsibility: Evolution of a definitional construct. *Business and Society*, 38(3), 268–295.

Clary, E. G., & Snyder, M. (1991). A functional analysis of altruism and prosocial behavior: The case of volunteerism. In M. S. Clark (Ed.), *Prosocial behavior* (pp. 119–148). Newbury Park, CA: Sage Publications, Inc.

Clary, E. G., Snyder, M., Ridge, R., & Copeland, J. (1998). Understanding and assessing the motivations of volunteers: A functional approach. *Journal of Personality and Social Psychology*, 74(6), 1516–1530.

CSR Hellas. (2014). *Responsible entrepreneurship guide – corporate volunteering, Hellenic corporate network social responsibility* (p. 3). ISSN: 2241-9179.

De Gilder, D., Schuyt, T., & Breedijk, M. (2005). Effects of an employee volunteering program on the workforce: The ABN-AMRO case. *Journal of Business Ethics*, 61, 143–152.

Deloitte Development. (2017). *Deloitte volunteerism survey*. Retrieved from https://www2.deloitte.com/content/dam/Deloitte/us/Documents/about-deloitte/us2017deloitte-volunteerism-survey.pdf

Dolnicar, S., Gruny, B., & Randle, M. (2007). *Segmenting the volunteer market: Learnings from an Australian study*. Wollongong: Faculty of Commerce, University of Wollongong.

Dolnicar, S., & Randle, M. (2004). What moves which volunteers to donate their time? An investigation of psychographic heterogeneity among volunteers in Australia. *Voluntas, 18*, 135–155.

Dury, S., De Donder, L., De Witte, N., Buffel, T., Jacquet, W., & Verté, D. (2015). To volunteer or not: The influence of individual characteristics, resources, and social factors on the likelihood of volunteering by older adults. *Nonprofit and Voluntary Sector Quarterly, 44*(6), 1107–1128.

El Akremi, A., Gond, J., Swaen, V., De Roeck, K., & Igalens, J. (2018). How do employees perceive corporate responsibility? Development and validation of a multidimensional corporate stakeholder responsibility scale. *Journal of Management, 44*(2), 619–657.

Ellen, P., Mohr, L., & Webb, D. (2000). Charitable programs and the retailer: Do they mix? *Journal of Retailing, 76*(3), 393–406.

European Youth Forum. (2007). *European chapter on the rights and the responsibilities of volunteers*. Brussels, Belgium.

Gazley, B., & Dignam, M. (2008). *The decision to volunteer: Why people give their time and how you can engage them*. Washington, DC: ASAE and the Center for Association Leadership.

Gómez, P., & Fernández, J. L. (2017). Brakes and barriers of corporate volunteering. *CIRIEC España, Revista de Economía Pública, Social y Cooperativa, 90*, 253–290.

Haski-Leventhal, D., & Bargal, D. (2008). The volunteer stages and transitions model: Organizational socialization of volunteers. *Human Relations, 61*(1), 67–102.

Holroyd, C., & Silver, A. (2001). *Corporate volunteering: Helping to build business and community sustainability – A handbook for corporations and business*. Bunbury, Western Australia: The Centre for Regional Development and Research.

Hustinx, L. (2010). I quit, therefore I am? Volunteer turnover and the politics of self-actualization. *Nonprofit and Voluntary Sector Quarterly, 39*(2), 236–255.

Hustinx, L., Cnaan, R., & Handy, F. (2010). Navigating theories of volunteering: A hybrid map for a complex phenomenon. *Journal for the Theory of Social Behaviour, 40*, 410–434.

Karl, K., Peluchette, J., & Hall, L. (2008). Give them something to smile about: A marketing strategy for recruiting and retaining volunteers. *Journal of Nonprofit & Public Sector Marketing, 20*(1), 71–96.

Kotler, P., & Lee, N. (2005). Best of breed: When it comes to gaining a market edge while supporting a social cause, "corporate social marketing" leads the pack. *Social Marketing Quarterly, 11*(3–4), 91–103. doi:10.1080/1524 5000500414480

Madison, T., Ward, S., & Royalty, K. (2012). Corporate social responsibility, organizational commitment, and employer- sponsored volunteerism. *International Journal of Business and Social Science, 3*(1), 1–14.

Pajo, K., & Lee, L. (2011). Corporate-sponsored volunteering: A work design perspective. *Journal of Business, 99*(3), 467–482.

Peloza, J., & Hassay, D. (2006). Intra-organizational volunteerism: Good soldiers, good deeds, and good politics. *Journal of Business Ethics, 64*, 357–379.

Quirk, D. (1998). *Corporate volunteering: The potential and the way forward*. Wellington, N.Z.: The Wellington Volunteer Centre.

Sanchez-Hernandez, M. I., & Gallardo-Vázquez, D. (2013). Approaching corporate volunteering in Spain. *Corporate Governance, 13*(14), 397–411. doi:10.1108/cg-02-2012-0009

Strigas, A. (2003). Motivational factors for student volunteers and the development of an incentive typology in sport settings. *Research Quarterly for Exercise and Sport, 74*(Suppl.), 90.

Strigas, A., & Jackson, N. (2003). Motivating volunteers to serve and succeed: Design and results of a pilot study that explores demographics and motivational factors in sport volunteerism. *International Sports Journal, 7*(1), 111–121.

Wei, Y., Donthu, N., & Bernhardt, K. L. (2012). Volunteerism of older adults in the United States. *International Review on Public and Nonprofit Marketing, 9*(1), 1–18.

Willems, J., & Dury, S. (2017). Reasons for not volunteering overcoming boundaries to attract volunteers. *The Service Industries Journal, 37*(11–12), 726–745. doi:10.1080/02642069.2017.1318381

Willems, J., Huybrechts, G., Jegers, M., Vantilborgh, T., Bidee, J., & Pepermans, R. (2012). Volunteer decisions (not) to leave: Reasons to quit versus functional motives to stay. *Human Relations, 65*, 883–900.

Wilson, J. (2012). Volunteerism research: A review essay. *Nonprofit and Voluntary Sector Quarterly, 41*(2), 176–212.

Zhang, Z., Wang, J., & Jia, M. (2020). Integrating the bright and dark sides of corporate volunteering climate: Is corporate volunteering climate a burden or boost to employees? *British Journal of Management, 32*(2), 495–511.

14 Governance, Corporate Social Responsibility, and Sustainability

The Development of the Corporate Environmental Sustainability Framework

Stavros Triantafyllidis

Introduction

This chapter aims to explore organizational governance and corporate social responsibility (CSR) through the lens of sustainability. Specifically, the focus of discussion is on specific sustainability mechanisms that may enhance governmental decision-making, organizational behavior, and CSR practices. The mechanism discussed includes environmental sustainability as an integrated philosophy of an organization that practices CSR (Rubino & Napoli, 2020). Specifically, in terms of acceptable environmental performance practices, we examine an organization's governance characteristics, such as the board of directors, executives, and owners, toward corporate environmental sustainability (CES). The theoretical frameworks used in this chapter include the stakeholder theory, agency, and resource dependence theory (RDT). The theories are used to support the interactions between governance and CSR to establish CES.

Ansoff (1965) used the term "stakeholder theory" to define a company's objectives based on the literature. A goal is to obtain the capability to balance the conflicting appeals of different stakeholders in the company. The stakeholder theory is a theory of organizational management and business ethics that addresses rights and values in administering an organization (Freeman, 1984). The performance of the company is the dependent construct, and the stakeholder interest is the independent construct. A study by Freeman (1983) categorized the development of the stakeholder concept into a corporate planning and business policy model and a CSR model of stakeholder management.

Stakeholder theory supports that an organization interacts with many other stakeholders, such as its consumers, employees, governments, community, service, and environmental agencies (Freeman, 1984). Accordingly, an organization is required to account for all its stakeholders, and, because they control the decision-making process directly, managers are

DOI: 10.4324/9781003152750-17

central to this system of relationships. Therefore, an essential requirement of a corporate governance system should be that it helps run a firm. All of its stakeholders, both financial and nonfinancial, will benefit from an essential role in this process being played by managers. About CSR, this position has excellent repercussions in terms of the broader range of foreseen managerial responsibilities.

Moreover, agency theory explains the relationships between agents and principals (Rubino & Napoli, 2020). The agent represents the principal in a particular business transaction. For example, in an organizational setting, the agents represent the best interests of the principal. The different parts of principals and agents may become sources of conflict, as some agents may not correctly act in the principal's best interests. The resulting miscommunication and disagreement may result in various problems and discord within organizations.

Finally, RDT assures that organizations are involved in business with each other in business-to-business (B2B) to acquire the necessary resources essential for sustaining their operations. For example, the board of directors in an organization may have a critical role in improving an organization's performance since its members can provide direction based on their experience and knowledge via their social networks, valuable connections with assets, and influential social capital. This will permit managers to enhance the firm's value by making use of specific pro-social strategies. This may occur in a firm where a director has influential roles with other companies and significant board experience. Given the support of governance and organizational behavior theories, this chapter integrates sustainability for investigating how governance and related CSR practices can embrace CES. Accordingly, the following sections illustrate the relationship between governance, CSR, and CES.

Literature Review

This section will present the relationships of governance and CSR with CES and sustainability. Accordingly, organizational awareness of social and environmental issues has increased, at both the government and the corporate levels (Kell, 2013). The social and ecological initiatives have developed to help organizations design their plans and implement their strategies according to their principles and core values. The organization's vision is to reflect CSR and CES to its mission, goals, and objectives. In the literature, many methods have been suggested at the local, national, and international levels (i.e., private associations and nongovernmental organizations, such as the European Commission) (Kell, 2013). Furthermore, the United Nations introduces the Global Compact Agenda (UNGC) at the 1999 World Economic Forum, which was the most expansive voluntary CSR initiative in the world (Kell, 2013; Rasche, 2009).

Specifically, the program has drawn attention from organizations world-wide and attracted a thousand participants (Rasche, 2009).

Corporate Environmental Sustainability

The natural environment is in a very dire situation. In the past decade, our planet and its natural resources are in critical condition due to the global climate crisis. The climate crisis reflects the increased average temperature of the planet Earth. According to research, the current average temperature is expected to increase by two degrees Celsius (Meehl & Stocker, 2007; Shneider, Ganopolski, & Rahmstorm, 2006). The increased temperature is referred to as global warming, which is the observed rise in the earth's climate system (Zhang, 2007). Also, climate change is another aspect of the worldwide climate crisis that correlates with global warming. It is defined as the change in the climate system's statistical properties when considered over long periods. (America's Climate Choices, 2010).

Certain human activities have also been identified as significant causes of recent climate change. Many organizations and industries generate pollutants, carbon dioxide (CO_2) emissions, water, and solid wastes to the natural environment. The generation of these toxic substances is bad for the environment. The most acceptable definition the last decades is the Brundtland report in 1987 by the World Commission on Environment and Development (WCED), which defined Sustainable development as "Humanity can make development sustainable to ensure that it meets the needs of the present without compromising the ability of future generations to meet their own needs" (WCED, 1987, par. 27). Goodman (1995) suggested that environmental sustainability implies sustainable production and consumption levels rather than sustained economic growth. On the consumption side, it holds the emissions within the natural environment's assimilative capacity without damage. On the other hand, the outcome percentages of renewable energy should be kept within regeneration rates on the production side.

An essential suggestion of this chapter is that there cannot be social sustainability or CSR without environmental sustainability. Environmental sustainability supplies the conditions for social sustainability to be approached. Accordingly, a new endeavor at the organizational level has been grown, the Corporate Environmental Sustainability (CES). CES is defined in the literature as "the actions were taken by companies to decrease their internal and external impacts on the natural environment, to improve sustainable consumption and production throughout the supply chain" (Naidoo & Gasparatos, 2018, p. 127). Sustainable consumption is defined as "the use of services and products that meet basic human needs and promote quality of life while minimizing natural resources and hazardous materials usage, as well as waste and emission generation in the whole product life cycle, so as not to affect the satisfaction of future generations' needs (Naidoo & Gasparatos, 2018, p. 127). Sustainable production is defined as "the continuous application of an integrated preventive environmental strategy applied to processes, products, and services to increase eco-efficiency and reduce risks to humans and the environment (Naidoo & Gasparatos, 2018, p. 127). The following sections will include further analysis of how governance, CSR, and CES can be work in concert.

Corporate Social and Environmental Responsibility

A macro-perspective of the organizations is to reduce these impacts to the environment by adopting green environmental practices. Based on the literature, recent research reports determine this activity as social environmental responsibility (SER) (Babiak & Trendafilova, 2010; Trendafilova & Babiak, 2013). Richard Holmes and Phil Watts (2000) defined (CSR) as the continuing commitment by businesses to behave ethically and contribute to economic development while improving the workforce's quality of life and their families and the local community and society. Likewise, CSR has been defined as a firm's commitment to declining or eliminating any catastrophic effects on society and increasing macro-perspective beneficial impact (Mohr, Webb, & Harris, 2001).

A study by Trendafilova, Babiak, and Heinze (2013) was conducted in these lines. Specifically, the researchers explored the institutional powers that affect the environmental sustainability in the professional sport sector and found that institutional forces such as scrutiny, regulations, and normative pressures drive sport organizations to address more and more environmental CSR.

There is a growing interest in the sport industry as far as the environment and CSR are concerned. The stakeholders are involved in environmentally friendly practices, primarily in sports in the US. Specifically, McCullough and Cunnigham (2011) examined the adoption of green practices by sport consumers in a baseball event. Another survey by McCullough and Cunnigham (2010) was conducted to develop a conceptual model that articulated why sport organizations engage in environmental-friendly practices. This study showed that the operational, political, and social pressures drive sports organizations to adopt green practices. The involvement of sport organizations in these practices is one of the characteristics of CSR.

Environmental Sustainability Solutions and Performance

There have been proposed several solutions in the literature to help alleviate negative impacts on the environment (Triantafyllidis et al., 2018; Triantafyllidis, 2018; Casper et al., 2012; Casper et al., 2014). Besides, there has been a heightening of environmental sustainability progress within organizations (Triantafyllidis, 2018). In the recent work by Triantafyllidis (2018), many solutions were communicated concerning the number of CO_2 emissions generated by sporting events. One recommendation is to assimilate advanced technologies into organizational facilities, including renewable energy sources and electronic car stations (Triantafyllidis, 2018).

In the global market industry, organizations, businesses, firms, and agencies increasingly implement CES strategies to enhance their environmental performance (Naidoo & Gasparatos, 2018). It has also been suggested for organizations related to sport and tourism that their tactics can achieve environmental performance in environmentally sustainable plans. For example, the venue's practices and choices could reduce CO_2 emissions derived from consumers and tourists (Triantafyllidis, 2018). From the sport consumer perspective, people are involved in daily pro-environmental behavior during sport events. An example could be the involvement of the fans in the recycling process (Inoue & Kent, 2012). From the organizational perspective, many sport organizations' stadiums in the United States are built based on sustainable green standards. For instance, the first stadium in the US that received LEED gold certification is Levi's Stadium, home to a professional football team (NFL), the San Francisco 49ers. Building projects must satisfy perquisites and earn certification levels (Stadium becomes first US, 2014). These practices and developments by sport organizations are examples of the sport events sector's response to climate change. Therefore, it would be essential to determine the environmentally friendly practices that a sport organization participates in. For instance, renewable energy sport facility buildings, with the LEED certification, energy save lighting, management of the water resources, recycling policies, a station for free recharge battery of the electric cars are some of the green practices that a company involves in (America's top 5 energy-efficient football stadiums, 2013).

CSR and CES applications in Sport

A big industry that affects the environment is the sport industry, especially in North America, including professional, collegiate, and youth leagues, and it is the largest on earth. Specifically, a sport event, such as American football, generates reliable wastewater (Pfahl, 2013; Godfrey, 2009). For instance, after the Super Bowl game, the amount of solid waste that went for recycling was 58,000 pounds (Crossman, 2008). Another example is an Ohio State University football game, which generates two tons of trash (Pfahl, 2013). As a result, the sport facilities and the sport events in North America greatly impact the environment.

Also, the economic impact of the sport industry in the US is very critical. The sport industry sector in the US is of vital importance. In (2013) the Economic Modeling Specialists Intl. (EMSI) showed that the sports industry as a whole brings $14.3 billion in earnings a year. The sector also contributes 456,000 jobs with an average salary of $39,000 per job (Burrow, 2013).

The uniqueness of sport events and sport facilities is that they concentrate many people in a confined space over a relatively short period. As a result, they can pose risks to the natural environment within which they operate (Chernushenko, 1994). Specifically, in the Super Bowl game, 70,000 people visited the event (Pfahl, 2013). The National Football League (NFL) holds the largest average sport league attendance globally (Reiche, 2013). Likewise, some sports are affected by the environment and view it as their responsibility to improve environmental damage that affects their sport (Laurence & Wells, 2012; Mair & Jago, 2010).

Moreover, a nonprofit organization has a mission to assist sport organizations in enhancing environmentally friendly practices. This nonprofit organization is the Green Sport Alliance. Based on the literature, it is known that the GSA is a watchdog that is utilized as an institutional force that exerts pressure on sport organizations to adopt environmentally friendly practices (Trendafilova et al., 2013). Organizations such as GSA can influence sport organizations to adopt ways that can protect the natural environment.

Organizational and Corporate Governance

In the literature, corporate governance is defined as "the system by which companies are directed and controlled" (Spitzeck & Hansen, 2010, p. 378). The agency theory has developed the goal of corporate governance. This view has been developed by stakeholder theory, which explains why stakeholders are essential for their survival. They need to be considered in the system by which companies are directed and controlled (Freeman, 1984). Also, agency theory illustrates that stakeholder interests have to align with governance focus, such as the involvement in corporate decision-making beyond the board of directors (Letza, Sun, & Kirkbride, 2004; Sison, 2008).

Conceptual Models of the Corporate Environmental Sustainability (CES)

Several conceptual models appear in the literature that suggests the corporate environmental sustainability process in the context of different industries. First, Bansal and Roth (2000) proposed a model for corporate ecological responsiveness. They collected data from other firms. The researchers examined why companies go green so they could create a model that explains corporate environmental responsiveness. Second, a study by Marshall, Cordano, and Silverman (2005) developed a model regarding the proactive ecological behavior in the U.S. wine industry.

Regarding this model's development, the researchers researched earlier environmental management sources that described the drivers who engage companies to adopt green practices. Third, a study by Lynes and Andrachuk (2008) developed a conceptual model of the external and internal influences, motivations, and catalysts on a firm's (Scandinavian airlines) level of engagement for Corporate Social-Ecological Responsibility (CSER). Finally, a study by Mair and Jago (2010) proposed a model for corporate greening that can be applied in different industry sectors. Accordingly, at the end of this chapter, we offer a model for the business sector of sport, event in tourism. Based on the literature in can be found some conceptual models for corporate greening in different industry sectors. For the sport industry, there is a lack of corporate greening models, such as the CES. For that reason, this chapter proposes a model that can be applied to sport events.

As far as the sport industry literature, very few models have been applied. Firstly, a study by Trendafilova et al. (2013) suggested a model for CSR adoption in professional sports. Also, a survey by McCullough and Cunnigham (2011) proposed a conceptual model for the reasons that motivate sport organizations to engage in environmentally friendly practices. An empirical study by Inoue and Kent (2012) explained how sport organizations persuade sport consumers to engage in pro-environmental behavior. This study suggested a model in which a sport team's positive green practices boost the sport consumers to adopt pro-environmental behavior from the internalization perspective.

Theoretical Frameworks

At this point, it would be necessary to make clear who the stakeholders are. Based on the literature, it has been defined by Freeman (1984) that stakeholder is any group or individual who can affect or is affected by the achievement of the company's objectives. The stakeholders of a company formed by employees, customers, suppliers, public interest groups, governmental bodies, stockholders, the owners, and the managers (Rogers and Dearing, 1988). These stakeholders can be separated into two stakeholder categories, the internal and the external stakeholders. The internal stakeholders work in the organization (e.g., employees, owners, and managers). The exterior is people who work and contribute to the organization outside of it (e.g., customers, sponsors, and suppliers).

Stakeholder Theory

Drawing from previous literature utilizing stakeholder theory, employees and spectators are vital for organizational survival (Spitzeck & Hansen, 2010). One view purports that stakeholders act instrumentally to support a corporation's success (Spitzeck & Hansen, 2010). Instrumental stakeholder theory will serve as the theoretical framework, given that this paper focuses on the relationship between stakeholders and their influence upon an organization's environmental sustainability initiatives (Spitzeck & Hansen, 2010). According to instrumental stakeholder theory, corporations only need to prioritize stakeholders who can alter the firm's worth (Spitzeck & Hansen, 2010). This includes external and internal stakeholders.

One widely accepted definition of a stakeholder originates from Freeman's (1983, 1984) work. Specifically, Freeman (1983, 1984) claims that a stakeholder is any group or individual who can affect or is affected by achieving the organization's objective. In this sense, a "stakeholder" is considered anyone or anything influenced by an organization's actions. This definition allows the term "stakeholder" to be applied broadly to individuals and groups. One study by Clarkson (1995) differentiates between two types of stakeholders, primary and secondary. Primary stakeholders are those individuals where an organization cannot survive and be sustained without their active participation and support. Secondary stakeholders affect and are affected by the organization but are not engaged in transactions with the organization and are not essential for organizational survival.

External Stakeholder

As stated previously, a stakeholder is defined as "any group or individual who can affect or is affected by the achievement of the organization's objectives" (Spitzeck & Hansen, 2010, p. 379). To draw from this interpretation, an external stakeholder is any group or individual outside of an organization's business who can affect or is affected by the achievement of the organization's objectives. As a result of having multiple stakeholders involved within organizational projects, most corporate sustainability measures go beyond the traditional administrative limits and necessitate the organization to take awareness of perceptions from a wide array of external and internal stakeholders (Sharma & Henriques, 2005).

In a study regarding stakeholder influences on sustainability practices in the Canadian forest products industry, external stakeholder influences contributed to increased sustainability practices by businesses involved (Sharma & Henriques, 2005). Concerning pollution control in the Canadian forest industry, some external stakeholders have raised awareness toward the undesirable health and environmental effects of emissions resulting from the inappropriate disposal of unwanted waste (Sharma & Henriques, 2005). External stakeholders have raised awareness by publishing books, local community movements, reporting emissions, and government agencies that act as regulators (Sharma & Henriques, 2005).

Babiak and Wolfe (2009) studied the internal and external factors of corporate social responsibility in professional sport in a more sport-related context. I find this study to be relatable to the current topic at hand for two reasons. First, corporate social responsibility can include initiatives that relate to environmental sustainability. Second, the study focuses on internal and external factors of corporate social responsibility, which have stakeholders. Regarding stakeholder managing, the study claims that "relations with stakeholders such as the media, players, various levels of government, sponsors, fans, and local communities can benefit from CSR activities" (Babiak & Wolfe, 2009, p. 723). Moreover, the study found that "the interconnectedness among organizations in the professional sport organizational field, namely external stakeholders (teams, municipal state governments, the media, and sponsors), is powerful, thus contributing to the increasing emphasis on community outreach programs" (Babiak & Wolfe, 2009). This goes to show how external stakeholders influence an organization's internal benefits and external programs.

Internal Stakeholders

A study regarding the review of determinate factors of environmental proactivity concludes that internal primary stakeholders motivate environmental proactivity the most compared to primary external stakeholders (Frooman & Murrell, 2005). Specifically, internal stakeholders are located within a business or organization; this includes employees, directors, and shareholders. Drawing from Freeman's (1983, 1984) initial assessment of stakeholders, an internal stakeholder refers to any group or individual inside an organization's business who can impact or is impacted by attaining the organization's objectives.

Moreover, internal stakeholders influence the organizational behavior in multiple ways. According to a study by Frooman and Murrell (2005), stakeholders implement two influence strategies, manipulation strategies and pathway strategies. Specifically, Manipulation strategies "focus on the leveraging of resources flowing into a firm to influence that firm" (Frooman & Murrell, 2005, p. 9). Furthermore, there are two types of manipulation strategies, precisely, coercion and compromise. Coercion and compromise "are negative in nature and involve either the threat to reduce a benefit or increase a cost to a firm" (Frooman & Murrell, 2005, p. 9). Compromise strategies "are positive in nature and involve an offer to either increase a benefit or reduce a cost to the firm" (Frooman & Murrell, 2005, p. 9). Internal stakeholders' compromise manipulation strategies essentially influence environmental sustainability initiatives at the corporate level (i.e., CES). This is because ecological sustainability involves the reduction of costs to the organization. For example, an organization can start using renewable energy to mitigate its overall expenditures.

Pathway strategies focus on the entity or individual who partakes in the actual manipulation. Similar to manipulation strategies, there are two types of pathway strategies, direct and indirect. Direct and indirect pathway strategies can be described as "either the stakeholder does the manipulation itself directly, or an ally of the stakeholder does the manipulation" (Frooman & Murrell, 2005). To highlight sport-related internal stakeholders, Pfahl (2013) discussed the term "Sustainability Teams". A sustainability team plans and designs policies regarding environmental sustainability and specifically CES. Sustainability teams are influenced mainly by internal organizational members, primary employees from different departments (Pfahl, 2013). Additionally, members of a sustainability team must be continuously in contact with various levels of the organization's leadership because executives and directors need the support of members to utilize its core voice (Pfahl, 2013).

Discussion

This study was built upon the stakeholder theory that includes supportive concepts from the agency and resource dependence theory. The stakeholder theory used theory to explain the connection between corporate governance, CSR, and CES. The chapter also highlights the crucial role stakeholders play in corporate organizational governance and their implications on CSR and CES. The theory also served as the foundation for explaining the process involved between stakeholders and their associated organization. Previous literature focuses on stakeholder's significant influence at the corporate levels' social responsibility. However, this chapter promotes CES's concept focuses on the relationship between stakeholders and corporate governance decisions toward environmental sustainability initiatives.

Moreover, this section has discussed the proposal of a conceptual model for CES applied in sport and tourism. Based on the stakeholder theory, there is an interaction between the company and the stakeholders. The sport and tourism organization and their stakeholders influence each other for the adoption of pro-environmental behavior. As a result, the stakeholders adopt pro-environmental behavior such as the sport organization. This concludes the creation of the green sport events. In other words, the sport organization and the sport consumers adopt green practices during sport events, resulting in the "CES Model" design.

Sport Organizational Internal and External Stakeholders

This CES model considers the perception of the audience of a sport organization. Specifically, this audience includes internal stakeholders associated with the sport team and external stakeholders who corporate (sponsors) or are emotionally involved with it (fans). Internal stakeholders are in a close relationship with the sport team – likewise, the CEO, the press manager, and the owner. The change of the perception about the environment by these people will immediately influence the sport organization's behavior. On the other hand, external stakeholders, such as the sponsors and the suppliers, are also critical. The financial survival of these stakeholders depends on the sport team. A similar outcome comes from the fans too. Fans are emotionally involved with their favorite team. The change of the behavior by the sport organization will influence the perception of the fans. As found in the literature, it can be supported that fans change their behavior based on their favorite sport team (Babiak & Wolfe, 2009; Madrigal & Dalakas, 2008; Wann & Branscombe, 1990; Trendafilova et al., 2014).

Implications

This CES model is relevant to scholars and practitioners for several reasons. First of all, this model is general and broad. As a result, it could be a springboard for other researchers interested in exploring the media's influence regarding environmentally friendly practices and CSR. Furthermore, this model can contribute to the exploration of environmental issues in sport events. For instance, researchers that examine the ecological and carbon footprint impacts in sport events could extend this specific conceptual model. Finally, scholars from mass communication departments could contribute to this model by conducting further and more in-depth research on the media and how they can influence and promote this decade's environmental gravity.

As far as the practitioners are concerned, the CES model can be used by all the sport organizations involved with sport events. Specifically, sport teams can use this model and educate fans about environmental issues and how to be involved in environmentally friendly practices. They can also start using the team's social media as a promoter of the natural environment and promote all these practices to sports consumers, such as recycling, water conservation, and hybrid cars. Based on the literature, other sport teams already get involved in these actions. Moreover, this paper analyzed the critical role of the theories. As a result, sport teams should follow and trust this model and get involved in green practices and promote them.

Limitations and Delimitations

One major limitation of the CES model is the extent to which data would be collected. Additionally, this study includes the assumption that stakeholder attitudes regarding environmental sustainability can be consistently measured, and the respondents that would be involved in the survey respond genuinely. One delimitation of the study is the restriction of individual stakeholders to collect data from. This study would only use stakeholders such as spectators/fans and internal personnel/collegiate athletic departments' employees.

Moreover, as far as the public is concerned, it would be critical to mention that not all people are educated or conscious of the fragile environment, climate change, and global warming. This paper's limitation is that these people who can contribute based on the CES model are conscious citizens and stakeholders. They know the environmental issue in modern society. Unfortunately, the number of aware people and using all green practices as a habit and their daily routine is small. Lastly, based on my conceptual model, the media is responsible for the lack of knowledge about Environmental Sustainability. As a result, this is the most critical limitation of my model. However, this paper raises the alarm to be aware of the danger of natural environmental disasters.

Future Research

Future research should aim at understanding how stakeholder attitudes influence behavioral intentions to partake in environmental sustainability. This is essential in understanding how attitudes truly impact behaviors. Additionally, future research should focus upon the degree collegiate athletic departments are involved with environmental sustainability measures. This can help identify the extent to which college athletic departments are willing to be involved with environmental sustainability. Moreover, future research should compare ecological sustainability initiatives across multiple collegiate athletic departments to understand trends. For example, whether geographic location factors into the extent collegiate athletic departments are involved with environmental sustainability.

Research to examine the financial benefits or costs of the adoption of pro-environmental behavior by sport organizations. Also, further research should be conducted as far as the media is concerned. The media is an important catalyst, so research should be done to examine how and what information they publish for climate change and global warming. Based on environmental science, it should be reviewed if the media show the source of climate change.

Moreover, the CES model has the potential for further research. The future inquiry might include interviews from CEOs of sport organizations and surveys completed by the organizations' employees. Furthermore, surveys will be given to the sport consumers before the sport event. A questionnaire will be formed with questions about how the fans are involved in it as far as the green practices are concerned. For instance, what type of car they drive? Is it hybrid? Type of questions such as are you aware of recycling, do you recycle during the sport events. The methodology added to this conceptual paper will contribute to a further understanding of the adoption of green practices by the sport organization and consumer behavior.

References

America's climate choices: Panel on advancing the science of climate change. (2010). *Advancing the science of climate change.* Washington, DC: The national Academies of Science, Engineering and Medicine.

America's top 5 energy-efficient football stadiums. (2013). Retrieved from www. ase.org/resources/americas-top-5-energy-efficient-football-stadiums

Ansoff, H. L. (1965). *Corporate strategy.* New York: McGraw-Hill.

Babiak, K., & Wolfe, R. (2009). Determinants of corporate social responsibility in professional sport: Internal and external factors. *Journal of Sport Management, 23,* 717–742.

Babiak, K., & Trendafilova, S. (2010). CSR and environmental responsibility: Motives and pressures to adopt green management practices. *Corporate Social Responsibility and Environmental Management, 18,* 11–24.

Bansal, P., & Roth, K. (2000). Why companies go green: A model of ecological responsiveness. *Academy of Management Journal, 43*(4), 717–737.

Burrow, G. (2013). *Not just a game: The impact of sports on U.S. Economy.* Retrieved from www.economicmodeling.com/2013/07/09/not-just-a-game-the-impact-of-sports-on-u-s-economy/

Casper, J. M., Pfahl, M. E., & McCullogh, B. (2014). Intercollegiate sport and the environment: Examining fan engagement based on athletics department sustainability efforts. *Journal of Issues in Intercollegiate Athletics, 7,* 65–91.

Casper, J. M., Pfahl, M. E., & McSherry, M. (2012). Athletics department awareness and action regarding the environ-ment: A study of NCAA athletics department sustainability practices. *Journal of Sport Management, 26*(1), 11–29.

Chernushenko, D. (1994). *Greening our games: Running sports events and facilities that won't cost the Earth.* Ottawa, Canada: Centurion Publishing and Marketing.

Clarkson, M. E. (1995). A stakeholder framework for analyzing and evaluating corporate social performance. *Academy of Management Review, 20*(1), 92–117.

Crossman, M. (2008). When the party's over. *Sporting News, 37,* 232.

Freeman, R. E. (1983). Strategic management a stakeholder approach. *Advances Strategic Management,* 31–60.

Freeman, R. E. (1984). *Strategic management: A stakeholder approach.* Marshall, MA: Pitman.

Frooman, J., & Murrell, A. J. (2005). Stakeholder influence strategies: The roles of structural and demographic determinants. *Business & Society, 44*(1), 3–31.

Godfrey, P. G. (2009). Corporate social responsibility in sport: An overview and critical issues. *Journal of Sport Management, 23,* 698–716.

Goodman, R. (1995). The concept of environmental sustainability. *Annual Review of Ecology and Systematics, 26,* 1–24.

Holmes, L., & Watts, R. (2000). *Corporate social responsibility: Making good business sense.* Conches-Geneva, Switzerland: World Business Council of Sustainable Development.

Inoue, Y., & Kent, A. (2012). Sport teams as promoters of pro-environmental behavior: An empirical study. *Journal of Sport Management*, 26, 417–432.

Kell, G. (2013). 12 Years later: Reflections on the growth of the UN global compact. *Business & Society*, 52(1), 31–52.

Laurence, H., & Wells, M. (2012). Event Management and the event manager. In H. Lawrence & M. Wells (Eds.), *Creating and managing successful sports events* (pp. 1–16). Dubuque, IA: Kendall/Hunt Publishing Company.

Letza, S., Sun, X., & Kirkbride, J. (2004). Shareholding versus stakeholding: A critical review of corporate governance. *Corporate Governance: An International Review*, 12, 242–262. https://doi.org/10.1111/j.1467-8683.2004.00367.x

Lynes, J. K., & Andrachuk, M. (2008). Motivations for corporate social and environmental responsibility: A case study of Scandinavian airlines. *Journal of International Management*, 14, 377–390.

Madrigal, R., & Dalakas, V. (2008). Consumer psychology of sport. In C. P. Haugtvedt, P. M. Herr, & F. R. Kardes (Eds.), *Handbook of consumer psychology* (pp. 857–876). New York: Tyler & Francis.

Mair, J., & Jago, L. (2010). The development of a conceptual model of greening in the business events tourism sector. *Journal of Sustainable Tourism*, 18(1), 77–94.

Marshall, R. S., Cordano, M., & Silverman, M. (2005). Exploring individual and institutional drivers of proactive environmentalism in the US wine industry. *Business Strategy and the Environment*, 14(2), 92–109.

McCullough, B. P., & Cunnigham, G. B. (2010). A conceptual model to understand the impetus to engage in and the expected organizational outcomes of green initiatives. *Quest*, 62, 348–363.

McCullough, B. P., & Cunnigham, G. B. (2011). Recycling intentions among youth baseball spectators. *International Journal of Sport Management and Marketing*, 10, 104–120.

Meehl, G., & Stocker, T. (2007). Quantifying the range of climate change. In M. Allen & G. B. Pant (Eds.), *Climate change 2007: Working group I: The physical science basis*. Cambridge, UK and New York, NY: Cambridge University Press. Retrieved from www.ipcc.ch/publications_and_data/ar4/wg1/en/ch10s10-5.html

Mohr, L. A., Webb, D. J., & Harris, K. E. (2001). Do consumers expect companies to be socially responsible? The impact of corporate social responsibility on buying behavior. *Journal of Consumer Affairs*, 35(1), 45–72.

Naidoo, M., & Gasparatos, A. (2018). Corporate environmental sustainability in the retail sector: Drivers, strategies and performance measurement. *Journal of Cleaner Production*, 203, 125–142.

Pfahl, M. (2013). The environmental awakening in sports. *Solutions*, 4, 67–76.

Rasche, A. (2009). "A necessary supplement" what the United Nations global compact is and is not. *Business & Society*, 48(4), 511–537.

Reiche, D. (2013). Climate policies in the U.S. at the stakeholder level: A case study of the national football league. *Energy Policy*, 60, 775–784. https://doi.org/10.1016/j.enpol.2013.05.039

Rogers, E., & Dearing, J. (1988). Agenda-setting theory research: Where has it been, where is it going? *Communication Yearbook*, 11, 555–594.

Rubino, F., & Napoli, F. (2020). What impact does corporate governance have on corporate environmental performances. An empirical study of Italian listed firms. *Sustainability*, 12(14), 5742.

Sharma, S., & Henriques, I. (2005). Stakeholder influences on sustainability practices in the Canadian forest products industry. *Strategic Management Journal*, 26(2), 159–180.

Shneider Von Deimling, T., Ganopolski, H., & Rahmstorm, S. (2006). Climate sensitivity estimated from ensemble simulations of glacial climate. *Climate Dynamics*, 27, 149–163.

Sison, A. J. G. (2008). *Corporate governance and ethics: An aristotelian perspective*. Cheltenham, UK: Edward Elgar Publishing Limited.

Spitzeck, H., & Hansen, E. G. (2010). Stakeholder governance: How stakeholders influence corporate decision making. *Corporate Governance: The International Journal of Business in Society*, 10(1), 378–391.

Stadium becomes first US venue of its kind to earn LEED gold certification. (2014, July 22). Retrieved November 11, 2014, from www.levisstadium.com/2014/07/stadium-becomes-first-us-venue-kind-earn-leed-gold-certification/

Trendafilova, S., & Babiak, K. (2013). Understanding strategic corporate environmental responsibility in professional sport. *Sport Management and Marketing*, 13(1/2), 1–26.

Trendafilova, S., Babiak, K., & Heinze, K. (2013). Corporate social responsibility and environmental sustainability: Why professional sport is greening the playing field. *Sport Management Review*, 16, 298–313.

Trendafilova, S., McCullough, B., Pfahl, M., Nguyen, S. N., Casper, J., & Picariello, M. (2014). Environmental sustainability in sport: Current state and future trends. *Global Journal on Advances in Pure & Applied Sciences*, 3, 9–14.

Triantafyllidis, S. (2018). Carbon dioxide emissions research and sustainable transportation in the sports industry. *Journal of Carbon Research*, 4(4), 57. https://doi.org/10.3390/c4040057

Triantafyllidis, S., Ries, R. J., & Kaplanidou, K. (2018). Carbon dioxide emissions of spectators' transportation in collegiate sporting events: Comparing on-campus and off-campus stadium locations. *Sustainability*, 10(1), 241. https://doi.org/10.3390/su10010241

Wann, D. L., & Branscombe, N. R. (1990). Die-hard and fair-weather fans: Effects of identification on BIRGing and CORFing tendencies. *Journal of Sport and Social Issues*, 14(2), 103–117. doi:10.1177/019372359001400203

World Commission on Environment and Development. (1987). *Our common future*. Oxford: Oxford University Press.

Zhang, Y. (2007). Warming of the climate system in unequivocal: Highlights of the fourth IPCC assessment report. *United Nation Chronicle*, 44(2). Retrieved from http://unchronicle.un.org/article/warming-climate-system-unequivocal-highlights-fourth-ipcc-assessment-report/

Index

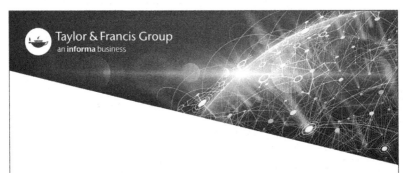

Printed in the United States
by Baker & Taylor Publisher Services